ces and Words

Punctuation and Mechanics

Tips for Multilingual Writers

Glossary and Index

up as you write. Use *Quick Access* tools to help you quickly find the information you need:

■ The **Divider Directory** to the left lists all of the tabbed parts and chapters in *Quick Access*.

■ **Quick Reference** boxes throughout the book give you easy access to the most common and important issues that will come up as you write.

■ A **detailed table of contents** for a tabbed section can be found on the back of each tabbed page.

■ The **Index** lists all the topics covered in the handbook. Find a topic, note the page number, and then use the page range given on the back of the extended tab to find your topic quickly.

■ The **Terms Glossary** defines important terms related to writing and grammar. Every word printed in small capital letters in *Quick Access* is defined in the glossary.

■ The one-of-a-kind **Quick Reference Card for Research and Documentation** inserted at the back of the book puts useful information from the book into a more portable format. Take the card with you to class, to the writing lab, or to the library as you do research.

■ Fold out the back cover of the book and on the inside you will have a **Quick View** of every tabbed part, chapter, and section of *Quick Access*.

■ On the other side of the back cover, you will find a list of **Response Symbols** and **Proofreading Marks** that your instructor may use on your paper. Refer to these lists to find out what section of the handbook will help you edit and proofread your work.

Three books
Two authors
One vision for handbooks

Lynn Troyka and **Doug Hesse** offer three books to suit your course and your students' needs:

The Simon & Schuster Handbook for Writers
Ninth Edition

- 960 pages
- Hardcover
- Full color

Quick Access
Sixth Edition

- 552 pages
- Spiral-bound, tabbed
- Full color

QA Compact
Second Edition

- 552 pages
- Spiral-bound
- Two-color

■ ■ ■ ■ ■ ■ ■ ■

Quick Access
Reference for Writers

SIXTH EDITION

LYNN QUITMAN TROYKA

DOUGLAS HESSE

Prentice Hall
Upper Saddle River   London   Singapore
Toronto   Tokyo   Sydney   Hong Kong   Mexico City

VP/Editorial Director: Leah Jewell
Editor in Chief: Craig Campanella
Executive Editor: Kevin Molloy
Project Manager, Editorial: Jessica A. Kupetz
Editorial Assistant: David Nitti
VP/Director of Marketing: Tim Stookesbury
Executive Marketing Manager:
   Megan Galvin-Fak
Senior Marketing Manager: Susan E. Stoudt
Marketing Assistant: Sara Fry
Assistant Managing Editor: Melissa Feimer
Text Permissions Specialist: Jane Scelta
Development Editor in Chief: Rochelle Diogenes
Development Editor: Leslie Taggart
Permissions Assistant: Peggy Davis
Senior Operations Specialist: Sherry Lewis
Manager, Image Rights and Permissions:
   Zina Arabia

Manager, Visual Research: Beth Brenzel
Manager, Cover Visual Research and
   Permissions: Karen Sanatar
Image Permissions Coordinator:
   Ang'John Ferreri
Image Researcher: Beth Brenzel
Senior Art Director: Nancy Wells
Art Director: Anne Nieglos
AV Project Manager: Maria Piper
Interior and Cover Designer: Anne DeMarinis
Cover Art: "Mulberry Tree" 1889 by Vincent Van
   Gogh © The Gallery Collection/Corbis
Full-Service Project Management: Karen Berry,
   Pine Tree Composition, Inc.
Copyeditor: Tally Morgan
Composition: Pine Tree Composition, Inc.
Printer/Binder: Courier Companies
Cover Printer: Lehigh Phoenix

This book was set in 10/12 Adobe Garamond.

Credits and acknowledgments borrowed from other sources and reproduced, with permission, in this textbook appear on the corresponding page within text or on page 513.

Library of Congress Cataloging-in-Publication Data

Troyka, Lynn Quitman
   Quick access reference for writers / Lynn Quitman Troyka ; Douglas Hesse. -- 6th ed.
      p. cm.
   Includes index.
   ISBN 0-205-66481-4
   1. English language—Rhetoric—Handbooks, manuals, etc.   2. English language—Grammar—
Handbooks, manuals, etc.   3. Report writing—Handbooks, manuals, etc.   I. Hesse, Douglas
Dean. II. Title.
   PE1408.T69565 2009
   808'.042—dc22

                                                                              2008053006

10 9 8 7 6 5 4 3

Prentice Hall
is an imprint of

www.pearsonhighered.com

Student ISBN-13:
978-0-205-66481-8
Student ISBN-10:
0-205-66481-4
Exam ISBN-13:
978-0-205-66501-3
Exam ISBN-10:
0-205-66501-2

Why Do You Need This New Edition?

The sixth edition of *Quick Access Reference for Writers* has been revised to provide more useful instruction and examples for writing students and instructors. Some of the useful features that you'll find only in the new edition are:

① **The most up-to-date coverage of documentation styles**: the sixth edition features the most current standards for MLA and APA documentation, which you'll need in first-year composition as well as in many courses in your field of study.

② New and revised **Quick Reference boxes** highlight the most important must-have concepts for easy use. These are key to finding the information you need in the handbook.

③ **New Chapters 4, 5, 6, and 7** are focused on writing in college and on the specific types of writing assignments you are likely to encounter. These chapters give not only general writing advice but also specific strategies for producing the most common

types of academic writing in first-year composition and other courses. This makes the sixth edition a great resource for any class, not just first-year composition.

④ **A new Chapter 21, "Creating a Writing Portfolio,"** offers direction on creating print and electronic portfolios, a popular assignment for many instructors and a helpful tool when applying for scholarships and jobs.

⑤ **Coverage and support for writing with new media,** including making oral presentations and using multimedia, writing blogs and wikis, and document and visual design.

⑥ **A new Quick Reference Card for Research and Documentation** puts all of the most important concepts for research in your pocket, so you'll have it when and where you need it.

⑦ **New and revised sample papers and examples** follow the most current standards for documentation and document design. These examples are handy when formatting your own papers for any discipline.

HOW TO USE *QUICK ACCESS*

We are confident you will find *Quick Access* an invaluable guide in your journey through college and beyond. The following list of *Quick Access* tools will help you find the information you need quickly and easily.

- **The QA Divider Directory** on the inside front cover lists all of the tabbed parts and chapters in *Quick Access*. Locate the general topic you need to reference and then turn to the tab and page indicated on the Divider Directory.

- **MyCompLab®** offers essential help with writing, grammar, and research and features a complete electronic version of *Quick Access*. You can register for access at www.mycomplab.com.

- **A list of supplementary material available with this book,** including information about the book's Web site, can be found in the Preface.

- **Quick Reference** boxes throughout the book offer easy access to some of the most common and important issues that will come up as you write. You will also find Quick Reference boxes highlighted in the book's Index.

- **Documentation source maps** are designed to clearly illustrate the process for citing different types of sources. Annotated replications of original sources, step-by-step guidelines, and use of color help students see where to pull information from a source and where to place it in a citation. Visual tools throughout the research and documentation sections simplify the research writing process.

- **The Terms Glossary** located in the final tabbed part is an easy way to find the definitions for common writing-related terms. Words and phrases called out in SMALL CAPITAL LETTERS throughout the book are defined in the Terms Glossary.

- **The one-of-a-kind Quick Reference Card for Research and Documentation,** at the end of the book, offers some of the most useful information from the book in a more portable format.

- **A list of Response Symbols and Proofreading Marks** is on the back cover foldout. Consult this list if your instructor uses revision and proofreading symbols when commenting on your writing.

The sample composite page to the right illustrates how to navigate the content of the book from page to page.

44j What is pronoun case?

Indicates new section of a chapter.

Case applies in different ways to pronouns and to nouns. For pronouns, case refers to three pronoun forms: **subjective** (pronoun SUBJECTS), **objective** (pronoun OBJECTS), and **possessive** (pronouns that are possessive). For nouns, case refers to only one noun form: possessive. (For using apostrophes in the possessive case, see Chapter 60.)

Words printed in bold or in small capital letters are discussed elsewhere in the book and are defined in the Terms Glossary.

Quick Reference 44.2

Choosing between *that* and *which*

In informal writing, you can use either *that* or *which* in a restrictive clause (a clause that is essential to the sentence's meaning), as long as you do so consistently in each piece of writing. However, in academic writing, your instructor and peers usually expect you to use *that*.

> The zoos **that most children like** display newborn and baby animals. [The point of this sentence is to identify the kind of zoos that children like. Therefore, the clause *that most children like* is essential to the meaning of the sentence; if you remove it, the meaning changes substantially.]

Use *which* in a **nonrestrictive clause** (a clause that isn't essential to the sentence's meaning).

> Zoos, **which most children like**, attract more visitors if they display newborn and baby animals. [This sentence concerns what attracts more visitors to zoos. The clause *which most children like* is not essential to the meaning of the sentence; if you remove it, the meaning of the sentence doesn't change substantially.]

Quick Reference boxes highlight key information.

🛇 **Alert:** The expression *he or she* operates as a single unit and therefore calls for a singular antecedent. Generally, however, try to avoid this awkward expression by switching to plural forms. ●

Alerts call attention to important rules and best practices.

🌐 **ESOL Tip:** The word *to* has several functions, each of which is discussed in Chapter 46. As part of the INFINITIVE *to eat*, the word *to* modifies (limits) the PRONOUN *nothing*. ●

ESOL icons call out information of particular use for multilingual students.

For more help with your writing, grammar, and research, go to **www.mycomplab.com**

mycomplab

A wealth of writing resources is available through MyCompLab.

To David, the love of my life

LYNN QUITMAN TROYKA

To Don and Coral Hesse

DOUG HESSE

PREFACE

This sixth edition of *Quick Access Reference for Writers* gives you "quick access" to all the information you need about the writing process, from writing research papers to documenting sources, and from writing for the Web to writing using visuals, and from mastering grammar to using correct punctuation. *Quick Access* is carefully designed for easy use and speedy entrée into all topics, as illustrated in the walkthrough of the text in this Preface.

Accessible and proven tone.   Lynn Troyka and Doug Hesse make topics accessible and welcome students into a conversation about becoming a better writer. *Quick Access* has been written and designed to be accessible and to suit a wide variety of student needs.

NEW focus on academic writing strategies in Part 1.   Four new chapters (4–7) guide students through specific strategies for the most common types of academic writing in first-year and other courses, including writing about experiences, observations, and readings.

Easy access to common errors integrated throughout the text.   Common errors that most writers make are often called out as **Alerts** or in **Quick Reference boxes** throughout the text.

Coverage and support for writing with technology.

- NEW Chapter 26, "Contributing to Blogs and Wikis," offers practical instruction for creating and contributing to online writing communities.

- Chapter 20, "Making Oral Presentations and Using Multimedia," explains how and why to use various strategies for effective oral presentations. This chapter also discusses how to use several types of multimedia and the pitfalls associated with them.

- Chapter 25, "Writing for the Web," shows students how to produce effective online texts for various audiences and purposes.

Support for multilingual writers integrated throughout and in a dedicated section.   Whether English is your native language or you are multilingual, you'll find quick answers in *Quick Access* to your questions about standard American English grammar, punctuation, and sentence correctness and style. Look for this symbol 🌐 to find these ESOL tips. In addition, there's an entire section devoted to questions of special concern to multilingual students.

Research and documentation sections that provide applicable strategies and are designed for utility.   We know from talking to instructors and students that the research and documentation sections of a handbook are the most often referenced. Therefore, we have taken great care in designing these sections to be as useful as possible.

- Research chapters emphasize the distinction between scholarly sources (such as those found in libraries and professionally edited databases) and less reliable sources, including strategies for recognizing and integrating credible sources.
- The book emphasizes research as a potentially important component of any writing situation, which teaches students to see the act of researching as valuable beyond only designated research papers.
- The use of computer-based research strategies is fully integrated throughout the book.
- Chapter 31, "Using Sources and Avoiding Plagiarism," helps students appreciate the importance of citing sources and provides useful strategies for avoiding plagiarism.

Completely updated MLA documentation, APA documentation, *Chicago Manual* (CM) documentation, and the Council of Science Editors (CSE) documentation.   These sections are designed to help students find the right models quickly and accurately. We have provided updated examples throughout.

Documentation coverage reflects the most current standards across the disciplines.

- MLA documentation reflects the anticipated 2009 updates to MLA style as outlined in the third edition of the *MLA Style Manual and Guide to Scholarly Publishing.*
- APA documentation reflects the latest (2007) guidelines for electronic sources.
- CSE documentation is completely updated to reflect the latest (2006) guidelines.

Student and professional writing samples.   *Quick Access* contains extensive samples of student writing, including five complete documents on fresh topics of interest, as well as new examples of professional writing.

A streamlined, open, functional design.   The book's layout serves to emphasize the most important topics, ideas, and examples, making finding critical information easy. Greater use of full-color images and illustrations throughout not only enhances interest for students but also conforms to the increased use of visual rhetoric in composition.

SUPPLEMENTS

The following supplements accompany *Quick Access,* Sixth Edition, to aid in teaching and learning:

For the Instructor

- **Instructor's Manual.** *Strategies and Resources for Teaching Writing with the Quick Access Reference for Writers* offers practical, hands-on advice for new and experienced composition instructors for organizing their syllabi, planning, and teaching.
- **Prentice Hall Resources for Writing.** This series is a specially designed set of supplements for the instructor that support timely classroom and composition topics. These supplements are available upon adoption of *Quick Access.*
  - *Teaching Writing Across the Curriculum* by Art Young is written for college teachers in all disciplines and provides useful advice on teaching writing across the curriculum.
  - *Teaching Civic Literacy* by Cheryl Duffy offers advice on how to integrate civic literacy into the composition classroom.
  - *Teaching Visual Rhetoric* by Susan Loudermilk provides an illustrated look at visual rhetoric and offers guidance on how to incorporate this topic into the classroom.
  - *Teaching Writing for ESL Students* by Ruth Spack addresses various strategies that can be employed to teach writing to nonnative speakers.

For the Instructor and Student

MyCompLab®   The new MyCompLab uniquely integrates proven resources and new assessment tools with a student's own writing. This seamless and flexible application, built for writers by writers, will help instructors and students accomplish everyday composition tasks more easily and effectively.

Student Workbook and Answer Key   Contains hundreds of additional exercises and activities with answers to help improve writing skills.

Prentice Hall WAC Resources   Includes *Papers Across the Curriculum* (edited by Judith Ferster), a series of sample student papers, and *A Prentice Hall Pocket Reader: Writing Across the Curriculum* (by Stephen Brown, University of Nevada Las Vegas). If you would like to put additional emphasis on WAC in your composition course(s), please contact your Pearson sales representative for more information.

Dictionary, Thesaurus, Writer's Guides, Workbooks, and Pocket Readers
The following resources can be packaged with *Quick Access,* Sixth Edition.

- *The New American Webster Handy College Dictionary*
- *The New American Roget's College Thesaurus*
- *A Writer's Guide to Research and Documentation*
- *A Writer's Guide to Oral Presentations and Writing in the Disciplines*
- *A Writer's Guide to Document and Web Design*
- *A Writer's Guide to Writing About Literature*
- *The Prentice Hall Grammar Workbook*
- *A Prentice Hall Pocket Reader: Argument, Patterns, Themes, Purposes, and Writing Across the Curriculum*

ACKNOWLEDGMENTS

With this sixth edition of *Quick Access Reference for Writers*, nicknamed *QA*, we heartily thank all those students who, to our great luck, have landed in our writing courses. We admire how they and their counterparts in classrooms around the world strive to write skillfully, think critically, and communicate successfully, in college and beyond. We especially thank the individual students who have given us permission to make them "published authors" by including their exemplary writing in this handbook.

Hundreds of students have contacted us by e-mail or letter with their reactions to and questions about *QA* or related matters. We deeply appreciate these messages. We take these comments seriously and use them to improve our teaching and this book. Any student now holding *QA* is welcome to get in touch with us at troykalq@nyc.rr.com, at dhesse@du.edu, or c/o Executive English Editor, Pearson Education, 1 Lake Street, Upper Saddle River, NJ 07458. We promise to answer.

A project as complicated as *Quick Access* cannot be completed without the expertise and dedication of many professionals. We would like to thank all the exceptional people at Pearson Prentice Hall who facilitated our work on *Quick Access*, Sixth Edition. We're especially grateful for the expertise of Kevin Molloy, Leslie Taggart, Dave Nitti, Jessica Kupetz, Paul Sarkis, Susan Stoudt, Megan Galvin, Joan Foley, Ann Marie McCarthy, Melissa Feimer, Anne Nieglos, Anne DeMarinis, Leah Jewell, Craig Campanella, Rochelle Diogenes, and Yolanda De Rooy. All have worked creatively, tirelessly, and with good cheer.

Doug values Lynn Troyka's vast knowledge, skill, dedication to teaching, and patience. He appreciates the support of all his colleagues at the University of Denver, but most specifically Eliana Schonberg, Amy Kho, Jennifer Karas, and Gregg Kvistad. He further states, "Carol Rutz, Cheryl Glenn, Erika Lindemann, and, always, Kathi Yancey have been exemplary professional and personal friends. Dan Graybill, Susan Bellas, and Laurence Bellas are constant sources of support and friendship. My children, Monica, Andrew, and Paige, amaze me with their creativity, as does the best writer I know: Becky Bradway, my wife."

Lynn is especially grateful to her coauthor Doug Hesse for his gentle friendship and invaluable participation in revising the *Quick Access Reference for Writers* for its sixth edition. Lynn also places on the record her gratitude to Ida Morea, her administrative assistant and special pal, Lynn's central support with her solid expertise and clever problem solving; Kristen Black, along with Dan, Lindsey, and Ryan, the beloved, ever-present joy of her life; Avery Ryan, Lynn's superb friend and "niece," along with Jimmy, Gavin, and Ian, for being irreplaceably woven into the texture of her life; and Edith Klausner, Lynn's sister and grand friend, a vital part of her life. Other exceptional folks include Susan Bartelstone; Florence Bolden; Rita and Hy Cohen; Esther DiMarzio; Alan, Lynne, Adam, and Josh Furman; Edie and Alan Lipp; JoAnn Lavery; Roberta Moore; Betty Renshaw; Magdelena Rogalskaja; Joseph W. Thweatt; Lisa and Nathaniel Wallace; Muriel Wolfe; and extraordinary Douglas Young III and his wife Anna. Principally, Lynn thanks her husband and sweetheart, David Troyka, for being her treasured companion and most discerning critic.

Lynn Quitman Troyka
Doug Hesse

Personal Message to Students
FROM LYNN QUITMAN TROYKA AND DOUG HESSE

As writers, many of you have much in common with both of us. Sure, we've been at it longer, so we've had more practice, and most rules have become cemented in our heads. However, we share with you a common goal: to put ideas into words worthy of someone else's reading time.

We also share the constant desire to become better writers. Given our extensive teaching experience, this probably sounds odd. However, writing is a lifelong enterprise. Just as we did, you'll write not only in composition classes, but also in other courses throughout college. Writing will likely be an important part of your career, of your role as a public citizen, and even of your personal life. It has certainly been central to ours. Whenever we get stuck in an unfamiliar writing situation or while learning new writing technology, we rummage through strategies we've developed over time. We talk to friends and colleagues, in person, by phone, and by e-mail, and they consult us, too.

We offer this book to you, then, as our partners in the process of writing. We hope that its pages help you give voice to your thoughts—now and years from now. We trust you'll find our advice useful in the wide range of writing situations you're bound to encounter in college and in life. You're always welcome to write us at troykalq@nyc.rr.com or dhesse@du.edu to share your reactions to this book and your experiences as writers. We promise to answer.

Each of us would like to end this message with a personal story.

From Doug: I first glimpsed the power of writing in high school, when I wrote sappy—but apparently successful—love poems. Still, when I went to college, I was surprised to discover all I didn't know about writing. Fortunately, I had good teachers and developed lots of patience. I needed it. I continue to learn from my colleagues, my students, and my coauthor, Lynn.

From Lynn: When I was an undergraduate, handbooks for writers weren't common. Questions about writing nagged at me. One day, browsing in the library, I found an incorrectly shelved, dust-covered book whose title included the words *handbook* and *writing.* I read it hungrily and kept checking it out from the library. Back then, I could never have imagined that someday I might write such a book myself. Now that we've completed the sixth edition of the *Quick Access Reference for Writers,* I'm amazed that I ever had the nerve to begin. This proves to me—and I hope to you—that anyone can write. Students don't always believe that. I hope you will.

With cordial regards,

Lynn Quitman Troyka   *Doug Hesse*

ABOUT THE AUTHORS

Lynn Quitman Troyka, Adjunct Professor in the Graduate Program in Language and Literature at the City College (CCNY) of the City University of New York (CUNY), has also taught at Queensborough Community College. Former editor of the *Journal of Basic Writing,* she has had her writing and research published in major journals and various scholarly collections. She also conducts workshops in the teaching of writing. Dr. Troyka is coauthor of the *Simon & Schuster Handbook for Writers*, Ninth Edition, Pearson Prentice Hall; *QA Compact,* Second Edition, Pearson Prentice Hall; the Canadian editions of her *Simon & Schuster Handbook for Writers* and *Quick Access Reference for Writers; Structured Reading,* Seventh Edition, Prentice Hall; and *Steps in Composition,* Eighth Edition, Prentice Hall.

Dr. Troyka is a past chair of the Conference on College Composition and Communication (CCCC); the Two-Year College Association (TYCA) of the National Council of Teachers of English (NCTE); the College Section of NCTE; and the Writing Division of the Modern Language Association (MLA). She received the 2001 CCCC Exemplar Award, the highest CCCC award for scholarship, teaching, and service; the Rhetorician of the Year Award; and the TYCA Pickett Award for Service.

"This information," says Dr. Troyka, "tells what I've done, not who I am. I am a teacher. Teaching is my life's work, and I love it."

Doug Hesse, Professor of English and Director of Writing at the University of Denver, previously held several positions at Illinois State University, including Director of the Honors and Writing Programs, and Director of the Center for the Advancement of Teaching. Dr. Hesse earned his PhD from the University of Iowa. He has also taught at the University of Findlay, Miami University (as Wiepking Distinguished Visiting Professor), and Michigan Tech.

Dr. Hesse is a past chair of the Conference on College Composition and Communication (CCCC), the nation's largest professional association of college writing instructors. A past president, as well, of the Council of Writing Program Administrators (WPA), Dr. Hesse edited that organization's journal, *Writing Program Administration.* He has been a member of the executive committee of the National Council of Teachers of English (NCTE) and chaired the Modern Language Association (MLA) Division on Teaching as a Profession.

He is the author of over fifty articles and book chapters, in such journals as *College Composition and Communication, College English, JAC, Rhetoric Review,* and the *Journal of Teaching Writing* and in such books as *Essays on the Essay; Writing Theory and Critical Theory; The Writing Program Administrator's*

Sourcebook; Literary Nonfiction; The Private, the Public, and the Published; and *Passions, Pedagogies, and 21st Century Technologies.* He is also coauthor with Lynn Quitman Troyka of the *Simon & Schuster Handbook for Writers*, Ninth Edition, Pearson Prentice Hall; and *QA Compact*, Second Edition, Pearson Prentice Hall. He has consulted at over forty colleges and universities.

The writing program he directs at the University of Denver is only one of twenty-five internationally to receive the CCCC Certificate of Excellence. "Of all these accomplishments," says Dr. Hesse, "the one that matters most to me was being named Distinguished Humanities Teacher. That one came from my students and suggests that, in however small a way, I've mattered in their education and lives."

Lynn Quitman Troyka

Doug Hesse

1 ▪ ▪ ▪ ▪ ▪ ▪

Thinking Like a Writer

1a Why is writing important?

We live in an age when people do more writing than they have at any other time in history. Not only have computers made it easier to produce clean texts, but they've also allowed average writers to create documents that twenty years ago would have required professional designers.

As people rely more and more on written communication, the ability to write well becomes more vital. Certainly this is true in college, where you can expect to write in a variety of courses across the curriculum, not just in English classes. It's also true in the world of work. A survey of business leaders found that "most professional employees are expected to write" and that "individual opportunity in the United States depends critically on the ability to present one's thoughts coherently, cogently, and persuasively on paper."*

Writing is a skill that takes you beyond classrooms and workplaces. It helps you participate as an informed citizen, from appealing a parking ticket to influencing the outcomes of elections. Furthermore, it helps you share ideas with friends, family members, and people with similar interests. You might write e-mails and text messages, keep journals, craft stories or poems, create or contribute to Web sites on topics that interest you, or write **blogs** (Web logs).

The opportunities to make a difference with your writing are limitless. Whether you are a student, an employee, an employer, a concerned citizen, or a member of another type of group, you have an important message to convey. Spend some time and energy improving your writing skills, and your efforts will bring you personal, academic, and professional rewards.

1b How do I think like a writer?

Thinking like a writer means practicing the mental skills that successful writers use whenever they write. In fact, the physical act of writing actually promotes thinking. It triggers brain processes that lead you to make new connections among ideas and helps you "see" things that you hadn't seen before.

---

*National Commission on Writing, *Writing: A Ticket to Work . . . or a Ticket Out?: A Survey of Business Leaders* (New York: College Entrance Examination Board, 2004), 9 Sept. 2005.

Figure 1.1 Different varieties and styles of writing

Above all, thinking like a writer involves considering the world around you. You pause to examine ideas. You challenge ideas instead of passively accepting them. You question conclusions instead of mindlessly agreeing with them. You engage in critical thinking. Finally, you learn to communicate these insights and observations to others.

1c   How do writers think about the writing situation?

Successful writers know they need to adjust their writing for different tasks, purposes, and audiences. Quick Reference 1.1 outlines the major elements you should think about in any writing situation.

Quick Reference 1.1

Elements of a writing situation

- Topic: What subject will you be writing about? (8d)
- Purpose: What should the writing accomplish? (8b)
- Audience: Who are the readers for this specific piece of writing? (8c)
- Context: When and how will your writing be read?
- Role: How do you want your audience to perceive you?
- Special requirements: Do you have requirements such as length, type of writing, format, or due dates?

Audience refers to people who read a specific piece of writing. When you write for yourself, you're free to focus only on what matters to you. Often you can choose the topic you're writing about, as well as the tone and style. If, however, you're writing for a specific audience, you need to maintain a keen awareness of its presence as you focus on your topic and writing style.

Different types of audiences will have different needs and expectations about your content and format. A humanities professor would generally expect a paper with a clear thesis, well-organized paragraphs, and a formal style. A communications director for a group such as Habitat for Humanity would usually expect an upbeat, easily readable, informative approach in the organization's newsletter. Someone leafing through a magazine like *Rolling Stone* would expect to find energetic prose, even slang, about contemporary rock music and youth politics.

The context of your purpose and audience can affect the writing situation. **Context** refers to the circumstances in which your readers will encounter your writing. For example, persuading people to buy fuel-efficient cars when gas costs $1 per gallon is a different and more difficult task than when it costs $4. Informing college students about child-care options, you will change the amount of information and how it is displayed if your message will appear on a poster in the student center rather than in a campus newspaper article.

It may surprise you to learn that you can take on different **roles** (personalities or identities) for different writing situations. For example, suppose you're trying to persuade readers to save energy. You might emphasize your concerns as a future parent who is personally worried about the future, or you might instead present yourself as an objective and impersonal analyst. You can support the role you select by using an appropriate writing style and tone (10c).

1d   What is critical thinking?

"Critical" in this context does not mean finding fault, as when one person criticizes another for doing something wrong. Rather, **critical thinking** is a deliberate process of actively summarizing, analyzing, inferring, synthesizing, and evaluating information, situations, or ideas.

Actually, critical thinking is something you do more often than you realize. For example, when you pick a college, you reflect on the information you gathered about the school. When you start a new job, you engage in critical thinking to learn and master how to do the work and to decide whether or not the job matches your abilities. Yet even though thoughts come naturally, awareness of how and why you think does not. Thinking about thinking is how you think critically.

Critical thinking means identifying the weaknesses, strengths, implications, and applications of an idea, a text, an image, and so on. Critical thinking begins with understanding, moves through analysis and synthesis, and ends with your evaluation of the idea or topic at hand. The steps you take during the critical thinking process rarely proceed in a rigid order. We describe each step separately in Quick Reference 1.2, but in reality, they interweave and loop back and forth.

Quick Reference 1.2   ■ ■ ■ ■ ■ ■ ■

Steps in the critical thinking process

1. **Comprehend** and **summarize**. Understand the **literal** meaning: the "plain" meaning on the surface of the material. Extract and restate its main message or central point. Accurately and objectively describe an image, event, or situation. Add nothing. Read "on the lines."

2. **Analyze**. Examine the material by breaking it into its component parts. Ask about the nature or meaning of each part and how it contributes to the overall meaning or effect.

3. **Infer**. Read "between the lines" to see what's not stated but implied. Consider examples, images, and other aspects of the material, and ask what they suggest about the writer's views.

4. **Synthesize**. Connect what you've summarized, analyzed, and inferred with your prior knowledge or experiences, with other ideas or perspectives, or with other readings, texts, or situations.

5. **Evaluate**. Read "beyond the lines." Judge the quality of the material or form your own informed opinion about it. Answer such questions as, "Is it reasonable? Fair? Accurate? Convincing? Ethical? Useful? Comprehensive? Important?"

2

Reading Critically

2a What is critical reading?

To read critically is to think about what you're reading—during the time that you're reading and afterward. To practice critical reading, study the advertisement in Figure 2.1 and apply the five steps in the critical thinking process outlined in Quick Reference 1.2.

Figure 2.1 Ad about fair housing

2b   What steps do I use to read critically?

Reading is an active process, a dynamic interaction between the page and your brain. Understanding how this interaction works can help you become a better reader.

Without being conscious of it, as you read you make split-second predictions. Your mind is constantly guessing what ideas and words are coming next. When your mind does see what has come next, it instantly confirms or revises its prediction and moves on. For example, when you glance through a magazine and read the title "The Heartbeat," your mind starts guessing: Is this a love story? Is this about how the heart pumps blood? Perhaps it tells the story of someone who had a heart attack? As you read the first few sentences, your mind confirms which guess was correct. If you see words like *romance* and *kisses,* you know that the material involves a human relationship. On the other hand, if you see words like *electrical impulse, muscle fibers,* and *contraction,* you know instantly that you're in the realm of physiology.

To make predictions efficiently, consider your **purpose** for reading. Are you reading to relax, to learn, or to do both? Your purpose for reading a popular novel or a Web page about a hobby will differ from your purpose for reading a college textbook, the terms of a loan, or a proposal for a business opportunity.

■ Determining literal meaning

Reading for **literal meaning** involves reading to comprehend. This isn't the time to go beyond what's "on the line." Your goal is to understand the content of the writing. In a news story, you want to know what happened. In an article, you want to grasp the topic or argument. In a work of fiction, you want to know the plot. In a business proposal, you want to understand what you're being asked to buy, sell, or do. Rushing through material to cover it, rather than to understand it, wastes your valuable time. Resist the temptation to add your own interpretation to the literal meaning of the material.

If you find reading on the literal level difficult, the cause might be a writer's complex style. Try breaking the sentences into shorter units or rewording them in a simpler style. Think about the vocabulary that the writer uses and what the words mean. Take your time.

SUGGESTIONS FOR IMPROVING YOUR READING COMPREHENSION

- Associate new material with what you already know, especially when you're reading about an unfamiliar subject. You might consult an easier book or a reference work (such as an encyclopedia) on the subject and read it before you tackle the more complex material. Some readers search the Internet for simplified material. This approach can be risky unless you make sure your sources are reliable and accurate (30e).

- Remain fiercely determined to concentrate, especially if your mind tends to wander. Arrange for silence or nondistracting music. Work alone or in a quiet library with others. Try to complete your reading at your best time of day.

- Allow sufficient time to read, reflect, and review. Balance your time for reading and studying with time for classes, work, social activities, community events, and family functions. Reading and studying take time. Few things prevent success as much as poor time management.

- As you encounter new words, try to figure them out from the context in which they appear. You'll find that the rest of the sentence or a nearby sentence often cues you to what the word means. Refer to an up-to-date college dictionary as a last resort if the context doesn't hint at a word's meaning.

- Work efficiently. Don't waste time looking up a word more than once. Write or tape a list of new words into each textbook or inside your dictionary, or paste the list into a computer document you create for that purpose. Take time as often as possible to look over the list to remind yourself of the meanings. This is a quick, easy way to build your vocabulary.

■ Making inferences

Making **inferences** refers to the process of reading "between the lines," detecting a writer's assumptions, telling the difference between fact and opinion, discovering a writer's bias, and recognizing a writer's tone. Without knowing it, you make inferences all the time. For example, if you watch a crowd come out of a movie theater very quietly, and some people are wiping their eyes, you can generally assume that the film had a sad ending.

A WRITER'S ASSUMPTIONS

Writers sometimes state their assumptions, but often readers must think hard to uncover assumptions that are unstated and unacknowledged. Consider, for instance, an essay with the following thesis statement and main supports: Policymakers need to ban private ownership of wild animals as pets. First, wild animals are dangerous to humans. Second, domestication is hazardous to the animals themselves.

What underlying assumptions can you discover by thinking critically about these ideas? First, the writer assumes that situations dangerous to people should be outlawed. Similarly, the writer assumes that situations dangerous to animals should be outlawed. Notice that these assumptions are debatable. For example, driving a car is dangerous to people, but we don't outlaw that activity.

To read critically, you need to sort out a writer's assumptions. A good beginning point is to ask "What else must the author believe in order to believe what he or she is stating?" Then you can read with greater understanding of the writer's stance on the subject—and greater insight into how the writer expects you to react. Most important, you can resist being manipulated by such assumptions.

FACT VERSUS OPINION

Some writers intentionally blur the difference between fact and opinion. **Facts** are statements that people can verify objectively by observation, experiment, or research. That Abraham Lincoln was the sixteenth president of the United States is a fact. That Abraham Lincoln was the greatest US president is an **opinion**—a statement with which you may or may not agree. Critical readers know the difference.

To differentiate between fact and opinion, you want to think beyond the obvious. For example, decide whether the following statement is a fact or an opinion: "All people desire a steady income." Although it's common for people to equate success with a constant stream of money, some individuals prefer a more freewheeling approach to life. They may work hard, save money, and then travel for months, not working at all. Thus the statement, though accurate for most people, isn't true for all. It is, therefore, an opinion.

A WRITER'S BIAS

When you make inferences, you may discover viewpoints based on **bias** rather than facts or evidence. If writers make rude or cruel remarks, you can infer that they dislike certain ideas or people. Someone who asserts strong viewpoints but does not back them up with evidence may well be guilty of bias; you frequently encounter writers like this on the Internet. Be critical of bias and **prejudice**, because they slant the material toward the writer's beliefs and attitudes and away from facts or proof. You might find that a writer uses positive language to cover up prejudice. For example, in the statement "Most women are too nice to succeed in business," *nice* sounds complimentary, but the underlying assumption is negative and prejudicial.

A WRITER'S TONE

By recognizing the **tone** that emerges from a writer's use of words and ways of presenting ideas, you're making inferences. Just as our voices emit certain tones when we're happy, bored, sad, or excited, so do our words. Tone can be serious, respectful, friendly, humorous, slanted, sarcastic, or angry. Consider the difference between "Would you please cease that activity?" and "Knock it off right now!" or "The experience was generally most pleasant" and "We had a great time."

A formal word choice usually imparts a tone of distant seriousness, while informal language is more intimate and immediate. Most reports, newspaper articles, and research documents contain language that is neutral in tone. The writer attempts to establish a sense of impartiality to convince readers that the facts contained in the document are true. Letters, personal Web sites, music lyrics, and similar writing adopt a conversational, informal tone. Such writing asks to be interpreted emotionally and subjectively; the author is treating readers or listeners as friends. When the tone doesn't fit the occasion, the writer may be seeking to manipulate readers rather than to have them think logically. For example, some editorial writers rely on sarcasm and strong emotional language to attempt to persuade readers and bypass their analytical censors.

◼ Identifying the evidence

For any opinions or claims, you next need to identify and analyze the evidence that the writer provides. Evidence consists of facts, examples, the results of formal studies, and the opinions of experts. A helpful step in analysis is to identify the kind of evidence used (or what evidence is missing).

- **Primary sources** are firsthand evidence based on your own or someone else's original work or direct observation. Primary sources can take the form of experiments, surveys, interviews, memoirs, observations, original creative works (for example, poems, novels, paintings and other visual art, plays, films, or musical compositions).
- **Secondary sources** report, describe, comment on, or analyze the experiences or work of others.

For a checklist to evaluate evidence, see 32c.

◼ Identifying cause and effect

Cause and effect describes the relationship between one event (cause) and another event that happens as a result (effect). The relationship also works in reverse: One event (effect) results from another event (cause). Whether you begin with a cause or with an effect, you're using the same basic pattern.

Cause A → produces → effect B

You may seek to understand the effects of a known cause:

More studying → produces → ?

Or you may seek to determine the cause or causes of a known effect:

? → produces → recurrent headaches

When you're analyzing a reading, look for any claims of cause and effect. For any that you find, think carefully through the relationship between cause

A and effect B. Just because A happened before B or because A and B are associated with each other doesn't mean A caused B. To establish that A causes B, every time A is present, B must occur. Or, put another way, B never occurs unless A is present. The need for repetition explains why the US Food and Drug Administration (FDA) runs thousands of clinical trials before approving a new medicine. Be aware, too, that multiple causes and effects are more likely to occur than a single cause influencing a single effect.

■ Making evaluations

Critical readers evaluate what they've read only after they have dealt with the literal and inferential meanings in the material. Making **evaluations** calls for reading "beyond the lines," to come to conclusions about whether a writer's reasoning is sound and the presentation and word choice are balanced. To help evaluate readings, ask yourself the following questions:

- Does the writer provide evidence for all claims?
- Is the evidence sufficient and appropriate (13d)?
- Does the writer omit any viewpoints contrary to the evidence?
- Does the writer make reasonable assumptions?
- If the writer claims one thing caused another, might there be alternative reasons?
- What biases might the writer have?

2c   How do close reading and active reading work?

The secret to reading closely and actively is **annotating**. When you annotate, you write notes to yourself in a text's margins, occasionally underlining or highlighting important passages or using asterisks and other special marks to focus your attention. To annotate an electronic document, you can try several strategies. You can take handwritten notes on a separate sheet of paper or type your notes in a separate computer file. You can print the document and write notes on the hard copy, as you can see in Figure 2.2 (p. 11). You can even annotate electronically using software functions such as underlining, highlighting, and inserting comments. Just be careful to note which words are your own and which are the author's. Remember, if you turn in a paper that quotes, paraphrases, or summarizes a writer's work without giving proper credit, you'll be committing PLAGIARISM* (Ch. 31), which can result in serious penalties.

---

*Words printed in SMALL CAPITAL LETTERS are discussed elsewhere in the text and are defined in the Terms Glossary at the back of the book.

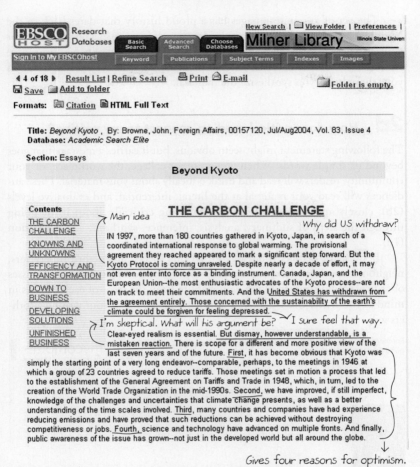

Figure 2.2 A student's annotations on an article printed from the *EBSCO Host* database

Close reading means annotating for content and meaning. You might, for example, number and briefly list the steps of a process or summarize major points in the margin. Where you underline or highlight, also jot key words or phrases in the margin. When you review, these marginal notes will jog your memory. Your goal is to extract meaning on the literal, inferential, and evaluative levels (2b).

Active reading means annotating to make connections between what you already know or have experienced and the material you're reading—in other words, synthesizing ideas. This is your chance to use your critical thinking skills to converse on paper with the writer.

The act of annotating pages has a proud history that dates back to the Middle Ages. However, if you can't bring yourself to write in a book, design for yourself a double-entry notebook. On one side of each sheet of paper, write close reading notes on the content; on the other side, enter active reading notes on your thoughts as you synthesize the material.

2d   How does critical reading connect to my writing?

The following statement might seem obvious, but it carries a message that goes beyond its simple words: When you write for college, the workplace, or your community, readers will read and think critically about your material. These audiences will read your material at the literal, inferential, and evaluative levels (2b), closely and actively (2c), while thinking critically about it, by going through the steps of summary, analysis, inference, synthesis, and evaluation (1d).

Because the people who read your writing (peers, instructors, supervisors, neighbors, specialized experts on your topic, and so on) use these processes of critical reading and thinking, you want to keep the steps of each process in mind as you write. Use Chapters 1 and 2 to help you read your writing as others will.

For more help with your writing, grammar, and research,
go to **www.mycomplab.com**

Viewing Images Critically

3a   How do I view images with a critical eye?

Our digital age surrounds us with images in publications, on computers, on television, and on cell phones. You can view images critically in the same way that you can read texts critically by using summary, analysis, inference, synthesis, and evaluation (see Quick Reference 1.2); by using literal, inferential, and evaluative reading (see pages 6–10); or by reading the questions in Quick Reference 3.1.

Quick Reference 3.1 ■ ■ ■ ■ ■ ■ ■

Some helpful questions for analyzing visual images

- What does the image show?
- What are its parts? Do the parts belong together (like a lake, trees, and mountains), or do they contrast with one another (like a woman in a fancy dress sitting on a tractor)?
- If there is a foreground and a background, what is in each?
- If the image is a scene, what seems to be going on? What might be its message?
- If the image seems to be part of a story, what might have happened before or after?
- If there are people in the image, how do they seem to relate to each other (friends, acquaintances, business associates, or strangers)?
- If there are contrasts in shading, coloring, or focus in the image, what is sharply in focus? Blurry? Bright? In shadows? Colorful? Drab? How do such differences, or their absence, call attention to various parts of the image?
- If there are words in the image, what is their relationship to it? Some words and images contrast for effect, such as a picture of a belching smokestack accompanied by a caption that says, "Fresh air."
- Are there any connections between the image and things you've experienced or learned from school, work, reading, visits to museums or other cultural sites, watching movies, plays, and television, and so on?
- Based on your observations, what is your evaluation of the image?

Look at Figure 3.1 with a critical eye.

- **Summarizing** the picture, as well as viewing it literally, you can see—at a minimum—a street full of older houses with modern skyscrapers in the distance.
- **Analyzing** the picture, as well as viewing it inferentially, you can "read between the lines" to see that it's fairly rich with layers of meaning. You can think about the meanings conveyed by the condition of the houses versus those of the modern buildings or about the lives of the people who live and work in each place. You can focus on the message of the comparative sizes of the houses and skyscrapers; on the contrast between this street and those you imagine at the base of the skyscrapers; on why the photographer chose this perspective; on how different captions might give the picture different meanings. For example, consider the difference between three

Figure 3.1 Images help us think visually.

different captions: "Progress," "Inequality," or "The Neighborhood." Many possible ideas may come to mind as you study the picture critically.

- **Synthesizing** the picture, you can connect what you've analyzed and inferred to what you associate with ideas you've learned from various life experiences.

- **Evaluating** the picture is the last step in viewing it critically. Resist evaluating prematurely because by going through the earlier steps of thinking and reading critically, your evaluation becomes informed by more than a noncritical personal reaction such as "I like the picture" or "I don't like the picture." In evaluating a visual critically, you can speak of how the visual "struck" you at first glance; how it did or did not gain depth of meaning as you analyzed it, looking at what could be inferred or imagined; and how it lent itself to synthesis within the realms of your personal experience and education.

For more help with your writing, grammar, and research,
go to **www.mycomplab.com**

4

Sources for College Writing

4a   How do writing situations in college vary?

College students explore many types of writing, and expecting one set of guidelines to work well for every single variety would be unrealistic. Analyzing the WRITING SITUATION (1c) and understanding the WRITING PROCESS (Chapters 8–11) are important and useful for all writing. But we've found that general advice is even more helpful when combined with strategies and guidelines for writing particular types of papers. How does writing a personal essay or memoir call for a process different from writing a summary? What are the important elements of a film review or a report?

The various types (or genres) of college writing differ in terms of length, PURPOSE, context, and special considerations. (See Chapters 14–18 for advice on writing in different disciplines, Chapter 19 on writing essay exams, Chapter 20 on writing oral presentations, and Chapter 21 on creating writing portfolios.) The writer's role may differ in each case. For example, the writer may be an impartial observer who stays in the background, or the writer's experience and personality may be the center of attention. The format and style can vary. Each genre also draws on different types of SOURCES, for example, experiences, observations, and readings.

4b   What sources can I use in college writing?

A **source** is any form of information that provides ideas, examples, information, or evidence. Usually, students think of readings as sources, and clearly they are crucial. In fact, finding written sources is the topic of Chapters 29 and 30, and documenting sources is covered in Chapters 33–40. Summaries, for example, are concise restatements of a reading's main points, while syntheses weave together the ideas from two or more sources. Critical responses to readings are common college writing assignments. Chapter 7 discusses the differences between the kinds of writing that depend on readings as sources.

Your own memories and experiences are a source, even though you may not think of them that way. In personal essays, memoirs, and literacy narratives, your personal experiences are a source of stories that you can reflect on and analyze. Chapter 5 suggests processes for writing from experience and memory.

A third kind of source is direct observation. For example, you might be asked to observe people in a particular setting, take notes on their behaviors, and write a paper that explains what you've seen. You might be asked to attend a lecture and summarize what the speaker had to say or to write a response to it. You might be asked to gather instances of a particular social or cultural phenomenon and, using analysis, inference, or synthesis, explore the meaning of that phenomenon. For example, an assignment that asks you to analyze how adolescents are portrayed in current television programs would require you to observe several television shows, take notes, and explain your findings. We explain some types of writing about observations in Chapter 6. Two other genres based on observation, the case study and the ethnography, are used frequently in business, education, and the social sciences; see 17b.

A fourth kind of source is statistical or quantitative information, which comes in the form of numbers ("217 people liked mushroom pizza"), as percentages ("14% liked mushroom pizza"), or other statistics. You might find this information in a published written source, or you might generate it yourself by conducting surveys or laboratory experiments.

Finally, note that many assignments mix sources. You might be asked to relate one of your experiences to a reading in which someone else reports their own. You might do a study (for example, of public displays of affection or crowd behaviors at sporting events) that combines direct observations with a survey. We've explained these types separately just to make them clearer.

For more help with your
writing, grammar, and research,
go to **www.mycomplab.com**

Writing About Experiences

5a How do I write memoirs and personal essays?

Memoirs express a writer's memories. While memoirs, like autobiographies, can cover most of a person's life, they often focus on smaller slices, such as a particular incident or a related set of incidents.

Students often think that, unless they're famous or something important or exciting has happened to them, their lives aren't worth writing about. Nothing could be further from the truth. What makes a memoir good is less what it's about than how the writer writes about it. Consider the following short example.

> I can remember my father driving our car into a filling station at the edge of Birmingham. Two miles after we passed a particular motel, he would turn onto Callahan drive, which was a gravel road.

There's nothing very interesting here, just some facts and a bare description. But consider this version, in which the author writes about driving from Tennessee to Alabama in the 1950s:

> After lunch, our father would fold up his map and tuck it in the felt visor until we pulled into the filling station on the outskirts of Birmingham. Are we there yet? We had arrived when we saw the Moon Winx Motel sign—a heart-stopping piece of American road art, a double-sided neon extravaganza; a big taxicab-yellow crescent with a man-in-the-moon on each side, a sly smile, a blue eye that winked, and that blatant misspelling that X that made us so happy. Two miles beyond the winking moon, the Chrysler's tires would crunch the bed of river pebbles on the Callahan drive. In morning light the pebbles were salmon, ochre, a calcium white—and the water-worn stones, from the one-time bed of the Tombiggee River, closed around our bare feet like cool pockets.

> —Emily Hiestand, *Angela the Upside-Down Girl*

The basic information is no more dramatic than in the first version. However, the careful description makes it interesting. The main purpose of a memoir is to create a vivid sense of the experience for its readers. Memoirs have an expressive or literary purpose.

Personal essays are closely related to memoirs. You'll still want to tell about an experience, but personal essays tend to contain more reflection and to make their points more explicitly than memoirs. They answer the question, "What does this experience mean?" or "How does my experience illustrate a particular idea?" Quick Reference 5.1 lists important points about these genres.

Try some of the following processes for writing memoirs and personal essays.

1. Generating ideas

- In your first draft, concentrate on getting the basic story down. Pretend you're writing to a friend who is interested in what you're saying.
- Try creating some detailed scenes, describing the physical setting and including some dialogue so readers will get a close sense of being there.
- Do some FREEWRITING or use other invention strategies about the significance of your story. What did you learn at the time? How about looking back now? How does the experience connect to other experiences,

Quick Reference 5.1

Important elements of memoirs and personal essays

- A well-told story. Your readers will want to know what happened. They will also need enough background and context so they can fully understand what happened and appreciate why it made an impression.

- Lively details. Help your readers see and hear, perhaps even smell, taste, and feel what you were experiencing. Recreate the place and time and the people who were involved. Give readers reason to like (or dislike) the places or people involved by the way you characterize them.

- Reflective or analytic paragraphs or passages. In addition to telling readers what happened, also tell them what you were thinking during the experience (take us inside your head at the time) or what you make of it now, looking backward.

- An effective writing style and tone (10c).

readings, or ideas you've encountered in the world around you (in movies or television, for example, or in work, school, or family life)?

2. **Shaping ideas**

- The basic shape of a memoir is a story; however, it will also probably have some commentary or reflection (when you "step back" and explain what it all means). You can put that reflection at the beginning, the middle, or the end, or you can scatter it in a few places. Choose the strategy that seems most effective.

- You can begin at the beginning of the story, of course. But you can also begin with some exciting or interesting part from the middle or the end, and then go back to the beginning to tell how it all started. You've probably seen movies that have flashbacks, which are examples of this technique.

- Try to have places in your story where you "slow down," creating a scene in detail, as well as where you "speed up," covering events quickly so you can get to the interesting stuff.

3. **Revising your memoir or personal essay**

- Do your story and its details convey your impression of the experience? A common piece of advice is to "show, not tell." Try this experiment. Temporarily leave out any explicit statements about the story and what it means, and show the draft to a friend or peer. Let them tell you what they see as the point or meaning. If they can't—or if their interpretation differs significantly from yours—you need to revise. Put the explicit statements back in for your final draft.

- Are there places where you need more specific detail?
- Are there places where the writing drags too much and needs to be cut?
- Are the reflective or analytic parts thoughtful and interesting, or are they formulaic or obvious?

5b   How do I write literacy narratives?

A literacy narrative is a specific kind of memoir in which you tell the story of how you developed as a reader and writer. Generally, these stories stretch from your earliest memories to the present day. First-year writing instructors sometimes assign literacy narratives, as do some education and social sciences instructors.

Quick Reference 5.2

Important elements of literacy narratives

- The elements important to memoirs and personal essays also matter for literacy narratives: a good story, lively details, and reflection.
- Examples of your previous reading, writing, or other language experiences. These may include book titles, papers you remember writing, specific people important in your development as a reader and writer, scenes from school or home, and so on.

Try some of the following processes for writing literacy narratives.

1. **Generating ideas**

   Several questions can help you generate ideas.

   - What are the earliest books or stories you can remember someone reading to you? The earliest you can remember reading yourself? Can you tell us about more than the titles? Why do you think you remember these stories?
   - If people read to you, what do you remember about them? Can you create word pictures of them?
   - Where did you read or write at different points in your life? Can you describe the settings vividly?
   - What were your favorite books? What topics did you like to read about? What particular writings do you remember?

- What were your worst experiences reading or writing? What made them bad?
- Who or what were your strongest influences on reading or writing—either for good or ill?
- How did reading and writing "fit in" (or not) with other activities in your life?
- Why do you think you became the type of reader and writer you are today—whatever kind that is?

2. Shaping ideas

The strategies for shaping literacy narratives are the same as those for shaping memoirs and personal essays. See page 18.

3. Revising your literacy narrative

Here are some questions to ask (or to have a peer response group ask (8c) when revising:

- Do all the incidents contribute effectively to the whole narrative? Are there any that need to be cut or shortened?
- Are there places that would be stronger if I created a more vivid scene?
- Are there smooth connections and transitions between the different elements?
- Have I reflected on the meaning of the experiences? Have I included some general observations on what my experiences "add up to" and tell about me as a reader and writer?

For more help with your
writing, grammar, and research,
go to **www.mycomplab.com**

Writing About Observations

6a   How do I write reports of observations?

Sometimes your assignment is to report about an event. You're asked to attend a presentation or lecture and summarize the talk. You go to a concert, play, or sporting event with the goal of explaining what happened. In these writing situations, your purpose is to inform, and your role is to be an objective reporter, much like a journalist. Other times you may be asked to describe a scene (a landscape, a theatre set, a classroom), a person, a process, an object (a sculpture, a building, a machine), or an image. We devote a separate section (3a) to viewing and analyzing images. Two other kinds of reports of observations are case studies and ethnographies (17b).

Quick Reference 6.1

Important elements of a report

- A clear description of what you observed, which is complete and appropriately detailed—but not excessively so
- Objectivity
- The format that your instructor requires

Try the following processes for writing a report of an observation.

1. **Generating and drafting ideas**
   - Take careful notes. The quality of your report will depend on the clarity and fullness of the details you generate.
   - If you're writing about an event, gather information needed to answer the journalist's questions, which are particularly useful for this kind of writing. Write your first draft as soon after the event as possible, while your notes are still fresh.
   - Ask questions, if possible, not only of speakers or performers but also of other people attending the event. Ask what they observed.
   - Be precise with descriptions, noting both major and seemingly minor details.

2. **Shaping ideas**
   - Orient your readers in the first paragraph. Provide all of the general information (who, what, when, where, how, and why) in your opening.
   - Provide details in body paragraphs. You can organize events or processes either by chronological order (the sequence in which things happened) or by categories or topics.
   - Organize reports about objects by giving a big picture, then moving either spatially (left to right, top to bottom, center to edge) or by features.

3. Revising your report of an observation

Ask yourself or peer reviewers the following questions.

- Have I maintained objectivity throughout? Would my report agree with the report of someone else writing about the same thing?
- Did I write an introduction that gives readers a good overall picture?
- Would everything be clear to an audience who hadn't observed what I did?
- Are there any places where I either need more detail or where I need to make the report more concise?
- Have I fulfilled all of the assignment's special considerations (Quick Reference 1.1 on page 3)?

6b How do I write reviews or evaluations?

A **review** is a report plus an evaluation: a reasoned judgment of whether something is good or bad, fair or unfair, true or false, effective or useless. You're familiar with movie, music, and product reviews, which are designed to help you decide whether to invest your time, attention, or money. Reviews in academic situations show how thoughtfully you can evaluate a presentation, performance, product, event, art work, or some other object of inquiry.

Quick Reference 6.2 ■ ■ ■ ■ ■ ■ ■

Important elements of reviews

- Two elements are required: a summary or description and an evaluation of the source's quality or significance. Your thesis needs to take the form of an evaluation.
- Reasons for your evaluation and evidence for those reasons
- Answers to any specific questions your instructor asks and attention to any special considerations of the assignment

---

Try the following processes to write reviews and evaluations.

1. Generating and drafting ideas

- The advice for reporting applies. In addition, you need to generate an assessment. This involves critical thinking (Chapter 2).
- Analyze the source, using strategies in 2b. Pay attention to both content and style.

- Synthesize, if appropriate. How does the source relate to other ones like it?

2. **Shaping ideas**
   - Provide an overview of the event and your thesis in the opening paragraph.
   - Summarize the source in the early part of the paper (a paragraph or two after your opening) so your audience understands it. Depending on the type of source you're writing about, this could include a summary of the plot, a description of the setting, a list of songs performed, a physical description of an image or object, and so on.
   - In each of your remaining body paragraphs, start with a topic sentence that makes an assertion about some feature, followed by an explanation or evidence. You may want to save details from your summary/description to include when you discuss particular features.

3. **Revising your review or evaluation**

   Answer the following questions, or ask peer reviewers to answer them.
   - Is basic information clear?
   - Have I included judgments?
   - Have I provided enough details and evidence to make my judgments convincing?

■ Interpretations

An interpretation makes an argument about what something means or why it's significant. You might be familiar with interpretations from studying fiction or poetry, and we talk more about that kind of writing in Chapter 16. However, interpretation is hardly restricted to readings. Consider the following different assignment questions:

- In the painting *Guernica,* what do you think Picasso wants his viewers to feel and understand?
- What is the atmosphere of a particular place (a coffee shop, a shopping mall, a club)?
- How are doctors and nurses portrayed on television?

Each of these examples involves both description and interpretation. When you're writing an interpretation, don't feel like you have to "guess the right answer," as if there's one and only one right meaning. Instead, the quality of your work will depend on generating interesting insights that you then support with reasons. Analysis and inference are especially important for interpretation; see Quick Reference 1.2 on page 4.

Quick Reference 6.3

Important elements of an interpretation

- A clear explanation of the event, phenomenon, or object that you're interpreting
- Statements about what the subject of your interpretation means or why it is significant
- Convincing support, including reasoning, to show why your interpretive statements should be persuasive

Try the following processes when writing an interpretation.

1. **Generating ideas**
   - Summarize and describe very carefully; the act of paying close attention can generate important insights.
   - Use strategies of analysis and inference (2b).
   - Don't be afraid to explore. Brainstorm as many possible interpretations as you can; many of them might be outlandish, but it's better to choose from several possible interpretations than to be stuck with the first thing that comes to mind.
   - Play "the believing game." Believe that you have the authority and expertise to generate an interpretation and boldly put it on paper.

2. **Shaping ideas**
   - Good interpretations have a thesis that states the meaning or significance that your paper will then go on to explain.
   - Body paragraphs will each offer an explanation for your interpretation, with support and reasoning showing readers why it is plausible.

3. **Revising your interpretation**
   - Play "the doubting game." Assume (for the purpose of thinking critically) that your interpretation is flawed. State the flaws. Then revise to address them.
   - Ask whether the balance of summary and interpretation is effective. Are there places where you need more reasoning or support?

7

■ ■ ■ ■ ■

Writing About Readings

7a How can I write about readings?

To respond to readings or other works such as films, music CDs, paintings, and performances, you may be asked to write summaries, critical responses, analyses or interpretations, and syntheses. Analyses take up certain aspects of the work and discuss the impact of those parts on the whole. Syntheses weave together information and ideas from several sources. In an interpretation, the writer infers a theme from a work (Ch. 16). Be careful to distinguish summary (7b, next) from synthesis (7d).

7b How do I write a summary?

To summarize is to extract the main messages or central points of a reading and restate them in a much briefer fashion. A summary doesn't include supporting evidence or details. It's the gist, the hub, the seed of what the author is saying. A summary does not include your personal reaction to the reading.

How you summarize depends on your situation and assignment. For example, you can summarize an entire 500-page book in a single sentence, in a single page, or in five or six pages. Typically, your instructor will tell you how long a summary needs to be; if he or she doesn't, it's reasonable for you to ask.

Following are examples of two different levels of summary based on the same source.

SUMMARY IN A SINGLE SENTENCE

Research finds that people with large numbers of choices are actually less happy than people with fewer choices (Schwartz).

SUMMARY IN 50 TO 100 WORDS

Boshoven 1

Kristin Boshoven

English 101

Professor Lequire

5 April 2008

Summary of "The Tyranny of Choice"

Research finds that people with large numbers of choices
are actually less happy than people with fewer choices.
Although the amount of wealth and number of choices have
increased during the past thirty years, fewer Americans report
themselves as being happy, and depression, suicide, and
mental health problems have increased. While some choice is
good, having too many choices hinders decision making,
especially among "maximizers," who try to make the best
possible choices. Research in shopping, education, and
medical settings shows that even when people eventually
decide, they experience regret, worrying that the options they
didn't choose might have been better (Schwartz).

Boshoven 2

Work Cited

Schwartz, Barry. "The Tyranny of Choice." *Chronicle of Higher
Education* (23 Jan. 2004): B6. Print.

Notice that the longer summary begins with the same sentence as the short one; leading a summary with the reading's main idea is effective. Notice that both summaries put ideas in the writer's own words and capture only the main idea.

One decision to make in summary writing is whether to refer to the author or to leave him or her out, as in the earlier examples. Check if your instructor has a preference. The second example above could be rewritten (the four dots are ellipses, showing material left out):

> In "The Tyranny of Research," Barry Schwartz summaries research that finds that people with large numbers of choices. . . . Schwartz contends that, while some choice is good, too many choices. . . .

Quick Reference 7.1   ∎ ∎ ∎ ∎ ∎ ∎ ∎

Important elements of summaries

- Inclusion of only the source's main ideas.
- Proportional summary of the source. Longer and more important aspects of the original need to get more space and attention in your summary.
- Use of your own words. If you need to use key terms or phrases from the source, include them in quotation marks, but otherwise put everything into your own words.
- Accurate documentation of the original source.

Try the following processes for writing summaries. (*Note:* For more help in writing a summary, see section 31h.)

1. **Generating ideas**
   - Identify TOPIC SENTENCES or main ideas, separating them from examples or illustrations. You want to focus on the main ideas.
   - Take notes in your own words, then put the source away. Write from your notes, going back to check the original only after you've written a first draft.

2. **Shaping ideas**
   - Begin with a sentence that summarizes the entire reading, unless you're writing a particularly long summary.
   - Follow the order of the original.

- Include a Works Cited (Chapter 34) or References (Chapter 37) page, depending on the required DOCUMENTATION STYLE.

3. Revising your summary

- Have I maintained objectivity throughout?
- Have I put ideas into my own words?
- Is the summary proportional?
- Is documentation accurate?
- Can I make any statements more CONCISE (Ch. 50)?

7c How do I write a critical response?

A **critical response** essay has two missions: to provide a SUMMARY of a source's main idea and to respond to that idea. In a critical response, also called a critique or a *review,* you present judgments about a particular work, supported by your underlying reasoning. For example, a movie, book, music, or art review should present the writer's carefully reasoned, well-supported opinion of the work. Critical responses and reviews may focus on the literary form, or genre, of a work (for example, "How well does this poem satisfy the conventions of a sonnet?"). Responses or reviews may focus on a work's accuracy, logic, or conclusions ("Is this history of rap music complete and accurate?"). Finally, responses or reviews may analyze a work's relation to other works ("Is the stage version of a certain play better or worse than the film version?") or a work's similarities to and differences from the "real" world ("To what extent do television comedies accurately portray American family life?").

Here is student Kristin Boshoven's short critical response to Barry Schwartz's essay, "The Tyranny of Choice," which was summarized above. Note that it incorporates the summary.

Kristin Boshoven

English 101

Professor Lequire

7 April 2008

Too Much Choice: Disturbing but Not Destructive

Barry Schwartz argues that people with large numbers of choices are actually less happy than people with fewer choices. Although the amount of wealth and choice has increased during the past thirty years, studies show that fewer Americans report themselves as being happy. Depression, suicide, and mental health problems have increased. While some choice is good, too many choices hinder decision making, especially among people who Schwartz calls "maximizers," people who try to make the best possible choices. Research in shopping, education, and medical settings shows that even when people eventually decide, they experience regret, worrying that the options they didn't choose might have been better.

Although Schwartz cites convincing evidence for his claims, he ultimately goes too far in his conclusions. Excessive choice does seem to make life harder, not easier, but it alone can't be blamed for whatever unhappiness exists in our society.

My own experience supports Schwartz's finding that that people who have thirty choices of jam as opposed to six often don't purchase any. About a month ago my husband and I decided to buy an inexpensive global positioning (GPS) device to use in our car. When we went to the store, we were confronted with twenty different models, and even though a helpful salesperson explained the various features to me, we couldn't make up our minds. We decided to do more research, which was a mistake. After weeks of reading reviews in

Boshoven 2

everything from *Consumer Reports* to the *New York Times*, we are close to making a decision. However, I have a sinking feeling that as soon as we buy something, we'll learn that another choice would have been better, or ours will drop $50 in price. In the meantime, we could have been enjoying the use of a GPS system for the past month if we had not worried so much. I could relate similar experiences trying to choose which movie to see, which dentist to visit, and so on. I suspect others could, too, which is why I find Schwartz's argument convincing at this level.

However, when he suggests that the increase of choice is a source of things like depression and suicide, he goes too far. Our society has undergone tremendous changes in the past forty or fifty years, and many of those changes are more likely to cause problems than the existence of too much choice. For example, workers in the 1950s through the 1970s could generally count on holding jobs with one company as long as they wanted, even through retirement. A 1950s autoworker, for example, might not have been thrilled with his job (and these were jobs held almost exclusively by men), but at least he could count on it, and it paid enough to buy a house and education for his family. The economic uncertainties of the past twenty years, and especially since 2001, have meant that workers—and now women as well as men—do not have the same job stability as decades ago.

Although I agree that too many choices can lead to anxiety and even unhappiness, there are larger factors. If Americans report more depression and suicide than they once did, a more likely candidate is economic and social uncertainty, not having too many kinds of cereal on the grocery store shelves.

Boshoven 3

Work Cited

Schwartz, Barry. "The Tyranny of Choice." *Chronicle of Higher Education* (23 Jan. 2004): B6. Print.

Quick Reference 7.2

Important elements of critical responses

- A clear and concise summary of the source.
- Statements of agreement, disagreement, or qualified agreement (you accept some points but not others), accompanied by reasons and evidence for your statements.

Try the following processes for writing critical responses.

1. **Generating ideas**
   - Use ACTIVE READING (2c) and CRITICAL READING (2b) to identify the main points and generate reactions to the source.
   - Use techniques for ANALYZING (11f), drawing INFERENCES (2b), and assessing reasoning processes (13d–g).
   - Discuss the source with another person. Summarize its content and elicit the other person's opinion or ideas. Deliberately debate that opinion or challenge those ideas. Discussions and debates can get your mind moving. (If in your writing you use that other person's ideas, be sure to give the person credit as your source; see Chapter 31.)

2. **Shaping ideas**
   - Write a SUMMARY of the main idea or central point of the material you're responding to.
   - Write a smooth TRANSITION between the summary and your response. This transitional statement, which bridges the two parts, need not be a formal THESIS STATEMENT (8g), but it needs to signal clearly the beginning of your response.
   - Respond to the source based on your prior knowledge and experience.

3. Revising your critical response

Respond to the following questions as you consider possible revisions.

* Have I combined summary and response? Have I explained my response in a way that readers will find thoughtful and convincing?
* Have I fulfilled all DOCUMENTATION requirements? See Chapters 33–40 for coverage of four DOCUMENTATION STYLES (MLA, APA, CM, and CSE). Ask your instructor which style to use.

7d   How do I write a synthesis?

A **synthesis** weaves ideas together. Unsynthesized ideas and information are like separate spools of thread, neatly lined up, possibly coordinated, but not woven together or integrated. Synthesized ideas and information are like threads woven into a tapestry. By synthesizing, you show evidence of your ability to bring ideas together.

One common synthesizing task is to connect two or more readings or source materials into a single piece of writing. You complete this synthesis after you have summarized, analyzed, and evaluated each of the source materials. Another common type of synthesis is to connect material to what you already know. When you synthesize, you draw on ideas from what you have read, listened to, and experienced. In so doing, you create a new final product that is your own.

Don't be afraid to synthesize. We're always surprised to learn that some students assume that what they think has no value. Nothing could be farther from the truth—simply use your life experiences, television watching, reading, and everything else you can think of.

Your goal in synthesizing multiple sources is to join two or more texts together into a single piece of writing. The resulting text should be more than just a succession of summaries. That is, avoid merely listing who said what about a topic. Such a list isn't a synthesis—it doesn't create new connections among ideas.

The following example shows how student Tom Mentzer synthesized two sources. Read source 1 and source 2 to familiarize yourself with the information he read.

SOURCE 1

Shishmaref is melting into the ocean. Over the past 30 years, the Inupiaq Eskimo village, perched on a slender barrier island 625 miles north of Anchorage, has lost 100 ft. to 300 ft. of coastline—half of it since 1997. As Alaska's climate warms, the permafrost beneath the beaches is thawing and the sea ice is thinning, leaving its 600 residents increasingly vulnerable to violent storms. One house has collapsed, and 18 others had to be moved to higher ground, along with the town's bulk-fuel tanks.

—Margot Roosevelt, "Vanishing Alaska"

SOURCE 2

Global temperatures have risen by about 0.6 degrees Celsius since the nineteenth century. Other measures of climate bolster the theory that the world is getting warmer: satellite measurements suggest that spring arrives about a week earlier now than in the late 1970s, for example, and records show that migratory birds fly to higher latitudes earlier in the season and stay later.

—John Browne, "Beyond Kyoto"

Now read Tom's synthesis. Notice that he used summary (7a) and paraphrase (31g) to synthesize the two sources. Also look at how the first sentence in his synthesis weaves the sources together with a new concept.

EXAMPLE OF A SYNTHESIS OF TWO SOURCES

Global warming is affecting both the natural and artificial worlds. Rising temperatures have accelerated spring's arrival and changed the migration patterns of birds (Browne 20). They have also changed life for residents of Arctic regions. For example, eighteen families in Shishmaref, Alaska, had to move their houses away from the coast because the permafrost under the beaches had thawed (Roosevelt 68).

—Tom Mentzer, student

In his synthesis, Tom also used in-text citations (in MLA STYLE) to signal to the reader which information he borrowed from the two sources. In the Works Cited list at the end of his paper, Tom listed full source information for both sources. To learn how to document your sources, see Chapters 33 through 40.

SOURCES LISTED ON TOM'S WORKS CITED PAGE

Browne, John. "Beyond Kyoto." *Foreign Affairs* 83.4 (2004): 20-32. *Ebsco Host*. Web. 20 Apr. 2007.

Roosevelt, Margot. "Vanishing Alaska." *Time* 4 Oct. 2004: 68-70. Print.

Try the following techniques to write a synthesis.

- Make comparisons with—or contrasts between—ideas and information. Do the sources generally agree or generally disagree? What are the bases of their agreement or disagreement? Are there subtle differences or shades of meaning or emphasis?

- Create definitions that combine and extend definitions you encounter in the separate sources.
- Use examples or descriptions from one source to illustrate ideas in another.
- Use processes described in one source to explain those in others.
- In revising, ask, "Have I truly synthesized the sources, or have I just written about one and then the other?"

7e   How do I write essays that apply theories or concepts?

Some essays apply theories or concepts from one source to another source or situation, usually for the purpose of interpretation or evaluation. Two examples will make this clearer.

1. How does Smith's theory of social deviance explain the behaviors of criminals in Jones' book?

2. Based on your own experiences, are Beaudoin's categories of high school cliques accurate?

The following advice will help you write essays of application.

1. Generating ideas

- Brainstorm a list of all the possible ways the specific source illustrates or "fits" the concept or theory. Use analysis (11f) or inference (2b).
- Brainstorm a list of ways the specific source disproves or complicates the concept or theory.

2. Shaping ideas

- Begin your essay with a brief summary of the theory or concept (7b), leading to a thesis that states how it applies to the specific situation or reading you're discussing.
- Your next paragraphs will need to summarize your specific source.
- Next, include paragraphs to support your thesis, giving reasons for your assertion.

3. Revising your essay of application

- Have you explained both sources accurately and efficiently?
- Have you written a strong thesis and provided reasons and support?

For more help with your writing, grammar, and research,
go to **www.mycomplab.com**

mycomplab

8

Planning and Shaping Writing

8a What is the writing process?

Many people assume that a real writer can magically write a finished product, word by perfect word. Experienced writers know that writing is a process, a series of activities that starts the moment they begin thinking about a topic and ends when they complete a final draft. In addition, experienced writers are aware that good writing is actually rewriting—again and yet again. Their drafts contain additions, deletions, rewordings, and rearrangements. Figure 8.1 shows how Lynn drafted and revised the first few sentences of this chapter.

As you work through the writing process as described in Quick Reference 8.1 (p. 36), remember that writing is a recursive activity, which means that writers often move back before moving ahead, skip a step and go back to it later, or finish a section but later decide to return to it. As the circles and arrows in Figure 8.2 show, planning is not over when drafting begins; drafting is not over when revising begins; editing might take you back to revising; and so on.

For example, consider that a college essay has an INTRODUCTORY PARAGRAPH* (11b), as many BODY PARAGRAPHS (11d) as you need to cover your topic, and a CONCLUDING PARAGRAPH (11g). As you're writing, you might discover you need to think of a new topic for one of your body paragraphs so that it's in line with

Many people assume that a real writer can ^magically^ write a finished product, ~~easily.~~ ^word by perfect word.^ Experienced writers know ~~better than~~ that⊙ writing is a process,~~that involves~~ a series of activities that starts ~~when the writers start~~ ^the moment they begin^ thinking ^about a topic^ and ends ~~with~~ a final draft. ^when they complete^

Figure 8.1 Draft and revision of the beginning of the first paragraph in 8a

---

*Words printed in SMALL CAPITAL LETTERS are discussed elsewhere in the text and are defined in the Terms Glossary at the back of the book.

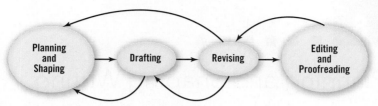

Figure 8.2 Visualizing the writing process

Quick Reference 8.1   ■ ■ ■ ■ ■ ■ ■

An overview of the writing process

- **Planning** means gathering ideas and thinking about a focus for your writing.
- **Shaping** means considering ways to organize your material.
- **Drafting** means writing your ideas in sentences and paragraphs.
- **Revising** means evaluating your draft and then rewriting it by adding, cutting, replacing, moving, and often totally recasting material.
- **Editing** means checking for correct grammar, spelling, punctuation, and mechanics.
- **Proofreading** means checking your final draft for typing errors or handwriting legibility, so that what you hand in is as clean as possible.

---

your introduction. Similarly, as you write your concluding paragraph, you might realize that a body paragraph or the introductory paragraph needs revision to flow smoothly with the style and tone of the rest of your essay. Paths differ for each writer and for the same writer in each new WRITING SITUATION (1c).

Here's our personal advice: Most writers struggle with ideas that are difficult to express, sentences that won't take shape, and words that aren't precise. Be patient with yourself; writing takes time. The more you write, the easier it will become.

8b What are the purposes for writing?

A writer's PURPOSE for writing is the motivating force behind what that writer wishes or is assigned to write. You need, therefore, to choose among the four major purposes of writing, listed in Quick Reference 8.2.

In this book, we concentrate on two major purposes: to inform a reader and to persuade a reader. These are the most common purposes for **academic writing**, the writing people do for college and scholarship. They're also the

Quick Reference 8.2

Purposes for writing

- To inform a reader
- To persuade a reader
- To express yourself or make connections with others
- To create a literary work

most common purposes for **workplace writing**, the writing that people do on the job, and for **civic writing** or **public writing**, the writing meant to communicate with or influence public audiences. The two remaining purposes listed in Quick Reference 8.2 contribute to human thought and culture, but they relate less to what most college writing involves.

■ Informing a reader

Informative writing, also called *expository writing,* seeks to give and explain information to readers. It expounds on—systematically tells about—observations, ideas, facts, scientific data, and statistics. Typically, you can find informative writing in textbooks, encyclopedias, technical and business reports, nonfiction books, Web sites maintained by professional organizations, newspapers, and many magazines. Chapter 12 explains qualities of effective informative writing. Here's an example of an informative paragraph.

> Poison is a stealth killer, effective in minuscule amounts, often undetectable. It's the treachery in the arsenic-tainted glass of wine. The fatal attraction: Snow White's poison apple, the death-defying art of the snake handler, the Japanese roulette practiced by those who eat fugu. Without poison, comic book superheroes and villains in plays and movies would be considerably duller. Spiderman exists by the grace of a radioactive spider bite. The rise of the Teenage Mutant Ninja Turtles can be traced to their fall (as pet turtles) into a sewer along with a container of toxic materials. Laertes used a poison-dipped sword to kill Hamlet, and Claude Rains's nasty mother kept sneaking poison drops into Ingrid Bergman's drinks in the Hitchcock thriller *Notorious.*
>
> —Cathy Newman, "The Poison Paradox"

■ Persuading a reader

Persuasive writing, also called *argumentative writing,* seeks to convince readers about a matter of opinion. Examples of persuasive writing include newspaper editorials, letters to the editor, opinion pieces in newspapers and magazines or on the Web, business proposals, legal arguments, reviews, sermons, books that argue a point of view, and advertising. Chapter 13, "Writing to Argue," explains how to write effective and engaging arguments. Here's an example of a persuasive paragraph.

> The most visible evidence that commercialism now dominates religious holidays in the United States comes from the push to spend money rather than honor special observances. Individuals and businesses buy and mail huge quantities of Christmas cards. How many people can resist the social and business pressures of sending cards? Furthermore, often exchanging expensive gifts has become standard practice on Christmas Day and for weeks beforehand. Many people go into credit card debt that lasts for half a year or longer merely to support the costly cycle of giving and receiving presents. The advertising industry makes huge profits from writing ads that set high expectations among children and adults alike.
>
> —Linda Brighteyes, student

8c   Who is my audience?

Your **audience** consists of everyone who will read your writing, whether you are writing for academic, business, or civic purposes. Throughout your life, you will address a variety of audiences, including

- Your peers (fellow students, professional colleagues, members of your community)
- A general audience (educated, experienced readers who don't have specialized knowledge of your topic)
- A specialized audience (people who have specialized knowledge of your topic)
- Your instructor or supervisor

Skilled writers adapt their work for different audiences. For example, you wouldn't explain photosynthesis to a six-year-old the same way you would explain it to a college biology major. If you're writing a sales report for your supervisor, you would comfortably use technical terms such as *product life cycle, breakeven quantity, nonprice competition,* and *markup* without fear of being misunderstood. In contrast, if general readers were your audience, you would want to avoid such specialized words unless you defined them clearly. The better you understand your audience for your writing situation, the better your chances of reaching its members successfully.

One way to analyze your audience is to ask yourself, "Who are its members? What are their ages and genders; their ethnic backgrounds, political views, and religious beliefs; their interests or hobbies; their roles (for example, student, parent, voter, wage earner, property owner, veteran)?" For more ways to analyze your audience, see Quick Reference 8.3.

Quick Reference 8.3

Ways to analyze your audience

Knowledge. Does the audience know less than you, as much as you, or more than you?

Beliefs. Does the audience agree with your point of view, disagree with your point of view, or have no opinion about the topic?

Interest. Is the audience eager to read about the topic, open to the topic, or resistant or uninterested in the topic?

Relation to you. Is the audience made up of personal friends or family members, acquaintances, coworkers, or people you've never met?

Situation. Are you writing for an audience in the classroom, in the workplace, or in a social situation?

ESOL Tip: As someone from another culture, you might be surprised—even offended—by the directness with which people speak and write in the United States. If so, we hope you'll read our open letter to multilingual writers about honoring one's native culture (pp. 477–478). The idea is that as you write for US audiences, you need to adapt to US writing style. Your own written-language traditions may expect elaborate or ceremonial language, call for you to introduce the central point in the essay's middle, and prefer more tactful and indirect discussions than US style. In contrast, US writing is direct, straightforward, and without digressive embellishments. College instructors in the United States expect ACADEMIC WRITING to contain a THESIS STATEMENT (usually at the end of the introductory paragraph—see 8g), to demonstrate a tightly organized presentation of information from one paragraph to the next, to make generalizations that are always backed up with strong supporting details, and to end with a logical concluding paragraph. In addition, you need to use standard English grammar, as spoken by most announcers on major television network news programs. ●

Writing for a peer-response group

Participating in a **peer-response group** (a team of students, coworkers, or other associates) makes you part of a respected tradition of colleagues helping colleagues. Professional writers often seek comments from other writers to improve their rough drafts. In many business areas, final drafts almost always result from many people sharing thoughts and ideas. As a member of a college peer-response group, you're not expected to be a writing expert. Rather, you're expected to offer responses as a practiced reader and a student writer who knows the difficulties of writing well. Hearing or reading comments from your peers can be very informative, surprising, and helpful. Use the guidelines in Quick Reference 8.4 to help ensure that your participation will be helpful to other writers.

Quick Reference 8.4   ■ ■ ■ ■ ■ ■ ■

Guidelines for participating in peer-response groups

One major principle needs to guide your participation in a peer-response group: Always take an upbeat, constructive attitude, whether you're responding to someone else's writing or receiving responses from others.

- Think of yourself as a coach, not a judge.
- Consider all writing by your peers as "works in progress."
- After hearing or reading a peer's writing, briefly summarize it to check that you understand what the person said or wrote.
- Start with what you think is well done. No one likes to hear only negative comments.
- Be honest in your suggestions for improvement.
- Give concrete and specific responses. General comments such as "This is good" or "This is weak" don't offer much help. Describe specifically what is good or weak.
- Follow your instructor's system for putting your comments in writing so that your fellow writer can recall what you said. If one member of your group is supposed to take notes, speak clearly so that the person's notes can be accurate. If you're the note taker, be accurate and ask the speaker to repeat what he or she said if the comment went by too quickly.

■ Writing for an instructor

As your audience, your instructor plays three roles. An instructor (1) represents either general or specialized readers, (2) acts as your writing coach, and (3) becomes the eventual evaluator of your final drafts.

Instructors know that few students are experienced writers or experts on their topics. Still, instructors expect your writing to show that you took serious time to learn something worthwhile about a subject and then to write about it clearly, within the constraints of academic writing. Instructors are experienced readers; they recognize a minimal effort almost at once.

You might wrongly assume that your instructor can mentally fill in what you haven't bothered to say fully. You might think that you would be wrong, even insulting, if you extended your discussion beyond simple statements. However, instructors—indeed, all readers—are not mind readers, and they question your knowledge and abilities if you don't write fully on a topic. Go beyond stating the obvious and show that you know how to develop your material beyond bare-bones basics.

■ Writing for a supervisor

Supervisors expect employees to carefully prepare memos, notes, lesson plans, briefs, presentations, or reports. Like instructors, supervisors may read your work through the eyes of its intended audience—if the audience is not the supervisors themselves. They may coach you through revisions, and they may evaluate your work, not directly with a grade (as an instructor would) but indirectly with periodic performance reviews. Supervisors, like instructors, recognize subpar work prepared minutes before a meeting or deadline. Before you begin an assignment, remember to find out what your supervisor (your audience) is looking for and write to those specifications.

8d How do I work with a writing topic?

Situations vary. Some college and workplace assignments are very specific about your topic. For example, "Explain how oxygen is absorbed in the lungs" or "Summarize the results of the market survey" leaves no room for choice. You need to write about those topics precisely, without going off in some other direction.

Writing-class assignments are rarely that specific. More often, your instructor asks you to select your own topic, to narrow a broad topic, or to broaden a narrow topic. As you do this, the overriding principle is always this: **What separates most good writing from bad is the writer's ability to move back and forth between general statements and specific details.**

■ Selecting your own topic

If you need to choose a topic, take time to think through your ideas. Avoid getting so deeply involved in one topic that you can't change to a more suitable topic in the time allotted. Not all topics are suitable for academic writing.

Think through potential topics by breaking each into its logical subsections. Then make sure you can supply sufficiently specific details to back up each general statement. Your topic needs to allow you to demonstrate your intellectual thinking and writing abilities. Conversely, make sure you don't drown your essay with so many details that your readers can't figure out what generalizations they are supporting. Work toward balance by finding a middle ground. That is, beware of topics so broad that they lead to vague generalizations (for example, "Education is necessary for success"). Also, beware of topics so narrow that they lead nowhere after a few sentences (for example, "Jessica Max attends Tower College").

■ Narrowing or broadening an assigned topic

Suppose that "marriage" is your assigned topic for a 1,000-word essay. Your topic would be too broad if you chose "What makes a successful marriage?" Conversely, it would be too narrow if you came up with "Alexandra and Gavin were married by a justice of the peace." You'd likely be on target with a topic such as "In successful marriages, husbands and wives learn to accept many of each other's faults." You could use 1,000 words to explain and give concrete examples of typical faults and discuss why accepting them is important.

Sara Cardini, the student whose essay appears in 12b, knew that her assigned topic, "Explain to an educated audience something you learned outside of a classroom," was too broad. She had to be specific. She wanted to discuss how she learned about a culture other than her own. She realized that her narrower topic, "Japanese culture," was still too broad. She thought of some even narrower topics, such as "Japanese music" or "Japanese schools." In the end, she chose "Japanese videos" and, even more specifically, a kind of Japanese animation called "anime" (commonly pronounced AN-a-may). Some extensive experiences had taught her about the topic, and she could think of both generalizations and specific details to use in her essay. In addition, Sara knew that if she needed to do research, she could find many sources in books and magazines and on the Internet.

8e   How can I collaborate with other writers?

Experience in collaborative writing has benefits beyond your college years because working well with others is a skill that employers value. Collaborative writing projects are common in the business and professional world. Marketing managers, for example, lead teams who conduct consumer research and then—as a group—write up their findings. Often, the size or complexity of a project means that only a team of people can accomplish it in the given amount of time.

Collaborative writing assignments are increasingly popular in college courses across the curriculum, especially in business, the sciences, and the social sciences. Even if they aren't required to write full papers, small groups are commonly asked to brainstorm a topic together before individual writing tasks, to discuss various sides of a debatable topic, or to share reactions to an essay or piece of literature the class reads.

Three qualities are essential to collaborative writing. The first is careful planning. Your group needs to decide when and how it will meet (in person, in a telephone call, in an online discussion); what steps it will follow and what the due dates will be; what software you'll use; and who will be responsible for what.

The second essential quality is a fair division of labor. Almost nothing causes bad feelings more quickly than when some group members feel like they're doing far more than their share. During early planning meetings, the group should figure out the tasks involved in the project and estimate how much time and effort each will take. (You can rebalance things during later meetings, if necessary.)

One basic way a group can divide tasks is according to the different steps in the writing process. One or more people can be in charge of generating ideas or conducting research; one or more can be in charge of writing the first draft; one or more can be in charge of revising; and one or more may be in charge of editing, proofreading, and formatting the final draft. However, it's hard to sep-arate these tasks cleanly, and we warn you that writing the first draft often re-quires more effort than any other element. This approach also means that some group members will be waiting for others to complete their parts.

A second way to divide tasks is to assign part of the project to each per-son. Many projects can be broken into sections, and using an outline (8h) can help you see what those sections are. Each person can then plan, write, revise, and edit a section, and the other members can serve as a built-in peer-response group to make suggestions for revision. This approach can have the advantage of distributing the work more cleanly at the outset, but it often takes a lot of work at the end to stitch the parts together. It can be difficult when several people try to complete this final editing and compilation.

In reality, you'll probably find your group using a combination of these two approaches. You'll also probably find it useful to assign people basic roles such as leader (or facilitator) and recorder (or secretary). These roles can change dur-ing the project, but in our experience groups find it efficient when someone takes responsibility for calling and leading meetings.

The third essential element of collaborative projects is clear communica-tion. Open and honest communication is vital, and people need to put aside their own egos to build a productive and trusting atmosphere. Keep notes for every meeting so that the group has a clear record of what was decided; one way to do this is to have someone send an e-mail summarizing each meeting. If people disagree over the group's decisions, the group should resolve that dis-agreement before moving on. You'll also find it effective to ask for regular re-ports from each group member.

8f   How can I find ideas for writing?

Do you ever worry that you have nothing to write about? You're not alone. The techniques listed here can help you uncover ideas and details to use in your writing. If one technique doesn't provide enough useful material, try another.

■ Keeping a journal or blog

Writing in a journal is like having a conversation with yourself. You can write about anything you like—your experiences, observations, dreams, creative ideas, reactions to your reading. Some people like the feeling and informality of pen in hand traveling over a notebook. Others keep a journal on a computer or even online in a BLOG (26a).

Why do it? First, writing every day gives you the habit of productivity. The more you write, the more you get used to the feeling of expressing yourself through words. Second, writing regularly in a journal helps you think through ideas that need time to develop. Third, your journal becomes a source of ideas when you need to choose your own writing topic (8d).

■ Freewriting

Freewriting means writing whatever comes into your mind about any topic that surfaces, without stopping to worry about whether your ideas are good or your spelling is correct. Such writing is a voyage of discovery in which you allow your thoughts to emerge as you write. **Focused freewriting** means starting with a favorite word or sentence from your journal, a quotation you like, or perhaps a topic you are studying for a course, and then freewriting with that focus in mind. When you freewrite, don't interrupt the flow. Keep writing. Don't censor your thoughts or insights. Don't review or cross out.

Sometimes, when you have finished freewriting and read over what you have written, you may think it seems mindless or uninspired. But on other occasions, your insights may startle or delight you.

■ Chatting

Chatting, in the traditional sense, means talking. Sometimes talking over possible topics with a friend or colleague can generate some ideas. Just be sure to write about those ideas soon afterward, before you forget them.

In a more recent sense, however, chatting also refers to "talking" online through instant messaging, e-mail, and other electronic forums. Exchanging ideas online not only stimulates your thinking but also acts as a writing warm-up. Figure 8.3 is an excerpt from an online chatting session.

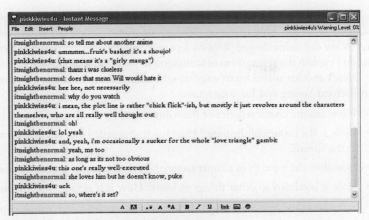

Figure 8.3 Online chatting session

Brainstorming

Brainstorming means listing everything you can think of about a topic. Let your mind roam freely, generating quantities of ideas before analyzing them. After you've brainstormed, look for patterns and ways to group your ideas. Discard items that don't fit into any group. Groups with the most items are likely to be topics you can write about successfully.

Here's some brainstorming by student writer Sara Cardini, whose essay on Japanese animation appears in 12b. Sara grouped the items marked with an asterisk and used them in her third paragraph.

types of anime: robot movies, comedies, romances

images move quickly*

big-eyed characters*

dubbing vs. subtitles

jazz and rock music*

diverse people like anime

colorful and complicated animation*

example: *Samurai X**

different from Disney cartoons

Asking and answering questions

Try exploring your topic by asking questions that journalists use: Who? What? Where? When? Why? How?

These were Sara Cardini's prewriting questions: *Who* are the people interested in anime? *What* are some common elements of anime? *Where* did anime originate? *When* did anime begin? *Why* do Japanese and American animation differ? *How* do I explain the anime form of animation to someone who has never seen it?

Here's another useful list of questions developed some years ago by rhetorician Richard Young and his colleagues.

- What are the characteristics of the topic?
- What is the history of the topic? How has it changed? How might it change in the future?
- How does the topic fit in a larger context? To what categories does it belong?
- How is it related to other things or ideas? How is it similar or different?

Sara also asked herself some of these questions to write her anime paper: *What* are the basic characteristics of anime? *What* is the history of anime? Has it changed? Do I expect it to change in the future? *How* is anime similar to or different from other kinds of animation? *How* is anime connected to Japanese culture?

■ Clustering

Clustering, also called *mapping,* is a visual form of brainstorming. Write your topic in the middle of a sheet and then circle it. Now, moving out from the center, use lines and circles to record your ideas. Continue using this method to subdivide and add details. For example, here's part of Sara's clustering for the second paragraph of her essay about Japanese anime (12b).

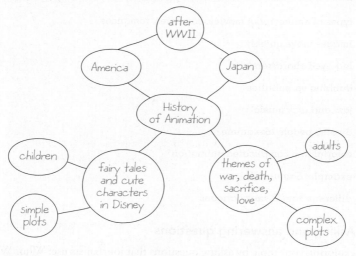

8g What is a thesis statement?

The essay forms the basis of most academic writing. A **thesis statement** is the central message of an essay. Your thesis statement both reflects the content of your essay and guides your writing. To compose a thesis statement, first write a simple statement that makes an **assertion**. An assertion names your topic and states your position on it. Writing an assertion focuses your thinking as you progress toward a fully developed thesis statement. As you are writing, if you find that your thesis statement and the content of your essay don't match, revise one or the other—or perhaps both.

Here's student writer Sara Cardini's assertion for her informative essay about Japanese anime (12b), followed by her progress toward a final version of her thesis statement.

I think Japanese animation is interesting. [This assertion is a start, but simply to proclaim something "interesting" is dull.]

Most people think cartoons are simple entertainment for kids, but there are exceptions to that rule. [This statement draws readers in by promising to show them how their expectations may be inadequate, and there really isn't a "rule" involved.]

Anime is a sophisticated Japanese cartoon style. [This statement is closer to a thesis statement because it is more specific. It promises to show that anime is sophisticated. However, the concept that anime differs from American cartoons is an important part of Sara's paper, and that concept is missing here.]

The purpose of this paper is to explain Japanese anime and how it differs from the style of American cartoons. [This version clearly states a main point of the paper, but it is inappropriate because it announces what the writer is going to do.]

Anime has traditions and features that distinguish it from American cartoons and make it appeal to adults as well as children. [The final version serves as Sara's thesis statement by effectively conveying the main ideas and point of her essay.]

Sara's final version fulfills the basic requirements for a thesis statement, as listed in Quick Reference 8.4.

Quick Reference 8.4

Basic requirements for a thesis statement

1. It states the essay's subject but does not repeat the title of the essay.
2. It indicates the essay's purpose but does not announce it with "The purpose of this essay is . . ."
3. It conveys the writer's point of view toward the subject.
4. It makes a general statement that leads to a set of main ideas and supporting details; that is, it's much more than a statement of fact that leads nowhere.
5. It uses specific language and avoids vague words.
6. It may give the major subdivisions of the topic.

8h How might outlining help me write?

An **outline** is a structured, sequential list of the contents of a text. Some writers always use outlines, while others never do. Some instructors require an outline with an assignment, while others don't. You need to experiment with what works best for you personally as well as remain aware of what your instructor calls for.

In some situations, writers like to outline before they write, in order to flesh out, pull together, and arrange material before DRAFTING (9a). In other situations, writers prefer to outline after they've written their first draft, to check the logic and flow of thought of the essay. They also outline while REVISING (10a). Outlines are excellent self-checking tools for revealing where information is missing, repeated, or off the topic.

An **informal outline** doesn't follow any of the numbering and lettering conventions of a formal outline. It often looks like a BRAINSTORMING list, with ideas jotted down in a somewhat random order. Here is part of an informal outline for the second paragraph of Sara Cardini's essay (12b).

SAMPLE INFORMAL OUTLINE

qualities of anime

quick movements

jazz and rock music

large eyes for characters

complicated drawings

Samurai X as an example

A traditional **formal outline** follows long-established conventions for using numbers and letters to show relationships among ideas. Although MLA STYLE doesn't officially endorse one outline style, most instructors who assign outlines prefer the traditional format shown in Quick Reference 8.5. Other instructors prefer a formal outline that shows the content of both the introductory paragraph and the concluding paragraph. Either type of formal outline can be a **sentence outline**, composed entirely of complete sentences, or it can be a **topic outline**, composed only of words and phrases. Quick Reference 8.5 shows a traditional sentence outline as well as a formal topic outline. Never mix the two styles in one outline.

Here are some tips to help you write successful outlines. Most important, formal outlines always need at least two subdivisions at each level—there must be no I without a II, no A without a B, and so on. If a level has only one subdivision, either integrate it into the higher level or expand it to at least two subdivisions. Second, keep all subdivisions at the same level of generality (that is, don't pair a main idea with a subordinate idea, and don't pair a subordinating idea with a supporting detail). Third, keep your word forms parallel at each level of generality. For a full discussion of PARALLELISM, see Chapter 52.

Quick Reference 8.5 · · · · · · · ·

Outline formats

TRADITIONAL FORMAL OUTLINE
Thesis statement: Give the thesis statement here.

I. First main idea
    A. First subordinate idea
        1. First reason or example
        2. Second reason or example
            a. First supporting detail
            b. Second supporting detail
    B. Second subordinate idea
II. Second main idea

continued >>

Quick Reference 8.5 (continued)

EXAMPLE OF A TRADITIONAL FORMAL SENTENCE OUTLINE
This outline goes with the third paragraph of Sara Cardini's essay (12b).

Thesis statement: Anime has traditions and features that distinguish it from American cartoons and make it appeal to adults as well as children.

I. Anime has distinctive qualities.

   A. Images move quickly.

   B. Soundtracks use jazz and rock.

   C. Characters have large eyes and sharp features.

   D. Art is colorful and complicated.

      1. *Samurai X* is an example of a popular anime.

      2. *Samurai X* is about a nineteenth-century warrior.

      3. The art in *Samurai X* looks like old Japanese prints.

EXAMPLE OF A TRADITIONAL FORMAL TOPIC OUTLINE
This outline goes with the third paragraph of Sara Cardini's essay (12b).

I. Anime qualities

   A. Quick images

   B. Jazz and rock soundtracks

   C. Characters' eyes and features

   D. Colorful, complicated art

      1. *Samurai X* as example

      2. *Samurai X* about nineteenth-century warrior

      3. *Samurai X* art like old Japanese prints

For more help with your writing, grammar, and research,
go to **www.mycomplab.com**

9

Drafting

9a What strategies can I use to write a first draft?

A first draft is always rough. Its goal is to give you something to improve by REVISING (10a). Here are three suggested alternatives for writing a first draft.

- Put aside all of the notes you made to get started. Write a **discovery draft**, which uses FOCUSED FREEWRITING to uncover ideas and make connections that spring to mind during FREEWRITING.
- Keep your notes from the techniques described in 8f at hand and write a structured first draft by working your way through your notes.
- Or combine the two approaches. When your notes can guide you, use them. When you feel stuck about what to say next, switch to a discovery draft.

The direction of drafting is forward: Keep pressing ahead. If you wonder about the spelling of a word or a point in grammar, highlight or underline it and check it later. If you can't think of an exact word, use a SYNONYM and mark it so you'll know to change it later. If you're worried about your sentence style or the order in which you present details, jot *Style?* or *Order?* in the margin and return to the issue later. If you're drafting on a computer, write notes to yourself in all capital letters and enclose them in square brackets so that you can find them later. No matter what, keep moving ahead. If you begin to run dry, reread what you've written to propel yourself to write further. Keep writing until you've managed to complete a first draft.

9b What can I do if I experience writer's block?

Writer's block is the inability to think of ideas or get words down on paper or on the screen. Not just students but even experienced writers occasionally fall victim to writer's block. Quick Reference 9.1 lists some strategies that experienced writers often use to overcome writer's block.

Once you've finished your first draft, move on to revising, EDITING, and proofreading.

Quick Reference 9.1

Ways to overcome writer's block

- **Avoid staring at a blank page.** Relax and move your hand across the page or keyboard while you think about your topic.

- **Visualize yourself writing.** Imagine yourself in a place where you usually write, busily moving your hand across the page or your fingers on the keyboard.

- **Imagine a scene or sound that relates to your topic.** Start to write by describing what you see or hear.

- **Write a letter or an e-mail.** Start with "Dear" and the name of a trusted friend or relative. Pretend you're writing to that person.

- **Talk to someone (in person, on the phone, or online).** Having a sounding board can help spark ideas and generate enthusiasm.

- **Write pretending that you're someone else.** Take on someone else's identity and write from that person's perspective. Pretend you're a confident expert in the subject matter, for example.

- **Start in the middle.** Write from the center of your essay out instead of from beginning to end. Start with the part or idea you find easiest or most engaging.

For more help with your
writing, grammar, and research,
go to **www.mycomplab.com**

10

Revising, Editing, and Proofreading

10a What strategies can I use to revise?

When you're **revising**, you're moving a draft from first to final version by adding, cutting, replacing, and rearranging material. You need to shift from suspending judgment to making judgments. Revision involves working with your draft at the level of ideas to achieve your purpose for your audience.

Although you want to review your work with a critical eye, don't be overly harsh with yourself. Most early drafts merely provide raw material for you to revise. For greatest efficiency, be systematic in evaluating your draft. Use the questions in Quick Reference 10.1 or guidelines supplied by your instructor. Every time you make a change, evaluate it on its own and also in the context of the surrounding material. Continue this process until you're satisfied that you've made all the improvements you can and your essay is in its final form.

Quick Reference 10.1 ■ ■ ■ ■ ■ ■ ■

Revision checklist

Your goal is to answer *yes* to each question on the following list. If you answer *no,* you need to revise your writing accordingly. The section numbers in parentheses tell you where to look in this handbook for help.

1. Is your essay topic suitable and sufficiently narrow? (8d)
2. Does your thesis statement communicate your topic, focus, and purpose (8g)
3. Does your essay show that you are aware of your audience? (8c)
4. Are there places where your reader would be confused or need more information?
5. Are there places where a skeptical reader would object to your argument or not be convinced?
6. Is your essay arranged effectively? (12a, 13g)
7. Have you checked for material that strays off the topic?
8. Does your introduction prepare your reader for the rest of the essay? (11b)
9. Do your body paragraphs express main ideas in topic sentences as needed? (11c) Are your main ideas clearly related to your thesis statement? (2d)
10. Do you provide specific, concrete support for each main idea? (11d)
11. Do you use transitions and other techniques to connect ideas within and between paragraphs? (11e)
12. Does your conclusion give your essay a sense of completion? (11g)

With computers, you can easily add, delete, or move anything, from a word or a sentence to a paragraph or an entire idea. As you try various revisions, use the "Save As" function on your computer to save your drafts under slightly different names, such as "Animation Draft 1," "Animation Draft 2," and so on. By saving several drafts of your paper, you can always return to an earlier version if you later decide you prefer something in one of your earlier drafts.

If you want to drop material, resist deleting it instantly. As handbook authors, we save almost everything. Doug typically keeps a file named "Junk"; Lynn keeps one named "Discarded Stuff."

In deciding that your draft is final, try to avoid being so impressed by the clean appearance of a nicely printed and formatted paper that you avoid making changes.

Here's part of a paragraph from one draft of the informative essay by student Sara Cardini. Using a revision checklist, Sara made several changes and added more specific, concrete details. For the final draft, see body paragraph 2 of Sara's essay (12b).

> *Animation developed differently in America and Japan after WWII.*
> ^While Americans considered animation entertainment
> *mainly*
> for children, the Japanese viewed it as ~~entertaining primarily~~
> ^
> for adults. Since the beginning of print, cartooning in Japan has
> *in this tradition*
> targeted adults, so anime was a natural step. ~~It's interesting how~~
> ^
> ~~graphic novels were important in Japan long before they were here,~~
> ~~but lately you see more and more graphic novels.~~/In America, aside
> from editorial cartoons and newspaper funny pages, comics were
> *adolescent males*
> aimed primarily at ~~boys~~. American animation in the 1940s and 1950s
> *The early work* ^,for example, came from fairy tales, or it featured
> was different. ~~Think~~ of Walt Disney. Japanese cartoons were *cute animal*
> ^ *young* ^ *characters.*
> developed for both ~~kids~~ and old ~~people~~, male and female audiences,
> ^
> and have taken on adult subjects often absent from American cartoons.
> *These subjects include war, death, sacrifice, and history.*

10b How do a thesis statement and an essay title help me revise?

Use your THESIS STATEMENT to guide your revision. At the end of every paragraph, ask yourself, "Does this paragraph relate to my thesis statement?" If your thesis statement does not match what your essay says, revise the thesis statement, the essay, or both.

Your essay title can also play an important part in revising, so don't wait until the last minute and merely tack on a title. Create at least a working title during your first draft. Use it consistently as a checkpoint as your essay evolves.

A **direct title** tells exactly what the essay will be about: for example, "The Characteristics of Japanese Animation." An **indirect title** hints at an essay's topic: "More Than Simple Cartoons?" This indirect title is too far from the subject, so it isn't suitable. However, indirect titles can be very effective as long as the connection is not too obscure. For example, this indirect title would work for Sara Cardini's essay: "Imagining That Walt Disney Had Been Japanese."

Alert: A title stands alone. Don't open an essay with a reaction to the title or with an opening sentence that is a continuation of the title. For example, the following would be an inappropriate opening for Sara's paper:

TITLE	The Appeal of Japanese Animation for Adults
INAPPROPRIATE OPENING	There certainly are many apparent reasons to like it. ●

10c How do I revise for style?

As you decide how to revise your draft to respond to your writing situation and audience, you should consider *how* you say something as well as *what* you're saying. You create the **style** of your writing by how you shape sentence structures and how you choose to address readers. **Tone** involves using the right words to deliver your meaning.

Style and tone

Style and tone operate together through a combination of the varying levels of formality and personality that you use. **Formality** in writing can be roughly divided into three categories.

- Formal writing is used for ceremonies, contracts, policies, and some literary writing. "Formal writing," by the way, doesn't mean dull and drab material. Indeed, lively language always enhances such messages.
- Informal writing is casual, colloquial, and sometimes playful; it is usually found in e-mails, text messages, Facebook postings, or on certain BLOGS.
- Semiformal writing, which sits between these poles, is the style and tone found in academic writing, as well as in much business and public writing. Its TONE is reasonable and evenhanded, its style is clear and efficient, and its word choices are appropriate for an audience expecting professional communication.

Generally, when you write for an audience about whom you know little, a somewhat more formal style and tone are appropriate, though an entirely formal presentation isn't desirable. If informal writings are T-shirts and jeans, and formal writings are tuxedos and evening gowns, then semiformal writings are business-casual attire. Here are examples of the levels of formality.

INFORMAL　It's totally sweet how gas makes stars.

SEMIFORMAL　Gas clouds slowly transform into stars.

FORMAL　The condensations of gas spun their slow gravitational pirouettes, slowly transmogrifying gas cloud into star.

—Carl Sagan, "Starfolk: A Fable"

■ Personality

Personality refers to how much the writer reveals about himself or herself. An *intimate style* and tone, which treats the reader as a close friend, includes specific personal experiences and opinions. A *familiar* or *polite style* includes some experiences or personal thoughts, but only of a kind you might share in a professional relationship with an instructor, supervisor, or colleague. In such writing, the reader can glimpse the writer behind the language, but not as fully as in intimate writing because the emphasis is on the ideas or subject matter. An *impersonal style* reveals nothing about the writer, so that the content is all that the reader notices.

As you consider *how* to say what you want to say, consult the topics and sections in this book listed in Quick Reference 10.2.

Quick Box 10.2　■ ■ ■ ■ ■ ■ ■

Elements that shape style and tone in writing

Sentence length and variety (52e)

Coordination and subordination (51)

Parallelism (52a–d)

Word order in sentences (52f, 52h)

Diction or word choice (54)

Figurative language (54e)

10d　What strategies can I use to edit?

Editing means finding and fixing errors you've made in grammar, spelling, punctuation, capitals, numbers, italics, and abbreviations. Some instructors call these *surface-level features.* You're ready to edit after you've revised the content and organization of your paper to your critical satisfaction. We urge you to edit slowly and methodically using the suggestions in Quick Reference 10.3 as a guide. Looking up advice and rules in this handbook takes concentration and time. You may also want to ask friends, classmates, or colleagues with a good "editing eye" to read your paper and circle anything they think you need to check for correctness.

Quick Reference 10.3

Editing checklist

Your goal is to answer *yes* to each question below. If you answer *no,* you need to edit. The numbers in parentheses tell you which chapters in this handbook to go to for more information.

1. Are your sentences concise? (Chapter 50)
2. Are your sentences interesting? Do you use parallelism, variety, and emphasis to increase the impact of your writing? (Chapter 52)
3. Have you used exact words? (Chapter 54)
4. Is your usage correct and your language appropriate? (Chapter 53)
5. Have you avoided sexist or stereotypical language? (Chapter 55)
6. Is your grammar correct? (Chapters 41–45)
7. Is your spelling correct? (Chapter 56)
8. Have you used commas correctly? (Chapter 57)
9. Have you used all other punctuation correctly? (Chapters 58–64)
10. Have you used capital letters, italics, abbreviations, and numbers correctly? (Chapters 65–68)
11. Have you used the appropriate citation and documentation formats? (Chapters 33–40)?

Using software programs to edit

When you are editing, use the features available in your word processing program (such as Word and WordPerfect), but note the following cautions.

- **Thesaurus programs** give you SYNONYMS for words. They can't, however, tell you which ones fit well into your particular sentences. Whenever a synonym is unfamiliar or hazy, look it up in your dictionary. You don't want to use words that strike you as attractive options but then turn out to distort your communication. For example, a synonym for *friend* is *acquaintance,* but these words have different connotations.
- **Grammar- or style-check programs** check your writing against the software's strict interpretations of rules of grammar, word use, punctuation, and other conventions. Can you always rely on those standards? No. These signals call attention to possible errors. The decision to make changes, however, is yours. Consult this handbook when you're not sure what a

program is suggesting or whether you're justified in deviating from the program's rules.

ESOL Tip: Be cautious when using electronic grammar-check programs because they're often unreliable. For example, although the sentence "**What** she has **is** high intelligence" is grammatically correct, some programs flag it as incorrect. ●

10e   What strategies can I use to proofread?

Proofreading is a careful, line-by-line reading of a final, clean version of your writing. Always proofread for errors and correct them before you hand in a paper or transmit your work to its intended audience. A neat, accurate paper conveys your positive attitude toward your work. Here are some proofreading strategies.

- Proofread with a ruler held just under the line you are reading so that you can focus on one line at a time.

- Start at the end of a paragraph or the end of your essay and read each sentence in reverse order or word by word, to avoid being distracted by the content.

- Read your final draft aloud so that you see and hear errors; look carefully for omitted letters and words as well as for repeated words.

- Keep lists of spelling, punctuation, or grammar errors that you often make. (For example, you may know you have trouble keeping *to, too,* and *two* straight.) Consult those lists before you revise, edit, and proofread so that you look specifically for those troublemakers.

Almost all writers proofread more effectively on the page than on the screen, so we recommend that you print a hard copy of your writing for proofreading purposes. If you are working onscreen, try highlighting a small section of your writing. This separates it visually from the rest of the screen and helps reduce the tendency to read too quickly and overlook errors.

When you proofread, use your word processing program's spell-checker, but don't rely solely on it. **Spell-check programs** show you words that don't match the dictionary in the software. These programs are a big help for spotting a misspelling or mistyping (called *typos*), but they won't call your attention to instances involving the wrong *word*—as when you typed *form* when you intended to type *from.* Proofread for words that are misused rather than misspelled—for example, *it's* for *its.* **Always read your work carefully after you use a spell-check program.**

For more help with your writing, grammar, and research,
go to **www.mycomplab.com**

11

■ ■ ■ ■ ■ ■

Composing Paragraphs

11a What is a paragraph?

A **paragraph** is a group of sentences that work together to develop a unit of thought. Paragraphing permits writers to divide material into manageable parts and arrange the parts in a unified whole. Paragraphing also cues your readers about shifts in ideas or emphasis. Much of the assigned writing you do typically consists of an introductory paragraph, a group of body paragraphs, and a concluding paragraph. In college, your instructors may call such writing *essays, compositions, themes, reports,* or *papers.* In other settings, your writing may take the form of letters, reports, proposals, Web pages, and so on (Chs. 22–26).

11b How can I write effective introductory paragraphs?

An **introductory paragraph** serves several functions. It prepares the reader for what lies ahead by giving background information or setting the stage in some other way. It also tries to arouse interest so that the reader will want to read on. Quick Reference 11.1 suggests some strategies for creating interest.

Quick Reference 11.1   ■ ■ ■ ■ ■ ■ ■

Strategies for writing introductory paragraphs

STRATEGIES FOR CAPTURING YOUR READER'S INTEREST

- Provide relevant background information about your topic.
- Relate a brief, interesting anecdote that applies to your topic.
- Give pertinent, perhaps surprising statistics about your topic.
- Ask a provocative question or two to lead in to your topic.
- Use a quotation that relates closely to your topic.
- Draw an analogy to clarify or illustrate your topic.
- Define a key term you use throughout your piece of writing.

continued >>

Quick Reference 11.1	(continued)

STRATEGIES TO AVOID

- Making obvious statements about the essay's topic or purpose: Do not say, "I am going to discuss some facts about animation."
- Apologizing, as in "I'm not sure I'm right, but here's what I think."
- Using overworked expressions, such as "Haste really does make waste, as I recently discovered."

You may be required to include a THESIS STATEMENT in the introductory paragraph (8g, 10b), especially in your college writing. Usually, the thesis statement appears in the last sentence or two of the introductory paragraph (see sample paragraphs 1 and 2). Experienced writers sometimes diverge from this basic pattern, depending on their writing PURPOSE. However, we recommend sticking to the basics and following your instructors' requirements or the style used at your workplace.

1   Alone one is never lonely, May Sarton says in her essay "The Rewards of Living a Solitary Life." Most people, however, are terrified of living alone. They are used to living with others—children with parents, roommates with roommates, friends with friends, husbands with wives. When the statistics catch up with them, therefore, they are rarely prepared. Chances are high that most adult men and women will live alone, briefly or longer, at some time.

—Tara Foster, student

2   Twenty-three years ago, an American philosophy professor named James Flynn discovered a remarkable trend: Average IQ scores in every industrialized country on the planet had been increasing steadily for decades. Despite concerns about the dumbing-down of society—the failing schools, the garbage on TV, the decline of reading—the overall population was getting smarter. And the climb has continued, with more recent studies showing that the rate of IQ increase is accelerating. Next to global warming and Moore's law, the so-called Flynn effect may be the most revealing line on the increasingly crowded chart of modern life—and it's an especially hopeful one. We still have plenty of problems to solve, but at least there's one consolation: Our brains are getting better at problem-solving.

—Steven Johnson, "Dome Improvement"

11c How do topic sentences work?

A **topic sentence** contains the main idea of a BODY PARAGRAPH and controls its content. A paragraph has UNITY when the connection between the main idea and its supporting details is clear. In student writing, topic sentences come most often at the beginning of a paragraph, but putting them at the end or implying them is fine.

Starting with a topic sentence

When a topic sentence starts a paragraph, readers immediately know what topic will be discussed.

3   The key to a successful franchise, according to many texts on the subject, can be expressed in one word: "uniformity." Franchises and chain stores strive to offer exactly the same product or service at numerous locations. Customers are drawn to familiar brands by an instinct to avoid the unknown. A brand offers a feeling of reassurance when its products are always and everywhere the same. "We have found out . . . that we cannot trust some people who are nonconformists," declared Ray Kroc, one of the founders of McDonald's, angered by some of his franchisees. "We will make conformists out of them in a hurry. . . . The organization cannot trust the individual; the individual must trust the organization."

—Eric Schlosser, *Fast Food Nation*

Ending with a topic sentence

When a topic sentence ends a body paragraph, readers sometimes feel more eager to read on to the next paragraph.

4   The once majestic oak tree crashes to the ground amid the destructive flames, as its panic-stricken inhabitants attempt to flee the fiery tomb. Undergrowth that formerly flourished smolders in ashes. A family of deer darts furiously from one wall of flame to the other, without an emergency exit. On the outskirts of the inferno, firefighters try desperately to stop the destruction. Somewhere at the source of this chaos lies a former campsite containing the cause of this destruction—an untended campfire. This scene is one of many that illustrate how human apathy and carelessness destroy nature.

—Anne Bryson, student

Implying a topic sentence

Some paragraphs convey a main idea without a specific topic sentence. Writers carefully construct these paragraphs so that details add up in such a way that the main idea is clear even though it is not explicitly stated.

5   Customers used to wait at the cash register for minutes before a checker would finally pay attention. Of course, the wait happened only when they actually had found the item they had come to buy. Most customers went away empty-handed. The manager had a practice of running ads for products that

were just about sold out. I would watch people pick through piles of shirts in a fruitless search for something other than an extra-small or an extra-extra-large.

—Armstrong Washington, student

A couple of possible main ideas implied by this paragraph are "The store manager was incompetent" or "The store operated very poorly."

11d   How can I use details to develop body paragraphs?

Use specific, concrete details to develop **body paragraphs** that support the generalization in the TOPIC SENTENCE. What separates most good writing from bad is the writer's ability to move back and forth between generalizations and specific details. To check that you have enough detail, try using RENNS, a memory device summarized in Quick Reference 11.2. You don't need to use details in the order of the letters in RENNS. Neither do you need to use all of the RENNS. For example, paragraph 6 uses only three. See if you can identify them before you read the analysis after the paragraph.

Quick Reference 11.2   ■ ■ ■ ■ ■ ■ ■

RENNS = specific, concrete details

R	**R**easons
E	**E**xamples
N	**N**ames
N	**N**umbers
S	**S**enses (sight, sound, smell, taste, touch)

---

6   Whether bad or good, in tune or not, whistling has its practical side. Clifford Pratt is working with a group of speech therapists to develop whistling techniques to help children overcome speech problems through improved breath control and tongue flexibility. People who have a piercing whistle have a clear advantage when it comes to hailing cabs, calling the dog or the children, or indicating approval during a sporting event. And if you want to leave the house and can't remember where you put your keys, there's a key chain on the market with a beep that can be activated by a whistle: You whistle and the key chain tells you where it is.

—Cassandra Tate, "Whistlers Blow New Life into a Forgotten Art"

Paragraph 6 uses several examples (E) of how whistling can be helpful: overcoming speech problems, hailing cabs, calling dogs and children, cheering at sporting events, and finding keys. It also uses specific names (N): *Clifford Pratt* (not the general term *researcher*), *children* (not the general term *people*), and *dogs* (not the general term *animals*). In addition, the paragraph uses sensory description (S): the feeling of breath control, tongue flexibility, and the sounds of whistles and a beeping key chain.

11e What strategies can I use to create coherent paragraphs?

A paragraph is *coherent* when its sentences are connected in content and relate to each other in form and language. **Coherence** creates a smooth flow of thoughts within each paragraph as well as from one paragraph to another. You can use transitional words and expressions, deliberate repetition, and parallelism to help make your writing coherent.

■ Using transitional expressions

Transitional expressions are words and phrases that express connections among ideas, both within and between paragraphs. As listed in Quick Reference 11.3, they do this by showing relationships, such as addition, contrast, or result. Here are some tips for using **transitions** effectively.

- Vary the transitional expressions within a category that you use. For example, avoid *for instance* every time you give an example.
- Always use each transitional expression within a category precisely, according to its exact meaning. For example, in the category of "contrast," the expression *in contrast* signals that a contrast with what came before is coming next.

> **NO** The jewels were valuable. Otherwise, the carpets were not. [*Otherwise* does not compare the carpets and jewels, which is the intention of these sentences.]

> **YES** The jewels were valuable. In contrast, the carpets were not. [*In contrast* means that one element (carpets) stands in contrast to another (the jewels). This comparison makes sense.]

In the following paragraph, notice the transitional words and expressions that are in boldface type.

Jaguars, **for example**, were **once** found in the United States from southern Louisiana to California. **Today** they are rare north of the Mexican

> ## Quick Reference 11.3 ▪▪▪▪▪▪▪
>
> ### Transitional words and expressions and the relationships they express
>
> | | |
> |---|---|
> | ADDITION | also, besides, equally important, furthermore, in addition, moreover, too |
> | COMPARISON | in the same way, likewise, similarly |
> | CONCESSION | granted, naturally, of course |
> | CONTRAST | at the same time, certainly, despite the fact that, however, in contrast, instead, nevertheless, on the contrary, on the other hand, otherwise, still |
> | EMPHASIS | indeed, in fact, of course |
> | EXAMPLE | a case in point, as an illustration, for example, for instance, namely, specifically |
> | PLACE | here, in the background, in the front, nearby, there |
> | RESULT | accordingly, as a result, consequently, hence, then, therefore, thus |
> | SUMMARY | finally, in conclusion, in short, in summary |
> | TIME SEQUENCE | eventually, finally, meanwhile, next, now, once, then, today, tomorrow, subsequently, yesterday |

7 border, with no confirmed sightings since 1971. They are rare, **too**, in Mexico, where biologist Carl Koford estimated their population at fewer than a thousand in a 1972 survey. Some biologists think the number is even smaller **today**. **Similarly**, jaguars have disappeared from southern Argentina and Paraguay.

—Jeffrey P. Cohen, "Kings of the Wild"

▪ Using deliberate repetition and parallelism

You can also achieve coherence through **deliberate repetition** of key words. Use it sparingly, however, or your writing will become monotonous. Paragraph 8 shows effective use of deliberate repetition. The word *work* is repeated throughout, and within a single sentence, *walking* and *without* are repeated for added coherence.

You can also use **parallelism** (Ch. 52) to link ideas and achieve coherence. Sentences are parallel when they repeat a grammatical structure. Notice, for example, that in paragraph 8, the middle supporting sentences all open with the same structure: *It was work.* Notice, too, the parallelism in the fourth sentence—*to swing, to tighten,* and *to walk.*

The world of *work* into which Jacinto and the other seven-year-olds were apprenticed was within sight and sound of the pueblo. **It was *work*** under blazing suns, in rainstorms, in pitch-black nights. **It was *work*** that you were always *walking to* or *walking from, work without wages* and *work without end.*

8   **It was *work*** that gave you a bone-tired feeling at the end of the day, so you learned **to swing** a machete, **to tighten** a cinch, and **to walk** without lost motion. Between seven and twelve you learned all this, each lesson driven home when your *jefe* said with a scowl: "*Así no, hombre; así.*" And he showed you how.

—Ernesto Galarza, *Barrio Boy*

11f   What strategies can I use to develop body paragraphs?

As you develop the supporting body paragraphs in your writing, you can use various **rhetorical strategies**, which are patterns and techniques for presenting ideas clearly and effectively. The specific strategies that you choose to use depend on what you want to accomplish.

In this section, you'll learn about rhetorical strategies one at a time. When you write, however, no paragraph is isolated, so rhetorical strategies often overlap in one paragraph. For example, in a paragraph explaining how to prepare a slide to study under a microscope, you would likely use the process pattern along with definition and description.

■ Composing a narration

Narrative writing tells what is happening or what has happened—it is storytelling. Narration is usually organized chronologically—first this, then that.

We walked down the path to the well-house, attracted by the fragrance of the honeysuckle with which it was covered. Someone was drawing water and my teacher placed my hand under the spout. As the cool stream gushed over one hand she spelled into the other the word *water,* first slowly, then rapidly. I stood still, my whole attention fixed upon the motions of her fingers. Sud-

9   denly I felt a misty consciousness as of something forgotten—a thrill of returning thought; and somehow the mystery of language was revealed to me. I knew then that "water" meant the wonderful cool something that was flowing over my hand. That living word awakened my soul, gave it light, hope, joy, set it free! There were barriers still, it is true, but barriers that could in time be swept away.

—Helen Keller, *The Story of My Life*

Composing a description

Descriptive writing paints a picture in words. It usually calls on the five senses. It may be organized spatially (from top to bottom, left to right, inside to outside, and so on). Paragraph 10 is organized spatially. Description can also be organized from general to specific (presenting a dominant impression followed by details) and from least to most important (arranging information so that it builds to a climax).

10   A combination of cries from exotic animals and laughter and gasps from children fills the air along with the aroma of popcorn and peanuts. A hungry lion bellows for dinner, his roar breaking through the confusing chatter of other animals. Birds of all kinds chirp endlessly at curious children. Monkeys swing from limb to limb, performing gymnastics for gawking onlookers. A comedy routine by orangutans employing old shoes and garments incites squeals of amusement. Reptiles sleep peacefully behind glass windows, yet they send shivers down the spines of those who remember the quick death many of these reptiles can induce. The sights and sounds and smells of the zoo inform and entertain children of all ages.

—Deborah Harris, student

Describing a process

Process writing tells how to do something. It gives instructions or advice. Most process writing is organized chronologically because sequence is very important. In fact, not only must you give the steps of the process in order, but you must include all the steps.

11   Carrying loads of equal weight like paint cans and toolboxes is easier if you carry one in each hand. Keep your shoulders back and down so that the weight is balanced on each side of your body, not suspended in front. With this method, you will be able to lift heavier loads and also to walk and stand erect. Your back will not be strained by being pulled to one side.

—John Warde, "Safe Lifting Techniques"

Composing an example or illustration

Writing developed with **examples** provides concrete, specific representations of the main idea. A single extended example is often called an **illustration**. If you use several examples, you can choose to arrange them from least to most important or the other way around. Choose according to your purpose and the meaning and impact you want to deliver.

He was one of the greatest scientists the world has ever known, yet if I had to convey the essence of Albert Einstein in a single word, I would choose *simplicity.* Perhaps an anecdote will help. Once, caught in a downpour, he took off his hat and held it under his coat. Asked why, he explained, with admirable logic, that the rain would damage the hat, but his hair would be none **12** the worse for its wetting. This knack of going instinctively to the heart of the matter was the secret of his major scientific discoveries—this and his extraordinary feeling for beauty.

—Banesh Hoffman, "My Friend, Albert Einstein"

■ Composing a definition

When you *define* something, you give its meaning. Many writers find that they often use **definition** with other rhetorical strategies. For instance, if you're explaining how to build a picture frame (process), you'll probably need to define the woodworking term *miter.*

You can also develop an entire paragraph by definition. To do this, discuss the meaning of a word or concept in more detail than a dictionary definition. You might, for example, tell what the word you are defining is *not* as well as what it *is,* as in paragraph 13.

Chemistry is that branch of science that has the task of investigating the materials out of which the universe is made. It is not concerned with the forms into which they may be fashioned. Such objects as chairs, tables, vases, bot- **13** tles, or wires are of no significance in chemistry; but such substances as glass, wool, iron, sulfur, and clay, as the materials out of which they are made, are what it studies. Chemistry is concerned not only with the composition of such substances but also with their inner structure.

—John Arrend Timm, *General Chemistry*

■ Composing a comparison and contrast

Writing developed by *comparisons* deals with similarities, and writing developed by *contrasts* deals with differences. **Comparison and contrast** writing is usually organized in one of two ways. **Point-by-point organization** moves back and forth between the items being compared, as in paragraph 14 (which moves between Mark and Wayne). **Block organization** discusses one item completely before discussing the next, as in paragraph 15 (sporting games are discussed completely before anything is said about business).

My husband and I constantly marvel at the fact that our two sons, born of the same parents and only two years apart in age, are such completely opposite human beings. The most obvious differences became apparent at their births. Our firstborn, **Mark**, was big and bold—his intense, already wise eyes, broad shoulders, huge and heavy hands, and powerful, chunky legs gave us the impression that he could have walked out of the delivery room on his own.

14   Our second son, **Wayne**, was delightfully different. Rather than having the football physique that Mark was born with, Wayne came into the world with a long, slim, wiry body more suited to running, jumping, and contorting. Wayne's eyes, rather than being intense like Mark's, were impish and innocent. When **Mark** was delivered, he cried only momentarily, then seemed to settle into a state of intense concentration, as if trying to absorb everything he could about the strange, new environment he found himself in. Conversely, **Wayne** screamed from the moment he first appeared. There was nothing helpless or pathetic about his cry either—he was darn angry!

—Roseanne Labonté, student

15   **Games** are of limited duration, take place on or in fixed and finite sites and are governed by openly promulgated rules that are enforced on the spot by neutral professionals. Moreover, they are performed by relatively evenly matched teams that are counseled and led through every move by seasoned hands. Scores are kept, and at the end of the game, a winner is declared. **Business** is usually a little different. In fact, if there is anyone out there who can say that the business is of limited duration, takes place on a fixed site, is governed by openly promulgated rules that are enforced on the spot by neutral professionals, competes only on relatively even terms, and performs in a way that can be measured in runs or points, then that person is either extraordinarily lucky or seriously deluded.

—Warren Bennis, "Time to Hang Up the Old Sports Clichés"

◼ Composing an analysis

Analysis examines and discusses separate parts of a whole. For example, paragraph 16 identifies a new type of zoo design and then analyzes why this design has developed, specifying three reasons for the "landscape revolution."

16   The current revolution in zoo design—the landscape revolution—is driven by three kinds of change that have occurred during this [past] century. First are great leaps in animal ecology, veterinary medicine, landscape design, and exhibit technology, making possible unprecedented realism in zoo exhibits. Second, and perhaps most important, is the progressive disappearance of wilderness—the very subject of zoos—from the earth. Third is knowledge derived from market research and from environmental psychology, making possible a sophisticated focus on the zoo-goer.

—Melissa Greene, "No Rms, Jungle Vu"

◼ Composing a classification

Classification groups items according to a shared characteristic. In writing a classification, you want to discuss or clarify each category in turn.

Many different kinds of signals are used by the coaches. There are flash signals, which are just what the name implies: The coach may flash a hand across his face or chest to indicate a bunt or hit-and-run. There are holding signals, which are held in one position for several seconds. There might be

17 the clenched fist, bent elbow, or both hands on knees. Then there are the block signals. These divide the coach's body into different sections, or blocks. Touching a part of his body, rubbing his shirt, or touching his cap indicates a sign. Different players can be keyed to various parts of the block so the coach is actually giving several signals with the same sign.

—Rockwell Stensrud, "Who's on Third?"

■ Composing an analogy

Analogy is a kind of comparison, identifying similarities between objects or ideas that are not usually associated with each other.

Casual dress, like casual speech, tends to be loose, relaxed, and colorful. It often contains what might be called "slang words": blue jeans, sneakers, baseball caps, aprons, flowered cotton housedresses, and the like. These garments could not be worn on a formal occasion without causing disapproval, but in ordinary circumstances they pass without remark. "Vulgar words" in dress, on the other hand, give emphasis and get immediate attention in almost any cir-

18 cumstances, just as they do in speech. Only the skillful can employ them without some loss of face, and even then they must be used in the right way. A torn, unbuttoned shirt, or wildly uncombed hair can signify strong emotions: passion, grief, rage, despair. They are most effective if people already think of you as being neatly dressed, just as the curses of well-spoken persons count for more than those of the customarily foul-mouthed.

—Alison Lurie, *The Language of Clothes*

■ Explaining cause and effect

Causes lead to an event or an effect; *effects* result from causes. Writing that shows **cause and effect** examines outcomes and reasons for outcomes.

Many collapses of the past appear to have been triggered, at least in part, by ecological problems: people inadvertently destroyed their environmental resources. But societies are not doomed to collapse because of environmental damage. Some societies have coped with their problems, whereas others have

19 not. But I know of no case in which a society's collapse can be attributed simply to environmental damage; there are always complicating factors. Among them are climate change, the role of neighbors (who can be friendly or hostile), and, most important, the ways people respond to their environmental problems.

—Jared Diamond, "Collapse: Ecological Lessons in Survival"

11g   How can I write effective concluding paragraphs?

The **concluding paragraph** of an essay ends the entire essay. Your conclusion needs to follow logically from your THESIS STATEMENT and BODY PARAGRAPHS. Never merely tack on a conclusion. Use it to provide a sense of completion, a finishing touch that enhances the whole essay. See Quick Reference 11.4 for ideas about writing conclusions. The conclusion reproduced in paragraph 20 (from the essay whose introductory paragraph was reprinted in paragraph 1) poses a challenging question and asks the reader to prepare for the future.

Quick Reference 11.4   ■ ■ ■ ■ ■ ■ ■

Strategies for writing concluding paragraphs

STRATEGIES FOR CAPTURING YOUR READER'S INTEREST

- Use one of the strategies suggested for introductory paragraphs (see Quick Reference 11.1), but not the same one used in the introduction.
- Ask the reader for awareness, action, or a similar outcome.
- Project into the future.
- Summarize the main points if the essay is longer than three pages.

STRATEGIES TO AVOID

- Introducing new ideas or facts that belong in the body of the essay
- Merely rewording the introduction
- Announcing what you have done, as in "In this paper, I have explained Japanese animation"
- Making absolute claims, as in "In this essay, I have proved that anime deserves our attention"
- Apologizing, as in "Even though I am not an expert, I feel the points I have made are valid"

---

20   You need to ask yourself, "If I had to live alone starting tomorrow morning, would I know how?" If the answer is no, you need to become conscious of what living alone calls for. If you face up to life today, you will not have to hide from it later on.

—Tara Foster, student

12

Writing to Inform

12a How can I arrange information in an informative essay?

To deliver your message most effectively, you want to arrange all elements of your text for the greatest clarity and impact. No one arrangement fits all essays. But all arrangements are based on the ancient principles of storytelling—that is, every piece of writing should have a beginning, a middle, and an end. Here are some guidelines for arranging informative essays.

1. **Introductory paragraph:** captures the reader's interest and leads into the subject of the essay (11b).

2. **Thesis statement:** states the central message of the essay or other type of document (8g, 10b). In academic essays, the thesis statement usually appears at the end of the introductory paragraph. In other writings, a thesis statement generally appears very near the beginning.

3. **Background information:** provides a context for the ideas that will be presented in the work that follows. Depending on the complexity of background information, you may present it in the introductory paragraph or devote another paragraph to it.

4. **Body paragraphs:** explain and expand on your message. Body paragraphs form the core of the writing. They usually open with a TOPIC SENTENCE (general statement) and are backed up by specific details. Generalizations come to life with RENNS (11d). Each paragraph should be unified (11c) and coherent (11e).

5. **Concluding paragraph:** ends the essay smoothly and flows logically from the rest of the essay (11g).

You can see how such an arrangement works in INFORMATIVE WRITING by studying the final draft of an essay by student writer Sara Cardini (12b). In Chapter 13, you can find a full discussion of arrangement in PERSUASIVE WRITING.

12b   Final draft of a student's informative essay

Places header at top right: name and page number	Cardini 1

Sara Cardini

Puts student name, course, date, flush left and double-spaced

Mr. Bantham

English 101

21 April 2008

Centers title

The Appeals of Japanese Animation for Adults

Includes attention-getting first line

    I confess that I am an animation addict. Like most people, I watched cartoons as a child, consuming daily doses of *Hey, Arnold* and *Doug* and watching *The Lion King* over and over again. Then in junior high, just about the time I was getting tired of cartoons, I discovered *Sailor Moon* and an entirely different approach to animation. *Sailor Moon* is just one of hundreds of animated television series to come from the creative minds of Japan. These series and thousands of films are called *anime* (commonly pronounced AN-ah-may). Because

Provides her credentials on topic

much anime is created for adults, I have continued to watch it as I have gotten older. In fact, my interest has grown so strong that I have studied Japanese, have attended anime conferences, and am now studying filmmaking. I am not alone in my interest. In recent years, anime has become hugely popular in the United States. Still, people who are unfamiliar with anime may wonder why adults would waste their time watching cartoons. Some

Offers a thesis

careful analysis makes the answer clear. Anime has traditions and features that distinguish it from American cartoons and make it sophisticated enough to appeal to adults.

Provides start of background in topic sentence

    Animation developed differently in Japan and America after World War II. Whereas Americans considered animation

continued >>

(Proportions shown in this paper are adjusted to fit the space limitations of this book. Follow the actual dimensions given in this book and your instructor's directions.)

Cardini 2

entertainment for children, the Japanese viewed it as mainly for adults. Since the beginning of print, cartooning in Japan has targeted adults, so anime was a natural step in this tradition. In America, aside from editorial cartoons and newspaper funny pages, comics were aimed primarily at adolescent males. The early work of Walt Disney, for example, came from fairy tales, or it featured cute animal characters. In Japan, animated cartoons take on adult subjects often absent from American cartoons. These subjects include war, death, sacrifice, love, Japan's historical past and future, and even occasionally sex and violence. The plot lines are often extremely complex. Stories that would be kept simple in a Disney film to avoid viewer confusion have no such restrictions in Japan.

Uses comparison and contrast to develop paragraph

Complex plots are but one of the distinctive features of anime. Anime images move quickly, with a style often more frantic than in American cartoons. Their soundtracks frequently use jazz and rock rather than symphonic music. Perhaps most striking are the large eyes and sharp features of the characters. People in anime are very stylized, not realistic. The drawing is colorful, more complicated, and often more abstract than most American cartoons. For example, a TV series called *Samurai X* is one of the most popular anime cartoons with both American and Japanese audiences. *Samurai X* is set in the nineteenth century and tells the story of one warrior's life. It is drawn beautifully in a way that looks both like older Japanese art prints and like more contemporary movies such as *Crouching Tiger, Hidden Dragon*.

Makes transition in topic sentence

Uses specific details to explain anime

Provides a concrete example

The unique style of anime comes largely because the films were produced for specific audiences. The animators were creating works only for a Japanese market, at least until quite

Focuses on audiences in topic sentence

continued >>

Cardini 3

Uses cause
and effect
to explain
differences

recently. Therefore, they did not take into account the traditions of other cultures. In contrast, US animation was produced for an international audience, which meant simpler, more easily understood topics that came out of familiar European traditions. For uninitiated viewers, then, anime provides a crash course in an Eastern culture quite different from Western culture. Nearly all serious anime fans own guides that explain such things as Japanese social hierarchies, clothing, dining habits, traditions,

Cites a very
specific
example

rituals, and mythology. To cite one small example, several anime cartoons feature a *hagoromo* or feathered cloak worn by a mythological figure known as the *tennyo*, a swan maiden. Knowing that this figure has a symbolic meaning for a Japanese viewer and is not just a random decoration or character adds to the depth of a scene in which it appears. Decoding some of these cultural references is undoubtedly some of the fun and challenge for the true *otakon*, or anime fan.

Steers readers
from familiar
to unfamiliar
in topic
sentence

Anime appears in all kinds of types and genres, from children's works like *Pokémon* to dark science fiction like *Ghost in the Shell*. Japanese television has many daily animated series that vary in terms of sophistication and

Uses
classification
to explain
types

audience. Some of these have extremely complex scripts, while others are painfully simplistic. Several of these television series now appear in America, with some of the best known

Provides
specific titles
as examples

including *Inuyasha* and *Evangelion*. A wide range of anime feature films are readily available on DVD in America, and many have even found their way into theaters. For example, *Akira* is a film about life thirty years after a nuclear war. A misfit boy, Tetsuo, accidentally discovers the government experiments that led to that war and then learns that scientists are starting similar experiments once again.

continued >>

Cardini 4

Probably the most famous theatrical anime in the United States was *Spirited Away*, directed by Hayao Miyasaki. In the film, a young girl named Chihiro and her parents are driving to a new home when they get lost and turn up at an abandoned theme park. They find a food stall, where her parents eat until they turn into pigs. Not knowing what to do, Chihiro wanders until she finds a boy who leads her to an enormous magical bath house. That place turns out to be a resort for the gods, who appear in all sorts of fantastic shapes and sizes. Chihiro disguises herself and gets a job as a maid. These events lead to a series of adventures, involving everything from a white dragon to a spirit named No Face to an enormous baby, until Chihiro is able to free her parents from the spell. Despite the strangeness of this plot and its characters, American audiences were attracted to the imaginative ideas and the intricate art of *Spirited Away*. The movie will likely become a classic.

One reason American adults enjoy anime is because they miss a form they loved as children. They long for animated art that goes to an adult level in terms of design, creativity, sophistication, and content. While there have been a few American cartoons aimed at adults *(The Simpsons, South Park)*, the animation is basic and the tone is usually satiric. In American filmmaking, serious topics and themes are usually reserved for real actors, not cartoons. There is no such barrier in anime.

As Americans come to embrace anime, the form may change. Some fans fear that the art of anime will be watered down in the bid for popularity and profits. Others celebrate the combination of styles as some American animators borrow from the Japanese. As an animation addict, I welcome more

Focuses on one prominent example in the topic sentence

Uses narrative to summarize the plot

Adds her perspective by commenting on the summary

States a reason in the topic sentence

Contrasts American cartoons with anime

Speculates about the future in concluding strategy

continued >>

Cardini 4

Uses final comment to return to her opening idea American animation for adults. Still, I would be disappointed if the distinct qualities of anime disappeared. I fervently hope the Japanese animators will maintain their exotic creativity.

For more help with your writing, grammar, and research, go to **www.mycomplab.com**

13

■ ■ ■ ■ ■ ■

Writing to Argue

13a What is an argument?

A written **argument** consists of a *claim* and *support* for the claim.

- The **claim** states the issue and then takes a position on a debatable topic (the position can be written as a THESIS STATEMENT).
- **Support** for the claim (EVIDENCE, reasons, and EXAMPLES) is presented factually and logically.

In daily life, you might think of an argument as a personal conflict or disagreement. Many radio and television programs and Web sites reinforce this impression by featuring people who seem more interested in pushing their own agendas than in trying to persuade reasonably. For ACADEMIC WRITING, as well as business and PUBLIC WRITING, however, arguments are ways of demonstrating CRITICAL THINKING. Arguments involve making and defending a position, a proposal, or an interpretation on a topic open to debate. So that you can argue your position effectively, you want to examine critically all sides of the topic. On difficult issues, your goal is to persuade an AUDIENCE to consider your ideas with an open mind, which means that your audience's viewpoints and values need to influence your decisions about content, organization, and style.

13b   What are common types of arguments?

Many people believe that all writing contains an element of argument. In this view, even seemingly informative pieces like summaries, reports, and analyses attempt to convince readers that the author has done a skillful job and that the result is worth their time and attention. But even if we concentrate just on those writings in which writers are explicitly trying to persuade readers, there are several different types of arguments. Understanding which type of argument you need to write can help you plan your approach.

Definition arguments persuade readers to interpret a particular term in a particular way. What some people might label a work of art, others might term pornography. Is assisted suicide "murder" or "a medical procedure"? What are the characteristics a film must have to be called a romantic comedy?

Evaluation arguments persuade readers that something is good or bad, worthwhile or a waste of time, better or worse than other things like it. Common examples are movie and music reviews. Evaluation arguments argue that a particular set of criteria are important for measuring a particular class of things (for example, "mysteries must keep the audience guessing until the end"), and they argue that the thing being evaluated meets or doesn't meet those criteria ("because you could figure out very early who was the thief, it was a bad film").

Cause and effect arguments take one of two different forms. One is to argue that an existing situation results from a particular cause or set of causes. For example, you might take the situation of homelessness and argue that certain causes are most responsible (such as mental illness or minimum wages that are too low). Another is to argue that a cause will result in a certain effect. For example, you might argue that if we built more nuclear power plants, we would reduce global warming.

Proposal arguments convince readers that a particular solution to a problem or a particular way of addressing a need is best. Such arguments must first prove the existence of a problem that is important enough to require attention. Second, they must offer a solution and demonstrate how it will be more feasible and effective than other possible solutions. To convince college administrators to build more student parking, you'd write a proposal argument.

13c   How do I choose a topic and develop a claim for an argument?

When you choose a topic for a written argument, be sure that it's open to debate. An essay becomes an argument when it makes a claim about or takes a position on information. An effective way to develop a position on a topic is to ask a question about it or to identify the controversy surrounding it.

FACT	Students at Calhoon College must study a foreign language.
DEBATABLE QUESTION	Should Calhoon College require students to study a foreign language?
ONE SIDE	Calhoon College should not require students to study a foreign language.
OTHER SIDE	Calhoon College should require students to study a foreign language.

Though you need to select one side of a debatable question to defend in your essay, you need to present and then refute opposing positions. As you do so, always maintain a respectful tone by avoiding insults, abstaining from exaggerations, and resisting sarcasm.

Often instructors assign an argument topic, including the claim to make. In such cases, you need to argue in support of that position. Even if you personally disagree with the position, readers expect you to reason logically about it. Indeed, experienced debate teams practice arguing all sides of an issue.

If you can choose your own topic, choose one that is suitable for college writing. Your readers expect you to select a topic of substance and to argue convincingly and reasonably about it. For example, "book censorship in public libraries" is worthy of a college-level essay; "the color of baseball caps" is not.

Alex Garcia, the student who wrote the argument essay that appears in section 13j, chose his own topic for a written argument in a first-year college writing class. Alex was a biology major who was fascinated by genetic engineering, especially of food. While researching this topic, he became interested in the broader issue of organic food and whether it was really better. When he found wide disagreements, he knew that the controversy would make a good topic for his argument. Here's how Alex progressed from topic to claim to thesis statement.

TOPIC	Whether organic foods are better than regular ones
MY POSITION	I think people should buy organic foods when they can.
THESIS STATEMENT (FIRST DRAFT)	It is good for people to buy organic foods. [This is a preliminary thesis statement. It clearly states the writer's position, but the word *good* is vague.]
THESIS STATEMENT (SECOND DRAFT)	In order to achieve health benefits and to improve the quality of the environment, organic foods should be purchased by consumers. [This revised thesis statement is better because it states not only the writer's claim but also a reason for the claim. However, it suffers from a lack of conciseness and from the unnecessary passive construction "should be purchased."]

THESIS STATEMENT (FINAL DRAFT)	Research shows that the health and environmental benefits of organic foods outweigh their extra costs. [This final version works well because it states the writer's claim clearly and concisely, with verbs all in the active voice. The writer now has a thesis statement suitable for the time and length given in his assignment. Also, it meets the requirements for a thesis statement given in Quick Reference 8.4.]

13d How do I support my argument?

Use reasons, examples, and evidence to support an argument's claim (see RENNS, Quick Reference 11.2). One good method for developing reasons for an argument is to ask yourself *why* you believe your claim. When you respond, "Because . . .," you offer **reasons** for your claim. Another method to find reasons is to list pros and cons about your claim. The lists usually contain reasons. Specifically, evidence consists of facts, statistics, expert testimony, personal experience, and so forth.

If you consult SOURCES to find supporting evidence, reasons, or examples, be sure to use correct DOCUMENTATION within the text of your essay and in your WORKS CITED or REFERENCES at the end of your paper (Chs. 33–34, 36–37). By doing this, you avoid PLAGIARISM, the adopting of someone else's ideas and trying to pass them off as your own.

13e What types of appeals can provide support?

An effective argument relies on three types of **persuasive appeals**: logical appeals, emotional appeals, and ethical appeals. The ancient Greeks called these appeals *logos, pathos,* and *ethos.*

When you use **logical appeals** (*logos*), you allow your readers, whether they agree or disagree with you, to respect your position on the topic. Sound reasoning involves using effective evidence (32c) and reasons, accurate deductive and inductive reasoning, and clear distinctions between fact and opinion. Sound reasoning avoids LOGICAL FALLACIES (13h).

One strategy for generating logical appeals is the **Toulmin model**, which was developed by philosopher Stephen Toulmin. Quick Reference 13.1 presents the elements in Toulmin's system for mounting an argument. The Toulmin model is also useful for analyzing others' arguments. For example, identifying the **warrants** (assumptions that are often unstated) is a good critical thinking strategy that is related to making INFERENCES.

The Toulmin model for argument

- **Claim:** A variation of a thesis statement. If needed, the claim is qualified or limited.

   Alex Garcia makes the following claim in his argument: The health and environmental benefits of organic foods outweigh their extra costs.

- **Support:** Reasons and evidence, moving from broad reasons to specific data and details, support the claim.

   Alex offers three main reasons: (1) Organic produce is safer for individuals; (2) Organic meats and dairy products are safer for society as a whole; and (3) Organic farming is better for the environment. He then provides evidence for each of those reasons, drawing on source materials.

- **Warrants:** The writer's underlying assumptions, which are often implied rather than stated. Warrants may also need support (also called *backing*).

   Alex's essay has several warrants, among them: (1) We should always make choices that increase our safety; and (2) Preserving the environment enhances our quality of life. (Notice that these warrants are debatable. For example, we routinely make choices that are less safe than other options; for example, going skiing or roller skating is more dangerous than staying at home. Quality of life is determined by many factors.)

When you use **emotional appeals** (*pathos*), you try to persuade your readers by appealing to their hearts more than their minds. Such appeals are generally more effective when you combine them with logical appeals. A person who asks for a raise and gives reasons like "I have a family to support" or "I need to pay medical bills" likely won't get very far. The person also needs to prove that his or her work contributions have gone above and beyond the job description, dramatically increased sales, or brought similar advantages. Emotional appeals can use descriptive language and concrete details or examples to create a mental picture for readers, which is an approach that leads them to feel or understand the importance of your claim. Figure 13.1 provides an example of emotional appeals. You want to appeal to your audience's values and beliefs through honest examples and descriptions that add a sense of humanity and reality to the issue you are arguing. You should avoid manipulating your readers with biased, SLANTED LANGUAGE. Readers see through such tactics and resent them.

When you use **ethical appeals** (*ethos*), you establish your personal credibility with your audience. Your readers need to trust and respect you before they

Sleeping Sickness
Untreated, It Inevitably Kills

Spread by tsetse flies, this dreaded tropical disease claims more than 66,000 lives a year in 36 African nations. Doctors Without Borders volunteer Rebecca Golden returned from Angola, where a desperate battle against sleeping sickness is being waged after years of war have wrecked that nation's health care system.

"The treatment is a form of arsenic and is extremely painful," says Rebecca. "I was visiting some children receiving their medicine and was amazed at their courage and strength. **When the arsenic entered their bloodstream, they curled their toes, turned their heads, and closed their eyes tightly.** Their choice was to die or take the treatment. They accepted it with such calm. After 20 years of war and lost family members, they seem to accept this as just another part of the survival process."

Your support helps Doctors Without Borders save lives. **In our battle against sleeping sickness and other diseases, your gift can make a vital difference.**

Every Dollar Counts

$35 – Supplies a basic suture kit to repair minor shrapnel wounds.

$75 – Provides 1,500 patients with clean water for a week.

$100 – Provides infection-fighting antibiotics to treat nearly 40 wounded children.

$200 – Supplies 40 malnourished children with special high-protein food for a day.

Visit www.doctorswithoutborders.org

Figure 13.1 An argument that appeals to emotions

can be open to your position. One effective way to make an ethical appeal is to draw on your personal experience, as long as it relates directly to your argument. (Some college instructors don't want students to write in the FIRST PERSON; check with your instructor so that you can adjust your style accordingly.) Alex Garcia creates an ethical appeal in his first paragraph when he identifies himself as a shopper with a limited budget who, nonetheless, chooses more expensive options. You can also establish your credibility by demonstrating that you know what you are talking about, showing—not merely claiming—that you are well informed about your topic. Arguing by considering a variety of perspectives and using reliable SOURCES for supporting evidence communicates that you are arguing fairly and honestly. Equally important, when you use a reasonable TONE, you communicate that you are being fair-minded.

13f   How do I consider my audience?

The PURPOSE of written argument is to convince your AUDIENCE, either to agree with you or to be open to your position. Therefore, you want to consider what your readers already know about your topic. Further, think about their values, viewpoints, and assumptions. Always use this information to develop your argument.

Unfortunately, some members of some audiences can be persuaded by purely sensational or one-sided claims. Witness the effects on some readers of highly charged advertising or of narrowly one-sided ultraconservative or ultraliberal assertions. However, such arguments rarely change the minds of people who don't already agree with them. Critical thinking quickly reveals their weaknesses, including a frequent use of LOGICAL FALLACIES (13h). That's why academic audiences expect a higher standard and value, above all, logical appeals and appropriate support.

In many instances, of course, you can't actually expect to change your reader's mind, which means your goal is to demonstrate that your point of view has merit. If you think that your audience is likely to read your point of view with hostility, you might consider using a ROGERIAN ARGUMENT. Rogerian argument, based on psychologist Carl Rogers's communication principles, suggests that even hostile readers can respect your position if you show that you understand their viewpoint and treat it with respect. Quick Reference 13.2 outlines Rogers's basic ideas.

Quick Reference 13.2   ■ ■ ■ ■ ■ ■ ■

The structure of a Rogerian argument

- **Introduction:** Sets the stage for the position that is argued in the essay.
- **Thesis statement:** States the topic and position you want to argue.
- **Common ground:** Explains the issue, acknowledging that your readers likely don't agree with you. Speculates and respectfully gives attention to the points of agreement you and your readers likely share concerning the underlying problem or issue about your topic. You might even acknowledge situations in which your readers' position may be desirable. This may take one paragraph or several, depending on the complexity of the issue.
- **Discussion of your position:** Gives EVIDENCE and reasons for your stand on the topic, as in a CLASSICAL ARGUMENT (13g).
- **Conclusion:** Summarizes why your position is preferable to your opponent's. You might, for example, explain why a particular situation makes your position desirable.

13g How can I structure an argument?

No single method is best for organizing an argument. The Toulmin model works in some situations, while the Rogerian structure works in others. Probably the most frequently used structure is the **classical argument** developed by the ancient Greeks and Romans. The student essay in 13j uses this structure. Quick Reference 13.3 lists its parts. Whatever structure you choose, readers expect your argument essay to have a clear introduction, body, and conclusion.

Quick Reference 13.3   ■ ■ ■ ■ ■ ■ ■

Structure of a classical argument

- **Introductory paragraph:** Sets the stage for the position argued in the essay. It gains the reader's interest and respect. In some cases, it provides background information on the topic or problem.

- **Thesis statement:** States the position that the writer wants to argue.

- **Evidence and reasons:** Supports the position that the writer wants to argue. Each piece of evidence or reason usually consists of a general statement backed up with specific details, including examples. Generally, each reason will be the topic sentence of a paragraph. Organize your reasons in a logical sequence that will be effective for your audience.

- **Rebuttal (objections and responses to them):** Presents the opposition's position and then argues against that position. Writers can position this information in one of three ways: after the introduction, before the conclusion, or in a point-counterpoint format throughout the essay's body.

- **Concluding paragraph:** Wraps up the essay, often with a summary of the argument, an elaboration of the argument's significance, or a call to action for the readers.

13h What are logical fallacies?

Logical fallacies are flaws in reasoning that lead to faulty, illogical statements. Logical fallacies often masquerade as reasonable statements in a written argument, but they represent either a writer's attempt to manipulate readers or errors in the writer's reasoning process.

- **Hasty generalization** occurs when someone draws a conclusion based on inadequate evidence. Stereotyping is a common example of hasty generalization. For example, it is faulty to come to the conclusion that *all college students leave bad tips at restaurants* based on a few experiences with some students who have.

- The **either-or fallacy**, also called the *false dilemma,* limits the choices to only two alternatives when more exist. For example, *Either stop criticizing the president or move to another country* falsely implies that completely supporting elected officials is a prerequisite for living in America, to the exclusion of other options.

- A **false analogy** claims that two items are alike when actually they are more different than similar. The statement *If we can put a man on the moon, we should be able to find a cure for cancer* is faulty because space science is very different from biological science.

- A **false cause** asserts that one event leads to another when in fact the two events may be only loosely or coincidentally related. A common type of false cause is called *post hoc, ergo propter hoc,* which is Latin for "after this, therefore because of this." For example, *Ever since we opened that new city park, the crime rate has increased* suggests that the new park caused a change in criminal activity. There are many more likely causes.

- **Slippery slope** arguments suggest that an event will cause a "domino effect," a series of uncontrollable consequences. Some argue that the anti–gun control and pro-choice movements use the slippery slope fallacy when they say that *any* limitation of individual rights will inevitably lead to the removal of other civil rights.

- A **personal attack**, also known as an *ad hominem attack,* criticizes a person's appearance, personal habits, or character instead of dealing with the merits of the individual's argument. The following example is faulty because the writer attacks the person rather than the person's argument: *If Senator Williams had children of her own, we could take seriously her argument against permanently jailing all child abusers.*

- The **bandwagon** effect, also known as an *ad populum appeal,* implies that something is right because everyone else is doing it. An example is a teenager asking, "Why can't I go to the concert next week? All my friends are going."

- **False authority** means citing the opinion of an "expert" who has no claim to expertise about the subject at hand. Using celebrities to advertise products unrelated to their careers is a common example of this tactic.

- An **irrelevant argument** is also called a *non sequitur,* which is Latin for "it does not follow." This flaw occurs when a conclusion does not follow from the premise: *Ms. Chu is a forceful speaker, so she will be an outstanding mayor.* Ms. Chu's speaking style does not reflect her administrative abilities.

- A **red herring** is a fallacy of distraction. Sidetracking an issue by bringing up totally unrelated issues can distract people from the truth. The following question diverts attention from the issue of homelessness rather than arguing about it: *Why worry about the homeless situation when we should really be concerned with global warming?*

- **Begging the question** is also called *circular reasoning.* The supporting reasons only restate the claim. For example, in the statement *We shouldn't increase our workers' salaries because then our payroll would be larger,* the idea of *increased salaries* and a *larger payroll* essentially state the same outcome; the reason simply restates the claim rather than supporting it.

- **Emotional appeals**, such as appeals to fear, tradition, or pity, substitute emotions for logical reasoning. These appeals attempt to manipulate readers by reaching their hearts rather than their heads. The following statement attempts to appeal to readers' pity rather than their logic: *This woman has lived in poverty all of her life; she is ill and has four children at home to care for, so she should not be punished for her crimes.*

- **Slanted language** involves biasing the reader by using word choices that have strong positive or negative connotations. Calling a group of people involved in a protest rally a *mob* elicits a negative response from readers, whereas referring to the group as *concerned citizens* receives a positive response.

13i How can I revise my argument essays?

Use the general revising and editing guidelines in Quick References 10.1, 10.2, and 10.3 plus the guidelines for revising a written argument in Quick Reference 13.4.

Quick Reference 13.4 ∎ ∎ ∎ ∎ ∎ ∎ ∎

Guidelines for revising a written argument

- Does your claim take a position on a debatable topic? (13c)
- Do your evidence and reasons support the claim? (13d)
- Is the evidence sufficient, representative, relevant, and accurate? (32c)
- Do you cite sources correctly? (Chs. 33–34, 36–37)
- Is your argument structured effectively? (13g)
- Do you use appropriate logical, emotional, and ethical appeals to convince your audience? (13e)
- Have you avoided logical fallacies? (13h)

13j   Final draft of a student's argument essay

Garcia 1

Alex Garcia

Professor Brosnahan

WRIT 1122

4 May 2008

Why Organic Foods Are Worth the Extra Money

A small decision confronts me every time I walk into the
grocery store. I see a display of enticing apples for around $1.79
per pound. Next to them is a similar display of the same kind
of apples, perhaps just a little smaller and just a little less
perfect. These sell for $2.29 per pound. The difference between
the two is the tiny sticker that reads "organic." Are those
apples worth the extra money, especially when my budget is
tight and the other ones appear just fine? Millions of shoppers
face this same decision whenever they decide whether to buy
organic food, and the right answer seems complicated, especially
when the United States Department of Agriculture (USDA) "makes
no claims that organically produced food is safer or more
nutritious than conventionally produced food." However, current
research shows that the health and environmental benefits of
organic foods outweigh their extra costs.

Organic foods are produced without using most chemical
pesticides, without artificial fertilizers, without genetic
engineering, and without radiation (USDA). In the case of
organic meat, poultry, eggs, and dairy products, the animals
are raised without antibiotics or growth hormones. As a result,
people sometimes use the term "natural" instead of "organic,"
but "natural" is less precise. Before 2002, people could never
be quite sure what they were getting when they bought

continued >>

Garcia 2

supposedly organic food, unless they bought it directly from a
farmer they knew personally. In 2002, the USDA established
standards that food must meet in order to be labeled and sold
as organic.

According to environmental scientist Craig Minowa,
organic foods tend to cost about 15% more than non-organic,
mainly because they are currently more difficult to mass-
produce. Farmers who apply pesticides often get larger crops
from the same amount of land because there is less insect
damage. Artificial fertilizers tend to increase the yield, size,
and uniformity of fruits and vegetables, and herbicides kill
weeds that compete with desirable crops for sun, nutrients, and
moisture. Animals that routinely receive antibiotics and
growth hormones tend to grow more quickly and produce more
milk and eggs. In contrast, organic farmers have lower yields
and, therefore, higher costs. These get passed along as higher
prices to consumers.

Fig. 1 A display of organic foods

continued >>

Garcia 3

Still, the extra cost is certainly worthwhile in terms of health benefits. Numerous studies have shown the dangers of pesticides for humans. An extensive review of research by the Ontario College of Family Physicians concludes that "Exposure to all the commonly used pesticides . . . has shown positive associations with adverse health effects" (Sanborn et al. 173). The risks include cancer, psychiatric effects, difficulties becoming pregnant, miscarriages, and dermatitis. Carefully washing fruits and vegetables can remove some of these dangerous chemicals, but according to the prestigious journal *Nature*, even this does not remove all of them (Giles 797). Certainly, if there's a way to prevent these poisons from entering our bodies, we should take advantage of it. The few cents saved on cheaper food can quickly disappear in doctors' bills needed to treat conditions caused or worsened by chemicals.

Organic meat, poultry, and dairy products can address another health concern: the diminishing effectiveness of antibiotics. In the past decades, many kinds of bacteria have become resistant to drugs, making it extremely difficult to treat some kinds of tuberculosis, pneumonia, staphylococcus infections, and less serious diseases ("Dangerous" 1). True, this has happened mainly because doctors have over-prescribed antibiotics to patients who expect a pill for every illness. However, routinely giving antibiotics to all cows and chickens means that these drugs enter our food chain early, giving bacteria lots of chances to develop resistance. A person who switches to organic meats won't suddenly experience better results from antibiotics; the benefit is a more gradual one for society as a whole. However, if we want to be able to fight

continued >>

Garcia 4

infections with effective drugs, we need to reserve antibiotics
for true cases of need and discourage their routine use in
animals raised for food. Buying organic is a way to persuade
more farmers to adopt this practice.

Another benefit of organic foods is also a societal one:
Organic farming is better for the environment. In his review of
several studies, Colin Macilwain concluded that organic farms
nurture more and diverse plants and animals than regular
farms (797). Organic farms also don't release pesticides and
herbicides that can harm wildlife and run into our water
supply, with implications for people's health, too. Macilwain
notes that those farms also can generate less carbon dioxide,
which will help with global warming; also, many scientists
believe that organic farming is more sustainable because it
results in better soil quality (798). Once again, these benefits
are not ones that you will personally experience right away.

Fig. 2 Organic farming betters the environment

continued >>

However, a better natural environment means a better quality of living for everyone and for future generations.

Some critics point out that organic products aren't more nutritious than regular ones. Physician Sanjay Gupta, for example, finds the medical evidence for nutritional advantages is "thin" (60). The *Tufts University Health and Nutrition Letter* also reports that the research on nutritional benefits is mixed, with one important study showing "no overall differences" ("Is Organic" 8). Nutritional value, which includes qualities such as vitamins and other beneficial substances, is a different measure than food safety. At this point, it seems that nutrition alone is not a sufficient reason to buy organic foods. Perhaps future research will prove otherwise; a 2007 study, for example, showed that organically raised tomatoes have higher levels of flavonoids, nutrients that appear to have many health benefits (Mitchell et al.). In the meantime, however, environmental quality and, most importantly, avoiding chemicals remain convincing reasons to purchase organic food, even if the same cannot yet be claimed for nutrition.

Despite the considerable benefits for purchasing organic products, there remains each consumer's decision in the grocery store. Are the more expensive apples ultimately worth their extra cost to me? It's true that there are no easily measurable one-to-one benefits, no way to ensure that spending fifty cents more on this produce will directly improve my quality of life by fifty cents. However, countless people are rightly concerned these days about our personal health and the health of the world in which we live, and I am one of them. It's nearly impossible to put a value on a sustainable, diverse

continued >>

Garcia 6

natural environment and having the physical health to enjoy it.
The long-term benefits of buying organic, for anyone who can
reasonably afford to, far outweigh the short-term savings in the
checkout line.

Garcia 7

Works Cited

"Dangerous Bacterial Infections Are on the Rise." *Consumer
      Reports on Health* (Nov. 2007): 1-4. Print.

Giles, Jim. "Is Organic Food Better for Us?" *Nature* 428.6985
      (2004): 796-97. Print.

Gupta, Sanjay, and Shahreen Abedin. "Rethinking Organics."
      Time (20 Aug. 2007): 60. Print.

"Is Organic Food Really More Nutritious?" *Tufts University
      Health and Nutrition Letter* (Sept. 2007): 8. Web. 25 Apr.
      2008.

Macilwain, Colin. "Is Organic Farming Better for the
      Environment?" *Nature* 428.6985 (2004): 797-98.

Minowa, Craig. Interview by Louise Druce. "FYI on Organics:
      Organic Q & A." Organic Consumers Assn. 29 June 2004.
      Web.

Mitchell, Alyson E., et al. "Ten-Year Comparison of the
      Influence of Organic and Conventional Crop
      Management Practices on the Content of Flavonoids
      in Tomatoes." *Journal of Agricultural Food Chemistry*
      55.15 (2007): 6154-59. Web. 30 Apr. 2008.

continued >>

Garcia 8

United States. Dept. of Agriculture. "Organic Food Labels and
Standards: The Facts." National Organic Program.
Jan. 2007. Web. 26 Apr. 2008.

Sanborn, Margaret, et al. *Pesticides Literature Review:
Systematic Review of Pesticide Human Health Effects.*
Toronto: Ontario College of Family Physicians, 2004.
Web. 28 Apr. 2008.

For more help with your writing, grammar, and research,
go to **www.mycomplab.com**

14

An Overview of Writing
Across the Curriculum

14a   What is writing across the curriculum?

Writing across the curriculum refers to the writing you do in college courses beyond first-year composition. Good writing in various subject areas, such as history, biology, and psychology, has many common features. However, there are
also important differences. A lab report for a chemistry course, for example, differs from a paper for a literature course. Quick Reference 14.1 summarizes different types of writing across the curriculum.

Quick Reference 14.1

Comparing the disciplines

Discipline	Types of assignments	Primary sources	Secondary sources	Usual documentation styles
HUMANITIES history, languages, literature, philosophy, art, music, theater	essays, response statements, reviews, analyses, original works such as stories, poems, auto-biographies	literary works, manuscripts, paintings and sculptures, historical documents, films, plays, photographs, artifacts from popular culture	reviews, journal articles, research papers, books	MLA, CM
SOCIAL SCIENCES psychology, sociology, anthropology, education	research reports, case studies, reviews of the literature, analyses	surveys, interviews, observations, experiments, tests and measures	journal articles, scholarly books, literature reviews	APA

continued >>

*Words printed in SMALL CAPITAL LETTERS are discussed elsewhere in the text and are de-
fined in the Terms Glossary at the back of the book.

Discipline	Types of assignments	Primary sources	Secondary sources	Usual documentation styles
NATURAL SCIENCES biology, chemistry, physics, mathematics	reports, research proposals and reports, science reviews	experiments, field notes, direct observations, measurements	journal articles, research papers, books	often CSE but varies by discipline

Quick Reference 14.2   (continued)

For more help with your
writing, grammar, and research,
go to **www.mycomplab.com**

15

Writing About the Humanities

15a What are the humanities?

The humanities consist of disciplines that seek to represent and understand human experience, creativity, thought, and values. These disciplines include literature, languages, philosophy, and history, although some colleges group history with the social sciences. Also, many colleges consider the fine arts (music, art, dance, theater, and creative writing) part of the humanities.

15b What types of papers do I write in the humanities?

Because the humanities cover an impressively broad range of knowledge, writing in the humanities covers many types and purposes.

■ Summaries

Occasionally your instructor will request an objective summary of a text; you might need to tell the plot of a novel or present the main points of an article (7a). Generally, however, a summary is a means to a greater end. For example, writing an interpretation often requires you to summarize parts of the source so that your points about it are clear.

■ Syntheses

SYNTHESIS relates several texts, ideas, or pieces of information to one another (7d). For example, you might read several accounts of the events leading up to the Civil War and then write a synthesis that explains what caused that war. Or you might read several philosophers' definitions of morality and then write a synthesis of the components of a moral life.

■ Responses

In a response, you give your personal reaction to a work, supported by explanations of your reasoning (7c). For example, do you think Hamlet's behavior makes sense? What is your reaction to America's dealings with Hitler in the 1930s? Do you agree with Peter Singer's philosophical arguments against using animals in scientific experiments? Before you begin writing a response, clarify whether your instructor wants you to justify it with references to a text.

■ Interpretations

An interpretation explains the meaning or significance of a particular text, event, or work of art (Quick Reference 16.1). For example, what does Plato's *Republic* suggest about the nature of a good society? What was the significance of the 9/11 tragedy for Americans' sense of security? Your reply isn't right or wrong; rather, you present your point of view and explain your reasoning. The quality of your reasoning determines how successfully you convey your point.

■ Narratives

When you write a NARRATIVE (11f), you construct a coherent story out of separate facts or events. In a history class, for example, you might examine news events, laws, diaries and journals, and related materials to create a chronological version of what happened. You might do the kind of work that a biographer does, gathering information about isolated events in people's lives, interviews with those people or others who knew them, letters or other writings, and related SOURCES, all to form a coherent story of their lives.

Some writing assignments in the humanities may ask you to write about your memories or experiences (Ch. 5). Generally, such writings will involve effectively telling a story, often accompanied by some reflection on or analysis of that story.

Figure 15.1

▦ Analyses

The humanities use a number of **analytical frameworks**, or systematic ways of investigating a work. Quick Reference 15.1 summarizes some common analytical frameworks used, most notably in literary analysis. Nearly all writing in the humanities depends on analysis to some extent.

Consider how you could use some of the frameworks in Quick Reference 15.1 to analyze the photograph in Figure 15.1.

Quick Reference 15.1	▪ ▪ ▪ ▪ ▪ ▪ ▪

Selected analytical frameworks used in the humanities

RHETORICAL	Explores how and why people use LOGICAL, EMOTIONAL, and ETHICAL APPEALS to create desired effects on specific audiences, in specific situations (Ch. 13).
CULTURAL OR NEW HISTORICAL	Explores how social, economic, and other cultural forces influence the development of ideas, texts, art, laws, customs, and so on. Also explores how individual texts or events provide broader understandings of the past or present.
DECONSTRUCTIONIST	Assumes that the meaning of any given text is not stable or "in" the work. Rather, meaning always depends on contexts and the interests of the people in power. The goal of deconstruction is to produce multiple possible meanings of a work, usually in order to undermine traditional interpretations.

continued >>

Quick Reference 15.1 (continued)

FEMINIST	Focuses on how women are presented and treated, concentrating especially on power relationships between men and women.
FORMALIST	Centers on matters of structure, form, and traditional literary devices (plot, rhythm, imagery, symbolism, and others; see Quick Box 16.2).
MARXIST	Assumes that the most important forces in human experience are economic and material ones. Focuses on power differences between economic classes of people and the effects of those differences.
READER-RESPONSE	Emphasizes how the individual reader determines meaning. The reader's personal history, values, experiences, relationships, and previous reading all contribute to how he or she interprets a particular work or event.

15c Which documentation style do I use in writing about the humanities?

Most fields in the humanities use the documentation style of the Modern Language Association (MLA), as explained and illustrated in Chapter 33. Some disciplines in the humanities use *Chicago Manual* (CM) style, as we explain in Chapter 39.

For more help with your writing, grammar, and research, go to **www.mycomplab.com**

Writing About Literature

16a What is literature?

Literature encompasses **fiction** (novels and stories), **drama** (plays, scripts, and some films), and **poetry** (poems and lyrics), as well as nonfiction with artistic qualities (memoirs, personal essays, and so on). Since ancient times, literature has represented human experience, entertained readers, and enlarged their perspectives about themselves, others, and different ways of living. The study of literature is one of the humanities (Ch. 15).

Writing about literature generates insights about your reading. It helps you understand other people, ideas, times, and places. It shows you how authors use language to stir the imaginations, emotions, and intellects of their readers. Finally, writing is a way to share your own reading experiences and insights with other readers.

Writing effective papers about literature involves more than summarizing the plot. It involves CRITICAL THINKING and SYNTHESIS. In such papers, you state a CLAIM (an observation or a position about the work of literature) and convince your readers that your thesis is reasonable. To be effective, a paper must be thorough and its claims must be well supported. For support, you make direct references to the work itself, by summarizing, paraphrasing, and quoting specific passages (Ch. 31) and by explaining precisely *why* and *how* the selected passages support your interpretation.

16b   How do I write different types of papers about literature?

When you read a literary work closely, look for details or passages that relate to your thesis. Mark up the text as you read by selectively underlining passages or by writing notes, comments, or questions in the margin.

■ Writing a personal response

A **personal response paper** is an essay in which you explain your reaction to a literary work or some aspect of it. You might write about why you did or did not enjoy reading a particular work, discuss whether situations in the work are similar to your personal experiences, explain whether you agree or disagree with the author's point of view and why, or answer a question or explore a problem that the work raised for you. For example, how do you react if a likable character breaks the law? As with all effective papers about literature, you need to explain your response by discussing specific passages or elements from the text.

■ Writing an interpretation

An interpretation explains the message or viewpoint that you think the work conveys. Most works of literature are open to more than one interpretation. Your task, then, is not to discover a single "right answer." Instead, your task is to determine a possible interpretation and provide an argument that supports it. The questions in Quick Reference 16.1 (referring to the complete poem on p. 102) can help you write an effective interpretation paper.

Quick Reference 16.1 ■ ■ ■ ■ ■ ■ ■

Questions for an interpretation paper

1. What is a central theme of the work? For example, in the poem "Blackberries," a central theme might be shame.

2. How do particular parts of the work relate to the theme? In "Blackberries," the smirking children in the car make the boy shamefully aware of his stained hands.

3. If patterns exist in the work, what might they mean? Patterns include repeated images, situations, and words. In "Blackberries," the words *consecrated, garland of thorns,* and *forgiveness* form a pattern.

4. What meaning does the author create through the elements listed in Quick Box 16.2?

5. Why might the work end as it does?

■ Writing a formal analysis

A formal analysis explains how elements of a literary work function to create meaning or effect. Your instructor may ask you to concentrate on one of these elements (for example, "How does the point of view in the story contribute to its meaning?") or to discuss how a writer develops a theme through several elements (for example, "How do setting, imagery, and symbolism reveal the author's viewpoint?"). The paper by student Michael Choi (16e) is an example of an interpretation based on a formal analysis. Quick Reference 16.2 (page 100) describes some of the major literary elements that you might expect to use in formal analyses.

■ Writing a cultural analysis

A **cultural analysis** relates a literary work to broader historical, social, cultural, or political situations. Instructors might ask you to explain how events or prevailing attitudes influenced the writing of a work or the way readers understand it. Quick Reference 16.3 (page 101) lists some common topics appropriate for a cultural analysis.

16c What special rules apply to writing about literature?

■ Using correct verb tenses

Always use the PRESENT TENSE when you describe or discuss a literary work or any of its elements: *Walter* [a character] **makes a difficult decision when he turns down Linder's offer to buy the house.** In addition, always use the present tense

Quick Reference 16.2 ■ ■ ■ ■ ■ ■ ■

Major elements to analyze in literary works

PLOT	Events and their sequence
THEME	Central idea or message
STRUCTURE	Organization and relationship of parts to each other and to the whole
CHARACTERIZATION	Traits, thoughts, and actions of the people in the work
SETTING	Time and place of the action
POINT OF VIEW	Perspective or position from which a narrator or a main character presents the material
STYLE	How words and sentence structure present the material
IMAGERY	Descriptive language that creates mental pictures for the reader
TONE	Author's attitude toward the subject of the work—and sometimes toward the reader—as expressed through choice of words, imagery, and point of view (10c)
FIGURES OF SPEECH	Unusual use or combination of words, such as METAPHOR or SIMILE, for enhanced vividness or effect
SYMBOLISM	The use of a specific object or event to represent a deeper, often abstract, meaning or idea
RHYTHM	Beat, meter
RHYME	Repetition of similar sounds for their auditory effect

for discussing what an author has done in a specific work: *Lorraine Hansberry, author of* A Raisin in the Sun, ***explores** not only powerful racial issues but also common family dynamics.* Always use a PAST-TENSE VERB to discuss historical events or biographical information: *Lorraine Hansberry's* A Raisin in the Sun **was the first play by an African American woman to be produced on Broadway.**

■ Using your own ideas and using secondary sources

Some assignments call only for your own ideas about a literary work. Other assignments call for you to use SECONDARY SOURCES. Secondary sources include books and articles in which experts discuss some aspect of the literary text or other material related to your topic. You can locate secondary sources by using the research process explained in Chapter 28.

Quick Reference 16.3

Major topics for cultural analyses

GENDER	How does a work portray women or men and define or challenge their roles in society?
CLASS	How does a work portray relationships among the upper, middle, and lower classes? How do characters' actions or perspectives result from their wealth and power—or from their poverty and powerlessness?
RACE AND ETHNICITY	How does a work portray the influences of race and ethnicity on the characters' actions, status, and values?
HISTORY	How does a work reflect—or challenge—past events and values in a society?
AUTOBIOGRAPHY	How did the writer's life experiences influence his or her work?
GENRE	How is the work similar to or different from other works of its type (for example, plays, sonnets, mysteries, comic novels, memoirs)?

16d How do I use documentation in writing about literature?

Documenting primary sources tells your readers exactly where to find the specific passages in the literary work from which you are quoting. Documenting secondary sources gives proper credit to the authors of those works and identifies you as someone who never intentionally or unintentionally steals from others. Unless your instructor requests another documentation style (Chs. 36–40), use MLA STYLE (Ch. 33) for writing about literature.

16e The final draft of a student's essay about literature

Working on the assignment

Michael Choi, a student in first-year English, fulfilled an assignment to write an interpretation of the images and metaphors in Yusef Komunyakaa's poem "Blackberries." When Michael first read the poem, several of the images puzzled him. He wondered how they connect to an apparently simple scene of a boy picking, eating, and selling blackberries. In the process of writing his essay, Michael came to understand how those previously puzzling images and metaphors help shape the poem's deeper meaning. His final draft is reproduced here.

■ Learning about the poet, Yusef Komunyakaa

Yusef Komunyakaa is an African American poet who was born in 1947 and raised in Louisiana. His father was a carpenter. Komunyakaa was educated at the University of Colorado, at Colorado State University, and at the University of California–Irvine. He served a tour of duty in Vietnam and was awarded the Bronze Star. In 1994, he won the Pulitzer Prize for poetry—one of the most prestigious honors a poet can receive in the United States—for his book *Neon Vernacular.* Here is his poem "Blackberries."

BLACKBERRIES
Yusef Komunyakaa

They left my hands like a printer's
Or thief's before a police blotter
& pulled me into early morning's
Terrestrial sweetness, so thick
The damp ground was consecrated 5
Where they fell among a garland of thorns.
Although I could smell old lime-covered
History, at ten I'd still hold out my hands
& berries fell into them. Eating from one
& filling a half gallon with the other, 10
I ate the mythology & dreamt
Of pies & cobbler, almost
Needful as forgiveness. My bird dog Spot
Eyed blue jays & thrashers. The mud frogs
In rich blackness, hid from daylight. 15
An hour later, beside City Limits Road
I balanced a gleaming can in each hand,
Limboed between worlds, repeating *one dollar.*
The big blue car made me sweat.
Wintertime crawled out of the windows. 20
When I leaned closer I saw the boy
& girl my age, in the wide back seat
Smirking, & it was then I remembered my fingers
Burning with thorns among berries too ripe to touch.

Student's essay about literature

Choi 1

Michael Choi

Professor May

English 100

8 November 2008

Images, Metaphors, and Meaning in "Blackberries"

In Yusef Komunyakaa's poem "Blackberries," the poet describes himself as "limboed between worlds" (line 18). At that moment, he is a boy standing beside City Limits Road--a symbolic line between the city and the country--selling berries that he has just picked. Yet the boy is also caught between his familiar natural world and a world of wealth and privilege. One of the poem's key issues is whether the boy is responsible for his situation. Komunyakaa uses a rich set of images and metaphors to suggest the boy's complicated position.

Some plain and direct images connect the boy to the world of nature. As he picks blackberries, the poet describes the "bird dog Spot" watching blue jays and thrashers (13-14), and he mentions "mud frogs" hiding in the dark (14-15). Readers form an impression of a rustic boy trying to earn some money from a countryside that is familiar and comfortable to him. He eats as he fills "gleaming" half-gallon cans (17) and dreams of "pies & cobbler" (12). The day is "thick" with "terrestrial sweetness" (4), and the atmosphere is peaceful, almost sleepy.

When the boy moves beyond the country to the City Limits Road to sell his harvest, however, his pleasant morning is shattered. After a customer drives up, the boy says, "The big blue car made me sweat" (19). Partly, he sweats because the

continued >>

Choi 2

car's air-conditioning makes him aware of heat that had not bothered him until that very moment. Komunyakaa uses the strong image that "Wintertime crawled out of the windows" to heighten the contrast between the artificial environment of the car and the natural environment of the boy (20). Even more

important, the boy sweats because he is suddenly self-conscious. He feels uncomfortable at the gap between himself and "the boy / & girl my age, in the wide back seat" (21-22). The emphasis on the air-conditioning and the width of the seat makes clear that these children come not only from the city but also from wealthier circumstances. When they smirk at him, he remembers his berry-stained fingers. Those stained hands are a metaphor for how different he is from the children in the car, both socially and economically. He feels ashamed.

Should he feel this way? Several complicated images and metaphors in the poem make this question difficult to answer. For example, at the beginning, the poet says that the berries "left my hands like a printer's" (1). This image not only calls attention to the inky stains on his hands but also likens berry picking to printing. Both are forms of honest manual labor. Furthermore, picking ripe berries is similar to the messy job of shedding ink-saturated type from a printing press--the typesetting method used before computers. This printing metaphor suggests a subtle connection between the boy's work and the poet's work. Komunyakaa immediately

continued >>

Choi 3

complicates the first image with a second that compares the boy's hands to a "thief's before a police blotter" (2). The common element between the two metaphors is the ink, which in the second is used for fingerprinting.

Note that the person whose fingerprints are being taken by the police is not simply a suspect but a thief (2). The person is already guilty of a crime. Has the boy been stealing berries that do not belong to him, and does he feel guilty when he is caught? This possible interpretation does not completely fit the encounter with the big blue car. The "smirking" response of the children in the car seems snobbish (23). Rather than accusing him of being a thief, the children make fun of him for getting dirty while picking berries, which they can buy in cool comfort. For his efforts, which even involve his "fingers / Burning with thorns" (23-24), the boy receives ridicule. The reader's sympathies lie with the boy selling the berries. Even if he did steal the berries, his crime does not seem that great.

Another set of metaphors, more mythic in nature, suggests an answer to the question of whether the boy should feel guilty. The boy reports that he "could smell old lime-covered / History" as he picks and eats (7-8). While lime might refer to a bright shade of green or to the citrus fruit, another meaning seems to apply here. The chemical substance lime has two uses. Farmers use it to reduce acidity in soil, where it serves as a kind of fertilizer. Alternatively, quicklime spread over the bodies of dead animals speeds their decomposition. To cover history in lime, therefore, means either to cultivate it or to bury it. Later, the boy states that he "ate the mythology & dreamt / Of pies & cobbler" (11-12). Obviously, no one can

continued >>

Choi 4

literally eat mythology. This metaphor suggests that the boy
is consuming the berries with little thought of any deeper
significance his actions might have. There is a mythic
dimension to picking blackberries, but the boy focuses on
pleasant physical sensations and, eventually, the chance to
make some money. Similarly, history is something to consume
or ignore. If the boy is a criminal (which seems unlikely),
maybe he is unaware that he is doing anything wrong.
Furthermore, perhaps no one owns the berries, and he is
merely "stealing" from nature.

The poem's most profound images and metaphors have
religious overtones. The poet describes the ground beneath the
berry bushes as "consecrated" (5). This powerful word choice
characterizes the ground as holy. The berries do not fall simply
among thorns but among "a garland of thorns" (6). The image of a
garland suggests the crown of thorns placed on the head of Jesus
after his trial, and these images draw out the deepest meaning of
the poet's being "limboed between worlds" (18). In some religious
traditions, limbo is a place where souls temporarily go before
entering heaven or where innocent but unbaptized babies
permanently dwell. In addition to standing between the world of
wealth and status that is represented by the car and the simpler
world of bird dogs and mud frogs, the boy stands outside
paradise. He has left and knows that he cannot go back.

Although mythic and religious elements are present in
"Blackberries," Komunyakaa's poem ultimately supports
interpretations on several levels. The poet uses religious
images to give depth to the boy's situation. When the boy picks
the berries, he is in a peaceful, natural environment that is
almost sacred, even if he does not realize it. When he sells the

continued >>

Choi 5

berries, he encounters a foreign world of wealth and privilege.
Because of his background, he cannot easily join that world.
Yet he cannot easily go back to his familiar ways because he
now sees his actions differently. He perceives that there may
be something wrong with picking blackberries. Whether or not
he should feel guilty, he does feel guilty. The poet is truly
limboed between worlds.

Choi 6

Work Cited

Komunyakaa, Yusef. "Blackberries." *Pleasure Dome: New and
Collected Poems.* Middletown: Wesleyan UP, 2001. 280–81.
Print.

For more help with your
writing, grammar, and research,
go to www.mycomplab.com

mycomplab

17

Writing in the Social Sciences

17a What are the social sciences?

The social sciences focus on the behavior of people as individuals and in groups.
The field includes disciplines such as economics, education, geography, political science, psychology, sociology, and at some colleges, history. In the social sciences, PRIMARY SOURCES include surveys and questionnaires, observations, interviews, and experiments.

Surveys and questionnaires systematically gather information from a representative number of individuals. To prepare a questionnaire, use the guidelines in Quick Reference 28.1. For advice on collecting information through observation, see 28c. We also explain interviewing strategies in 28c, especially in Quick Reference 28.2.

The social sciences sometimes use data from experiments as a source. For example, if you want to learn how people react in a particular situation, you can set up that situation artificially and bring individuals (known as "subjects") into it to observe their behavior. With all methods of inquiry in the social sciences, you are required to treat subjects fairly and honestly, not in ways that could harm their body, mind, or reputation.

17b What are different types of papers in the social sciences?

Instructors will sometimes assign the same kinds of writing in the social sciences as in the humanities (15c). Four additional types of papers are case studies, ethnographies, research reports, and research papers (or reviews of the literature).

▤ Case studies

A **case study** is an intensive study of one group or individual. Case studies are important in psychology, social work, education, medicine, and similar fields in which it's useful to form a comprehensive portrait of people in order to understand them and, in some cases, to help them. For example, if you learn that a certain teaching style is effective, you might do a case study of a student in order to understand how it works in a particular instance.

A case study is usually presented in a relatively fixed format, but the specific parts and their order vary. Most case studies contain the following components:

1. Basic identifying information about the individual or group
2. A history of the individual or group
3. Observations of the individual's or group's behavior
4. Conclusions and perhaps recommendations as a result of the observations

▤ Ethnographies

Ethnographies are comprehensive studies of people interacting in a particular situation. Ethnographies commonly are written in courses in business, education, or the social sciences, with anthropology and sociology being prime examples. A sociologist might compose an ethnography of a classroom, for instance, in order to understand the interactions and relationships among students. The level of details needed in ethnographies has been described by anthropologist Clifford Geertz as "thick description." The more details you have, the better, since you can't be sure which ones will be important until you analyze and reflect on the information.

▨ Research reports

Research reports explain your own original research based on primary sources. These may result from interviews, questionnaires, observations, or experiments. Research reports in the social sciences often follow a prescribed format:

1. Statement of the problem
2. Background, sometimes including a review of the literature
3. Methodology
4. Results
5. Discussion of findings

▨ Research papers (or reviews of the literature)

More often for students, social science research requires you to summarize, analyze, and synthesize SECONDARY SOURCES (15b). These sources are usually articles and books that report or discuss the findings of other people's primary research. To prepare a **review of the literature**, comprehensively gather and analyze the sources that have been published on a specific topic. *Literature* in this sense simply means "the body of work on a subject." Sometimes a review of the literature is a part of a longer paper, usually in the "background" section of a research report. Other times the entire paper might be an extensive review of the literature.

17c What documentation style should I use in the social sciences?

The most commonly used DOCUMENTATION STYLE in the social sciences is that of the American Psychological Association (APA). We describe APA documentation style and provide a sample student paper in Chapters 36–38. *Chicago Manual* (CM) documentation style is sometimes used in the social sciences (Chapter 39).

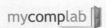

18

Writing in the Natural Sciences

18a What are the natural sciences?

The natural sciences include disciplines such as astronomy, biology, chemistry, geology, and physics. The sciences seek to describe and explain natural phenomena. The *scientific method,* commonly used in the sciences to make discoveries, is a procedure for gathering information related to a specific hypothesis. Quick Reference 18.1 gives guidelines for using this method.

Quick Reference 18.1

Guidelines for using the scientific method

1. Formulate a tentative explanation (a *hypothesis*) for a scientific phenomenon.
2. Read and summarize previously published information related to your hypothesis.
3. Plan a method of investigation to test your hypothesis.
4. Experiment, following exactly the investigative procedures you have outlined.
5. Observe closely the results of the experiment, and write notes carefully.
6. Analyze the results. Do they confirm the hypotheis?
7. Write a report of your research. At the end, you can suggest additional hypotheses that might be investigated.

18b How do I write different types of papers in the natural sciences?

Two major types of papers in the sciences are reports and reviews.

Science reports

Science reports tell about observations and experiments. When they describe laboratory experiments, as is often true in academic settings, they're usually called laboratory reports. Formal reports feature the eight elements identified in Quick Reference 18.2. Less formal reports, which are sometimes assigned in

Quick Reference 18.2

Parts of a science report

1. **Title.** Precisely describes your report's topic.

2. **Abstract.** Provides a short overview of the report to help readers decide whether or not your research is of interest to them.

3. **Introduction.** States the purpose behind your research and presents the hypothesis. Any needed background information and a review of the literature appear here.

4. **Methods and materials.** Describes the equipment, material, and procedures used.

5. **Results.** Provides the information obtained from your efforts. Charts, graphs, and photographs help present the data in a way that is easy for readers to grasp.

6. **Discussion.** Presents your interpretation and evaluation of the results. Did your efforts support your hypothesis? If not, can you suggest why not? Use concrete evidence in discussing your results.

7. **Conclusion.** Lists conclusions about the hypothesis and the outcomes of your efforts, paying particular attention to any theoretical implications that can be drawn from your work. Be specific in suggesting further research.

8. **List of references.** Presents references cited in the review of the literature, if any. Its format conforms to the requirements of the DOCUMENTATION STYLE in the particular science that is your subject.

introductory college courses, might not include an abstract or a review of the literature. Ask your instructor which sections to include in your report.

■ Science reviews

A science review is a paper that discusses published information on a scientific topic or issue. The purpose of the review is to summarize for readers all the current knowledge about the topic or issue. Sometimes the purpose of a science review is to synthesize, to tie in a new interpretation of the old material. In such a review, the writer must present EVIDENCE to persuade readers that the new interpretation is valid.

If you're required to write a science review, you want to (1) choose a very limited scientific issue currently being researched; (2) use information that is current—the more recently published the articles, books, and journals you consult, the better; (3) accurately paraphrase (31g) and summarize (31h) material; and (4) document your sources (28d). If your review runs longer than two or three pages, you might want to use headings to help your reader understand the organization and idea progression of your paper.

18c Which documentation style do I use in the natural sciences?

Documentation styles differ among the various sciences. A common style is that of the Council of Science Editors (CSE), described in Chapter 40.

For more help with your
writing, grammar, and research,
go to **www.mycomplab.com**

mycomplab

19

Writing Under Pressure

19a Why do I need to practice writing under strict time limits?

All writers, student and professional, sometimes find themselves having to produce effective writing in a limited time.

19b How do I prepare for essay exams?

Begin preparing for exams well before the day of the test. Attend class diligently and take good notes. Be an active reader, annotating your textbook and putting concepts into your own words.

Perhaps the best preparation comes from writing practice exams, which will give you experience in writing under pressure about course material. Your instructors may offer questions they used in previous years, or they may provide a number of questions to guide your studying. Alternatively, you and your classmates may generate your own exam questions using cue words and key content words drawn from your course material. Finally, ask each instructor whether an exam is "open book" so that you'll know if you can use books or notes during the test.

Writing essay exams is like writing other essays, but with firm limitations on the time available. Therefore, you need to go through all of the steps in the WRITING PROCESS (Chs. 8–10), but at a highly stepped-up speed. In addition to following the steps of the writing process, follow these time-tested strategies for writing essay exams.

- **Relax.** Never begin writing immediately. Instead, take a deep breath and let it out slowly to relax and focus your thoughts.

- **Read.** Read the test from beginning to end without skimming, so that you understand the questions completely. If you have a choice among topics, and equal credit is given to each, select the topics you know the most about.

- **Plan your time.** If the instructor indicates what percentage of your grade each question will affect, allot your time to your greatest advantage. Make sure to allow time for planning, DRAFTING, and proofreading.
- **Underline cue words.** These words tell you what you must do in your essay. Look for words such as *analyze, classify,* and *criticize.* An essay question might read like this:

   Analyze Socrates' discussion of "good life" and "good death." [Separate the concepts of "good life" and "good death" into parts and discuss each part.]

   Quick Reference 19.1 lists some common cue words with their meanings.
- **Circle key content words.** Look for the keywords or major terms in a statement or question. An essay question might ask:

   Justify the existence of **labor unions** in the **US economy**. [The key content words are *labor unions* and *US economy*.]

- **Use your time fully.** The best writers use every second available to write and polish. (Trust us, we've been in that spot often and have never regretted working right up to the time limit.)

Quick Reference 19.1 ■ ■ ■ ■ ■ ■ ■

Some common cue words

Cue Word	Meaning
ANALYZE	Separate into parts and discuss each.
CLASSIFY	Arrange in groups based on shared characteristics or functions.
CRITICIZE	Give your opinion and explain why you approve or disapprove of something.
COMPARE	Show similarities and differences.
DEFINE	Tell what something is to differentiate it from similar things.
DISCUSS	Consider in an organized way the various issues or elements involved.
EXPLAIN	Make clear a complex thing or process that needs to be illuminated or interpreted.
INTERPRET	Explain the meaning of something.
REVIEW	Evaluate or summarize critically.
SUMMARIZE	Lay out the major points of something.
SUPPORT	Argue in favor of something.

For more help with your writing, grammar, and research, go to **www.mycomplab.com**

20

Making Oral Presentations and Using Multimedia

20a What are oral presentations?

Oral presentations—speeches often supported with multimedia tools—are common not only in academic disciplines across the curriculum but also in work and public settings. Preparing a presentation and drafting a paper involve similar processes (Chapters 8–13). This chapter will provide additional information for preparing presentations and using multimedia tools.

20b How does my situation focus my presentation?

You need to adjust presentations to fit PURPOSES, AUDIENCES, roles, and any special considerations. Consider three different situations.

- You want to address a group of students to inform them about a film club you're starting.
- You need to persuade a management group at work to adopt a new set of procedures for making purchasing decisions.
- You plan to give a toast at a friend's wedding to express your feelings and to entertain the wedding guests.

Different approaches will be successful in each instance because your purpose and audience are different.

20c How do I adapt my message to my listening audience?

Adapting your presentation to your listeners means holding their interest and being responsive to their viewpoints. Consult the strategies for analyzing AUDIENCES in Quick Reference 8.3. Especially consider your listeners' prior knowledge of your topic. Are they *uninformed, informed,* or *mixed*? Quick Reference 20.1 suggests how to adapt your message to each type of audience.

Adapting an oral presentation to your audience

UNINFORMED AUDIENCE	Start with the basics and then move to a few new ideas. Define new terms and concepts and avoid unnecessary technical terms. Use visual aids and give examples. Repeat key ideas—but not too often.
INFORMED AUDIENCE	Never give more than a quick overview of the basics. Devote most of your time to new ideas and concepts.
MIXED AUDIENCE	In your introduction, acknowledge the more informed audience members who are present. Explain that you're going to review the basic concepts briefly so that everyone can build from the same knowledge base. Move as soon as possible toward more complex concepts.

20d How do I organize my presentation?

As with essays, an oral presentation has three parts: introduction, body, and conclusion (8a). Within the body, you present your major points, with two to three supports for each point. Drafting a SENTENCE OUTLINE (8h) gets you close to your final form and forces you to sharpen your thinking.

■ Introducing yourself and your topic

All audience members want to know three things about a speaker: Who are you? What are you going to talk about? Why should I listen? To respond effectively to these unasked questions, try these suggestions.

- Grab your audience's attention with an interesting question, quotation, or statistic; a bit of background information; a compliment; or an anecdote. If necessary to establish your credibility—even if someone has introduced you—briefly and humbly mention your qualifications as a speaker about your topic.
- Give your audience a road map of your talk: Tell where you're starting, where you're going, and how you intend to get there. Your listeners need to know that you won't waste their time.

■ Following your road map

Listening to a presentation is very different from reading an essay. Audiences generally need help following the speaker's line of reasoning. Here are some strategies to keep your listeners' minds from wandering.

- Signal clearly where you are on your road map by using cue word transitions such as *first, second,* and *third; subsequently, therefore,* and *furthermore;* or *before, then,* and *next.*
- Define unfamiliar terms and concepts and follow up with strong, memorable examples.
- Occasionally tell the audience what you consider significant, memorable, or especially relevant and why. Do so sparingly, at key points.
- Provide occasional summaries at points of transition. Recap what you've covered and say how it relates to what's coming next.

■ Wrapping up your presentation

Demonstrate that you haven't let key points simply float away. Try ending with these suggestions.

- Never let your voice volume fall or your clarity of pronunciation falter because the end is in sight.
- Do not introduce new ideas at the last minute.
- Signal that you are wrapping up your presentation using verbal cues, such as "In conclusion" and "Finally." When you say "finally," mean it!
- Make a dramatic, decisive statement; cite a memorable quotation; or issue a challenge. Allow a few seconds of silence, and then say "thank you." Use body language, such as stepping slightly back from the podium, and then sit down.

20e How do I incorporate multimedia into my oral presentation?

Multimedia elements such as visual aids, sound, and video can reinforce key ideas in your presentation by providing illustrations or concrete images for the audience.

■ Using traditional visual aids

Here are various types of visual aids and their uses. When using them, always make text or graphics large enough to be read easily at a distance.

Posters can dramatize a point, often with color or images. Make sure a poster is large enough for everyone in your audience to see it.

Dry-erase boards are preferable to chalkboards because colors on them are visually appealing. Use them to roughly sketch an illustration or to emphasize a technical word.

Handouts are useful when the topic calls for a longer text or when you want to give your audience something to refer to later. Short, simple handouts work best during a presentation, but longer, more detailed ones are more effective at the end. Always include DOCUMENTATION information for any SOURCES used in preparing the handout. A strategic handout can be a useful backup just in case other technologies are missing or broken. Finally, remember to wait until everyone has one before you begin speaking about it.

Transparencies need to be used with an overhead projector. You can prepare them in advance and write on them for emphasis during your presentation.

■ Using electronic media

PowerPoint, the most widely used presentation software, is a program that can create digital slides. (A similar program, "Impress," is free from www.openoffice.org.) These slides can contain words, images, or combinations of both; they can even include sound or movie clips. To project your slides during a presentation, you need an LCD projector connected to your computer and a separate screen.

To design PowerPoint slides, follow the principles of unity, variety, balance, and emphasis discussed in Chapter 24. Never present so much information on each slide that your audience pays more attention to reading it than to listening to you. Also, never simply read large amounts of text from your slides; your audience will quickly—and rightfully—become bored. People have coined the phrase "death by PowerPoint" in despair at presenters who simply repeat what's written on slides.

Figure 20.1 is an example of an effective PowerPoint slide prepared for a presentation about a community service project. The slide is clearly titled, is well balanced, and has an image to capture attention. It presents the points concisely and clearly.

A brief sound file (for example, a sentence or two from a speech) or a video clip (perhaps 20 to 30 seconds of footage from an event) can occasionally help you illustrate a point. These clips can be as simple as a CD or a DVD, or as complicated as Wave or QuickTime files on a computer. Always keep them brief and be absolutely sure that your audience will recognize immediately that they enhance your message and aren't just for show.

■ Planning for multimedia in your presentation

Few things are more frustrating for you or annoying to your audience than technical problems during a presentation. Beforehand, make sure all of your visual aids and multimedia will work well—and have a backup plan at hand in case

Figure 20.1 A sample PowerPoint slide

they fail during your presentation. Learn how to use the technology and rehearse carefully with it so that you can use it seamlessly during your presentation.

20f What presentation styles can I use?

Presentation style is the way you deliver what you have to say. You may memorize your talk, read it, map it, or speak without notes. Memorized talks often sound unnatural. Unless you've mastered the material well enough to recite it in a relaxed way, choose another presentation style. Reading your presentation aloud can bore your audience. If you have no choice but to read, avoid speaking in a monotone. Vary your pitch and style so that people will find it interesting to listen to you. In general, avoid speaking without notes until you have considerable experience giving speeches, unless otherwise instructed by your professor or someone in your workplace.

We recommend mapping your presentation. Mapping means creating a brief outline of your presentation's main points and examples, then using that outline to cue yourself as you talk.

Your body language can either add to or detract from your message. Eye contact is your most important nonverbal communication tool because it communicates confidence and shows respect for your listeners. Smile or nod at your audience as you begin. Gestures, if not overdone, contribute to your message by adding emphasis; they are best when they appear to be natural rather than forced or timed. If you use a podium, stand squarely behind it before you begin speaking. When gestures aren't needed, rest your hands on the podium—don't scratch your head, dust your clothing, or fidget.

20g How do I make a collaborative presentation?

A common practice in many academic settings—and in business and public situations, too—is to present an oral report as part of a group. All members of the group are required to contribute in some way to the collaborative enterprise. Here are some guidelines to follow.

- Make sure, when choosing a topic or a position about an issue, that most members of the group are familiar with the subject.
- Lay out clearly each member's responsibilities for preparing the presentation.
- Agree on firm time limits for each person, if all members of the group are expected to speak for an equal amount of time. If there is no such requirement, people who enjoy public speaking can take more responsibility for delivery, while others can do more of the preparatory work or contribute in other ways.
- Allow enough time for practice. Good delivery requires practice. Plan at least four complete run-throughs of your presentation, using visuals if you have them. Though each member can practice his or her own part alone, schedule practice sessions for the entire presentation as a group. This will help you work on transitions, make sure the order of presenters is effective, clock the length of the presentation, and cut or expand material accordingly.
- As you practice your presentation, have different group members watch in order to make suggestions or videotape the practices.

For more help with your writing, grammar, and research,
go to **www.mycomplab.com**

mycomplab

21

Creating a Writing Portfolio

21a What is a writing portfolio?

A portfolio is a collection of your writings that you present to others in order to achieve some purpose. You might be familiar with artists who make portfolios of their work in order to show gallery owners or prospective employers. Writing portfolios are similar. Students frequently need to submit them for part or all of a course grade or at the end of their majors or program. Portfolios can even help job candidates show their skills and experiences in a sample of their best work.

Making a successful portfolio requires four key steps: collecting all of your writings, selecting the works to include, writing an introduction to those works, and designing the presentation format, which can be paper-based or digital.

21b What do I need to collect for a portfolio?

Save everything you write: every paper and project, every exam or lab report, even every draft. You can't put together a good portfolio if you don't have plenty of works to choose from, including plenty to ignore. Because computer storage is so cheap and plentiful, it's easy to keep electronic copies of everything. It's a good idea to keep paper copies, too, especially when they have instructors' comments or grades; some portfolios, such as those submitted for awards or graduate school admissions, even require instructors' comments.

21c How do I choose works to include in a portfolio?

Selection is crucial to an effective portfolio. You need to choose the pieces that best satisfy basic requirements for the number of works or pages. Beyond that, the portfolio's purpose will guide your selection.

■ Portfolios that demonstrate your general writing ability

Consider this kind of assignment: "Present three works that best display your strengths as a writer." Clearly, you're going to choose your best writing, which sounds simple. However, you might also judge whether you can choose pieces that show the range of your abilities.

◼ Portfolios that demonstrate a particular quality or set of qualities

Consider another kind of situation: "Create a portfolio of three works that demonstrates how you're able to write for different audiences and purposes, and in different roles." In this case, you need to choose works that reflect different writing situations.

◼ Portfolios that demonstrate improvement

Consider a third kind of portfolio: "Select four examples of your writing from this semester that demonstrate how your writing has developed." In this case, your instructor wants to see your improvement. One way to do this is to choose writings from the beginning, middle, and end of the course. Another way is to choose both early and revised drafts from the same paper.

21d How do I write a portfolio introduction, reflection, or analysis?

A statement or essay in which you introduce or explain the works you're presenting is an important part of most portfolios. This writing, which may range from a few paragraphs to several pages, depending on the situation and requirements, should include certain basic elements. You want to introduce yourself as a writer; you want to introduce the works that follow; and you want to make some points about them, especially about how they satisfy the portfolio's purpose. It's helpful to think of the reflective introduction as an argument.

1. Make a claim about your writing.
2. Use SUMMARIES, PARAPHRASES, or QUOTATIONS from papers in the portfolio that support the claim.
3. Discuss how the summary, paraphrase, or quotations support your claim.

Repeat this pattern for as many claims as you have about your portfolio.

EXCERPT FROM A REFLECTIVE INTRODUCTION

During the 2008 spring semester, I completed five papers in English 101, revising each of them several times with response from my peers and feedback from my instructor. At times the process was frustrating; I came into the course feeling confident about my writing, but I learned that there's always room for improvement. This portfolio includes three papers I've chosen to represent my current strengths as a writer.

Claim

Summary One quality apparent in these papers is my ability to adjust writings for different audiences, both academic and general. For example, "Analyzing the Merits of Organic Produce" addresses an academic readership, specifically members of the scientific community reading a review of the literature. This can be seen in my consistent use of APA citation style and a scholarly tone suitable

Quotation for experts, as in my opening sentence, "Research on the health values of organic produce over nonorganic reveals that this issue

Discussion remains unresolved" (Johnson, 2006; Akule, 2007). The paper begins bluntly and directly because I decided scholars would require little orientation and would value my getting right to the point. Stressing that "research . . . reveals" emphasizes my ethos as a careful scholar, a quality reinforced by my including two citations. Academic readers will value this ethos more than they would an opinionated or informal one. The objective and cautious tone of "remains unresolved" differs from a more casual phrase like "is messy."

Summary In contrast, my paper "Is That Organic Apple Really Worth It?" is aimed at a more general audience, such as readers of a weekly news magazine. That paper uses scenes and examples designed to engage readers with a friendly tone. On pages seven and eight, for example, I include an interview with organic grower Jane Treadway in which I describe the setting. . . .

Quick Reference 21.1   ■ ■ ■ ■ ■ ■ ■

Items to include in a portfolio

Cover page. Include a title, your name and contact information, the course, and the date. The cover page may include images or graphical elements, if appropriate.

Contents. List all of the pieces included in the portfolio, beginning with the reflective introduction, along with their page numbers. In some portfolios, the contents appear on the cover.

Reflective introduction. Introduce and argue for your collection.

Writing 1 [Including a draft for Writing 1 if appropriate]
Writing 2 [Including a draft for Writing 2, if appropriate]

And so on, for all the writings in the portfolio.

21e How do I present a paper portfolio?

Paper portfolios can come in several formats, from a set of papers stapled or clipped together to writings collected in a folder or a binder. Follow any specific directions from your instructor. Clarify whether you should revise and reprint your writings or whether the portfolio should contain only the original works, perhaps with your instructor's comments. Add page numbers so that readers can locate your writings. Generally, your portfolio will contain the elements identified in Quick Reference 21.1. For an example of a cover page that includes contents, see Figure 21.1.

"Paths to Progress"

Portfolio by

Alba Carmen

WRIT 1133: Writing and Research

Casey Sampson, Instructor

May 30, 2008

Contents

Figure 21.1 Print portfolio cover page, with contents

21f How do I create a digital portfolio?

A **digital portfolio** is a collection of several texts in electronic format that you've chosen to represent the range of your skills and abilities. Unlike paper portfolios, digital versions contain links between—and within—individual texts; they can be modified and shared easily and cheaply; and they can be put online for public reading. Figure 21.2 shows the opening screen of one student's digital portfolio for a first semester writing course. Note that all the titles function as links to the papers themselves.

Digital portfolios can take several forms. In the simplest ones, you just upload your work into an online course management program, such as BlackBoard. More sophisticated digital portfolios involve your own design efforts, including images, sounds, and video. Importantly, you create links between files. In the following example, the blue underlined text is a link that readers can click to take them directly to the paper.

> One quality apparent in these papers is my ability to adjust writings for different audiences, both academic and general. For example, "Analyzing the Merits of Organic Produce" addresses an academic readership.

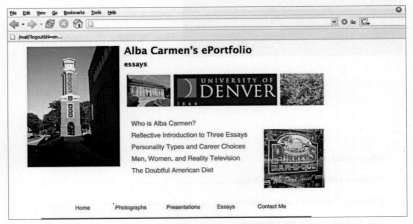

Figure 21.2 Opening screen of a student's digital portfolio

 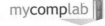

22

Writing for Work

22a   Who writes in the workplace and why?

If you're working, chances are good that you're writing. Writing infuses most job situations, from corporate offices, not-for-profit agencies, schools, and health care facilities to farms and factories. People write to coworkers inside organizations; they write to customers, vendors, or service providers outside them. Even people who work independently (such as consultants, therapists, artists, and craftspeople) keep records, apply for grants, correspond with customers, and advertise their services. In this chapter, we offer guidance for several common work-related writing tasks.

22b   What are important features
of work-related correspondence?

Correspondence is the general name for written communications, such as e-mails, memos, and letters, that you send to specific individuals. Your goal is to communicate plans, procedures, or purchases; share or ask for information; request specific actions; or influence decisions.

Work-related correspondence needs to appear professional, focused, and well informed. Avoid slang, abbreviations, informal words, or informal expressions. Use standard EDITED AMERICAN ENGLISH* grammar, spelling, and punctuation. Also, find out whether your organization prefers somewhat formal or very formal language for both internal and external correspondence. Remember, too, that when a business document takes on legal significance, even your most casually written messages can become official evidence in a court case. Write all your business materials, therefore, with such a possibility in mind. Quick Reference 22.1 (p. 126) provides general guidelines for writing work-related correspondence.

🌐 **ESOL Tip:** In some cultures, work-related correspondence is often sprinkled with elaborate language, many descriptive details, and even metaphors. Most American organizations, however, prefer correspondence that is clear and gets to the point quickly. ●

---

*Words printed in SMALL CAPITAL LETTERS are discussed elsewhere in the text and are defined in the Terms Glossary at the back of the book.

Quick Reference 22.1

Guidelines for work-related correspondence

- Address the recipient by name.
- Use GENDER-NEUTRAL LANGUAGE.
- Announce the PURPOSE of your communication at the outset.
- Be clear, concise, and specific.
- Be honest, positive, and natural, using a personal touch.
- Never spread gossip, personal opinion, put-downs, jokes, or chain letters.
- Edit ruthlessly for CONCISENESS and correctness.

22c   How do I write work-related e-mail?

Business e-mail has purposes and AUDIENCES quite different from those of the informal e-mail messages you exchange with friends and family. You might sprinkle informal e-mails with slang or with abbreviations like LOL (laughing out loud) or BTW (by the way). However, we recommend that you avoid these casual practices in work settings.

The "Cc" or "Copies" space is for the e-mail addresses of other people who need to see your message, even when they aren't expected to respond. When you use the "Bcc" (blind copy) space, you're sending a copy to someone without your primary recipients' knowing about it. Generally, it's considered rude to send blind copies, but rare situations might call for it. For example, you might choose to blind-copy a long list of e-mail addresses so your recipients don't have to scroll through lots of names.

For the body of your e-mail, single-space the text, and double-space between paragraphs and before your complimentary closing. Start paragraphs flush left at the margin. When you need to include a separate document with your e-mail, such as a report, compose it as a separate document in your word processing program, and attach it to your e-mail using the "Attachments" function. Figure 22.1 is an example of a professional e-mail. Quick Reference 22.2 (page 128) explains important qualities of email.

22d   What is netiquette?

Netiquette, a word coined from *Net* and *etiquette,* demands that you use good manners as you write e-mail. For example, always use gender-neutral language. Always address business recipients by their full names, including any title such

```
To:       sherrel.ampadu@jpltech.com
From:     Chris Malinowitz <cmalinowitz@chateauby.com>
Subject:  Confirming Meeting Arrangements
Cc:       dmclusky@chateauby.com
Bcc:
Attached: C:\Documents and Settings\Desktop\Chateau Menus.doc
```

Dear Ms. Ampadu:

I am writing to confirm the final arrangements for your business meeting on June 17, 2008, at our conference center.

As you directed, we will set the room in ten round tables, each seating six. We will provide a podium and microphone, an LCD projector and screen, and a white board with markers. I understand that you will be bringing your own laptop. Our technician can help you set up.

You indicated that you would like to provide lunch and refreshments at two breaks. Attached please find our menus. You will need to make your lunch selections at least 48 hours in advance.

If you have any questions or wish to make any changes, I would be pleased to accommodate your needs. Thank you for choosing The Chateau at Brickyard.

Sincerely,

Chris Malinowitz
Catering Director, The Chateau at Brickyard

Figure 22.1 Professional e-mail

as *Ms., Mr.,* or *Dr.* Also, use titles and last names, especially when you're communicating with people you've never met or corresponded with before. After you get to know people well, you might decide to lower your LEVEL OF FORMALITY. We suggest waiting until after those to whom you're writing begin to end their messages with their first names, especially when those people hold positions higher than yours.

Know your workplace's policy covering issues such as use of business e-mail accounts for personal purposes, the length and tone of most e-mail, your legal responsibilities concerning your e-mail, and restrictions on visiting WEB SITES unrelated to work. Increasingly, businesses monitor their employees' e-mail.

Quick Reference 22.2 summarizes some key points about writing business e-mail.

Guidelines for writing business e-mail

- Write a specific, not general, topic on the Subject line.

- Start your e-mail with a sentence that tells what your message is about.

- Put the details of your message in the second paragraph. Supply any background information that your recipients may need.

- Conclude your e-mail by asking for certain information or a specific action, if such is needed, or by restating your reason for writing.

- Never write in all capital letters or all lowercase letters. Not only are they annoying to read, but all capital letters are considered the written equivalent of shouting. All lowercase letters suggest laziness and a lack of respect.

- Keep your message brief and your paragraphs short.

- Be cautious about what you say in a business e-mail. After all, the recipient can forward any e-mail to others without your permission, even though this practice is considered unethical.

- Forward an e-mail message only if you've asked the original sender for permission.

- At the end of your message, before your full name and position, use a commonly accepted complimentary closing, such as *Sincerely, Cordially,* or *Regards.*

22e How do I format and write memos?

Memos are usually exchanged internally (within an organization or business). Today e-mail takes the place of most memos, unless the correspondence requires a physical record or signature. The guidelines for writing e-mail (22c) also pertain to memos. The appropriate form of communication—paper memos or e-mail—depends on what's customary in your work environment.

The standard format of a memo includes two major parts: the headings and the body.

To:	[Name your audience—a specific person or group.]
From:	[Give your name and your title, if any.]
Date:	[Give the date on which you write the memo.]
Re:	[State your subject as specifically as possible in the "Subject" or "Re" line.]

Here are some guidelines for preparing a memo.

- **Introduction:** State your purpose for writing and why your memo is worth your reader's attention. Either here or at the conclusion, mention whether the recipient needs to take action.
- **Body:** Present the essential information on your topic. If you write more than three or four paragraphs, use headings to divide the information into subtopics (24d).
- **Conclusion:** End with a one- to two-sentence summary, a specific recommendation, or what action is needed and by when. Finish with a "thank you" line.

22f   How do I format business letters?

Letters are used for formal and contractual correspondence when you want to establish a physical record of your communications. Cover letters (also called "letters of transmittal") accompany resumes, packages, reports, or other documents. Increasingly, e-mail is taking the place of business letters in less formal situations (22c). Here are guidelines for the format and content of your business letters.

- **Paper:** Use 8½-by-11-inch paper. The most suitable colors are white and off-white. Fold your business letters horizontally into thirds to fit into a standard number 10 business envelope (9½ by 4 inches). Never fold a page in half and then into thirds.
- **Letterhead:** Use the official letterhead stationery (name, address, and logo, if any) of the business where you're employed. If no letterhead exists, center your full name, address, and phone number at the top of the page, and use a larger font than for the content of your letter. Keep it simple.
- **Format:** Without indents, use single spacing within paragraphs and double spacing between paragraphs, which is called **block style**. Figure 22.4 (p. 135) shows a job application letter in business format.
- **Recipient's name:** Use the full name of your recipient whenever possible. If you can't locate a name, either through a phone call to a central switchboard or on the Internet, use a specific category—for example, "Dear Billing Department," placing the key word "Billing" first (not "Department of Billing"). Always use gender-neutral language.

22g   How do I write business reports?

Reports inform others inside or outside the workplace. Internal reports are designed to convey information to others in your workplace. They serve various purposes. If you attend a professional meeting, you might provide a report of what you learned for your supervisor and colleagues who weren't there. If you are working on a lengthy project, you may report on your progress so that others can understand what you have completed, what remains, and what problems or delays you anticipate, if any. If you have conducted extensive consumer research through telephone interviews with potential customers, you might summarize and analyze your findings in a report. In each of these cases, follow the principles of reporting (6a), analyzing (1d), and interpreting information (15c). Being clear and concise are vital.

External reports inform audiences beyond the workplace. Generally, they have a secondary function of creating a good impression of the company or organization. Probably the most common examples are annual reports, in which companies summarize for investors their accomplishments during the previous years, especially their profits and losses. However, other kinds of external reports are also common. For example, a school principal may write a report to parents that explain students' results on a statewide achievement test. Figure 22.2 shows a section of one company's report.

Because external reports are written for more general audiences, you will need to explain many terms and concepts that would be clear to your coworkers. Document design, whether in print or on the computer screen, is also important (Chapter 24). Notice how the report in Figure 22.2 uses images and color.

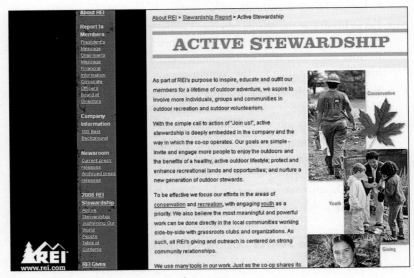

Figure 22.2 A company's external report

22h How do I write business proposals?

Proposals persuade readers to follow a plan, choose a product or service, or implement an idea. A marketing specialist might propose a new product line. A teacher might propose a change in the curriculum. A leader of a not-for-profit organization might propose a way to increase funding. Proposals generally describe a project, the steps for completing it, and its cost.

Readers evaluate proposals based on how well the writers have anticipated and answered their questions. If some readers have a high level of knowledge about the subject of the proposal, and others have little, then you need to explain the basic information and offer a glossary of terms. Here are some guidelines for preparing a proposal.

INTRODUCTION	Explain the project's purpose and scope. Describe the problem that the project seeks to solve, and lay out your solution. Include dates for beginning and completing the work. Project the outcomes and the costs. Be accurate and precise.
BODY	What is the product or service? What resources are needed? What are the phases of the project? What is the detailed budget? Precisely how is each phase to be completed? By what date is each phase to be completed? How will the project be evaluated?
CONCLUSION	Summarize the benefits of this proposal. Thank readers for their time. Offer to provide further information.

22i How do I write a resumé?

A **resumé** details your accomplishments and employment history. Its purpose is to help a potential employer determine whether you'll be a suitable candidate. To make a favorable impression, follow the guidelines for writing a resumé in Quick Reference 22.3. Figure 22.3 (p. 134) presents a sample resumé.

22j How do I write a job application letter?

A **job application letter** always needs to accompany your resumé. Avoid repeating what's already on the resumé. Instead, connect the company's expectations to your experience by emphasizing how your background has prepared you for the position. Your job application letter, more than your resumé, reflects

Quick Reference 22.3

■ ■ ■ ■ ■ ■ ■

Guidelines for writing a traditional, scannable, or plain-text resumé

- At the beginning, include your name, address, e-mail address, and telephone number.

- Make the resumé easy to read. Label the sections clearly, and target the resumé to the position you want. Help employers see your most significant attributes quickly and easily.

- Adjust your resumé to fit your purpose. For example, if you're applying for a job as a computer programmer, you'll want to emphasize different facts than you would if you were applying for a job selling computers in an electronics store.

- Use headings to separate blocks of information. Include the following headings, as appropriate: "Position Desired" or "Career Objective"; "Education"; "Experience"; "Licenses and Certifications"; "Related Experience"; "Honors and Awards"; "Publications and Presentations"; "Activities and Interests"; and "Special Abilities, Skills, and Knowledge."

- When you list your work experience, place your most recent job first; when listing education, place your most recent degrees, certificates, or enrollments first.

- Write telegraphically. Start with verb phrases, not with the word *I*, and omit *a, an,* and *the.*

- Include only relevant information.

- Tell the truth. Even if you get the job, an employer who discovers you lied will likely fire you.

- Include references, or state that you can provide them on request.

- Try to fit all of the information on one page. If you need a second page, make sure the most important information is on the first page.

- Use high-quality paper that is white, off-white, or light beige.

- Proofread carefully; even one spelling error or one formatting error can eliminate you from consideration.

- Scannable resumés are designed to be scanned by machines that digitize their content. Sophisticated software then searches the database to match key terms to position requirements. As a result, scannable resumés need to be simpler: don't use columns, different fonts, lines or other graphics, or bold or italic fonts. Choose a clean sans serif font such as Arial or Geneva in a 10–12 point size. Include keywords that the computer can

continued >>

Quick Reference 22.3 (continued)

match to the job. Here is the keyword list Monica Schickel created for the scannable version of the resume in Figure 22.3:

KEYWORDS

Publications experience, graphic design, editing, photography, supervisor, editing, customer service, digital media, excellent Spanish, Adobe creative suite, Photoshop, InDesign, Quark, CSS, Dreamweaver, Web design, illustrator, proofread, Excel, Access, Publisher, newspaper, layout, sales, willing to relocate

- Plain-text resumés can be pasted directly into e-mails (for companies that won't open attachments for fear of viruses) or into application databases. Use the same standards as for scannable resumés, but omit any dashes before items in a list. Every line of text should start at the left margin.

your energy and personality. See Figure 22.4 (p. 135) for a sample letter. Here are guidelines for writing a job application letter.

- Use one page only.
- Overall, think of your letter as a polite sales pitch about yourself and what benefits you can bring to the company. Don't be shy, but don't exaggerate.
- Use the same name, content, and format guidelines as for a business letter (22f).
- Address the letter to a specific person. If you can't discover a name, use a gender-neutral title such as "Dear Personnel Director." Quick Reference 22.4 (p. 136) provides help for writing gender-neutral salutations.
- Open your letter by identifying the position for which you're applying.
- Mention your qualifications and explain how your background will meet the job requirements.
- Make clear that you're familiar with the company or organization; your research will impress the employer.
- End by being specific about what you can do for the company. If the job will be your first, give your key attributes—but make sure they're relevant. For instance, you might state that you're punctual, self-disciplined, eager to learn, and hardworking.
- State when you're available for an interview and how the potential employer can reach you.
- Edit and proofread the letter carefully. If you have to hand-correct even one error, print out the letter again.

MONICA A. SCHICKEL

1817 Drevin Avenue
Denver, CO 80208
Cell phone: (303) 555-7722
E-mail: mnsschl@wordnet.com
Professional portfolio: www.schickelgraphics.net

OBJECTIVE: Entry level position as a graphic designer or publications assistant

EXPERIENCE

9/08 – present   **Publications Intern** (half-time; paid), *Westword* (Denver, CO)
- Design advertisements
- Prepare photographs for publications
- Lay out the "Tempo" section
- Fact-check, edit, and proofread articles

6/06 - 8/08   **Customer Service Representative,** Wells Fargo Bank (Aurora CO).
- Sold accounts to customers; made all sales goals
- Created promotional posters

4/03 - 8/05   **Evening Assistant Manager,** McDonalds Restaurant (Longmont, CO).
- Supervised 7 cooks and counter workers
- Assured food and service quality

EDUCATION

8/07 – present   Bachelor of Arts, The University of Denver, expected June 2009
Major: Graphic Arts; Minor: Digital Media Studies

8/05 – 5/07   AA General Education, Front Range Community College, May 2007

SKILLS AND SELECTED EXPERIENCES

- Expert in complete Adobe Creative Suite
- Expert in complete Microsoft Office Suite
- Excellent Spanish language skills
- Illustrator and photographer; have completed several commissions (see portfolio, above)
- Vice President, Student Residence Halls Association
- Cartoonist and Designer, *The DU Clarion* (campus newspaper)
- Excellent customer service skills

REFERENCES: Available on request

Figure 22.3 Sample resumé

Monica A. Schickel
1817 Drevin Avenue
Denver, CO 80208

Cell phone: (303) 555-7722
E-mail: mnsschl@wordnet.com
Professional portfolio: www.schickelgraphics.net

May 3, 2009

Jaime Cisneros
Publications Director
R.L. Smith Consulting
2000 Wabash Avenue
Chicago, IL 60601

Dear Mr. Cisneros:

Please consider my application for the graphic designer position currently being advertised on your company's Web site. I believe that my professional experiences, education, and skills prepare me well for this opportunity.

I am currently completing a paid internship at Westword, a weekly features and entertainment magazine in Denver, CO, where I have worked as an effective member of a creative team. My responsibilities have included designing advertisements, laying out sections, and editing photographs. Other related experience includes commissions as an illustrator and photographer. My professional portfolio demonstrates the range and quality of my work. As the enclosed resumé notes, I have additional experience in business environments.

Next month I will earn a BA in graphic design from The University of Denver, where my course of study has included extensive work in graphic design, photography, drawing, and illustration. Simultaneously, I will complete a minor in digital media studies that has included courses in Web design, video editing, and sound editing. I have expertise in all the standard software applications that would be relevant to your position.

I would be pleased to provide further information and to interview at your convenience. The opportunities at R.L. Smith closely match my background and goals, and the prospect of joining your team in Chicago is exciting. I look forward to discussing how I can contribute to your publications department.

Sincerely,

Monica A. Schickel

Monica A. Schickel

Figure 22.4 Sample job application letter

Guidelines for writing a gender-neutral salutation

1. Telephone or send an e-mail to the company to which you're sending the letter. State your reason for making contact, and ask for the name of the person to whom you should address your letter.

2. Address men as "Mr." and women as "Ms.," unless you're specifically told to use "Miss" or "Mrs." If your recipient goes by another title, such as "Dr." or "Professor," use it.

3. If you can't identify a proper name and must use a title alone, keep the title generic and gender-neutral.

   NO   Dear Sir: [sexist]
            Dear Sir or Madam: [sexist for both genders]

   YES Dear Human Resources Officer:
            Dear Sales Manager:

   For more information about gender-neutral language, see 55b.

ESOL Tip: In some cultures, job applications may include personal information, such as an applicant's age, marital status, number of children, religion, or political beliefs. In North America, however, this is not standard practice. Such personal information does not help an employer determine how well you can perform a particular job, so avoid including it in your application. ●

For more help with your
writing, grammar, and research,
go to **www.mycomplab.com**

mycomplab

23 ■ ■ ■ ■ ■ ■

Public Writing

23a What is public writing?

PUBLIC WRITING is intended for people who are reading for reasons other than work, school, or professional obligations. Instead, they read out of interest or a desire to keep informed. Some public writing is also known as CIVIC WRITING because you're writing to affect actions or beliefs among other citizens in a democratic society.

Examples of writing for the public include a letter or e-mail to refute a newspaper editorial, a program for a play or concert, a brochure to draw new members into a service organization, a proposal to build a town park, a fund-raising letter for a worthy cause, a script for a radio announcement, a Web site for a hobby or social cause that interests you, or an e-mail urging your representative to vote for a certain bill.

In public writing, you're likely writing for an AUDIENCE that you don't know personally. You're also discussing subjects that affect others, not only you. For these reasons, public writing requires that you take special care in analyzing your audience and establishing your credibility. "Establishing credibility" means using the three types of appeals discussed in 13e to convince readers that they need or want to listen to you.

23b How do I write a report for the public?

Reports for the public vary in length, format, and content. To write a public report, follow the guidelines in Quick Reference 23.1.

Quick Reference 23.1

Guidelines for writing a public report

- Decide your purpose. Will you only inform, or will you also analyze the information you present? Or—going one step further—will you make a recommendation based on the information and your analysis?

- State your findings objectively. Though you may later bring in your opinion by recommending a course of action, your credibility depends on your first reporting accurately.

- Organize the formal report using the following sections. Depending on the purpose of your report, however, you might combine or expand any of these sections.

  Executive summary: Provides a very brief summary of the entire report, including conclusions or recommendations

  Introduction: Explains the purpose of the report, describes the problem studied, and often describes or outlines the organization of the entire report

  Methods: Describes how the data were gathered

  Results: Presents the findings of the report

  Discussion: States the implications of your findings

  Conclusion: Makes recommendations or simply summarizes the findings

A policy brief is a kind of public report in which experts put technical information into a form that nonexperts and decision makers can understand. Most policy briefs these days are published on the Internet. The usual purpose of policy briefs is to persuade people with facts and analysis that support a specific decision. Readers of your policy brief need to perceive you as objective and careful, basing your position on logic and evidence. If you want to use a policy brief in a research paper, carefully analyze the quality of the source (29h, 30e). Figure 23.1 shows the opening of a policy brief.

23c   How do I write letters to my community or its officials?

Letters to your community or its officials allow you to influence opinions or actions. When you respond to a previous piece of writing in a publication, always begin by referring precisely to the source, using title, section, and date, if possible.

Many letters to the editor (and increasingly these are sent as e-mails) propose solutions to a community problem. Follow the general guidelines for writing ARGUMENTS (Ch. 13). Use the format for a business letter or e-mail, and keep the following guidelines in mind when writing to propose a solution:

- Briefly explain the specific problem you're attempting to solve.
- Tell how your solution will solve all elements of the problem.
- Briefly address the possible objections or alternatives to your proposed solution.
- State why your solution offers the most advantages of all of the alternatives.

The Future
of Children
PRINCETON-BROOKINGS

POLICY BRIEF   SPRING 2006

Fighting Obesity in the Public Schools
Ron Haskins, Christina Paxson, and Elisabeth Donahue

> Childhood obesity is a growing national problem. Federal, state, and local policymakers and practitioners recognize the need to take strong action. Public schools are playing a central role in fighting childhood obesity despite both political and financial constraints. But schools should do even more to reduce the availability of junk food, make school meals more nutritious, and increase students' daily exercise.

Figure 23.1 Opening of a policy brief

In the letter in Figure 23.2, a citizen argues for preserving a city park in its present form.

23d   What other types of public writing exist?

Many people write simply to express themselves or to entertain others. The most obvious examples of such writing are fiction, poetry, plays, film scripts, journals, and scrapbooks. In addition, many people produce newsletters, brochures, or similar documents, using not only words, but also graphic designs and images (Ch. 24). Writing for the Internet is perhaps the broadest form of public writing. On the Internet, you might post reviews, create Web sites, or keep a blog, an online journal that a writer updates on a fairly regular basis. Chapter 25 provides information on writing for the Web, and Chapter 26 discusses blogs.

To the Editor:

Re "Parking Plan Threatens Green Space" (news article, May 14):

For well over a century, Lincoln Park has provided a welcome oasis in downtown Springfield. In this park, office workers eat lunches, schoolchildren play on the way home, and evening concerts and other events unite the community.

It is very shortsighted, then, that the City Council now considers converting a third of the park into additional parking.

I acknowledge that parking downtown has gotten difficult. As the manager of a small shop, I know that our customers sometimes have trouble finding a parking place. However, the park itself is one of the reasons our downtown has become more popular in the past decade.

Ironically, destroying the park's attractive green space will reduce the need for more parking which will hurt business.

A better solution is for the city to purchase the vacant property at the corner of Main and Jefferson and build a multistory garage. No doubt this option is more expensive than using the park. However, the land would be available cheaply, a multistory garage would actually provide more parking than the park land, and a preserved park would bolster business, thereby increasing tax revenues. I'm sure most citizens would prefer to leave future generations a legacy of trees, grass, and inviting beaches rather than a debt of sterile concrete.

Joel C. Bradway
Springfield, May 17, 2005

Figure 23.2 Letter printed in a community newspaper

24

■ ■ ■ ■ ■ ■

Designing
Documents

24a   What is document design?

Document design refers to the visual appearance of a document (how it looks), as opposed to the content of the document (what it says). Designing documents includes everything from choosing typefaces and heading styles to selecting and placing graphics to determining the use of color. Note all of the elements in the poster in Figure 24.1.

Document design is important for several reasons, not least because first impressions count. A well-designed document shows that you respect your readers and have spent time formatting your work so that it's attractive and helps you achieve your PURPOSE.

Some documents follow formats that are fairly standardized. Certain kinds of writing for work, such as letters, memos, and e-mail messages, follow customary patterns (Ch. 22). Papers you write in academic settings usually follow guidelines established by the Modern Language Association (Ch. 33), the American Psychological Association (Ch. 36), the *Chicago Manual of Style* (Ch. 39), or the Council of Science Editors (Ch. 40). Check with your instructor about which style to use. Some instructors encourage—or even require—design elements such as photos, illustrations, and diagrams. However, before spending time and effort incorporating extensive design elements into academic work, ask your instructor whether design elements are appreciated.

Other document types invite more design creativity. Consider once again the public service announcement in Figure 24.1. Flyers, brochures, annual reports, and reports on special projects give you considerable room for originality. Overall, the best design is always the one appropriate to the purpose and WRITING SITUATION at hand.

You don't have to be a graphic artist to produce well-designed materials. With modest tools and knowledge, you can produce simple yet effective documents. Quick Reference 24.1 (page 142) lists types of software that you can use for document design.

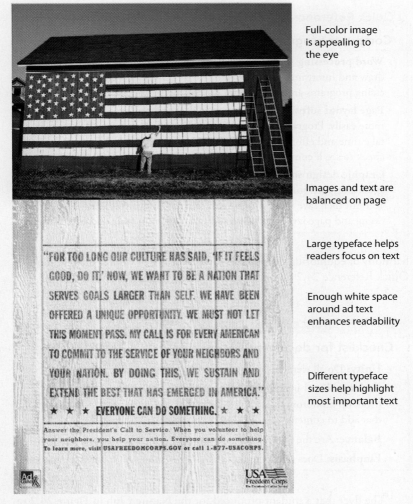

Full-color image
is appealing to
the eye

Images and text are
balanced on page

Large typeface helps
readers focus on text

Enough white space
around ad text
enhances readability

Different typeface
sizes help highlight
most important text

Figure 24.1 A thoughtfully designed poster

24b What are basic principles of design?

The basic principles of design are unity, variety, balance, and emphasis. **Unity** results from repetition and consistency. **Variety** comes from a logical, appropriate break from unity that adds interest. **Balance** refers to a sense of

Computer programs used in designing documents

Word processing software: Allows you to vary typefaces and fonts (24c), draw and insert images, and create charts, graphs, and tables. Word processing programs are sufficient for formatting most basic documents.

Page layout software: Enables you to design sophisticated documents more easily. Programs such as Adobe InDesign and Microsoft Publisher take time and effort to learn. They can also be expensive, so you might check to see if computers on campus have this software.

Graphic design software: Allows you to create and edit graphics and images using such software as Macromedia FreeHand and Adobe Photoshop. You can then save images in formats that are compatible with word processing and page layout software and insert them in your documents.

harmony or equilibrium. **Emphasis** directs the eye to what is most important. Quick Reference 24.2 describes how to check for these principles.

Quick Reference 24.2   ■ ■ ■ ■ ■ ■ ■

Checklist for document design

- **Unity:** Do all elements in my document work together visually?
- **Variety:** Have I introduced design elements, where appropriate, that break up monotony, such as headings that add to clarity or illustrations that add to content?
- **Balance:** Are the parts of my document in proportion to one another?
- **Emphasis:** Does my document design draw attention to key information?

The flyer that a student produced for the Nature Club in Figure 24.2 reflects the four design principles.

24c How do I design with text?

Text consists of letters and words. To format text, you need to decide which typeface—a particular style of type, such as Verdana or New Century Schoolbook—you'll use. Also called fonts, typefaces fall into two major categories. **Serif** fonts have little "feet" or finishing lines at the top and bottom of each letter; **sans serif** fonts (*sans* is French for "without") don't. Times New Roman is serif; Arial is sans serif. Serifs at the bottoms of letters help guide readers' eyes through lines of text; therefore, on documents to be printed on paper, use serif fonts for longer segments of text. Reserve sans serif for short, isolated lines such as headings and captions. For online texts, sans serif fonts are often used for the body of a Web page; some researchers report they are easier to read on the screen.

Fonts come in different sizes (heights) that are measured in "points" (there are 72 points in an inch). For body text in longer documents, use 10- to 12-point serif typefaces. Remember that fonts set a tone, so avoid using playful fonts (Comic Sans MS) or simulated handwriting fonts (Monotype Corsiva) in academic and business writing.

The Nature Club

Welcome!
The Nature Club is open to all members of the campus community. Our purpose is to share our common enjoyment of nature and to address environmental concerns. We meet the first Wednesday of each month, 7:00 p.m., in 114 Mercer Hall.

Spring Speakers

James Franklin
Biology
"Prairie Wildlife"
January 15

Sarah Minkowski
Political Science
"Alaskan Refuges and Energy Policy"
February 12

Ceasar Sanchez
The Nature Conservancy
"The Last Best Places"
March 12

Sherita Jones
State House of Representatives
"Pending Environmental Legislation"
April 9

Upcoming Special Events

- Fund-raising Dance for The Nature Conservancy
  February 19

- Salt River Canoeing
  April 18

- Camping and Hiking in Grand Teton National Park
  June 3–10

For more information, contact

Jesse Langland, President
The Nature Club
jk14@0000.edu

Figure 24.2 A flyer illustrating four key design principles

8 point   12 point   16 point   24 point

Highlighting text

Highlighting draws attention to key words or elements of a document. You can highlight in various ways, but the one guideline that applies in all cases is this: Use moderation.

BOLDFACE, ITALICS, AND UNDERLINING

Italics and underlining—they serve the same purpose—have special functions in writing (for example, to indicate titles of certain works; see Chapters 34 and 37), but they're also useful for emphasis and for headings. **Boldface** is reserved for heavy emphasis.

BULLETED AND NUMBERED LISTS

You can use bulleted and numbered lists when you discuss a series of items or steps in a complicated process or when you want to summarize key points or guidelines. A bulleted list identifies items with small dots or squares. Lists provide your reader with a way to think of the whole idea you are communicating. For this reason, they work particularly well as summaries.

COLOR

Adding color to a document can change it dramatically. Take time, however, to think about your reasons for adding color to a specific project. How does color suit the type of document? How will it help you accomplish your purpose? Use color sparingly for variety and emphasis.

▉ Justifying

When you make your text lines even in relation to the left or right margin, you're justifying them. There are four kinds of justification, or ways to line up text lines on margins: left, right, centered, and full, as shown below.

Left-justified text (text aligns on the left)

Right-justified text (text aligns on the right)

Center-justified text (text aligns in the center)

Full-justified text (both left and right justified to full length, or measure, of the line of type)

Most academic and business documents are left-justified, which means that the right ends of the lines are unjustified, or ragged. Center, right, and full justification are useful for designing shorter documents (flyers, posters, and so on) because they can attract attention.

▉ Indentation

When you move text in from the left margin, you are indenting. Using the ruler line in your word processing program to control indentations makes it easier to make global changes in your indentation. The top arrow of the bar sets the paragraph indentation, and the bottom arrow sets the indentation for everything else in the paragraph. MLA-STYLE Works Cited pages and APA-STYLE

References pages use hanging indentations: The first line of an entry starts at the left margin, and every following line is indented. Indent bulleted and numbered lists to make them stand out.

24d How do I use headings?

Headings clarify how you've organized your material and tell your readers what to expect in each section. Longer documents, including handbooks (like this one), reports, brochures, and Web pages, use headings to break content into chunks that are easier to digest and understand. In ACADEMIC WRITING, APA style favors headings and MLA style tends to discourage them. Following are some guidelines for writing and formatting headings.

- **Create headings in a slightly larger type than the type size in the body of your text.** You can use the same or a contrasting typeface, as long as it coordinates visually and is easy to read.
- **Keep headings brief and informative.** Your readers can use them as cues.
- **Change the format for headings of different levels.** Think of levels in headings the way you think of items in an OUTLINE (8h). First-level headings show the main divisions of a document. Second-level headings divide material that appears under first-level headings, and so on. Changing the format for different levels of headings creates a clear outline for the reader.
- **Use parallel structure.** All headings at the same level should be grammatically similar. For example, you might make all first-level headings questions and all second-level headings noun phrases. Quick Reference 24.3 presents common types of headings.

Quick Reference 24.3

Common types of headings

- **Noun phrases can cover a variety of topics.**
  Executive Branch of Government
- **Questions can evoke reader interest.**
  When and How Does the President Use the Veto Power?
- **Gerunds and *-ing* phrases can explain instructions or solve problems.**
  Submitting the Congressional Budget
- **Imperative sentences can give advice or directions.**
  Identify a Problem

24e How should I incorporate visuals?

Visuals, also called *graphics,* can enhance document design when used appropriately. A visual can condense, compare, and display information more effectively than words, but only if its content is suitable.

■ Charts, graphs, and tables

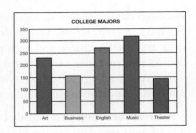

- **Bar graphs** compare values, such as the number of different majors at a college, as shown in the graph at right.

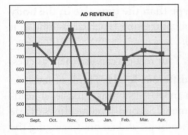

- **Line graphs** indicate changes over time. For example, advertising revenue is shown over an eight-month period in the graph at left.

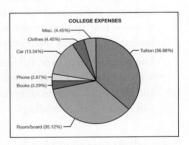

- **Pie charts** show the relationship of each part to a whole, such as a typical budget for a college student, as shown in the chart at right.

- **Tables** present data in list form, as shown below, allowing readers to grasp a lot of information at a glance.

TABLE 1   TOTAL NUMBER OF COMPUTER LAB USERS, BY SEMESTER

Semester	Number of Users	Percentage of Student Population
Spring 2008	2,321	25.8%
Summer 2008	592	6.6
Fall 2008	3,425	38.1

In academic or business documents, especially lengthy ones, number figures and tables, if there are more than one, and number them sequentially.

◼ Images

Clip art refers to pictures, sketches, and other graphics available on some word processing programs. It can also be downloaded from the Internet. Though  clip art is rarely, if ever, appropriate in academic writing and business writing, it can add interest to flyers, posters, newsletters, and brochures designed for certain audiences.

You can download **photographs** from a digital camera or scan them from printed photos, books, and articles. Several Internet image libraries or WEB SITES contain thousands of photographs available free or for a minimal charge. If you use a photograph you didn't take, you must always cite the source; see Quick Reference 24.4. Once a photograph is in your computer, you can place it in your document, usually with an "Insert" or "Import" command. A modest software program, such as the pictures toolbar in Microsoft Word, can help you adjust a photograph by cropping it (trimming the top, bottom, or sides), rotating it, or making it larger or smaller. With a powerful program like Adobe Photoshop you can modify colors or create special effects. The following example shows how cropping affects an image.

Quick Reference 24.4 offers guidelines and additional help in using visuals in your documents.

Quick Reference 24.4　　◼ ◼ ◼ ◼ ◼ ◼ ◼

Guidelines for using visuals

- **Design all visuals to be simple and uncluttered.**
- **Include a heading or title for each visual.** Doing so helps readers quickly understand what they're seeing.

continued >>

Quick Reference 24.4   (continued)

- **Never use unnecessary visuals.** For example, a chart that summarizes your findings might convey more to readers than a basic piece of clip art.

- **Consider your audience and their sensibilities.** You don't want to offend your readers, nor do you want them to be confused.

- **Credit your source if a visual isn't your own.** Always avoid PLAGIARISM by crediting your SOURCE. If you plan to use a visual for anything other than a class project, you need to obtain written permission from the copyright holder. Check for information about who owns rights to the image by looking for a copyright notice (often at the beginning or end of the document) or a credits list. For a Web page, look at the top or bottom of the document (25g).

24f   What is page layout?

Layout is the arrangement of text, visuals, color, and space on a page. You'll want to arrange these elements so that you follow the basic principles of design (24b). Quick Reference 24.5 explains how to position text and visuals.

Quick Reference 24.5   ■ ■ ■ ■ ■ ■ ■

Guidelines for positioning text and visuals

- Consider the size of visuals in placing them so that they don't cluster at the top or the bottom of a page. In other words, avoid creating a page that's top-heavy or bottom-heavy.

- To create balance in a document, imagine it as divided into halves, quarters, or eighths. As you position text or images in the spaces, see which look full, which look empty, and whether the effect seems visually balanced.

- Use the "Table" feature of your word processing program to position text and visuals exactly where you want them. Turn off the grid lines when you're done so that the printed copy shows only the text and visuals.

- Avoid splitting a chart or table between one page and the next. If possible, the entire chart or table needs to fit on a single page. If it runs slightly more than a page, look for ways to adjust spacing or reduce wording. If you have no choice but to continue a chart or table, then on the second page, repeat the title and add the word "continued" at the top.

- Print copies of your various layouts and look at them from different distances. Ask others to look at your layouts and tell you what they like best and least about each.

■ Using white space

White space, the part of your document that has neither text nor visuals, allows readers to read your document more easily and to absorb information in chunks rather than in one big block. White space indicates breaks between ideas and thereby focuses attention on the key features of your document. Flyers, brochures, posters, reports, Web pages, and similar documents tend to make extensive and varied use of white space because they rely heavily on graphics.

For more help with your
writing, grammar, and research,
go to **www.mycomplab.com**

mycomplab

25 ■ ■ ■ ■ ■ ■

Writing for the Web

25a   What are Web sites and Web pages?

Web sites on the World Wide Web are composed of Web pages. Web pages are common in academic, business, and public settings. They inform, entertain, and persuade through text, images, color, and often sound and video. Because Web sites allow readers to jump from page to page to find information within a site and beyond, they provide readers with exceptional flexibility.

25b   What is the Web writing process?

The **Web writing process** has five parts: (1) writing the content, (2) creating the structure of the content, (3) designing the layout of the material on the computer screen, (4) checking whether the Web material is usable, and (5) loading the Web site on a **server**, a computer that is always online and available to Internet users.

25c   How do I plan content for my Web site?

The Web differs from other media in distinct ways that affect your writing.

* Web writing calls for smaller blocks of text than print writing. Web readers prefer not to scroll down long sections of information.

- Web writing highlights the connections or links between related Web sites.
- Web writing emphasizes visual elements like color and pictures.

25d How do I create a structure for my Web site?

Web structure is the organization of the content and documents that site creators include in a Web project. Almost all Web sites have a **home page**, a page that introduces the site and provides links to the other pages that the site contains. The home page functions like a table of contents in print or like the entryway to a building. It should be appealing and give visitors to the home page clear directions for navigating from page to page. Here are some guidelines for creating a site's structure.

- Determine all of the pages your site might contain and whether these pages should be grouped into categories (groups of pages all on the same topic).
- Generate a list of categories. You might use the planning techniques of BRAINSTORMING, FREEWRITING, and CLUSTERING discussed in Chapter 8.
- Draft a map of your Web site to show how all the pages fit together. To plan a Web structure, draw a map of all your separate documents and the best way they connect to one another. Figure 25.1 shows two possible structures.
- Plan **hyperlinks**, which are direct electronic connections between two pages. Combinations of hyperlinks are the glue that holds Web writings together.

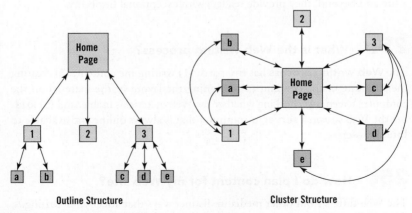

Outline Structure   Cluster Structure

Figure 25.1 Two possible Web structures

25e How do I design Web pages?

Once you've drafted a map of your Web site, you begin designing and creating your individual Web pages. Most guidelines and principles that contribute to good design in printed documents apply equally to Web design. Use the basic design principles of unity, variety, balance, and emphasis discussed in Chapter 24.

Begin by planning a Web page's general appearance. Make decisions about the placement of text and graphics, the use of color and white space, and what you want to emphasize. Early in your planning process, you might look at some Web sites that seem similar to what you have in mind. For example, if you're creating a site for a club or an organization, look at Web sites for clubs or organizations you know of or have heard about. Figure 25.2 is the home page of the National Museum of the American Indian. Readers can tell in a glance what kinds of information the Web site contains and then go directly to the pages that interest them.

Links   Featured events   Keyword search box

Figure 25.2 The home page of the National Museum of the American Indian

Here's some general advice about designing Web pages.

- **Choose an appropriate title.** Make sure your page has a title that tells readers exactly what they'll find there.
- **Keep backgrounds and texts simple.** Strive for a clean, uncluttered look. Dark text on a plain light background is easiest to read, with white being the preferred background. In contrast to print documents, sans serif fonts tend to be easier to read on computer screens than serif fonts. Avoid multiple typefaces, sizes, and colors, multiple images and graphics, and busy backgrounds.
- **Use images to attract attention to important elements and to please the reader.** Readers will tend to look first at pictures and graphics on a page.
- **Unify the pages in your site.** Keep the overall appearance of pages within one site consistent in terms of layout, typefaces, graphics, and color. Consider using a **navigation bar**, a set of links on every Web page that allows users to get back to the site's home page and to major parts of the site.
- **Provide identifying information.** Generally, the bottom of a page includes the date the page is updated (revised or added to), along with contact information for the site's creator or administrator.

25f How do I use Web writing software?

Web sites are written in a computer program language. The original language format is called HTML, for hypertext markup language. HTML editors are programs that generate tags, or codes, in much the same way that word processing programs generate boldface type or other formatting. Some HTML editors are Adobe Dreamweaver and Microsoft Expression Web.

The most important codes are those for links. Highlight the words you want to serve as the link and then provide the URL of the page you want users to see when they click on the link.

25g How do I incorporate images into Web pages?

Web pages can include many different kinds of graphics. For example, small icons such as colored balls can mark off a list of items (the way bullets are used in print documents, including this handbook). You can also use photographs imported from a digital camera, inserted using a scanner, or downloaded from the Internet, along with CLIP ART and other graphics.

Keep in mind that graphics, especially photographs, can take a long time to download, especially for people using a slow connection. Using a feature in programs like Adobe Photoshop or the picture editor in Microsoft Word, you can reduce the size of an image file.

Be careful and respectful when copying images from the Internet. E-mail the site's creator to ask permission. Generally, you'll be given free permission if you're writing for a class project or another educational purpose, but other uses may require a fee. The person granting permission may request a certain DOCUMENTATION format, or an instructor may provide guidelines for citing graphic sources. If in doubt, use MLA STYLE (Ch. 33) or APA STYLE (Ch. 36).

25h How do I edit and test usability?

Before you publish your Web page (before you upload it to a server), edit and proofread it as carefully as you would a print document. (See Quick Reference 10.3.) The key difference between editing a Web page and editing a print document is that you also need to check that all of the interactive parts of your Web page are working properly. Before you finalize your Web page, use the checklist in Quick Reference 25.1.

Quick Reference 25.1

■ ■ ■ ■ ■ ■ ■

Editing checklist for a Web site

- **Are any images broken?** Broken images show up as small icons instead of the pictures you want. The usual cause of broken images is mistyping the file name or failing to upload the image.

- **Do all the links work?** Missing, mistyped, or mislabeled files can cause broken links.

- **Is the Web site user-friendly?** Ask your friends, classmates, or colleagues to report any sections in which information is unclear or difficult to find. They can also provide feedback about your content.

25i How do I display my Web page?

To display your finished Web page, you need two things: First, you need space on a Web server, a centralized computer that is always online. Second, you need the ability to load all of your files to that server.

■ Finding space on the Web

If you have a commercial Internet service provider (ISP), such as America Online or Earthlink, you may be able to use it to post your Web site. Your college may offer Web space to its students, and some services on the Internet offer free

Web space. Try searching for "free Web hosting." Note that if you use "free" Web space, the provider may insert advertising on your page.

You'll also need some kind of file transfer protocol (FTP) program to upload the HTML files to your Web server. The host of your space should be able to advise you on the best way to upload files and which FTP program to use.

■ Uploading image or sound files

If you've used graphics, pictures, icons, or sound on your Web page, you'll also need to upload those files to the Web server where your page is now located.

After you have uploaded your Web site to a server, check it once again to make sure that all of the links are working.

25j How do I maintain my Web site?

Check your site at least weekly. You need to make sure your links still work, and you may also want to add new information, links, or features. Include a date at the bottom of your home page to let visitors know when you last updated the site.

For more help with your writing, grammar, and research,
go to **www.mycomplab.com**

Contributing to Blogs and Wikis

26a How do I write in a blog?

A Web log, or **blog**, is a Web site that displays a series of posts, or items. Posts are usually diary-like entries or observations but may also be images, videos, audio files, and links. Most blogs focus on a particular topic. For example, Slashdot (http://slashdot.org/) advertises itself as "news for nerds," and Theme Park Insider (http://www.themeparkinsider.com/) focuses on news about various theme parks in the United States.

Most blogs have a similar design. The content of a blog, a post about a particular topic, is in the center of the screen. The most recent post appears at the top of a page, followed by previous ones as a reader scrolls down. Many blogs contain a comment feature that allows others to respond to the original blog post. Some blogs also have a blogroll, which is a list of links to other blogs that focus on similar topics. Figure 26.1 shows a typical blog design.

Some instructors have students keep blogs as a course requirement. This follows the tradition of having students keep journals as a regular way of writing about course content. The twist is that others can easily read and comment on each person's postings. If you're assigned to produce a course blog, your instructor will provide specific directions.

If you'd like to create your own blog, decide on a type and purpose. Some blogs, such as Digg (http://digg.com), collect links and ask others to comment on those links. Other blogs, such as Reuters (http://blogs.reuters.com/us/) invite much longer response posts about current news stories or happenings around the Web. Still other blogs provide original material or refer to happenings in somebody's life.

Next, you'll want to figure out how much control you want over your blog's appearance. Some software allows you to easily start blogging almost immediately with little worry or knowledge. For example, Blogger is a popular online community that gets you started with only a few mouse clicks. However,

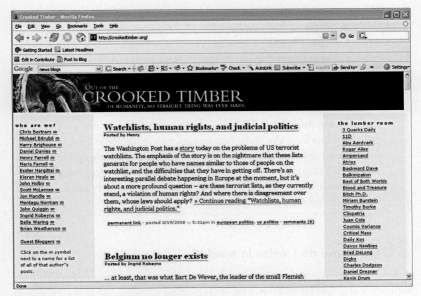

Figure 26.1 A typical blog design

if you would like to have more control, you may need to buy server space and set up the software yourself.

You need to find an AUDIENCE who cares about your perspective. You might participate in blogs and network with others, eventually gaining the attention of people who are interested in what you have to say. Most importantly, have something interesting to say. Quick Reference 26.1 contains some guidelines.

Quick Reference 26.1 ■ ■ ■ ■ ■ ■ ■

Guidelines for writing in a blog

- **Pick a unique title for your blog.** People and Internet search engines will recognize your blog if it has a good title.

- **Decide whether to use your own name or a made-up username.** You can protect your privacy to some degree if you have a pseudonym (literally, a "false name") or username. Especially if you're writing about controversial topics or taking controversial positions, you might not want employers, instructors, or even relatives to know your identity. Of course, an anonymous username doesn't give you license to be irresponsible or unethical. On the other hand, the advantage of your real name is that you get credit (and, we suppose, blame) for your writings. Think carefully about this decision.

- **Observe netiquette.** Remember, the Internet is available around the world to people in many cultures and of many ages. What might seem normal in your life isn't necessarily normal to someone else online. So be respectful in your posts, avoid vulgar language or SHOUTING (typing in all capital letters), and if you disagree with somebody, try to find common ground or evidence to the contrary rather than make *ad hominem* (13h) attacks.

- **Link, show, and share.** Include links in your posts to other, similar posts or items from the Web. Post images, videos, or audio files, but do respect copyrights. And share your posts and blog with others through the use of a blogroll or by participating on other blogs. Blogging is a way to share your ideas and experiences with others so that they might share their ideas and experiences with you.

26b How do I write in a wiki?

A **wiki** is a technology that allows anybody to change the content of a Web page without using special Web writing or uploading software. *Wiki* is a Hawaiian word meaning "fast," and the name refers to how quickly people using this technology can collaborate and revise information. One of the more popular wiki applications is the online encyclopedia, Wikipedia, shown in Figure 26.2.

Wikis and blogs serve different purposes. Wikis are designed to allow collaborative writing and presentation rather than individual commentary and response. A wiki entry, or node, is updated and presented immediately as the content of a Web site. Whatever was written at a particular node before it was edited is deleted, and the new content replaces it.

Wikis can be useful tools for collaborative writing projects because group members can all view a draft at the same time. Individuals can easily make contributions and changes. However, as you can imagine, this can also lead to complications. If you're using a wiki for a college project, you'll want to review strategies in section 8e for writing with others.

There is usually no need to create a wiki if one already exists to serve a particular purpose. Contributing to the existing wiki is usually time better spent. However, if you want to create a wiki for an unmet need—such as providing information for an upcoming election, creating a collaborative space for a business, or designing a study aid for a course—setting one up is fairly easy.

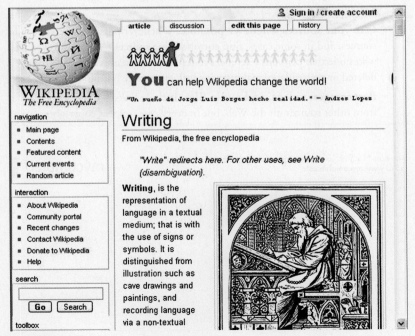

Figure 26.2 A screen capture from Wikipedia. Use caution when considering Wikipedia content, and ask your instructor whether he or she will permit you to use it for scholarly research.

Simple software like Pbwiki (http://pbwiki.com/education.wiki) will allow you quickly to start creating your own wiki without worrying about server space. If you need more control, you will have to install specialized software such as TikiWiki, MediaWiki, or SnipSnap on a dedicated Web server. In either case, you should observe the guidelines in Quick Reference 26.2 for writing or revising a wiki node.

Quick Reference 26.2

Guidelines for writing in a wiki

- **Revise with respect for others.** When revising a node, always consider ways to preserve what the person before you has written. The strength of a wiki is its ability to allow people to share their expertise, so try to maintain what others have said. Instead of deleting material, you might add qualifications, for example, words like "possibly" or phrases such as "in some cases" or "some have argued." You could then add another section to the node entitled "opposing arguments" (13g) that suggests an alternative viewpoint.

- **Cite your sources whenever possible.** Whenever possible, cite your sources, and in some cases, find corroborating sources. Any addition to a wiki node that contains references to reputable sources is less likely to be deleted or revised later, making your influence more lasting.

- **Post images, videos, and audio files.** Include links and references from other sources on the Web, but in every case, respect copyrights.

For more help with your writing, grammar, and research, go to **www.mycomplab.com**

27

Starting a Research Project

27a What is research?

Research is a systematic process of gathering information to answer a question. You do this all the time. You're doing research when you're trying to decide which college to attend, which MP3 player to buy, or which travel arrangements will make the best vacation. People wanting to start small businesses usually have to research the local business climate and present their findings to lenders to get a loan. Citizens wanting to oppose a new construction project have to research the effects of the project and present their findings in a careful way to a group of elected officials.

How much research you will do for a piece of writing in a college course can vary, depending on your audience, purpose, and type of writing (1c; 4a). You might be familiar with RESEARCH PAPERS* or TERM PAPERS, which are dense with information from sources that the writer synthesizes to support a thesis. Chapter 28 will help you with extended formal research projects.

However, any essay might potentially benefit from even a little research. Authors of memoirs often do research to recall a fact or detail from their past—the price of groceries twenty years ago, for example, or the history of a church they attended as children. For other writers, finding a crucial fact might improve an argument. Consider the original and revised sentences below.

ORIGINAL	Many families are homeless.
RESEARCHED	According to the US Department of Housing and Urban Development, of the 750,000 homeless people in America, nearly 40 percent are families (Eaton-Robb).

WORK CITED

Eaton-Robb, Pat. "Number of Homeless Families Rises." *USA Today*. USA Today, 10 Oct. 2007. Web. 23 Oct. 2007.

In the second version, the writer specifically answers the research question, "How many families are homeless?" Whenever writing has a vague

---

*Words printed in SMALL CAPITAL LETTERS are discussed elsewhere in the text and are defined in the Terms Glossary at the back of the book.

reference like "a lot" or "many" or "some," research can improve it with more precise information. Your ETHICAL APPEALS are stronger, and the specific details persuade readers.

27b   What are reasons for doing research?

Writers do research for several reasons and at different points in the writing process.

- **To find a single fact.** Sometimes you simply need to answer a direct question of "how much?" or "when?" or "where?" or "who?"

   Example: How does the cost of college today compare to the cost twenty years ago?

- **To understand an issue or situation more broadly.** Sometimes you need to learn basic information as well as the range of viewpoints or opinions on a particular topic.

   Example: What are the effects of globalization?

- **To synthesize current information.** You may need to bring together the most current information. A **review of the literature** is a synthesis of the latest knowledge on a particular topic.

   Example: What treatments are now possible for Alzheimer's disease?

- **To identify a specific opinion or point of view.** You might want to find out what the people who disagree with you believe and, more importantly, why. You can then explain why your position is better. Of course, you might also look for experts who support your view.

   Example: What are the arguments in favor of censoring cable television programs?

- **To create new knowledge.** Researchers make new knowledge as well as find knowledge others have already created. This is the kind of research that chemists and biologists do, of course, but so do psychologists, sociologists, journalists, and others. Examples are experiments, surveys, interviews, ethnographies, and observations. For instance, if you were writing a guide to coffee houses in a certain area, you'd need to visit all of them, take notes, and present your findings to readers. Field research (28c) is a general name for this kind of research.

Research is an absorbing, creative activity. It lets you come to know a subject deeply and leads to fresh insights. The entire process, especially when repeated in a number of courses and settings, helps shape you into a self-reliant learner.

27c How do I choose a research topic?

Sometimes college instructors assign specific topics; other times you get to choose. When you need to select your own research topic, several guidelines will help you choose a good one.

- Select a topic that interests you. It will be your companion for quite a while, perhaps most of a semester.
- Choose a sufficiently narrow topic that will allow you to be successful within the time and length given by the assignment. Avoid topics that are too broad, such as "emotions." A better choice would be "how people perceive and respond to anger in others."
- Choose a topic that your readers will perceive as significant and worthwhile.
- Choose a topic worth researching. Avoid trivial topics that prevent you from investigating ideas, analyzing them critically, and creating a synthesis of complex concepts.

> **NO** Types of cars that are popular among teenagers
>
> **YES** The effect of SUVs on the environment

A good academic topic allows you to demonstrate your critical thinking abilities. There are two broad ways of doing so. First, you might choose a topic on which intelligent people have formed different opinions. Then you might analyze your sources and draw on your own experiences to decide which position appears best. The purpose of such a paper would be to attempt to persuade readers that you've considered the various positions and reached a reasonable conclusion (Ch. 13).

Alternatively, you might choose to inform readers in a paper that synthesizes several sources related to a complex subject. Writing a SYNTHESIS (7d) means pulling together extensive information from varied sources to examine essential points that relate to a topic. Your goal is to clarify complicated or scattered information for your readers.

The freedom to choose any topic you want can sometimes lead to what is called "research topic block." Don't panic. Instead, use some of the following strategies for generating ideas.

- Talk with others. Ask instructors or other experts in your area of interest what issues currently seem "hot" to them. Ask them to recommend readings or the names of authorities on those issues.
- Browse through some textbooks in your area of interest. Read the table of contents and major headings. As you narrow your focus, note the names of important books and experts, often mentioned in reference lists at the end of chapters or at the back of the book.

- Read encyclopedia articles about your area of interest and its subcategories. Never, however, stop with the encyclopedia—it is too basic for college-level research.
- Browse the library or a good bookstore. Stroll through the shelves to find subjects that interest you. Look at books as well as popular magazines and browse academic journals in fields that interest you.
- Browse the Internet. Many Web search engines provide a list of general categories (30d). Click on a general category to get subcategories. Browsing increasingly specific subcategories can turn up an interesting topic.

27d What is a research question?

A **research question** provides a clear focus for your research and a goal for your WRITING PROCESS. Without such a question, your research writing can become an aimless search for a haphazard collection of facts and opinions. For example, you can more successfully research the question "How do people become homeless?" than you can research the broad topic of "homelessness." Some research questions can lead to a final, definitive answer (for example, "How does penicillin destroy bacteria?"). Other research questions cannot (for example, "Is Congress more responsible than the Supreme Court for setting social policy?").

You may need to refine your question. Consider the following example.

1. Why can't a rich country like the United States eliminate homelessness?
2. Is it true that many families—not just adults—are homeless?
3. Is the homelessness problem getting better or worse?
4. What are we doing to solve the problem of homelessness?

From the first, very broad question, a succession of more specific questions emerges. Even the last, focused question is quite complicated, but at least it provides a clear direction for your writing.

The answer to your research question usually, but not always, appears in your THESIS STATEMENT. Sometimes the thesis statement simply alludes to your answer, especially when the answer is long or complicated.

27e How do I plan a research project?

If you feel overwhelmed by the prospect of research writing, you're not alone. The best approach is to divide your project into a series of steps, which makes the process far less intimidating. Managing projects over time is a vital life skill, and you might find it helpful to create a checklist like the one in Quick Reference 27.1 for other situations.

Quick Reference 27.1

Sample schedule for a research project

Assignment received _____

Assignment due date _____

PLANNING   FINISH BY (DATE)

1. Start my research log (27f).   _____
2. Choose a topic suitable for research (27c).   _____
3. Draft my research question (27d).   _____
4. Understand my writing situation (1c).   _____
5. Take practical steps:
   a. Gather materials and supplies.   _____
   b. Learn how to use my college library.   _____
6. Determine what documentation style I need to use (28e). _____

RESEARCHING

7. Plan my "search strategy," but modify as necessary (28a). _____
8. Decide the kinds of research I need to do:
   a. Field research (28c). If yes, schedule tasks.   _____
   b. Library-based sources (Ch. 29).   _____
9. Web sources (Ch. 30)
10. Locate and evaluate sources (29h, 30e).   _____
11. Compile a working bibliography (28e) or annotated   _____
    bibliography (28f).
12. Take content notes from sources I find useful (28g). _____

WRITING

13. Draft my thesis statement (8g).   _____
14. Outline, as required or useful (8h).   _____
15. Draft my paper (32b).   _____
16. Use correct in-text citations (33b-c, 36b-c, 39a, 40a).
17. Revise my paper (32c).   _____
18. Compile my final bibliography (Works Cited or   _____
    References), using the documentation style required
    (34a-b, 37a-b, 39b, 40b).

27f What is a research log?

To set up a **research log** (a diary of your research process), follow these steps.

- Create a "Research Log" file or folder on the computer or use a separate notebook.
- Record each step in your search for information. Enter the date; your search strategies; the gist of the information you discovered; the details of exactly where you found it; and exactly where you filed your detailed notes.
- Note the next step you think you should take when you return to your research.
- Decide when you're ready to move away from gathering material to organizing it or writing about it.
- Write down your thoughts and insights as you move through the research and writing processes.

Although much of what you write in your research log will never find its way into your paper, whatever you read and reread in the log will greatly increase your efficiency as a researcher.

For more help with your writing, grammar, and research, go to **www.mycomplab.com**

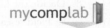

28

Developing a Search Strategy

28a What is a search strategy?

A **search strategy** is an organized procedure for locating and gathering information to answer your specific research question. Using a search strategy guarantees that you'll work systematically rather than haphazardly, and you'll find what you're looking for more quickly. Following are three frequently used search strategies. If no single strategy meets your requirements, you can create one of your own. As you work through useful SOURCES, you can switch or combine strategies.

EXPERT METHOD	Useful when your topic is specific and narrow. Start with articles or books by an expert in the field. You might want to interview an expert on the topic.
CHAINING METHOD	Useful when your topic is a general one. Start with reference books and bibliographies in current articles or WEB SITES; use them to link to additional sources. Keep following the links until you reach increasingly expert sources. Alternatively, talk with people who have some general knowledge of your topic and ask them to refer you to experts they might know.
QUESTIONING METHOD	Useful when you have a topic. Brainstorm to break your overall research question into several smaller questions, then find sources to answer each of them. This method has the advantage of allowing you to see if your sources cover all the areas important to your research question. Generating a list of questions like this can give your search a direction and purpose.

Start and complete your search as soon as possible after you get your assignment. Early in your process you may discover sources that take time to obtain (for example, through an interlibrary loan) or are hard to locate (for example, a business document).

One more piece of advice: Avoid getting too far along in your search until you're reasonably certain that you're going in a useful direction. Rather than spend endless hours simply gathering sources, read and analyze some of your materials to make sure your topic is a good one. Your research log can be useful for this purpose.

28b What is a source?

A **source** is any form of information that provides ideas, examples, or evidence. Sources are either primary or secondary. A **primary source** is original work such as an experiment, observation, interview, survey, or other research project; FIELD RESEARCH (28c) you carry out yourself; or a document such as a letter, diary, novel, poem, short story, autobiography, or journal.

A **secondary source** reports, describes, comments on, or analyzes someone else's work. This information comes to you secondhand. That is, someone other than the primary source relays the information, adding a layer between you and the original material. This doesn't mean secondary sources are inferior. However, you need to evaluate secondary sources carefully to make sure that what's being relayed to you isn't distorted or biased in the process.

⦿**ESOL Tip:** In the United States, PLAGIARISM is a major offense in ACADEMIC WRITING. In some cultures, it is customary to take material from scholarly authorities on your topic. However, this practice is forbidden in the United States unless you use quotation marks around the exact words and then state where you found those words. For detailed information on how to avoid plagiarism, see Chapter 31. ⦿

Suppose you are researching student attitudes toward marriage. Surveying several students would be primary research. Consulting scholars' books and articles about students and marriage would be secondary research. Your decision to use primary or secondary sources depends on your research question or the nature of your assignment.

As you locate, assemble, and evaluate sources related to your topic, expect to accumulate much more information than you'll actually use. Indeed, the quality of your paper depends partly on your ability to eliminate inadequate or repetitive sources and recognize what is valuable material.

28c   What is field research?

Field research involves going into real-life situations to observe, survey, interview, or participate in some activity firsthand. A field researcher might, for example, go to a factory, a lecture, a day-care center, or a mall—anywhere that people engage in everyday activities. A field researcher might also interview experts and other relevant individuals. Finally, field researchers might observe and describe objects, such as the architecture of a building. Because field research yields original data, it's a PRIMARY SOURCE.

■ Surveying

Surveys use questions to gather information about peoples' experiences, situations, opinions, or attitudes. Responses to multiple-choice or true/false questions are easy for people to complete and for researchers to summarize and report as totals or averages. Open-ended questions, in which people are asked to write responses, require more effort. However, they sometimes can provide more complete or accurate information. For advice, see Quick Reference 28.1.

When you report findings from a survey, keep within your limitations. For example, if the only people who answer your survey are students at a particular college or people at a particular shopping mall, you can't claim your results represent "all college students" or "all North Americans."

Quick Reference 28.1

Guidelines for developing a questionnaire

1. Define what you want to learn.
2. Identify the appropriate types and numbers of people to answer your survey so that you get the information you need.
3. Write questions to elicit the information.
4. Use appropriate language when phrasing questions so that they are easy to understand.
5. Make sure that your wording does not imply what you want to hear.
6. Decide whether to include open-ended questions that allow people to write their own answers.
7. Test a draft of the questionnaire on a small group of people. If any question is misinterpreted or difficult to understand, revise and retest it.

■ Observing people and situations

CASE STUDIES and ETHNOGRAPHIES (17b) are examples of researching people in specific situations. For observations of behavior (for example, the audience at a sporting event or elementary school children at play during recess), you can take notes during the activity. Try to remain objective so that you can see things clearly. One strategy is to take notes in a two-column format. On the left, record only objective observations; on the right, record comments or possible interpretations. Figure 28.1 is an example of a double-column note strategy.

■ Interviewing

You might interview ordinary people to gather opinions and impressions. An expert can offer valuable information, a new point of view, and firsthand facts, statistics, and examples. Probably the best place to start is with the faculty at your college, people with expertise in many areas who may suggest additional sources, or experts. Even your family and friends might be useful if they have been involved with an issue you're researching. Corporations, institutions, or professional organizations often have public relations offices that can answer questions or make referrals.

Make every attempt to conduct interviews in person so that you can observe body language and facial expressions as you talk. However, if distance is a problem, you can conduct interviews over the phone or online. Quick Reference 28.2 provides specific suggestions for conducting interviews.

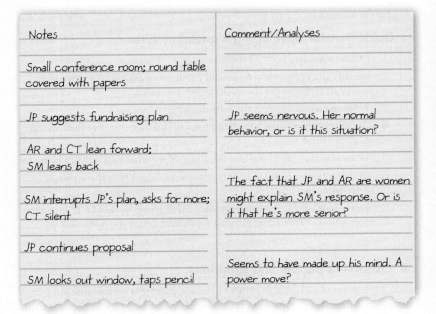

Notes	Comment/Analyses
Small conference room; round table covered with papers	
JP suggests fundraising plan	JP seems nervous. Her normal behavior, or is it this situation?
AR and CT lean forward; SM leans back	
SM interrupts JP's plan, asks for more; CT silent	The fact that JP and AR are women might explain SM's response. Or is it that he's more senior?
JP continues proposal	
SM looks out window, taps pencil	Seems to have made up his mind. A power move?

Figure 28.1 A double-column note

Quick Reference 28.2

Taking notes during research interviews

- Arrange the interview well in advance, conduct background research, prepare specific questions, and show up on time.
- Rehearse how to ask your questions without reading them (perhaps highlight the key word in colored ink). Looking your interviewee in the eye as you ask questions establishes ease and trust. If you're interviewing on the telephone, be organized and precise.
- Create a shortcut symbol or letter for key terms you expect to hear during the interview. This cuts down on the time needed to look away from your interviewee.
- Take careful notes, listening especially for key names, books, or other print or online sources.
- Use standard 8½-by-11-inch paper so that you have room to write.
- Bring extra pens or pencils.
- Never depend on recording an interview. People have become reluctant to permit such recording.

28d   What documentation style should I use?

A **documentation style** is a system for providing information about each source you use. Documentation styles vary from one academic discipline to another. The humanities often use MLA (Modern Language Association) STYLE (Ch. 33). The social sciences frequently use APA (American Psychological Association) STYLE (Ch. 36). Biology and other natural sciences often use CSE (Council of Science Editors) STYLE (Ch. 40). CM (*Chicago Manual*) STYLE (Ch. 39) is used in various disciplines, generally in the humanities. If you don't know which style to use, ask your instructor. Use only one documentation style in each piece of writing.

Determining the documentation style you need to follow when you're developing your SEARCH STRATEGY (28a) helps guarantee that you'll write down the exact details you need to document your sources. You'll need to document all SECONDARY SOURCES. If you're doing primary research, your instructor may have special requirements, such as asking you to submit your research notes or results from observations, questionnaires, surveys, interviews, or anything else that produces primary data.

28e   What is a working bibliography?

A **working bibliography** is a preliminary list of the sources you gather in your research. It contains information about each source and where others might find it. Following is a list of basic elements to include (for more detailed information about documenting specific types of sources, see Chapters 31, 33, 36, 39, and 40).

Books	Periodical Articles	Online Sources
Author(s)	Author(s)	Author(s) (if available); editor or sponsor of site
Title	Title	Title of document and title of site
Publisher and place of publication	Name of periodical, volume number, issue number	Name of database or online source
Year of publication	Date of issue	Date of electronic publication
Call number	Page numbers of article	Electronic address (URL)
		Date you accessed the source

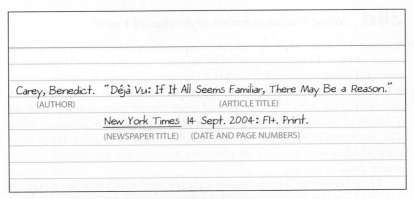

Figure 28.2 Sample bibliography note card in MLA style

Begin your working bibliography as soon as you start identifying sources. If your search turns up very few sources, you may want to change your topic. If it reveals a vast number of sources, you'll want to narrow your topic or even choose a different one. Expect to add and drop sources throughout the research process. As a rough estimate, your working bibliography needs to be about twice as long as the list of sources you end up using.

You can record your working bibliography on note cards or on a computer. On the one hand, note cards have the advantage of being easy to sift through and rearrange. You can also carry them with you when you do library research. At the end of your WRITING PROCESS, you can easily sort and alphabetize them to prepare your final bibliography. Write only one source on each card. Figure 28.2 shows a bibliography note card in MLA format.

On the other hand, putting your working bibliography on a computer saves you from having to type your list of sources later. If you use a computer for this purpose, clearly separate one entry from another. You can organize the list alphabetically, by author, or group the entries according to your subtopics.

Whichever method you use, when you come across a potential source, immediately record the information exactly as you need it to fulfill the requirements of the DOCUMENTATION STYLE your assignment requires. Spending a few extra moments at this stage can save you hours of work and frustration later on.

28f What is an annotated bibliography?

An **annotated bibliography** includes not only publishing information about your sources but also a brief summary and perhaps a commentary. Figure 28.3 shows part of an annotated bibliography using APA-style documentation.

McKenna, K. Y., Green, A. S., & Gleason, M. E. (2003). Relationship formation
 on the Internet: What's the big attraction? *Journal of Social Issues*,
 58, 9-31.

> Two studies show that people who share "true selves" over
> the Internet often form closer relationships than when they meet
> face to face. One study surveyed Internet users. A second study
> found that students who meet first on the Internet tend to like
> each other better than students who meet first in person.

Miyake, K., & Zuckerman, M. (1993). Beyond personality impressions.
 Journal of Personality, 61(3), 411-436.

> This research study examines how both physical and vocal
> attractiveness affect judges' responses to individuals. The
> researcher found that, for five different personality measures,
> judges rate more attractive people more highly.

Figure 28.3 Section from an annotated bibliography in APA style

28g How do I take content notes?

When you write **content notes**, you record information from your sources.

- If you're making content notes on index cards, put a heading on each card that gives a precise link to one of your bibliography items. Always include the source's title and the page numbers from which you're taking notes.

- On the computer, keep careful track of what ideas came from each source. One strategy is to open a new file for each source. Later, after you've taken notes on many of your sources, you can determine what subtopics are important for your paper. You can then open a new file for each topic and use the Cut and Paste functions to gather notes from all of your sources under each topic.

- On every note card or every note in your computer file, do one of three things: (1) copy the exact words from a source, enclosing them in quotation marks; (2) write a paraphrase of the source; or (3) write a summary of the source. Keeping track of the kind of note you're taking will help you avoid plagiarism. You might use the code *Q* for QUOTATION, *P* for PARAPHRASE, and *S* for SUMMARY. Or you might use a different typeface or ink color.

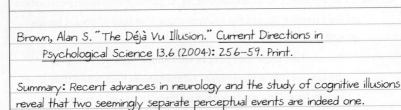

Brown, Alan S. "The Déjà Vu Illusion." *Current Directions in Psychological Science* 13.6 (2004): 256–59. Print.

Summary: Recent advances in neurology and the study of cognitive illusions reveal that two seemingly separate perceptual events are indeed one.

Comment: This is the part that grabs my attention. How could this be?

Figure 28.4 Handwritten content note card in MLA style

- As you are taking notes, separately record your own reactions and ideas, but take care to differentiate your ideas from those in your sources. You might write your own thoughts in a different color ink (note card) or font (computer); you might use the back of your note cards or a computer's "Comment" feature. You can also record your thinking in your research log.

Figure 28.4 shows one of Andrei Gurov's note cards for his research paper in 35b.

29

Finding and Evaluating Library-Based Sources

29a   How do I find library-based sources?

In an age when the Web contains billions of pages of information, it might seem almost prehistoric to talk about libraries. After all, the **library** is where generations of college students have traditionally gone to find SOURCES: books and PERIODICALS organized by CATALOGS and INDEXES. However, notice that we've referred to "library-based" and not necessarily the library itself. In many respects, the function that a library performs is even more important than the physical building. Librarians and scholars have systematically gathered and organized sources so that students and researchers can find the best ones efficiently and reliably. Many libraries give you remote access to their holdings via the Internet, so you might use library-based sources but never set foot in the building.

Still, the building itself continues to be a vital place for all research. One key advantage of going to the library is your chance to consult with librarians face to face. Helping is their profession. Never hesitate to ask questions about how to proceed or where to find a resource.

Catalogs list sources—usually books, but also films, recordings, and documents—that the library owns (29c). **Indexes** list articles in periodicals; each index covers a specific topic area (29d). Catalogs and indexes exist mainly in electronic format, but some are still in print format. **Databases** always exist electronically (29b). They consist of one or more indexes and contain extensive lists of articles, reports, and books. You can access and search electronic catalogs, indexes, and databases from computers in the library or by connecting to the library online.

29b How do I use databases?

Each entry in a DATABASE contains bibliographic information, including a title, author, date of publication, and publisher (in the case of books or reports) or periodical (in the case of articles). The entry might also provide an abstract or summary of the material. Sources that you identify through scholarly databases are almost always more reliable and appropriate than sources you find by simply browsing the Web. The reliability of scholarly databases stems from their origins: Only experts and professionals who recognize works of merit compile them.

Most college libraries subscribe to one or more database services, such as EBSCO, ProQuest, and FirstSearch. Your library's Web site will show the resources it has available. Because the college pays for these services, you don't have to, but you'll need an ID or password to use them. Commonly, your student number serves as your ID, but check with a librarian to see what's required at your college. Figure 29.1 shows an example of a college library Web site.

■ Using keywords

When searching for sources in library databases, **keywords** (also called descriptors or identifiers) are your pathway to success. Keywords are the main words in a source's title or the words that the author or editor has identified as central. Keywords allow you to access sources listed in electronic databases, BOOK CATALOGS, and periodical indexes, as well as on the World Wide Web or elsewhere on the Internet.

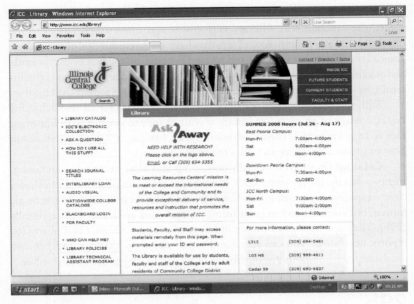

Figure 29.1 A college library Web site

When you search using keywords, chances are that much of what turns up won't be relevant to your topic. The two main ways to make keyword searches more efficient are using guided searches (answers to prompts) and using **Boolean expressions** (keyword combinations).

■ Using guided searches

Guided searches (also called advanced searches) allow you to search a database or search engine by answering prompts provided in an on-screen form. A typical search involves selecting a range of dates of publication (for example, after 2006 or between 1990 and 1995) and specifying only a certain language (such as English) or a certain format (such as books). Figure 29.2 is an example of a search for sources that have *déjà vu* in their titles and use *false memory* as another keyword but are not about *crime*.

■ Using Boolean expressions

Using BOOLEAN EXPRESSIONS means that you search a database or search engine by typing keyword combinations that narrow and refine your search. To combine keywords, use the words *AND, OR,* and *NOT* (or symbols that represent those words). Boolean expressions, generally placed between keywords, instruct the search engine to list only those Web sites in which your keywords

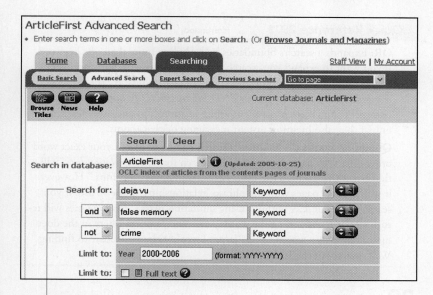

Users can list the keywords
they want to search for or
not to search for

Figure 29.2 A guided search

appear in certain combinations and to ignore others. Quick Reference 29.1
explains a few ways to search with keywords more effectively, using the subject
"relationships" as an example.

Quick Reference 29.1

Refining keyword searches with Boolean expressions

AND or the + ("plus") symbol: Narrows the focus of your search because
both keywords must be found. If you were researching the topic of the
APA paper in 38b (the role of physical attractiveness in new relationships
over the Internet), try the expression *relationships AND attractiveness AND
Internet.* Many search engines, such as Google.com, don't require the word
AND between terms. Figure 29.3 (p. 176) illustrates the results.

NOT or the − ("minus") symbol: Narrows a search by excluding texts
containing the specified word or phrase. If you want to eliminate instant
messaging from your search, type *relationships AND attractiveness AND
Internet NOT instant messaging.*

continued >>

Quick Reference 29.1 (continued)

OR: Expands a search's boundaries by including more than one keyword. If you want to expand your search to include sources about relationships begun through either instant messaging or chat rooms, try the expression *relationships AND attractiveness AND Internet AND instant messaging OR chat rooms.* You'll get pages mentioning relationships and attractiveness only if they also mention instant messaging or chat rooms.

Quotation marks (" "): Direct a search engine to match your exact word order on a Web page. For example, a search for *"online relationships"* will find pages that contain the exact phrase "online relationships." However, it won't return pages with the phrase "relationships online." Also, if you search for *James Joyce* without using quotation marks, most engines will return all pages containing the words *James* and *Joyce* anywhere in the document; however, a search using "James Joyce" brings you closer to finding Web sites about the Irish writer.

29c How do I find books?

A library's **book catalog,** which lists its holdings (its entire collection), exists as a computer database in almost every modern library. To find a book, you can search by author, by title, by subject, or by keyword. Figure 29.4 shows the home page for a typical book catalog, this one at the Library of Congress. Note

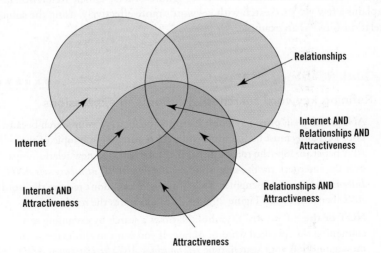

Figure 29.3 A Venn diagram showing overlaps among *relationships, attractiveness,* and *Internet.*

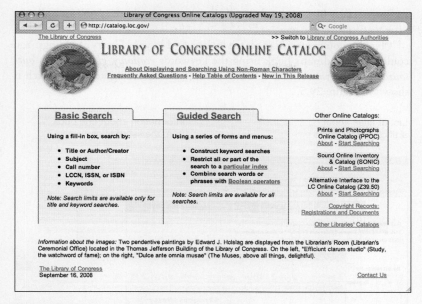

Figure 29.4 Library of Congress online catalog

that it allows you to search by title, author, subject, CALL NUMBER, or keyword; to search particular indexes; or to search using Boolean expressions.

Suppose a source recommends that you find a book by the author Thomas L. Friedman, but you don't know its title. A screen on your library's computer will have a place for you to type *Friedman, Thomas* in a space for "author." (Usually, you enter last name, then first name, but check which system your library uses.) If your library owns any books by Thomas Friedman, the computer will display their titles and other bibliographic information, such as the library call number. Then you can use the call number to request the book or to find it yourself.

Among the books you might find when searching for "Friedman, Thomas" is *The World Is Flat: A Brief History of the Twenty-first Century* (New York: Farrar, Straus and Giroux, 2005). Suppose you know that book's title but not its author and want to see if your library owns a copy. A screen on your library's computer will have a place for you to type in the title; in some systems, you don't type articles (*a, an, the*) so that in this case, you would type in only *"World Is Flat Brief History Twenty-first Century."*

Suppose, however, you don't know an author's name or a book title. You have only a research topic. In this case, you need to search by subject, using the terms listed in the *Library of Congress Subject Headings (LCSH)*. The *LCSH* is a multivolume catalog available, primarily in book form, in the reference section of every library. A version of the information in the *LCSH* is online at http://authorities.loc.gov.

Finally, you may wish to search by keyword in your library's holdings. You could find Friedman's book using the keywords *economy, globalization, outsourcing, employment,* and so on. A sample book catalog keyword search is shown in Figure 29.5.

List of titles about
artificial intelligence

Information about one book
from the list of titles

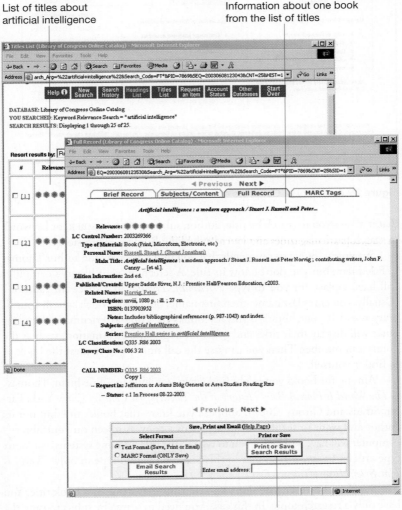

Options for saving this page

Figure 29.5 A book catalog keyword search

An entry in the library's book catalog contains a great deal of useful information: a book's title, author, publisher, date and place of publication, and length, along with its location in the library. A full-record catalog entry (a complete set of information about the source rather than a brief listing that may have only author, title, and call number) lists additional subjects covered in that book. The list of additional subjects can provide valuable clues for further searching.

Some libraries allow you to print out this information, send it to your e-mail account, or download and save it. Whether you choose one of these options or copy the information directly into your WORKING BIBLIOGRAPHY, it's crucial to record the **call number** exactly as it appears, with all numbers, letters, and decimal points. The call number tells where the book is located in the library's stacks (storage shelves). If you're researching in a library with open stacks (shelves that are accessible without special permission), the call number leads you to the area in the library where all books on the same subject can be found.

A call number is especially crucial in a library or special collection with closed stacks (a library where you fill in a call slip, hand it in at the call desk, and wait for the book to arrive). Such libraries don't permit you to browse the stacks, so you have to rely entirely on the book catalog.

29d How do I find periodicals?

Periodicals are magazines and journals published at set intervals during the year. To use periodicals efficiently, consult periodical indexes, most of which exist as online databases that are updated frequently.

Different kinds of periodicals will meet different research purposes. Quick Reference 29.2 describes several important types.

General databases index articles in journals, magazines, and newspapers. Large libraries have many general databases. Here is a list of some common ones:

- *Academic Search Premier* covers thousands of general and scholarly publications in the social sciences, humanities, education, computer sciences, engineering, language and linguistics, arts and literature, medical sciences, and ethnic studies. Most of the sources in this database are available in full text. This database is suitable for academic research projects, as long as you take care to focus on journal articles and well-regarded general publications.

- *General Reference Center Gold* covers current events, popular culture, business and industry, the arts and sciences, and sports published in newspapers, reference books, and general interest periodicals.

- *LexisNexis Academic* provides abstracts of news, business, and legal information. Sources include foreign news publications, regional US news

Types of periodicals

Type	Characteristics	Useful for
Journal	Scholarly articles written by experts for other experts; usually focus on one academic discipline or field; published relatively infrequently; examples are *College Composition and Communication* and *American Journal of Public Health*.	The most reliable expert research on a particular subject; detailed articles and extensive bibliographies that can point to other sources or experts; may also have book reviews
News magazines	Short to modest length articles on current events or topics that are of interest to a broad readership; have lots of photographs and graphics; may have opinions or editorials, as well as reviews; generally are published weekly; examples are *Time* and *U.S. News and World Report*	Easily understandable and timely introductions to current topics; often can point to more expert sources, topics, and keywords
Special interest or "lifestyle" magazines	Written for audiences (including fans and hobbyists) interested in a particular topic; include news and features on that topic; generally published monthly, with entertainment as an important goal; examples include *Outside, Rolling Stone, Wired*	Providing "how to" information on their topics of focus, as well as technical information or in-depth profiles of individuals, products, or events; many include reviews related to emphasis; the more serious examples are well-written and reliable
"Intellectual" or literary magazines	Publish relatively longer articles that provide in-depth analysis of issues, events, or people; may include creative work as well as nonfiction; aimed at a general, well-educated audience; usually published monthly; examples include *The Atlantic, Harper's, The New Yorker*	Learning about a topic in depth but in a way more accessible than scholarly journals; becoming aware of major controversies and positions; learning who experts are and what books or other sources have been published; reading arguments on topics

continued >>

Quick Reference 29.2   (continued)

Type	Characteristics	Useful for
Trade magazines	Focus on particular businesses, industries, and trade groups; discuss new products, legislation, or events that will influence individuals or businesses in that area; examples include *National Hog Farmer, Sound and Video Contractor*	Specialized information focusing on applying information or research in particular settings; seeing how specific audiences or interest groups may respond to a particular position
Newspapers	Publish articles about news, sports, and cultural events soon after they happen; contain several sections, including opinions and editorials, lifestyle (home, food, movies, etc.), sports and so on; most appear daily, though some smaller ones are weekly or twice-weekly; examples are *The Washington Post, The Rocky Mountain News, The DeWitt, Iowa, Observer*	Very current information on things as they happen; national newspapers (such as *The New York Times)* cover world events and frequently have analysis and commentary; local newspapers cover small happenings you likely won't find elsewhere; opinion sections and reviews are stimulating sources of ideas and positions

services, radio and television transcripts, federal and state case law, medical, legislative and industry news, and so on.

Specialized databases are more appropriate than general ones for most college-level research. Specialized databases list articles in journals published by and for expert, academic, or professional readers. Some examples include *Art Abstracts, MLA International Bibliography, PsycINFO,* and *Business Abstracts.* Many specialized databases include the abstract, or summary, that is printed at the beginning of each scholarly article.

You search periodical indexes by using keywords. Figure 29.6 shows three screens from a keyword search of *PsycINFO* on *déjà vu.* Andrei Gurov consulted this source while working on the paper that appears in 38b.

Keyword search

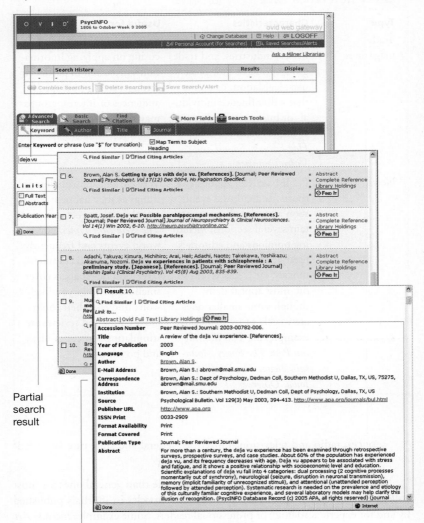

Partial search result

One article selected from database

Figure 29.6 Keyword search of *PsycINFO*

■ Locating the articles themselves

Periodical indexes help you find the titles of specific articles on your topic. Once you have a title, though, how do you get your hands on the article itself? Often you can find an online full-text version of the article to read, download, or print. A full-text version may be either in HTML format or PDF; the listing will tell you which one. If you have a choice, we recommend using the PDF version, which is easier to cite because it has the layout of a print article.

Sometimes, however, you need to find a printed copy of the periodical. Often the listing in the database will tell you whether your library owns a copy and what its call number is. Otherwise, you'll need to check if the periodical is listed in the library's CATALOG.

In either case, search for the periodical name you want (for example, *American Literature* or *The Economist*), not for the article's author or title. Then use the periodical's call number to find it in the library. To find the specific article you want, look for the issue in which the article you're looking for is printed. For advice on locating sources that you library doesn't own, see 29f.

29e   How do I use reference works?

Reference works include encyclopedias, almanacs, yearbooks, fact books, atlases, dictionaries, biographical reference works, and bibliographies. *General* reference works provide information on a vast number of subjects, but without much depth. *Specialized* reference works provide information on selected topics, often for more expert or professional audiences.

■ General reference works

Reference works are the starting point for many college and other advanced researchers—but they're no more than a starting point. **General reference works** contain basic information and are therefore insufficient for academic research. Still, they help researchers identify useful keywords for subject headings and online catalog searches. In addition, they are excellent sources for finding examples and verifying facts. Most widely used reference works are available in electronic versions. Check your library's Web site to see if the reference work you want is available online through a subscription or license the library has purchased. For example, your library may have a subscription to the *Gale Virtual Reference Library*, which allows libraries to choose up to 1,000 reference books available to users online. Alternatively, you can search the Web. (For example,

Encyclopaedia Britannica is at http://www.britannica.com.) Be aware that often you have to pay a fee for works you don't access through the library.

GENERAL ENCYCLOPEDIAS

Articles in multivolume general encyclopedias, such as the *Encyclopaedia Britannica,* summarize information on a wide variety of subjects. The articles can give you helpful background information and the names of major figures and experts in the field. Best of all, many articles end with a brief BIBLIOGRAPHY of major works on the subject.

ALMANACS, YEARBOOKS, AND FACT BOOKS

Often available both in print and online, almanacs, yearbooks, and fact books are huge compilations of facts in many subject areas. They're excellent for verifying information from other sources and in some cases for finding supporting facts and figures on the subject you're investigating. Examples include the *World Almanac, Facts on File* (which is indexed online by LexisNexis), and the annual *Statistical Abstract of the United States* (accessed online through http://www.census.gov).

ATLASES AND GAZETTEERS

Atlases (such as the *Times Atlas of the World*) contain maps of our planet's continents, seas, and skies. Gazetteers (such as the *Columbia Gazetteer of the World,* available online for a fee at http://www.columbiagazetteer.org) provide comprehensive geographical information on topography, climates, populations, migrations, natural resources, and so on.

DICTIONARIES

Dictionaries define words and terms. In addition to general dictionaries, specialized dictionaries exist in many academic disciplines.

BIOGRAPHICAL REFERENCE WORKS

Biographical reference books give brief factual information about famous people—their accomplishments along with pertinent events and dates in their lives. Biographical references include the *Who's Who* series and the *Dictionary of American Biography.*

BIBLIOGRAPHIES

Bibliographies are guides to sources on particular topics. They list books, articles, documents, films, and other resources and provide publication information so that you can find those sources. Annotated or critical bibliographies describe and evaluate the works that they list.

■ Specialized reference works

Specialized reference works provide authoritative and specific information on selected topics, often for more expert researchers. These works are usually appropriate for college-level research because the information is more advanced and detailed.

Here are a few examples of specialized references:

Dictionary of American Biography
Encyclopedia of Banking and Finance
Encyclopedia of Chemistry
Encyclopedia of Religion
Encyclopedia of the Biological Sciences
International Encyclopedia of Film
New Grove Dictionary of Music and Musicians
Oxford Companion to the Theatre

29f What if my library doesn't have a source I need?

Almost no library owns every book or subscribes to every periodical. However, many libraries are connected electronically to other libraries' book catalogs, giving you access to additional holdings. Often you or a librarian can request materials from other libraries through interlibrary loan (generally free of charge).

29g How do I find government documents?

Government publications are available in astounding variety. You can find information on laws and legal decisions, regulations, population, weather patterns, agriculture, national parks, education, and health, to name just a few topics. Since the mid-1990s, most government documents have been available through the World Wide Web. The Government Printing Office (GPO) maintains its *Catalog of U.S. Government Publications* online at http://www.gpoaccess.gov/index.html. The GPO site has a searchable database. Information about legislation is also available at the Web site THOMAS, a service of the Library of Congress, which you can access at http://thomas.loc.gov/. A directory of all federal government sites that provide statistical information is at http://www.fedstats.gov.

The LexisNexis database service provides access to a huge number of other governmental reports and documents. For example, it includes the Congressional Information Service (CIS), which indexes all papers produced by congressional panels and committees.

29h   How do I evaluate sources?

Finding a source is only part of your effort. You need to decide whether the information in the source might help you answer your research question. Your next step is to evaluate the quality, accuracy, and reliability of each source you find. Use the criteria in Quick Reference 29.3 to evaluate each source with a cold, critical eye.

Quick Reference 29.3   ■ ■ ■ ■ ■ ■ ■

Evaluating sources

- **Is the source authoritative?** Generally, encyclopedias, textbooks, and academic journals (*The American Scholar, Journal of Counseling and Development*) are authoritative. Books published by university presses (Indiana University Press) and by publishers that specialize in scholarly books are also trustworthy. Material published in newspapers, in general-readership magazines (*Time, U.S. News & World Report*), and by large commercial publishers (Prentice Hall) may be reliable, but you want to apply the other criteria in this list with special care, cross-checking names and facts. Web sites maintained by professional organizations, such as the National Council of Teachers of English at http://www.ncte.org, are authoritative.

- **Is the author an expert?** Biographical material in the article or book may tell you if the author is an expert on the topic. Look up the author's expertise in a biographical dictionary, search on the Internet, see if he or she has an appropriate degree in this field or professional affiliation, or learn if the author is often cited by other professionals in the field and published in journals.

- **Is the source current?** Check the publication date. Research is ongoing in most fields, and information is often modified or replaced by new findings.

- **Does the source support its information sufficiently?** Are its assertions or claims supported with sufficient evidence? If the author expresses a point of view but offers little evidence to back up that position or resorts to LOGICAL FALLACIES, reject the source.

- **Is the author's tone balanced?** Use your CRITICAL THINKING skills when you evaluate a source (1d and Ch. 2). If the TONE (2b) is unbiased and the reasoning is logical, the source is probably useful. Some warning signs of biased tone are name-calling, sarcasm, stereotyping, or absolute assertions about matters that are open to interpretation ("always," "everyone," and so on).

 **ESOL Tip:** The definition of "authority" can differ across cultures. However, in the United States, a source must meet specific criteria to be considered authoritative. A source is not reliable simply because the author or speaker is an influential or well-known member of the community, claims to have knowledge about a topic, or publishes material in print or online. When considering whether to use a source for your research, ask yourself the questions in Quick Reference 29.3. ●

For more help with your
writing, grammar, and research,
go to **www.mycomplab.com**

mycomplab

30

Researching the Web Wisely

30a Why do I need to use the Web "wisely"?

SOURCES from the library or from library DATABASES have the advantage of being selected by experts. Although you still have to evaluate them, they have passed a screening process. On the other hand, anyone can put anything on the Web. This makes the Web a rich source of information, but it also makes finding what you need difficult, and it opens the possibility of encountering inaccurate or biased materials.

30b How do I search the Web?

The principles for searching the Web are much like those for searching databases (29b). Once you use a BROWSER to get on the Web, you can search for sites by using a search engine or by typing an address—called a **URL**, for Universal (or Uniform) Resource Locator—into the search box. **Search engines** are programs designed to hunt the Internet for sources on specific topics that you identify by using KEYWORDS (30c) or through subject directories (30d). Common examples of search engines are Google (www.google.com) and Yahoo! (www.yahoo.com). Figure 30.1 shows the opening page of Google.com.

Choices for keeping personal records at Google.com

URL for Google.com
http://www.google.com

Choices within Google.com

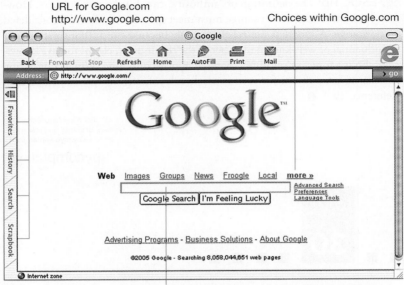

Enter keywords here and click "Google Search"

Figure 30.1 Opening page of Google.com

30c How do I use keywords?

In the same way you use keywords to find materials in library databases (29b), you use them to find information on the Internet. To conduct a keyword search, type a word or group of words in the search box on the opening page of the search engine, and click on the Search or Enter button.

30d How do I use subject directories?

Subject directories provide a good alternative to keyword searches. These directories are lists of topics (education, computing, entertainment, and so on) or resources and services (shopping, travel, and so on), with links to Web sites on those topics and resources. Most search engines have one or more subject directories. In addition, there are independent subject directories. Some examples are *Educator's Reference Desk* (http://www.eduref.org), *Librarians' Index to the Internet* (http://lii.org), *Library of Congress* (http://www.loc.gov), and *Refdesk.com* (http://www.refdesk.com).

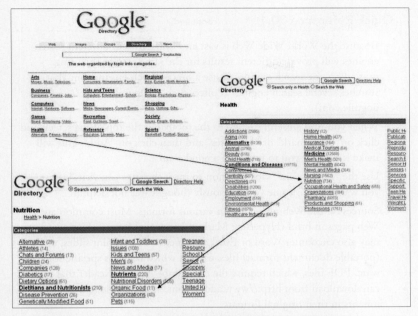

Figure 30.2 A Google subject directory for "Organic Food"

Clicking on a general category in a subject directory will take you to lists of increasingly specific categories. Eventually, you'll get a list of Web pages on the most specific subtopic you select. These search engines also allow you to click on a category and enter keywords for a search. For example, suppose that you are using Google.com to search for information on organic food. As Figure 30.2 shows, you would first go to Google's general category of "Health." Under "Health" you would find the category of "Nutrition," and within "Nutrition" you would find a link to "Organic Food," a page that lists dozens of additional categories and dozens of sources.

Quick Reference 30.1 summarizes the information in this section.

Quick Reference 30.1 ■ ■ ■ ■ ■ ■ ■

Tips on using search engines and directories

- Use keyword combinations or BOOLEAN EXPRESSIONS (Quick Reference 29.1) unless you have a very specific, narrow topic with unique keywords. A search for even a moderately common topic may produce thousands of hits, many of which won't be relevant to your topic. You might also switch to a subject directory.

continued >>

Quick Reference 30.1   (continued)

- Because the World Wide Web is vast and unorganized, different search engines will provide different results for the same search. Try using more than one search engine, or use a **meta-search engine**, one that searches several search engines at once, such as Dogpile (http://dogpile.com).

- When you find a useful site, go to the toolbar at the top of the screen and click on "Bookmark" or "Favorites" and then click on "Add." This will make it easy for you to return to a good source.

- Use the "History" or "Go" function to track the sites you visit, in case you want to revisit one you previously thought was not helpful.

- Sources on the Web may come in various formats. Most common are Web pages in html (Hypertext Markup Language) format. However, you may also encounter Word or Excel documents, PowerPoint slides, or PDF (portable document format) files, each of which requires specific software. PDF files, which require the free Adobe Acrobat Reader that you can download from http://www.adobe.com, allow people to preserve documents in their original formats.

30e How do I evaluate Web sources?

You need to evaluate Web sources particularly carefully for two reasons. First, since anyone can post anything on the Web, some sources may very well be plagiarized. Second, many sources on the Web have been written by individuals posing as experts and giving false or misleading information.

An important question to ask about any WEB SITE is why the information exists and why it was put on the Internet. Be sure to question the motives of the site's author, especially if you're being asked to take a specific action. Quick Reference 30.2 summarizes how to judge the reliability of Web sites.

Quick Reference 30.2

Judging the reliability of a Web site

Reliable sites are . . .

- **From educational, not-for-profit, or government organizations.** One sign is an Internet address ending in *.edu, .org, .gov,* or a country abbreviation such as *.ca* or *.uk.* However, if any of these organizations fail to list their sources, don't use them. Be aware that many colleges and universities now host student Web sites, which also end in *.edu.*

- **From expert authors.** Experts have degrees or credentials in their field that you can check. See if their names appear in other reliable sources, in bibliographies on your topic, or in reference books in your college's library. Check whether the site's author gives an e-mail address for questions or comments.

- **From reliable print sources.** Online versions of the *New York Times, Time* magazine, and other publications that are produced by the publisher are just as reliable as the print versions.

- **Well supported with evidence.** The information is presented in a balanced, unbiased fashion.

- **Current.** The site's information is regularly updated.

Questionable sites are . . .

- **From commercial organizations** that end in *.com* or personal pages. These sites may or may not list sources. If they fail to, don't use them. If they do, check that the sources are legitimate, not a front for some commercial enterprise.

- **From anonymous authors or authors without identifiable credentials.** Chat rooms, discussion groups, bulletin boards, and similar networks are questionable when they don't give credentials or other qualifying information.

- **Secondhand excerpts and quotations.** Materials that appear on a site that is not the official site of the publisher (such as a quotation taken from the *New York Times*) may have been edited in a biased or inaccurate manner. Such sources may be incomplete or inaccurate.

- **Unsupported or biased.** These sites carry declarations and assertions that have little or no supporting evidence.

- **Outdated.** The site's information hasn't been updated in a year or more.

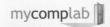

Using Sources and Avoiding Plagiarism

31a What is plagiarism?

To use SOURCES well, you need to learn how to incorporate others' words and ideas into your own papers accurately, effectively, and honestly. This last skill is especially important, so that you avoid **plagiarism**, which is presenting another person's words, ideas, or visual images as if they were your own. Plagiarizing, like stealing, is a form of academic dishonesty or cheating. It's a serious offense that can be grounds for a failing grade or expulsion from a college. Beyond that, you're hurting yourself. If you're plagiarizing, you're not learning.

Plagiarism isn't just something that college instructors get fussy about. In the workplace, it can get you fired. Plagiarism at work also has legal implications; using someone else's intellectual property without permission or credit is a form of theft that may land you in court. Furthermore, plagiarism in any setting—academic, business, or civic—hurts your credibility and reputation. Quick Reference 31.1 lists the major types of plagiarism.

Never assume that your instructor won't detect plagiarism. Instructors have a keen eye for writing styles that differ from the ones students generally produce and from your own style in particular. Instructors can access WEB SITES that check your work against that of all online paper providers, look up sources, or check with their colleagues.

Quick Reference 31.1 ■ ■ ■ ■ ■ ■

Types of plagiarism

You're plagiarizing if you . . .

- Buy a paper from an Internet site, another student or writer, or any other source.
- Turn in any paper that someone else has written, whether the person has given it to you, you've downloaded it from the Internet, or you've copied it from any other source.
- Change selected parts of an existing paper and claim the paper as your own.

continued >>

Quick Reference 31.1   (continued)

- Neglect to put quotation marks around words that you quote directly from a source, even if you document the source.

- Copy or paste into your paper any key terms, phrases, sentences, or longer passages from another source without using documentation to tell precisely where the material came from.

- Use ideas from another source without correctly citing and documenting that source, even if you put the ideas into your own words.

- Combine ideas from many sources and pass them off as your own without correctly citing and documenting the sources.

- Take language, ideas, or visual images from anyone (colleagues, companies, organizations, and so on) without obtaining permission or crediting them.

ESOL Tip: Perhaps you come from a country or culture that considers it acceptable for students to copy the writing of experts and authorities. Some cultures, in fact, believe that using another's words, even without citing them, is a sign of respect or learning. However, this practice is considered unacceptable in American and most Western settings. ●

31b How do I avoid plagiarism?

The first step in avoiding plagiarism is to learn the techniques of quoting (31f), paraphrasing (31g), and summarizing (31h) source materials. The second step is to master how to document sources correctly. A third step is to take advantage of the learning opportunities your instructor may build into research assignments. Many instructors require students to hand in a WORKING BIBLIOGRAPHY (28e) or ANNOTATED BIBLIOGRAPHY (28f). Your instructor may ask to see your research log (27f), your working notes, copies of your sources, or working drafts of your paper. Quick Reference 31.2 suggests some practical steps you can take to avoid plagiarism.

Quick Reference 31.2   ■ ■ ■ ■ ■ ■ ■

Strategies for avoiding plagiarism

- Acknowledge when you're using the ideas, words, or images of others. Always document the sources.

- Become thoroughly familiar with the documentation style your instructor requires you to use (Chs. 33–40).

continued >>

> **Quick Reference 31.2** (continued)
>
> - Write down all of the facts that you need to document a source the first time you consult it, or you risk not finding it again.
> - Follow a consistent notetaking system. Use different colors, or some other coding system, to distinguish three different types of material.
>
>   Quotations from a source (documentation required)
>
>   Material you have paraphrased, summarized, or otherwise drawn from a source (documentation required)
>
>   Your own thoughts, triggered by what you have read or experienced (no documentation required)
>
> - Write clear, even oversized quotation marks when you are quoting a passage directly. Make them stand out so that you can't miss them later.
> - Consult your instructor if you're unsure about any aspect of the documentation process.

31c How do I avoid plagiarism when using Internet sources?

You might be tempted to download a paper from the Internet. Don't. That kind of intellectual dishonesty can get you into real trouble. Even if you have absolutely no intention of plagiarizing, being careless can very easily lead to trouble. Quick Reference 31.3 suggests some ways you can avoid plagiarism when you're working on the Internet.

> **Quick Reference 31.3** ■ ■ ■ ■ ■ ■ ■
>
> ### Guidelines for avoiding plagiarism when using Internet sources
>
> - Never cut material from an online source and paste it directly into your paper without taking great care. You can too easily lose track of which language is your own and which comes from a source.
> - Keep material that you downloaded or printed from the Internet separate from your own writing, whether you intend to quote, summarize, or paraphrase the material. Be careful how you manage copied files. Use another color or a much larger font as a visual reminder that this isn't your work.

continued >>

- Copy or paste downloaded or printed material into your paper only when you intend to use it as a direct quotation or visual. Immediately place quotation marks around the material (later you may decide to set off a long passage as a block quotation; only then would you remove the quotation marks). Be sure to document the source at the same time as you're copying or pasting the quotation into your paper, or you may forget to do it later or do it incorrectly.

- Summarize or paraphrase materials *before* you include them in your paper. Document the sources of summarized passages at the same time as you insert them in your paper.

- Use an Internet service to check a passage you're not sure about. If you're concerned that you may have plagiarized by mistake, try submitting one or two sentences that concern you to http://www.google.com. To make this work, always place quotation marks around the sentences you want to check when you type them into the search window.

31d   What don't I have to document?

You don't have to document common knowledge or your own thinking. Common knowledge is information that most educated people know, although they might need to remind themselves of certain facts by looking them up in a reference book. For example, you would not need to document statements like these:

- Bill Clinton was the US president before George W. Bush.
- Mercury is the planet closest to the sun.
- Water boils at 212° F.
- All of the oceans on our planet contain salt water.

A very important component of a research paper that doesn't need documentation is *your own thinking,* which is based on what you've learned as you built on what you already knew about your topic. It consists of your ANALYSIS, SYNTHESIS, and evaluation of new material as you read or observe it.

You must document everything that you learn from a source, including ideas and specific language. Expressing the ideas of others in your own words doesn't release you from the obligation to tell exactly where you got those ideas using correct documentation. Consider the following example.

SOURCE

Park, Robert L. "Welcome to Planet Earth." *The Best American Science Writing 2001*. Ed. Jesse Cohen. New York: Ecco-Harper, 2001. 302–08. Print. [source information arranged in MLA documentation style]

ORIGINAL (PARK'S EXACT WORDS)

The widespread belief in alien abductions is just one example of the growing influence of pseudoscience. Two hundred years ago, educated people imagined that the greatest contribution of science would be to free the world from superstition and humbug. It has not happened. (304)

PLAGIARISM EXAMPLE

Belief in alien kidnappings illustrates the influence of pseudoscience. In the nineteenth century, educated people imagined that science would free the world from superstition, but they were wrong.

Even though the student changed some wording in the example above, the ideas aren't original to her. To avoid plagiarism she's required to document the source. The underlined phrases are especially problematic examples of plagiarism because they're Park's exact wording.

CORRECT EXAMPLE (USING QUOTATION, PARAPHRASE, AND DOCUMENTATION)

Robert Park calls people's beliefs in alien kidnapping proof of "the growing influence of pseudoscience" (304). Centuries of expectation that science would conquer "superstition and humbug" are still unfulfilled (304). [citation arranged in MLA documentation style]

In this revision, the writer has properly cited Park's ideas through a combination of quotation and paraphrase. Sections 31e–31i explain exactly how to use sources effectively and document them correctly.

31e How should I integrate sources into my writing?

Before trying to integrate sources into your writing, you need to analyze and synthesize your material (Chs. 2 and 7). Analysis is the process of breaking ideas down into their component parts so that you can think them through separately. Do this while reading and reviewing your notes. Synthesis, the process of making connections among different ideas, seeking relationships that tie them together, uses QUOTATION (31f), PARAPHRASE (31g), and SUMMARY (31h).

31f   How can I use quotations effectively?

A **quotation** is the exact words of a source enclosed in quotation marks (Ch. 61). Well-chosen quotations can lend a note of authority and enliven a document with someone else's voice.

Avoid adding too many quotations, however. If more than a quarter of your paper consists of quotations, you've probably written what some people call a "cut-and-paste special." Doing so gives your readers—including instructors—the impression that you haven't bothered to develop your own thinking and that you're letting other people do your talking. Quick Reference 31.4 provides guidelines for using quotations.

Quick Reference 31.4   ■ ■ ■ ■ ■ ■ ■

Guidelines for using quotations

- Use quotations from authorities on your subject to support or refute what you've written.
- Never use a quotation to present your THESIS STATEMENT or a TOPIC SENTENCE.
- Select quotations that fit your message. Choose a quotation only for the following reasons.

  Its language is particularly appropriate or distinctive.

  Its idea is particularly hard to paraphrase accurately.

  The source's authority is especially important to support your thesis or main point in a paragraph.

  The source's words are open to interpretation.

- Never allow quotations to make up a quarter or more of your paper. Instead, rely on paraphrase (31g) and summary (31h).
- Quote accurately. Always check a quotation against the original source— and then recheck it.
- Integrate quotations smoothly into your writing.
- Avoid plagiarism (31a–31c).
- Document quotations carefully.

■ Making quotations fit smoothly with your sentences

When you use quotations, the greatest risk you take is that you'll end up with incoherent, choppy sentences. You can avoid this problem by making the words you quote fit smoothly with three aspects of your writing: grammar, style, and logic. Here are some examples of sentences that don't mesh well with quotations, followed by revised versions.

SOURCE

Goleman, Daniel. *Emotional Intelligence.* New York: Bantam, 1995. Print. [source information arranged in MLA documentation style]

ORIGINAL (GOLEMAN'S EXACT WORDS)

These two minds, the emotional and the rational, operate in tight harmony for the most part, intertwining their very different ways of knowing to guide us through the world. [from page 9]

INCOHERENT GRAMMAR PROBLEM

Goleman explains how the emotional and rational <u>minds</u> <u>"intertwining</u> their very different ways of knowing to guide us through the world" (9).

INCOHERENT STYLE PROBLEM

Goleman explains how the <u>emotional and rational minds based on</u> <u>reason</u> work together by "intertwining their very different ways of knowing to guide us through the world" (9).

INCOHERENT LOGIC PROBLEM

Goleman explains how the emotional and rational minds <u>work together</u> <u>by</u> "their very different ways of knowing to guide us through the world" (9).

ACCEPTABLE USE OF THE QUOTATION

Goleman explains how the emotional and rational minds work together by "intertwining their very different ways of knowing to guide us through the world" (9).

■ Using brackets to add words

What do you do when a quotation doesn't fit smoothly with your writing? You can add a word or two to the quotation, in brackets—[ ]—so that it fits seamlessly with the rest of your sentence. Make sure, however, that your bracketed additions don't distort the meaning of the quotation.

ORIGINAL (GOLEMAN'S EXACT WORDS)

In many or most moments, these minds are exquisitely coordinated; feelings are essential to thought, thought to feeling. [from page 9]

QUOTATION WITH EXPLANATORY BRACKETS

"In many or most moments, these minds [emotional and rational] are exquisitely coordinated; feelings are essential to thought, thought to feeling" (Goleman 9). [citation arranged in MLA documentation style]

■ Using ellipsis to delete words

Another way to fit a quotation smoothly into your sentence is to use ellipsis. Delete the part of the quotation that seems to be causing the problem, and mark the omission by using ellipsis points (60d). When you use ellipsis to delete troublesome words, make sure that the remaining words accurately reflect the source's meaning and that your sentence still flows smoothly.

ORIGINAL (GOLEMAN'S EXACT WORDS)

But when passions surge, the balance tips: it is the emotional mind that captures the upper hand, swamping the rational mind. [from page 9]

QUOTATION USING ELLIPSIS

Goleman contends that "when passions surge, . . . the emotional mind . . . captures the upper hand" (9). [Citation arranged in MLA documentation style]

■ Integrating author names, source titles, and other information

A huge complaint instructors have about student research papers is that sometimes quotations are simply stuck in, for no apparent reason. Without context-setting information in the paper, the reader can't know exactly what logic leads the writer to use a particular quotation. Furthermore, always make sure your readers know who said each group of quoted words.

SOURCE

Wright, Karen. "Times of Our Lives." *Scientific American* Sept. 2002: 58-66. Print. [source information arranged in MLA documentation style]

ORIGINAL (WRIGHT'S EXACT WORDS)

In human bodies, biological clocks keep track of seconds, minutes, days, months and years. [from page 66]

INCORRECT (DISEMBODIED QUOTATION)

The human body has many subconscious processes. People don't have to make their hearts beat or remind themselves to breathe. "In human bodies, biological clocks keep track of seconds, minutes, days, months and years" (Wright 66).

CORRECT

The human body has many subconscious processes. People don't have to make their hearts beat or remind themselves to breathe. However, other processes are less obvious and perhaps more surprising. Karen Wright observes, for example, "In human bodies, biological clocks keep track of seconds, minutes, days, months and years" (66).

Another strategy for working quotations smoothly into your paper is to integrate the author's name, the source title, or other information. You can prepare your reader for a quotation using one of these methods.

- Mention in your sentence (before or after the quotation) the name of the author you're quoting.
- Mention in your sentence the title of the work you're quoting from.
- Give additional authority to your material. If the author of a quotation is a noteworthy figure, refer to his or her credentials.
- Add your own introductory analysis to the quotation, along with the name of the author, the title of the source, and/or the author's credentials.

Here are some examples, using the original quotation from Karen Wright, of effective integration of an author's name, source title, and credentials, along with an introductory analysis.

AUTHOR'S NAME

Karen Wright explains that "in human bodies, biological clocks keep track of seconds, minutes, days, months and years" (66).

AUTHOR'S NAME AND SOURCE TITLE

Karen Wright explains in "Times of Our Lives" that "in human bodies, biological clocks keep track of seconds, minutes, days, months and years" (66).

AUTHOR'S NAME AND CREDENTIALS

Karen Wright, an award-winning science journalist, explains that "in human bodies, biological clocks keep track of seconds, minutes, days, months and years" (66).

AUTHOR'S NAME WITH STUDENT'S INTRODUCTORY ANALYSIS

Karen Wright reviews evidence of surprising subconscious natural processes, explaining that "in human bodies, biological clocks keep track of seconds, minutes, days, months and years" (66).

31g How can I write good paraphrases?

A **paraphrase** precisely restates in your own words the written or spoken words of someone else. Select for paraphrase only passages that carry ideas you need to reproduce in detail. Because paraphrasing calls for a very close approximation of a source, avoid trying to paraphrase more than a paragraph or two; for longer passages, use summary (31h). Quick Reference 31.5 offers advice for paraphrasing.

Quick Reference 31.5

Guidelines for writing paraphrases

- Paraphrase the words of authorities on your subject to support or counter what you write in your paper.
- Never use a paraphrase to present your THESIS STATEMENT or a TOPIC SENTENCE.
- Say what the source says, but no more.
- Reproduce the source's sequence of ideas and emphases.
- Use your own words, phrasing, and sentence structure to restate the material. If some technical words in the original have only awkward synonyms, you may quote the original words—but do so very sparingly.
- Read your sentences over to make sure they don't distort the source's meaning.
- Expect your material to be as long as the original or even slightly longer.
- Integrate your paraphrase into your writing so that it fits smoothly.
- Avoid PLAGIARISM (31a–31c).
- Document your paraphrase carefully.

Here is an example of an unacceptable paraphrase and an acceptable one. The first paraphrase is unacceptable because the underlined words have been plagiarized.

SOURCE

Hulbert, Ann. "Post-Teenage Wasteland?" *New York Times Magazine* 9 Oct. 2005: 11–12. Print. [source information arranged in MLA documentation style]

ORIGINAL (HULBURT'S EXACT WORDS)

[T]he available data suggest that the road to maturity hasn't become as drastically different as people think—or as drawn out, either. It's true that the median age of marriage rose to 25 for women and almost 27 for men in 2000, from 20 and 23, respectively, in 1960. Yet those midcentury figures were record lows (earnestly analyzed in their time). Moreover, Americans of all ages have ceased to view starting a family as the major benchmark of grown-up status. When asked to rank the importance of traditional milestones in defining the arrival of adulthood, poll respondents place completing school, finding full-time employment, achieving financial independence and being able to support a family far above actually wedding a spouse or having kids. The new perspective isn't merely an immature swerve into selfishness; postponing those last two steps is good for the future of the whole family. [from page 11]

UNACCEPTABLE PARAPHRASE (UNDERLINED WORDS ARE PLAGIARIZED)

Data suggest that the road to maturity hasn't changed as much as people think. True, the median age of marriage was 25 for women and 27 for men in 2000, up from 20 and 23 in 1960. Yet those 1960 figures were record lows. Furthermore, Americans have stopped regarding beginning a family as the signpost of grown-up status. When they were asked to rank the importance of traditional benchmarks for deciding the arrival of adulthood, people rated graduating from school, finding a full-time job, gaining financial status, and being a breadwinner far above marrying or having kids. This new belief isn't merely immature selfishness; delaying those last two steps is good for the future of the whole family (Hulburt 11).

ACCEPTABLE PARAPHRASE

According to Ann Hulburt, statistics show that people are wrong when they believe our society is delaying maturity. She acknowledges that between 1960 and 2000, the median age at which women married rose from 20 to 25 (for men it went from 23 to 27), but points out that the early figures were extreme lows. Hulburt finds that Americans no longer equate adulthood with starting a family. Polls show that people rank several other "milestones" above marriage and children as signaling adulthood. These include finishing school, securing a full-time job, and earning enough to be independent and to support a family. Hulburt concludes that we should regard postponing marriage and children not as being selfish or immature but as investing in the family's future (11). [citation arranged in MLA documentation style]

The first attempt to paraphrase is unacceptable because the writer has simply changed a few words. What remains is plagiarized: It retains most of the original language, has the same sentence structure as the original, and uses no quotation marks. The documentation is correct, but its accuracy doesn't make up for the unacceptable paraphrasing.

The second paraphrase is acceptable. It captures the meaning of the original in the student's own words.

31h How can I write good summaries?

A **summary** differs from a paraphrase (31g) in one important way: Whereas a paraphrase restates the original material in its entirety, a summary provides only the main point of the original source. As a result, a summary is much shorter than a paraphrase. Summarizing is the technique you'll probably use most frequently in writing research papers. Read Quick Reference 31.6 to learn how to summarize effectively.

Quick Reference 31.6

■ ■ ■ ■ ■ ■ ■

Guidelines for writing summaries

- Summarize the work of authorities on your subject to support or refute what you write in your paper.
- Identify the main points and condense them in your own words, taking care not to alter the meaning of the original source.
- Never use a summary to present your THESIS STATEMENT or a TOPIC SENTENCE.
- Keep your summary short.
- Integrate your summary smoothly into your writing.
- Avoid PLAGIARISM (31a–31c).
- Document your sources precisely and carefully.

As you summarize a source, don't be tempted to include your personal interpretation or judgment. Your own opinions don't belong in a summary. Here's an example of an unacceptable summary and an acceptable one.

SOURCE

Tanenbaum, Leora. *Catfight: Women and Competition.* New York: Seven Stories, 2002. Print. [source information arranged in MLA documentation style]

ORIGINAL (TANENBAUM'S EXACT WORDS)

Until recently, most Americans disapproved of cosmetic surgery, but today the stigma is disappearing. Average Americans are lining up for procedures—two-thirds of patients report family incomes of less than $50,000 a year—and many of them return for more. Younger women undergo "maintenance" surgeries in a futile attempt to halt time. The latest fad is Botox, a purified and diluted form of botulinum toxin that is injected between the eyebrows to eliminate frown lines. Although the procedure costs between $300 and $1000 and must be repeated every few months, roughly 850,000 patients have had it performed on them. That number will undoubtedly shoot up now that the FDA has approved Botox for cosmetic use. Even teenagers are making appointments with plastic surgeons. More than 14,000 adolescents had plastic surgery in 1996, and many of them are choosing controversial procedures such as breast implants, liposuction, and tummy tucks, rather than the rhinoplasties of previous generations. [from pages 117–118]

UNACCEPTABLE SUMMARY (UNDERLINED WORDS ARE PLAGIARIZED)

Average Americans are lining up for surgical procedures. The latest fad is Botox, a toxin injected to eliminate frown lines. This is an insanely foolish waste of money. Even teenagers are making appointments with plastic surgeons, many of them for controversial procedures such as breast implants, liposuction, and tummy tucks (Tanenbaum 117-18).

ACCEPTABLE SUMMARY

Tanenbaum explains that plastic surgery is becoming widely acceptable, even for Americans with modest incomes and for younger women. Most popular is injecting the toxin Botox to smooth wrinkles. She notes that thousands of adolescents are even requesting controversial surgeries (117-18). [citation arranged in MLA documentation style]

The unacceptable summary has several major problems: It doesn't isolate the main point. It plagiarizes by taking much of its language directly from the source. Finally, the unacceptable summary includes the writer's interpretation ("This is an insanely foolish waste of money") rather than objectively representing the original. The acceptable summary concisely isolates the main point, puts the source into the writer's own words, calls attention to the author by including her name in the summary, and remains objective throughout.

31i   Which verbs can help me weave source material into my sentences?

Use the verbs in Quick Reference 31.7 appropriately according to their meanings in your sentences. For example, *says* and *states* are fairly neutral introductory verbs; you're just reporting the source's words. On the other hand, while still fairly neutral, *claims* or *contends* introduces a slight skepticism; you're suggesting that you may not share the source's certainty. *Demonstrates* or, even stronger, *proves* indicates that you find the source conclusive on a particular point.

Quick Reference 31.7 ■■■■■■■

Useful verbs for integrating quotations, paraphrases, and summaries

acknowledges	contrasts	illustrates	recommends
agrees	declares	implies	refutes
analyzes	demonstrates	indicates	rejects
argues	denies	insists	remarks
asserts	describes	introduces	reports
begins	develops	maintains	reveals
believes	discusses	means	says
claims	distinguishes	notes	shows
comments	between/	notices	specifies
compares	among	observes	speculates
complains	emphasizes	offers	states
concedes	establishes	points out	suggests
concludes	explains	prepares	supports
confirms	expresses	promises	supposes
considers	finds	proves	wishes
contends	focuses on	questions	writes
contradicts	grants	recognizes	

For more help with your writing, grammar, and research,
go to **www.mycomplab.com**

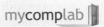

32

Drafting and Revising a Research Paper

32a How does the writing process apply to research papers?

DRAFTING and REVISING a research paper is like drafting and revising any piece of writing (Chs. 9–10). Yet to write a research paper, you need extra time for planning, drafting, thinking, redrafting, rethinking, and creating a final draft because you need to demonstrate all of the following:

- You've followed the steps of the research process presented in Chapters 27–30.
- You understand the information that you've located during your research.
- You've evaluated the SOURCES you've used in your research.
- You haven't plagiarized your material from someone else (31a–31c).
- You've used sources well in your writing, correctly employing QUOTATIONS, PARAPHRASES, and SUMMARIES (31f–31h).
- You've moved beyond summary to SYNTHESIS so that your sources are interwoven with each other and with your own thinking, not merely listed one by one (Ch. 7).
- You've used DOCUMENTATION accurately (For MLA STYLE, see Chapters 33–35; for APA STYLE, see Chapters 36–38; for other documentation styles, see Chapters 39–40.)

32b How do I draft a research paper?

Expect to write several drafts of your research paper. The first draft is your first chance to discover new insights and fresh connections. Here are some ways to write your first draft.

- Some researchers work with their notes at hand. They organize the notes into broad categories by making a separate group for each topic. As patterns begin to emerge, these writers might move material from one category to another. Each category becomes a section of the first draft. This method can reveal any gaps in information that call for additional research. Of course, you may discover that some of your research doesn't fit your topic and thesis. Put it aside; it might be useful in a later draft.

- Some writers generate a list of questions that their paper needs to address, then answer each question, one at a time, looking for the content notes that will help them. For example, writing on the topic of organic foods, some possible questions might be, "What are organic foods? What benefits do people see for eating them? Why do they cost more than regular foods? Does everyone agree that they are beneficial?" Generating and answering questions can be a way of turning a mass of information into manageable groupings.

- Some researchers finish their research and then slowly review half of the information they've gathered. Next, setting aside that information, they write a partial first draft by drawing on the information they remember from their reading. Then they use the same process with the second half of the information that they've gathered. Finally, with their two partial drafts and all their research notes in front of them, they write a complete first draft.

- Some researchers stop at various points during their research and use FREEWRITING to get their ideas into words. Researchers who use this method say that it helps them to recognize when they need to adjust their research question or change the emphasis of their search. After a number of rounds of researching and freewriting, these researchers find that they can write their complete first draft relatively easily.

- Some writers review their sources and create an OUTLINE before drafting (8h). Some find a FORMAL OUTLINE helpful, while others use a less formal approach.

32c How do I revise a research paper?

Before you write each new draft, read your previous draft with a sharp eye. Assess all of the features listed in Quick Reference 32.1. For best results, take a break of a few days (or at least a few hours) before beginning this process. This gives you distance from your material and a clearer vision of what you need to revise. For a more objective point of view, consider asking a few people you respect to read and react to your first, or perhaps your second, draft.

> ## Quick Reference 32.1
>
> ### Revision checklist for a research paper
>
> If the answer to a question in this checklist is no, you need to revise. The section numbers in parentheses tell you where to find helpful information.
>
> #### WRITING
>
> ✔ Does your introductory paragraph lead effectively into the material? (11b)
>
> ✔ Have you met the basic requirements for a written thesis statement? (8g)
>
> ✔ Do your thesis statement and the content of your paper address your research question(s)? (27d)
>
> ✔ Have you developed effective body paragraphs? (11d)
>
> ✔ Do your ideas follow sensibly and logically within each paragraph and from one paragraph to the next? (11e)
>
> ✔ Does the concluding paragraph end your paper effectively? (11g)
>
> ✔ Does your paper satisfy a critical thinker? (2d)
>
> #### RESEARCH
>
> ✔ Have you included appropriate and effective evidence and deleted irrelevant or insignificant evidence? (13d)
>
> ✔ Have you used quotations, paraphrases, and summaries well? (31f–31h)
>
> ✔ Have you integrated your source material well without plagiarizing? (31a–31c)
>
> #### FORMAT AND DOCUMENTATION
>
> ✔ Have you used the correct format in your parenthetical references? (Chs. 33 and 36)
>
> ✔ Does each of your parenthetical references tie into an item in your Works Cited list (MLA style) or References list (APA style) at the end of your paper? (Chs. 34 and 37)
>
> ✔ Does the paper exactly match the format you've been assigned to follow? Check margins, spacing, title, headings, page numbers, font, and so on. (Chs. 35 and 38)

One key to revising any research paper is to examine carefully the evidence you've included. **Evidence** consists of facts, statistics, expert studies and opinions, examples, and stories. Use RENNS (11d) to see if you can develop paragraphs more fully. Identify each of the points you have made in your paper, including your THESIS STATEMENT and all your subpoints. Then ask the following questions.

- **Is the evidence sufficient?** To be sufficient, evidence can't be thin or trivial. As a rule, the more evidence you present, the more convincing your thesis will be to readers.

- **Is the evidence representative?** Representative evidence is customary and normal, not based on exceptions.

- **Is the evidence relevant?** Relevant evidence relates directly to your thesis or topic sentence. It illustrates your reasons straightforwardly and never introduces unrelated material.

- **Is the evidence accurate?** Accurate evidence is correct, complete, and up to date. It comes from a reliable source. Equally important, you present it honestly, without distorting or misrepresenting it.

- **Is the evidence reasonable?** Reasonable evidence is not phrased in extreme language and avoids sweeping generalizations. Reasonable evidence is free of LOGICAL FALLACIES (13h).

For more help with your writing, grammar, and research,
go to **www.mycomplab.com**

mycomplab

33

MLA In-Text Citations

33a What is MLA documentation style?

A DOCUMENTATION STYLE* is a standard format that writers follow to tell read-ers what SOURCES they used and how to find them. Different disciplines follow different documentation styles. The one most frequently used in the humani-ties (Ch. 15) is from the Modern Language Association (MLA), a professional organization of several thousand English professors.

MLA style requires you to document your sources in two connected, equally important ways.

1. Within the body of the paper, use parenthetical documentation, as de-scribed in this chapter.

2. At the end of the paper, provide a list of the sources you used in your paper. Title this list "Works Cited," as described in Chapter 34.

Important MLA Style Changes

The guidelines and examples in this chapter have been adapted from the Third Edition of *The MLA Style Manual and Guide to Scholarly Pub-lishing* (2008). According to the MLA's Web site, this edition of the *MLA Style Manual* provides documentation style guidelines that will be used in MLA publications beginning in 2009. Thus, the guidelines in the sixth edition of the *MLA Handbook for Writers of Research Papers* should only be followed until the seventh edition is released in spring 2009. If you need more information regarding MLA style updates, check http://www.mla.org.

See Quick Reference 34.1 on page 218 for more guidance on these requirements.

---

*Words printed in SMALL CAPITAL LETTERS are discussed elsewhere in the text and are defined in the Terms Glossary at the back of the book.

33b   What is MLA in-text parenthetical documentation?

MLA-style **parenthetical documentation** (also called **in-text citations**) places source information in parentheses within the sentences of your research papers. This information—given each time that you quote, summarize, or paraphrase source materials—signals materials used from outside sources and enables readers to find the originals. (See Chapter 31 for information on how to quote, paraphrase, and summarize.)

If you include an author's name (or, if none, the title of the work) in the sentence to introduce the source material, you include in parentheses only the page number where you found the material:

> According to Brent Staples, IQ tests give scientists little insight into intelligence (293). [Author name cited in text; page number cited in parentheses.]

For readability and good writing technique, try to introduce the names of authors (or titles of sources) in your own sentences. If you don't include this information in your sentence, you need to insert it in the parentheses, before the page number. There is no punctuation between the author's name and the page number:

> IQ tests give scientists little insight into intelligence (Staples 293).
> [Author name and page number cited in parentheses.]

When possible, position a parenthetical reference at the end of the quotation, summary, or paraphrase it refers to—preferably at the end of a sentence, unless that would place it too far from the source's material. When you place the parenthetical reference at the end of a sentence, insert it before the sentence-ending period.

If you're citing a quotation enclosed in quotation marks, place the parenthetical information after the closing quotation mark but before sentence-ending punctuation.

> Coleman summarizes research that shows that "the number, rate, and direction of time-zone changes are the critical factors in determining the extent and degree of jet lag symptoms" (67). [Author name cited in text; page number cited in parentheses.]

The one exception to this rule concerns quotations that you set off in block style, meaning one inch from the left margin. (MLA requires that quotations longer than four typed lines be handled this way.) For block quotations, put the parenthetical reference after the period.

Bruce Sterling worries that people are pursuing less conventional medical treatments, and not always for good reasons:

> Medical tourism is already in full swing. Thailand is the golden shore for wealthy, sickly Asians and Australians. Fashionable Europeans head to South Africa for embarrassing plastic surgery. Crowds of scrip-waving Americans buy prescription drugs in Canada and Mexico. (92)

If you're quoting part of a paragraph or one complete paragraph, don't indent the first line of quoted words more than ten spaces. But if you quote more than one paragraph, indent the first line of each paragraph—including the first if it's a complete paragraph from the source—an additional three spaces (thirteen spaces in all).

33c What are additional MLA guidelines for parenthetical citations?

The directory at the beginning of this tab corresponds to the numbered examples in this section. Most of these examples show the author's name or the title included in the parenthetical citation, but remember that it's usually more effective to include that information in your sentence.

1. One Author—MLA

Give an author's name as it appears on the source: for a book, on the title page; for an article, directly below the title or at the end of the article.

> IQ tests give scientists little insight into intelligence (Staples 293).
> [Author name and page number cited in parentheses.]

2. Two or Three Authors—MLA

Give the names in the same order as in the source. Spell out *and*. For three authors, use commas to separate the authors' names.

> As children get older, they begin to express several different kinds of intelligence (Todd and Taylor 23).

> Another measure of emotional intelligence is the success of inter- and intrapersonal relationships (Voigt, Dees, and Prigoff 14).

3. More Than Three Authors—MLA

If your source has more than three authors, you can name them all or use the first author's name only, followed by *et al.*, either in a parenthetical reference or in your sentence. *Et al.* is an abbreviation of the Latin *et alii*, meaning "and others." In MLA citations, don't underline or italicize *et al.* No period follows *et,* but one follows *al.*

> Emotional security varies, depending on the circumstances of the social interaction (Carter et al. 158).

4. More Than One Source by an Author—MLA

When you use two or more sources by the same author, include the relevant title in each citation. In parenthetical citations, use a shortened version of the title. For example, in a paper using two of Howard Gardner's works, *Frames of Mind: The Theory of Multiple Intelligences* and "Reflections on Multiple Intelligences: Myths and Messages," use *Frames* and "Reflections." Shorten the titles as much as you can without making them ambiguous to readers, and start with the word by which the work is alphabetized in your WORKS CITED list. Separate the author's name and the title with a comma, but don't use punctuation between the title and page number.

> Although it seems straightforward to think of multiple intelligences as multiple approaches to learning (Gardner, *Frames* 60-61), an intelligence is not a learning style (Gardner, "Reflections" 202-03).

When you incorporate the title into your own sentences, you can omit a subtitle. After the first mention, you can shorten the main title as well.

5. Two or More Authors with the Same Last Name—MLA

Use each author's first initial and full last name in each parenthetical citation. If both authors have the same first initial, use the full name in all instances.

> According to Anne Cates, psychologists can predict how empathetic an adult will be from his or her behavior at age two (41), but other researchers disagree (T. Cates 171).

6. Group or Corporate Author—MLA

When a corporation or other group is named as the author of a source you want to cite, use the corporate name just as you would an individual's name.

> A five-year study shows that these tests are usually unreliable (Boston Women's Health Collective 11).

7. Work Cited by Title—MLA

If no author is named, use only the title. If the title is long, shorten it. Here's an in-text citation for an article titled "Are You a Day or Night Person?"

> The "morning lark" and "night owl" descriptions typically are used to categorize the human extremes ("Are You" 11).

8. Multivolume Work—MLA

If you use more than one volume of a multivolume work, include the relevant volume number in each citation. Separate the volume number and page number with a colon followed by a space.

> Although Amazon forest dwellers had been exposed to these viruses by 1900 (Rand 3: 202), Borneo forest dwellers escaped them until the 1960s (Rand 1: 543).

9. Novel, Play, Short Story, or Poem—MLA

Literary works frequently appear in different editions. When you cite material from literary works, providing the part, chapter, act, scene, canto, stanza, or line numbers usually helps readers locate what you are referring to better than page numbers alone. Unless your instructor tells you not to, use arabic numerals for these references, even if the literary work uses roman numerals. For novels that use them, give part and/or chapter numbers after page numbers. Use a semicolon after the page number but a comma to separate a part from a chapter.

> Flannery O'Connor describes one character in *The Violent Bear It Away* as "divided in two--a violent and a rational self" (139; pt. 2, ch. 6).

For plays that use them, give act, scene, and line numbers. Use periods between these numbers. For short stories, use page numbers.

> Among the most quoted of Shakespeare's lines is Hamlet's soliloquy beginning "To be, or not to be: that is the question" (3.1.56).

> The old man in John Collier's "The Chaser" says about his potions, "I don't deal in laxatives and teething mixtures . . ." (79).

For poems and songs, give canto, stanza, and/or line numbers. Use periods between these numbers.

> In "To Autumn," Keats's most melancholy image occurs in the lines "Then in a wailful choir the small gnats mourn / Among the river swallows" (3.27-28).

10. Bible or Sacred Text—MLA

Give the title of the edition you're using, the book (in the case of the Bible), and the chapter and verse. Spell out the names of books in sentences, but use abbreviations in parenthetical references.

> He would certainly benefit from the advice in Ephesians to "get rid of all bitterness, rage, and anger" (*New International Version Bible*, 4.31).

> He would certainly benefit from the advice to "get rid of all bitterness, rage, and anger" (*New International Version Bible*, Eph. 4.31).

11. Work in an Anthology or Other Collection—MLA

You may want to cite a work you have read in a book that contains many works by various authors and that was compiled or edited by someone other than the person you're citing. Your in-text citation should include the author of the selection you're citing and the page number. For example, suppose you want to cite the poem "Several Things" by Martha Collins, in a literature text edited by Pamela Annas and Robert Rosen. Use Collins's name and the title of her work in the sentence and the line numbers (see item 9) in a parenthetical citation.

> In "Several Things," Martha Collins enumerates what could take place in the lines of her poem: "Plums could appear, on a pewter plate / A dead red hare, hung by one foot. / A vase of flowers. Three shallots" (2-4).

12. Indirect Source—MLA

When you want to quote words that you found quoted in someone else's work, put the name of the person whose words you're quoting into your own sentence. Give the work where you found the quotation either in your sentence or in a parenthetical citation beginning with *qtd. in.*

> Martin Scorsese acknowledges the link between himself and his films: "I realize that all my life, I've been an outsider. I splatter bits of myself all over the screen" (qtd. in Giannetti and Eyman 397).

13. Two or More Sources in One Reference—MLA

If more than one source has contributed to an idea, opinion, or fact in your paper, cite them all. An efficient way to credit all is to include them in a single parenthetical citation, with a semicolon separating each block of information.

> Once researchers agreed that multiple intelligences existed, their next step was to try to measure or define them (West 17; Arturi 477; Gibbs 68).

14. An Entire Work—MLA

References to an entire work usually fit best into your own sentences.

> In *Convergence Culture*, Henry Jenkins explores how new digital media create a culture of active participation rather than passive reception.

15. Electronic Source with Page Numbers—MLA

The principles that govern in-text citations of electronic sources are exactly the same as the ones that apply to books, articles, or other sources. When an electronically accessed source identifies its author, use the author's name for parenthetical references. If no author is named, use the title of the source. When an electronic source has page numbers, use them exactly as you would the page numbers of a print source.

> Learning happens best when teachers truly care about their students' complete well-being (Anderson 7).

16. Electronic Source Without Page Numbers—MLA

Many online sources don't number pages. Simply refer to those works in their entirety. Try to include the name of the author in your sentence.

> In "What Is Artificial Intelligence?" John McCarthy notes that the science of artificial intelligence includes efforts beyond trying to simulate human intelligence.

For more help with your writing, grammar, and research, go to **www.mycomplab.com**

34

MLA Works Cited List

34a What are MLA guidelines for a Works Cited list?

In MLA-style DOCUMENTATION, the **Works Cited** list gives complete bibliographic information for each SOURCE used in your paper. Include only the sources from which you quote, paraphrase, or summarize. Quick Reference 34.1 gives general information about the Works Cited list. The rest of this chapter gives models of many specific kinds of Works Cited entries.

Quick Reference 34.1 ■ ■ ■ ■ ■ ■ ■

Guidelines for an MLA-style Works Cited list

TITLE
Use "Works Cited" (without quotation marks) as the title.

PLACEMENT OF LIST
Start a new page numbered sequentially with the rest of the paper, following the Notes pages, if any.

continued >>

Quick Reference 34.1 (continued)

CONTENT AND FORMAT

Include all sources quoted from, paraphrased, or summarized in your paper. Start each entry on a new line and at the regular left margin. If the entry uses more than one line, indent the second and all following lines one-half inch or five spaces from the left margin. Double-space all lines.

SPACING AFTER PUNCTUATION

Use one space after a period, unless your instructor asks you to use two. Always put only one space after a comma or a colon.

ARRANGEMENT OF ENTRIES

Alphabetize by author's last name. If no author is named, alphabetize by the title's first significant word (ignore *A, An,* or *The*).

AUTHORS' NAMES

Use first names and middle names or middle initials, if any, as given in the source. Don't reduce to initials any name that is given in full. For one author or the first-named author in multiauthor works, give the last name first. Use the word *and* with two or more authors. List multiple authors in the order given in the source. Use a comma between the first author's last and first names and after each complete author name except the last, which ends with a period: Fein, Ethel Andrea, Bert Griggs, and Delaware Rogash.

Include *Jr., Sr., II,* or *III* but no other titles or degrees before or after a name. For example, an entry for a work by Edward Meep III, MD, and Sir Richard Bolton would start like this: Meep, Edward, III, and Richard Bolton.

CAPITALIZATION OF TITLES

Capitalize all major words and the first and last words of all titles and subtitles. Don't capitalize ARTICLES (*a, an, the*), PREPOSITIONS, COORDINATING CONJUNCTIONS, or *to* in INFINITIVES in the middle of a title.

SPECIAL TREATMENT OF TITLES

Use quotation marks around titles of shorter works (poems, short stories, essays, articles). Use italics for the titles of longer works (books, periodicals, plays).

When a book title includes the title of another work that is usually in italics (such as a novel, play, or long poem), the preferred MLA style is not to italicize the incorporated title: *Decoding* Jane Eyre. For an alternative that MLA accepts, see item 20 on p. 227.

If the incorporated title is usually enclosed in quotation marks (such as a short story or short poem), keep the quotation marks and italicize the complete title of the book: *Theme and Form in "I Shall Laugh Purely": A Brief Study.*

Drop *A, An,* or *The* as the first word of a periodical title.

continued >>

Quick Reference 34.1 (continued)

PLACE OF PUBLICATION

If several cities are listed for the place of publication, give only the first. MLA doesn't require US state names. For an unfamiliar city outside the United States, include an abbreviated name of the country or Canadian province.

PUBLISHER

Use shortened names as long as they're clear: *Random* for *Random House.* For companies named for more than one person, name only the first: *Prentice* for *Prentice Hall.* For university presses, use the capital letters *U* and *P* (without periods): Oxford UP, U of Chicago P

PUBLICATION MONTH ABBREVIATIONS

Abbreviate all publication months except *May, June,* and *July.* Use the first three letters followed by a period (*Dec., Feb.*) except for *September* (*Sept.*).

PAGE RANGES

Give the page range—the starting page number and the ending page number, connected by a hyphen—of any paginated electronic source and any paginated print source that is part of a longer work (for example, a chapter in a book, an article in a journal). A range indicates that the cited work is on those pages and all pages in between. If that is not the case, use the style shown next for discontinuous pages. In either case, use numerals only, without the word *page* or *pages* or the abbreviation *p.* or *pp.*

Use the full second number through 99. Above that, use only the last two digits for the second number unless it would be unclear: 103-04 is clear, but 567-602 requires full numbers.

DISCONTINUOUS PAGES

A source has discontinuous pages when the source is interrupted by material that's not part of the source (for example, an article beginning on page 32 but continued on page 54). Use the starting page number followed by a plus sign (+): 32+.

MEDIUM OF PUBLICATION

Include the medium of publication for each Works Cited entry. For example, every entry for a print source must include "Print" at the end, followed by a period (if required, certain supplementary bibliographic information like translation information, name of a book series, or the total number of volumes in a set should follow the medium of publication). Every source from the World Wide Web must include *Web* at the end, followed by a period and the date of access. The medium of publication also needs to be included for broadcast sources (*Television, Radio*), sound recordings (*CD, LP, Audiocassette*), as well as films, DVDs, videocassettes, live performances, musical scores and works of visual arts, and so on. (See examples 34–96.)

continued >>

> **Quick Reference 34.1**   (continued)
>
> **ISSUE AND VOLUME NUMBERS FOR SCHOLARLY JOURNALS**
> Include both an issue and volume number for each Works Cited entry for
> scholarly journals. This applies both to journals that are continuously paginated
> and those that are not.
>
> **URLs IN ELECTRONIC SOURCES**
> Entries for online citations should include the URL only when the reader
> probably could not locate the source without it. If the entry requires a URL,
> enclose it in angle brackets <like this>. Put the URL before the access date
> and end it with a period. If your computer automatically creates a hyperlink
> when you type a URL, format the URL to look the same as the rest of the entry.
> In some applications, like Microsoft Word, you can use the command
> "remove hyperlink," which you can find on the "Insert" menu or by right-
> clicking on the hyperlink. If a URL must be divided between two lines, only
> break the URL after a slash and do not use a hyphen.

34b   What are MLA guidelines for sources in a Works Cited list?

The directory at the beginning of this tab corresponds to the numbered examples in this section. Not every possible documentation model is here. You may
find that you have to combine features of models to document a particular
source. You will also find more information in the *MLA Handbook for Writers
of Research Papers*. Figure 34.1 (p. 222) provides another tool to help you find
the Works Cited model you need: a decision-making flowchart.

BOOKS

Citations for books have three main parts: author, title, and publication information (place of publication, publisher, date of publication, and medium of
publication). Figure 34.2 (p. 223) illustrates where to find this information
and the proper citation format.

1. Book by One Author—MLA

Bradway, Becky. *Pink Houses and Family Taverns*. Bloomington: Indiana UP,
    2002. Print.

2. Book by Two or Three Authors—MLA

Edin, Kathryn, and Maria Kefalas. *Promises I Can Keep: Why Poor Women Put
    Motherhood before Marriage*. Berkeley: U of California P, 2005. Print.

MLA

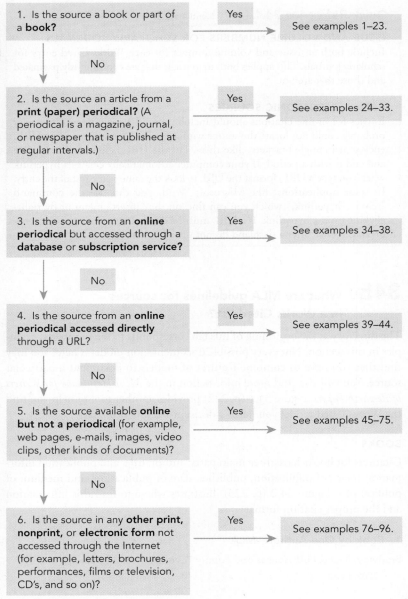

1. Is the source a book or part of a **book?** — Yes → See examples 1–23.

No ↓

2. Is the source an article from a **print (paper) periodical?** (A periodical is a magazine, journal, or newspaper that is published at regular intervals.) — Yes → See examples 24–33.

No ↓

3. Is the source from an **online periodical** but accessed through a **database** or **subscription service?** — Yes → See examples 34–38.

No ↓

4. Is the source from an **online periodical accessed directly** through a URL? — Yes → See examples 39–44.

No ↓

5. Is the source available **online but not a periodical** (for example, web pages, e-mails, images, video clips, other kinds of documents)? — Yes → See examples 45–75.

No ↓

6. Is the source in any **other print, nonprint, or electronic form** not accessed through the Internet (for example, letters, brochures, performances, films or television, CD's, and so on)? — Yes → See examples 76–96.

Figure 34.1 MLA Works Cited visual directory

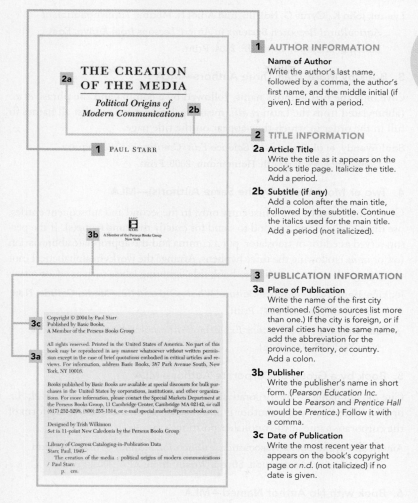

1 AUTHOR INFORMATION

Name of Author
Write the author's last name, followed by a comma, the author's first name, and the middle initial (if given). End with a period.

2 TITLE INFORMATION

2a Article Title
Write the title as it appears on the book's title page. Italicize the title. Add a period.

2b Subtitle (if any)
Add a colon after the main title, followed by the subtitle. Continue the italics used for the main title. Add a period (not italicized).

3 PUBLICATION INFORMATION

3a Place of Publication
Write the name of the first city mentioned. (Some sources list more than one.) If the city is foreign, or if several cities have the same name, add the abbreviation for the province, territory, or country. Add a colon.

3b Publisher
Write the publisher's name in short form. (*Pearson Education Inc.* would be *Pearson* and *Prentice Hall* would be *Prentice.*) Follow it with a comma.

3c Date of Publication
Write the most recent year that appears on the book's copyright page or *n.d.* (not italicized) if no date is given.

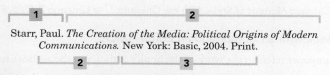

Starr, Paul. *The Creation of the Media: Political Origins of Modern Communications.* New York: Basic, 2004. Print.

Figure 34.2 Locating and citing source information in a book

Lynam, John K., Cyrus G. Ndiritu, and Adiel N. Mbabu. *Transformation of Agricultural Research Systems in Africa: Lessons from Kenya*. East Lansing: Michigan State UP, 2004. Print.

3. Book by More Than Three Authors—MLA

Give only the first author's name, followed by a comma and the phrase *et al.* (abbreviated from the Latin *et alii*, meaning "and others"), or list all names in full in the order in which they appear on the title page.

Saul, Wendy, et al. *Beyond the Science Fair: Creating a Kids' Inquiry Conference*. Portsmouth: Heinemann, 2005. Print.

4. Two or More Works by the Same Author(s)—MLA

Give author name(s) in the first entry only. In the second and subsequent entries, use three hyphens and a period to stand for exactly the same name(s). If the person served as editor or translator, put a comma and the appropriate abbreviation (*ed.* or *trans.*) following the three hyphens. Arrange the works in alphabetical (not chronological) order according to book title, ignoring labels such as *ed.* or *trans.*

Jenkins, Henry. *Convergence Culture: Where Old and New Media Collide*. New York: New York UP, 2006. Print.

---. *Fans, Bloggers, and Gamers: Exploring Participatory Culture*. New York: New York UP, 2006. Print.

5. Book by a Group or Corporate Author—MLA

Cite the full name of the corporate author first, omitting the first articles *A, An,* or *The*. When a corporate author is also the publisher, use a shortened form of the corporate name at the publisher position.

American Psychological Association. *Publication Manual of the American Psychological Association*. 5th ed. Washington: APA, 2001. Print.

6. Book with No Author Named—MLA

If there is no author's name on the title page, begin the citation with the title. Alphabetize the entry according to the first significant word of the title (ignore *A, An,* or *The*).

The Chicago Manual of Style. 15th ed. Chicago: U of Chicago P, 2003. Print.

7. Book with an Author and an Editor—MLA

If your paper refers to the work of the book's author, put the author's name first.

Brontë, Emily. *Wuthering Heights*. Ed. Richard J. Dunn. New York: Norton, 2002. Print.

If your paper refers to the work of the editor, put the editor's name first.

Dunn, Richard J., ed. *Wuthering Heights*. By Emily Brontë. New York: Norton, 2002. Print.

8. Translation—MLA

Kundera, Milan. *The Unbearable Lightness of Being*. Trans. Michael Henry Heim. New York: Harper, 1999. Print.

9. Work in Several Volumes or Parts—MLA

If you are citing only one volume, put the volume number before the publication information. If you wish, you can give the total number of volumes at the end of the entry. MLA recommends using arabic numerals, even if the source uses roman numerals (*Vol. 6* rather than *Vol. VI*).

Chrisley, Ronald, ed. *Artificial Intelligence: Critical Concepts*. Vol. 1. London: Routledge, 2000. Print. 4 vols.

10. Anthology or Edited Book—MLA

Use this model if you are citing an entire anthology. In the following example, *ed.* stands for "editor," so use *eds.* when more than one editor is named; also see items 9, 11, and 12.

Purdy, John L., and James Ruppert, eds. *Nothing but the Truth: An Anthology of Native American Literature*. Upper Saddle River: Prentice, 2001. Print.

11. One Selection from an Anthology or an Edited Book—MLA

Give the author and title of the selection first and then the full title of the anthology. Information about the editor starts with *Ed.* (for "Edited by"), so don't use *Eds.* when there is more than one editor. Give the name(s) of the editor(s) in normal order rather than reversing first and last names. Give the page range of the selection at the end.

Trujillo, Laura. "Balancing Act." *Border-Line Personalities: A New Generation of Latinas Dish on Sex, Sass, and Cultural Shifting*. Ed. Robyn Moreno and Michelle Herrera Mulligan. New York: Harper, 2004. 61-72. Print.

12. More Than One Selection from the Same Anthology or Edited Book—MLA

If you cite more than one selection from the same anthology, you can list the anthology as a separate entry with all of the publication information. Also list each selection from the anthology by author and title of the selection, but give only the name(s) of the editor(s) of the anthology and the page number(s) for each selection. Here, *ed.* stands for "editor," so it is correct to use *eds.* when more than one editor is named. List selections separately in alphabetical order by author's last name.

Bond, Ruskin. "The Night Train at Deoli." Chaudhuri 415-18.

Chaudhuri, Amit, ed. *The Vintage Book of Modern Indian Literature*. New York: Vintage, 2004. Print.

Vijayan, O.V. "The Rocks." Chaudhuri 291-96.

13. Signed Article in a Reference Book—MLA

A "signed article" means that the author of the article is identified. If the articles in the book are alphabetically arranged, you don't need to give volume and page numbers.

Burnbam, John C. "Freud, Sigmund." *The Encyclopedia of Psychiatry, Psychology, and Psychoanalysis*. Ed. Benjamin B. Wolman. New York: Holt, 1996. Print.

14. Unsigned Article in a Reference Book—MLA

Begin with the title of the article. If you're citing a widely used reference work, don't give full publication information. Instead, give only the edition and year of publication.

"Ireland." *The New Encyclopaedia Britannica: Macropaedia*. 15th ed. 2002. Print.

15. Second or Later Edition—MLA

If a book is not a first edition, the edition number is on the title page. Place the abbreviated information (*2nd ed., 3rd ed.,* etc.) between the title and the publication information. Give only the latest copyright date for the edition you are using.

Gibaldi, Joseph. *MLA Handbook for Writers of Research Papers*. 6th ed. New York: MLA, 2003. Print.

16. Introduction, Preface, Foreword, or Afterword—MLA

Give first the name of the writer of the part you're citing and then the name of the cited part, capitalized but not underlined or in quotation marks. After the book title, put *By* and the book author's full name, if different from the writer of the cited material. If the writer of the cited material is the same as the book author, use only the last name after *By*. After the publication information, give inclusive page numbers for the cited part, using roman or arabic numerals as the source does.

Hesse, Doug. Foreword. *The End of Composition Studies*. By David W. Smit. Carbondale: Southern Illinois UP, 2004. ix-xiii. Print.

When the introduction, preface, foreword, or afterword has a title, include it in the citation before the section name.

MLA

Fox-Genovese, Elizabeth. "Mothers and Daughters: The Ties That Bind."
Foreword. *Southern Mothers*. Ed. Nagueyalti Warren and Sally Wolff.
Baton Rouge: Louisiana State UP, 1999. iv-xviii. Print.

17. Unpublished Dissertation or Essay—MLA

State the author's name first, then the title in quotation marks (not under-lined), then a descriptive label (such as *Diss.* or *Unpublished essay*), followed by the degree-granting institution (for dissertations), and finally the date. Treat published dissertations as books.

Stuart, Gina Anne. "Exploring the Harry Potter Book Series: A Study of
Adolescent Reading Motivation." Diss. Utah State U, 2006. Print.

18. Reprint of an Older Book—MLA

Republishing information can be found on the copyright page. Give the date of the original version before the publication information for the version you are citing.

O'Brien, Flann. *At Swim-Two-Birds*. 1939. Normal: Dalkey Archive, 1998. Print.

19. Book in a Series—MLA

Mukherjee, Meenakshi. *Jane Austen*. New York: St. Martin's, 1991. Print. Women
Writers Ser.

20. Book with a Title Within a Title—MLA

The MLA recognizes two distinct styles for handling normally independent titles when they appear within an italicized title. When using the MLA's pre-ferred style, do not italicize the embedded title or set it within quotation marks.

Lumiansky, Robert M., and Herschel Baker, eds. *Critical Approaches to Six*
Major English Works: Beowulf *Through* Paradise Lost. Philadelphia: U of
Pennsylvania P, 1968. Print.

However, MLA also accepts a second style for handling such embedded titles. In this alternative style, you can set the normally independent titles within quotation marks and italicize them.

Lumiansky, Robert M., and Herschel Baker, eds. *Critical Approaches to Six*
Major English Works: "Beowulf" Through "Paradise Lost." Philadelphia:
U of Pennsylvania P, 1968. Print.

Use whichever style your instructor prefers.

21. Bible or Sacred Text—MLA

Bhagavad Gita. Trans. Juan Mascaro. Rev. ed. New York: Penguin, 2003. Print.

The Holy Bible: New International Version. New York: Harper, 1983. Print.

The Qur'an. Trans. Abdullah Yusuf Ali. 13th ed. Elmhurst: Tahrike Tarsile
Qur'an, 1999. Print.

22. Government Publication—MLA

For government publications that name no author, start with the name of the
government or government body. Then name the government agency. *GPO* is
a standard abbreviation for *Government Printing Office,* the publisher of most
US government publications.

United States. Cong. House. Committee on Resources. *Coastal Heritage Trail*
Route in New Jersey. 106th Cong., 1st sess. H. Rept. 16. Washington: GPO,
1999. Print.

---. ---. Senate. Select Committee on Intelligence. *Report on the U.S.*
Intelligence Community's Prewar Intelligence Assessment of Iraq.
108th Cong., 1st sess. Washington: GPO, 2004. Print.

23. Published Proceedings of a Conference—MLA

Rocha, Luis Mateus, et al., eds. *Artificial Life X: Proceedings of the Tenth*
International Conference on the Simulation and Synthesis of Living
Systems. Bloomington, IN. 3–7 June 2006. Cambridge: MIT P, 2006. Print.

PERIODICAL PUBLICATIONS—PRINT VERSIONS

Citations for periodical articles contain three major parts: author, title of article, and publication information. Figure 34.3 shows a citation for an article
from a scholarly journal (see item 27).

24. Signed Article in a Weekly or Biweekly Periodical—MLA

Brink, Susan. "Eat This Now!" *US News and World Report* 28 Mar. 2005: 56-58.
Print.

25. Signed Article in a Monthly or Bimonthly Periodical—MLA

Fallows, James. "The 1.4 Trillion Question." *The Atlantic* Jan.-Feb. 2008: 36-48.
Print.

26. Unsigned Article in a Periodical—MLA

"The Price Is Wrong." *Economist* 2 Aug. 2003: 58-59. Print.

27. Article in a Scholarly Journal—MLA

Both volume and issue number are provided for readers who will use online
databases to find and read the source.

MLA

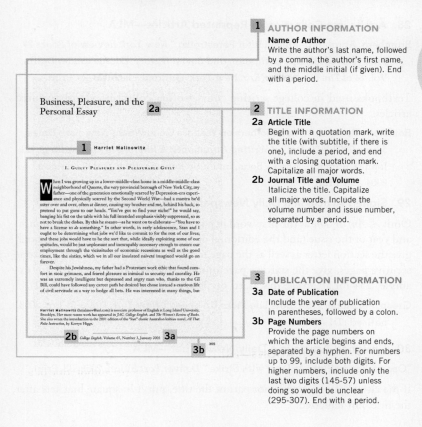

1 AUTHOR INFORMATION

Name of Author
Write the author's last name, followed by a comma, the author's first name, and the middle initial (if given). End with a period.

2 TITLE INFORMATION

2a Article Title
Begin with a quotation mark, write the title (with subtitle, if there is one), include a period, and end with a closing quotation mark. Capitalize all major words.

2b Journal Title and Volume
Italicize the title. Capitalize all major words. Include the volume number and issue number, separated by a period.

3 PUBLICATION INFORMATION

3a Date of Publication
Include the year of publication in parentheses, followed by a colon.

3b Page Numbers
Provide the page numbers on which the article begins and ends, separated by a hyphen. For numbers up to 99, include both digits. For higher numbers, include only the last two digits (145-57) unless doing so would be unclear (295-307). End with a period.

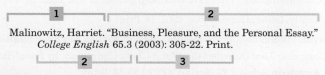

Malinowitz, Harriet. "Business, Pleasure, and the Personal Essay." *College English* 65.3 (2003): 305-22. Print.

Figure 34.3 Locating and citing source information for a journal article

Adler-Kassner, Linda, and Heidi Estrem. "Rethinking Research Writing: Public Literacy in the Composition Classroom." *WPA: Writing Program Administration* 26.3 (2003): 119–31. Print.

MLA

28. Article in a Collection of Reprinted Articles—MLA

Brumberg, Abraham. "Russia after Perestroika." *New York Review of Books* 27 June 1991: 53–62. Rpt. in *Russian and Soviet History*. Ed. Alexander Dallin. Vol. 14 of *The Gorbachev Era*. New York: Garland, 1992. 300–20. Print.

Textbooks used in college writing courses often collect previously printed articles.

Rothstein, Richard. "When Mothers on Welfare Go to Work." *New York Times* 5 June 2002: A20. Rpt. in *Writing Arguments: A Rhetoric with Readings*. Ed. John D. Ramage, John C. Bean, and June Johnson. New York: Longman, 2004. 263. Print.

29. Signed Article in a Daily Newspaper—MLA

Omit *A, An,* or *The* as the first word in a newspaper title. Give the day, month, and year of the issue (and the edition, if applicable). If sections are designated, give the section letter as well as the page number. If an article runs on nonconsecutive pages, give the starting page number followed by a plus sign (for example, *23+* for an article that starts on page 23 and continues on page 42).

Green, Penelope. "The Slow Life Picks Up Speed." *New York Times* 31 Jan. 2008, natl. ed.: D1+. Print.

30. Unsigned Article in a Daily Newspaper—MLA

"Oscars Ready Plans to Deal with Strike." *Denver Post* 31 Jan. 2008: B3. Print.

If the city of publication is not part of the title, put it in square brackets after the title, not italicized.

31. Editorial, Letter to the Editor, or Review—MLA

After the author's name or title, provide information about the type of publication.

"Primary Considerations." Editorial. *Washington Post* 27 Jan. 2008: B6. Print.

Finanger, Emily. Letter. *Outside* Feb. 2008: 14. Print.

Shenk, David. "Toolmaker, Brain Builder." Rev. of *Beyond Big Blue: Building the Computer That Defeated the World Chess Champion*, by Feng-Hsiung Hsu. *American Scholar* 72 (Spring 2003): 150–52. Print.

32. Article in a Looseleaf Collection of Reprinted Articles—MLA

Give the citation for the original publication first, followed by the citation for the collection.

Hayden, Thomas. "The Age of Robots." *US News and World Report* 23 Apr. 2001, 44+. Print. *Applied Science 2002*. Ed. Eleanor Goldstein. Boca Raton: SIRS, 2002. Art. 66.

33. Abstract in a Collection of Abstracts—MLA

To cite an abstract, first give information for the full work: the author's name, the title of the article, and publication information about the full article. If a reader could not know that the cited material is an abstract, write the word *Abstract,* not italicized, followed by a period. Give publication information about the collection of abstracts. For abstracts identified by item numbers rather than page numbers, use the word *item* before the item number.

Marcus, Hazel R., and Shinobu Kitayamo. "Culture and the Self: Implications
    for Cognition, Emotion, and Motivation." *Psychological Review* 88 (1991):
    224–53. *Psychological Abstracts* 78 (1991): item 23878. Print.

PERIODICALS—ONLINE VERSIONS FROM SUBSCRIPTION SERVICES

Online periodicals fall into two categories: (1) those you access through a DATABASE or subscription service paid for by your library or company, such as EBSCO or FirstSearch, or an online service to which you personally subscribe (examples 34–38); and (2) those you access directly by entering a specific URL (examples 39–44). Of course, many other online sources are not from periodicals; we explain them in examples 45–75.

Alert: Online periodical articles are frequently available in both "HTML" (hypertext mark-up language) and "PDF" (portable document format) versions. If you have the choice, use the PDF version because they show exactly how the article appears in print, including page numbers, images, and so on. As a result, PDFs are easier to cite. ●

34. Subscription Service: Article with a Print Version—MLA

Jackson, Gabriel. "Multiple Historic Meanings of the Spanish Civil War."
    Science and Society 68.3 (2004): 272–76. *Academic Search Elite*. Web.
    7 Mar. 2005.

VandeHei, Jim. "Two Years after White House Exit, Clinton Shaping
    Democratic Party." *Washington Post* 21 June 2003, final ed.: A1. *Academic*
    Universe. Web. 5 May 2005.

Figure 34.4 (p. 232) illustrates citing an article that has a print version but has been accessed through a subscription service.

35. Subscription Service: Material with No Print Version—MLA

Siemens, Raymond G. "A New Computer-Assisted Literary Criticism?"
    Computers and the Humanities 36.3 (2002): n. pag. America Online. Web.
    12 Nov. 2002.

MLA

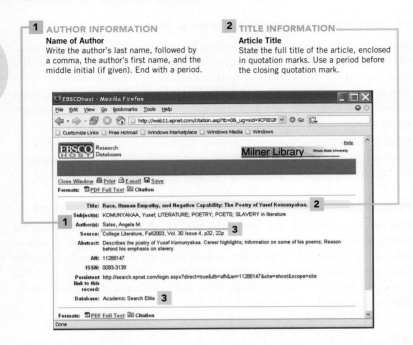

1 AUTHOR INFORMATION

Name of Author
Write the author's last name, followed by a comma, the author's first name, and the middle initial (if given). End with a period.

2 TITLE INFORMATION

Article Title
State the full title of the article, enclosed in quotation marks. Use a period before the closing quotation mark.

3 PUBLICATION INFORMATION

3a Name of Periodical
Provide the journal title (italicized).

3b Volume and Issue Numbers
Leave one space after the journal title and provide the volume and issue numbers, separated by a period.

3c Date of Publication
Provide the year of publication, in parentheses, followed by a colon.

3d Page Numbers
Provide the inclusive page numbers for the complete article, not just the portion you used. End with a period.

3e Title of Database
Italicize the name of the database. End with a period.

3f Medium of Publication
Provide the medium of publication consulted (*Web*), followed by a period.

3g Date of Access
Provide the day, month, and year that you accessed the article online. End with a period.

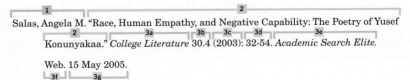

Salas, Angela M. "Race, Human Empathy, and Negative Capability: The Poetry of Yusef Konunyakaa." *College Literature* 30.4 (2003): 32-54. *Academic Search Elite.* Web. 15 May 2005.

Figure 34.4 Locating and citing source information for a journal found in an online database

36. Subscription Service: Abstract with a Print Version—MLA

Marcus, Hazel R., and Shinobu Kitayamo. "Culture and the Self: Implications
    for Cognition, Emotion, and Motivation." *Psychological Abstracts* 78 (1991).
    PsycINFO. Web. 10 Apr. 2004.

This entry is for the same abstract shown in item 34, but here it is accessed from
an online database (*PsycINFO*) by means of a library subscription service. The
date the source was accessed is 10 Apr. 2004.

37. Subscription Service Access with a Keyword: Article in a Periodical with a Print Version—MLA

Electronic versions of sources that also appear in print start with information
about the print version. Here is an entry for a journal article accessed through
a computer service; it also has a print version.

Wynne, Clive D. L. "'Willy' Didn't Yearn to Be Free." Editorial. *New York Times*
    27 Dec. 2003: n. pag. *New York Times Online*. America Online. Web. 29
    Dec. 2003. Keyword: nytimes.

Information applying to the print version of this article in the *New York Times*
ends with the publication date, and information about the online version starts
with the title of the database, *New York Times Online. America Online* is the service through which the database was accessed, and 29 Dec. 2003 is the access
date. The keyword *nytimes* was used to access *New York Times Online*.

38. Subscription Service Access Showing a Path—MLA

When you access a source by choosing a series of keywords, menus, or topics,
end the entry with the "path" of words you used. Use semicolons between items
in the path, and put a period at the end.

Futrelle, David. "A Smashing Success." *Money.com* 23 Dec. 1999. America
    Online. Web. 26 Dec. 1999. Path: Personal Finance; Business News;
    Business Publications; Money.com.

PERIODICALS—ONLINE VERSIONS ACCESSED DIRECTLY

You can access some online versions of periodicals directly, without going
through a paid subscription service. Newspapers and magazines often publish
some of their articles from each issue online this way. Often, however, you can't
access every single article—or any older articles—without being a subscriber.

39. Online Version of a Print Magazine Article—MLA

The example is for the online version of the same article cited in 25, above. In
addition to the print information, include the date you accessed the online

MLA

version. (If the page numbers from the print version are available, include them, too, after the publication date.)

Fallows, James. "The $1.4 Trillion Question." *The Atlantic.com*. Atlantic
 Monthly Group, Jan.-Feb. 2008. Web. 2 May 2008.

If the article is unsigned, begin with the title.

"Too Smart to Marry." *The Atlantic.com*. Atlantic Monthly Group, 14 Apr. 2005.
 Web. 7 Mar. 2005.

40. Online Version of a Print Journal Article—MLA

Hoge, Charles W., et al. "Mild Traumatic Brain Injury in U.S. Soldiers
 Returning from Iraq." *New England Journal of Medicine* 358.5 (2008):
 453-63. Web. 10 Sept. 2008.

41. Periodical Article Published Only Online—MLA

Many periodicals are published only online; others have "extra" online content that doesn't appear in print. Figure 34.5 illustrates how to cite an article that appears only online.

Ramirez, Eddy. "Comparing American Students with Those in China and
 India." *U.S. News and World Report*. U.S. News and World Report, 30 Jan.
 2008. Web. 4 Mar. 2008.

Shipka, Jody. "This Was (Not!!) an Easy Assignment." *Computers and
 Composition Online*. Computers and Composition Online, Fall 2007.
 Web. 2 May 2008.

42. Online Version of a Print Newspaper Article—MLA

If the article is signed, begin with the author's name, last name first.

Wilson, Janet. "EPA Fights Waste Site near River." *Los Angeles Times*. Los
 Angeles Times, 5 Mar. 2005. Web. 7 Mar. 2005.

If the article is unsigned, begin with the article title.

"EBay to Cut 1,000 Jobs, Will Buy Bill Me Later." *SF Gate*. San Francisco
 Chronicle, 6 Oct. 2008. Web. 6 Oct. 2008.

43. Online Editorial or Letter to the Editor—MLA

"Garbage In, Garbage Out." Editorial. *Los Angeles Times*. Los Angeles Times,
 2 Feb. 2008. Web. 22 Mar. 2008.

Ennis, Heather B. Letter to the Editor. *U.S. News and World Report*. U.S. News
 and World Report, 20 Dec. 2007. Web. 22 Dec. 2007.

MLA

1 AUTHOR INFORMATION

Name of Author
Write the author's last name, followed by
a comma, the author's first name, and the
middle initial (if given). End with a period.

2 TITLE INFORMATION

Article Title
State the full title of the article, enclosed
in quotation marks. Use a period before
the closing quotation mark.

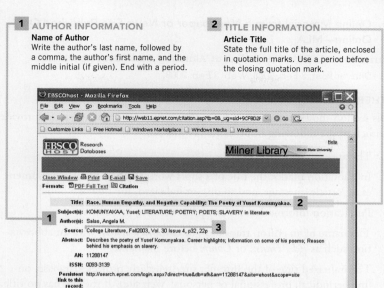

3 PUBLICATION INFORMATION

3a Name of Periodical
Provide the journal title (italicized).

3b Volume and Issue Numbers
Leave one space after the journal title
and provide the volume and issue numbers,
separated by a period.

3c Date of Publication
Provide the year of publication, in
parentheses, followed by a colon.

3d Page Numbers
Provide the inclusive page numbers for the
complete article, not just the portion you
used. End with a period.

3e Title of Database
Italicize the name of the database. End with
a period.

3f Medium of Publication
Provide the medium of publication consulted
(*Web*), followed by a period.

3g Date of Access
Provide the day, month, and year that you
accessed the article online. End with a period.

Salas, Angela M. "Race, Human Empathy, and Negative Capability: The Poetry of Yusef
Konunyakaa." *College Literature* 30.4 (2003): 32-54. *Academic Search Elite.*

Web. 15 May 2005.

Figure 34.5 Locating and citing source information for a journal article published only online

44. Online Material from a Newspaper or News Site Published Only Online—MLA

Harris, Edward. "Rain Forests Fall at 'Alarming' Rate." *denverpost.com.*
Denver Post, 3 Feb. 2008. Web. 3 Feb. 2008.

OTHER INTERNET SOURCES

This section shows models for other online sources. For such sources, provide as much of the following information as you can.

1. The author's name, if given.

2. In quotation marks, the title of a short work (Web page, brief document, essay, article, message, and so on); or italicized, the title of a book.

3. Publication information for any print version, if it exists.

4. The name of an editor, translator, or compiler, if any, with an abbreviation such as *Ed., Trans.,* or *Comp.* before the name.

5. The italicized title of the Internet site (scholarly project, database, online periodical, professional or personal Web site). If the site has no title, describe it: for example, *Home page.*

6. The date of electronic publication (including a version number, if any) or posting or the most recent update.

7. The name of a sponsoring organization, if any.

8. The medium of publication: Web.

9. The date you accessed the material.

10. The URL in angle brackets (< >), only when the reader probably could not locate the source without it. If you must break a URL at the end of a line, break only after a slash and do not use a hyphen.

45. Online Book—MLA

Chopin, Kate. *The Awakening.* 1899. *PBS Electronic Library.* 10 Dec. 1998. PBS.
Web. 13 Nov. 2004.

46. Online Book in a Scholarly Project—MLA

Herodotus. *The History of Herodotus.* Trans. George Rawlinson. 1947. *Internet Classics Archive.* Ed. Daniel C. Stevenson. 11 Jan. 1998. MIT. Web. 15 May 2006.

47. Online Government-Published Book—MLA

Start with the name of the government or government body, and then name the government agency, the title, the work's author (if known), the publication date, the medium of publication, the access date, and, if the reader needs it, the URL.

United States. Cong. Research Service. *Space Stations*. By Marcia S. Smith. 12 Dec. 1996. Web. 4 Dec. 2007.

MLA also permits an alternative format, with the author's name first, then title, then government body.

Huff, C. Ronald. *Comparing the Criminal Behavior of Youth Gangs and At-Risk Youths*. United States. Dept. of Justice. Natl. Inst. of Justice. Oct. 1998. Web. 5 Aug. 2008.

48. Professional Home Page—MLA

Provide as much of the following information as you can find as well as the medium of publication.

1. The name of the person who created or put up the home page. If first and last names are given, reverse the order of the first author's name.

2. For a professional home page, the name of the sponsoring organization.

3. The date you accessed the material.

Association for the Advancement of Artificial Intelligence. Web. 17 Mar. 2008.

49. Personal Home Page—MLA

Follow guidelines for professional home pages, with the following changes. Give the name of the person who created the page, last name first. Include the page's title, if there is one, italicized; if there is no title, add the description *Home page,* not italicized, followed by a period.

Hesse, Doug. Home page. Web. 1 Nov. 2007 <http://portfolio.du.edu/dhesse>.

50. Page from a Web Site—MLA

Provide as much information as you can (see Figure 34.6).

"Protecting Whales from Dangerous Sonar." *National Resources Defense Council*. NRDC, 9 Nov. 2005. Web. 12 Dec. 2005.

"Abridged History." *Maine Organic Farmers and Gardeners Association*. Maine Organic Farmers and Gardeners Assn., 2007. Web. 13 Dec. 2007.

51. Entire Internet Site—MLA

WebdelSol.Com. Ed. Michael Neff. 2008. Web. 4 Aug. 2008.

52. Academic Department Home Page—MLA

Write the name of the academic department, followed by the words *Dept. home page.* (Do not put any words in quotations or in italics.) Also include the name of the institution, the medium of publication, and the date you accessed the page.

Writing. Dept. home page. Grand Valley State U. Web. 26 Feb. 2008.

1 TITLE

Title of the Work
State the full title of the work cited, enclosed in quotation marks. Use a period before the closing quotation mark.

2 PUBLICATION INFORMATION

2a Title of the Overall Web Site
Provide the title of the Web site (italicized), followed by a period.

2b Publisher or Sponsor of the Web Site
Leave one space after the title of the overall Web site and provide the publisher or sponsor of the Web site. If this information is not available, use *N.p.* End with a comma.

2c Date of Publication
Provide the available date (day, month, and year) of publication, followed by a period. If no date is available, use *n.d.*

2d Medium of Publication
Provide the medium of publication consulted (*Web*), followed by a period.

2e Date of Access
Provide the day, month, and year that you accessed the article online. End with a period.

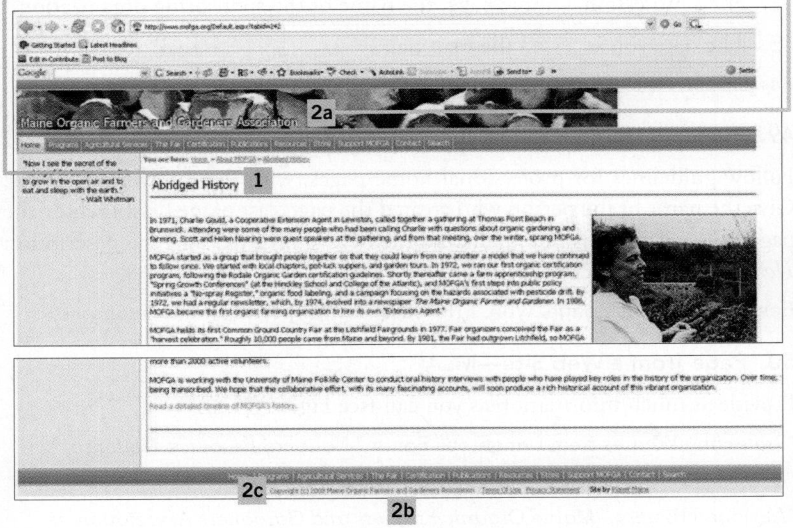

"Abridged History." *Maine Organic Farmers and Gardeners Association.* Maine Organic Farmers and Gardeners Assn., 2008. Web. 13 Feb. 2008.

Figure 34.6 Locating and citing source information for a Web page

53. Course Home Page—MLA

St. Germain, Sheryl. Myths and Fairytales: From *Inanna* to *Edward Scissorhands*. Course home page. Summer 2003. Dept. of English, Iowa State U. Web. 20 Feb. 2005. <http://www.public.iastate.edu/ ~sgermain/531.homepage.html>.

54. Government or Institutional Web Site—MLA

Home Education and Private Tutoring. Pennsylvania Department of Education, 2005. Web. 5 Aug. 2008.

55. Online Poem—MLA

Browning, Elizabeth Barrett. "Past and Future." *Women's Studies Database Reading Room*. U of Maryland. Web. 9 June 2003.

56. Online Work of Art—MLA

van Gogh, Vincent. *The Starry Night*. 1889. Museum of Mod. Art, New York. Web. 5 Dec. 2003. Keyword: Starry Night.

In this example, the keyword "Starry Night" is what a researcher types into a search box at the museum's Web site.

57. Online Image or Photograph—MLA

As with images from print publications (see item 88), include information about the photographer and title, if known. Otherwise, describe the photograph briefly and give information about the Web site, the medium of publication, and the access date.

Bourke-White, Margaret. "Fort Peck Dam, Montana." 1936. Gelatin silver print. Metropolitan Museum of Art, New York. Web. 5 Aug. 2008.

58. Online Interview—MLA

Pope, Carl. Interview by Amy Standen. *Salon.com*. Salon Media Group, 29 Apr. 2002. Web. 27 Jan. 2005.

59. Online Video or Film Clip—MLA

Reeves, Matt, dir. *Cloverfield*. Trailer. Bad Robot, 2008. Web. 18 Jan. 2008.

60. Online Cartoon—MLA

Harris, Sidney. "We have lots of information technology." Cartoon. *New Yorker* 27 May 2002. Web. 9 Feb. 2007.

61. Online Television or Radio Program—MLA

Chayes, Sarah. "Concorde." *All Things Considered.* Natl. Public Radio. 26 July
2000. Web. 7 Dec. 2001.

62. Online Discussion Posting—MLA

Give the author's name (if any), the title of the message in quotation marks, and
then *Online posting.* Give the date of the posting and the name of the bulletin
board, if any. Then give the publication medium, the access date and, in angle
brackets, the URL if needed.

Firrantello, Larry. "Van Gogh on Prozac." Online posting. 23 May 2005. *Salon
Table Talk.* Web. 7 June 2005. <http://tabletalk.salon.com/
webx?50@931.xC34anLmwOq.1@.773b2ad1>.

Be cautious about using online postings as sources. Some postings contain
cutting-edge information from experts, but some contain trash. Unfortunately,
it is nearly impossible to find out whether people online are who they claim
to be.

63. Real-Time Communication—MLA

Give the name of the speaker or writer, a title for the event (if any), the forum,
date, publication medium, access date, and URL if needed.

Berzsenyi, Christyne. Online discussion of "Writing to Meet Your Match: Rhetoric,
Perceptions, and Self-Presentation for Four Online Daters." *Computers and
Writing Online.* 13 May 2007. AcadianaMoo. Web. 13 May 2007.

64. E-Mail Message—MLA

Start with the name of the person who wrote the e-mail message. Give the
title or subject line in quotation marks. Then describe the message, including
the recipient's name. Add the date. Finally, write the medium of delivery
(*E-mail*).

Thompson, Jim. "Bob Martin's Opinions." Message to June Cain. 11 Nov. 2004.
E-mail.

65. Part of an Online Book—MLA

Teasdale, Sara. "Driftwood." *Flame and Shadow.* Ed. A. Light. N.p., 1920.
Project Gutenberg. 1 July 1996. Web. 18 Aug. 2008.

66. Online Review—MLA

Travers, Peter. Rev. of *No Country for Old Men,* dir. Joel Coen and Ethan
Coen. *RollingStone.* Rolling Stone, 1 Nov. 2007. Web. 25 Nov. 2007.

67. Online Abstract—MLA

Avery, Christopher, et al. "A Revealed Preference Ranking of U.S. Colleges and Universities." NBER Working Paper No. W10803. Oct. 2004. Abstract. Web. 2 Oct. 2008.

68. Posting on a Blog—MLA

McLemee, Scott. "To Whom It May Concern." *Quick Study*. 1 Jan. 2008. Web. 14 May 2008.

69. Online Sound Recording or Clip—MLA

Komunyakaa, Yusef. "My Father's Love Letters." *Poets.org Listening Booth*. Academy of American Poets, 5 May 1993. Web. 19 Aug. 2008.

70. Online Advertisement—MLA

Samsung. Advertisement. *RollingStone*. 8 Nov. 2005. Web.

71. Online Manuscript or Working Paper—MLA

deGrandpre, Andrew. "Baseball Destined to Die in Hockey Town." 2002. Unpublished article. Web. 7 Mar. 2005.

72. Podcast—MLA

A podcast is an audio recording that is posted online. Thus, the publication medium is *Web*. Include as much of the following information as you can identify: author, title, sponsoring organization or Web site, date posted, and date accessed.

"Business Marketing with Podcast: What Marketing Professionals Should Know." *Podblaze*. The Info Gurus, 13 Oct. 2005. Web. 19 Oct. 2005.

73. Online Slide Show—MLA

Erickson, Britta, narr. *Visionaries from the New China*. July 2007. Web. 11 Sept. 2008.

74. Online Photo Essay—MLA

Nachtwey, James. "Crime in Middle America." *Time* 2 Dec. 2006. Web. 5 May 2007.

75. Online Map, Chart, or Other Graphic—MLA

"Hurricane Rita." Graphic. *New York Times Online*. New York Times. 24 Sept. 2005. Web. 24 Sept. 2005.

MLA

OTHER PRINT, NONPRINT, AND ELECTRONIC SOURCES

76. Published or Unpublished Letter—MLA

Begin the entry with the author of the letter. Note the recipient, too.

Irvin, William. Letter to Lesley Osburn. 7 Dec. 2007. Print.

Williams, William Carlos. Letter to his son. 13 Mar. 1935. *Letters of the Century:*
    America 1900–1999. Ed. Lisa Grunwald and Stephen J. Adler. New York:
    Dial, 1999: 225–26. Print.

77. Microfiche Collection of Articles—MLA

A microfiche is a transparent sheet of film (a *fiche*) with microscopic printing
that needs to be read through a special magnifier. Each fiche holds several pages,
with each page designated by a grid position. A long document may appear on
more than one fiche.

Wenzell, Ron. "Businesses Prepare for a More Diverse Work Force." *St. Louis*
    Post Dispatch 3 Feb. 1990: 17. Microform. *NewsBank: Employment* 27 (1990):
    fiche 2, grid D12.

78. Map or Chart—MLA

Colorado Front Range Mountain Bike Topo Map. Map. Nederland: Latitude 40,
    2001. Print.

79. Report or Pamphlet—MLA

Use the format for books, to the extent possible.

National Commission on Writing in America's Schools and Colleges. *The*
    Neglected "R": The Need for a Writing Revolution. New York: College
    Board, 2003. Print.

80. Legal Source—MLA

Include the name of the case, the number of the case (preceded by *No.*), the
name of the court deciding the case, and the date of the decision.

Brown v. Board of Ed. No. 8. Supreme Ct. of the US. 8 Oct. 1952. Print.

81. Interview—MLA

Note the type of interview, for example "Telephone" or "Personal" (face-to-
face). For a published interview, give the name of the interviewed person first,
identify the source as an interview, and then give details as for any published
source: title; author, preceded by the word *By;* and publication details.

Friedman, Randi. Telephone interview. 30 Aug. 2008.

Winfrey, Oprah. "Ten Questions for Oprah Winfrey." By Richard Zoglin. *Time*
15 Dec. 2003: 8. Print.

82. Lecture, Speech, or Address—MLA

Kennedy, John Fitzgerald. Greater Houston Ministerial Assn. Rice Hotel,
Houston. 12 Sept. 1960. Address.

83. Film, Videotape, or DVD—MLA

Give the title first, and include the director, the distributor, and the year. For
older films that were subsequently released on tape or DVD, provide the original release date of the movie *before* the type of medium. For video downloads,
include the download date and the source. Other information (writer, producer, major actors) is optional but helpful. Put first names first.

It Happened One Night. Screenplay by Robert Riskin. Dir. and Prod. Frank Capra.
Perf. Clark Gable and Claudette Colbert. 1934. Sony Pictures, 1999. DVD.

84. Musical Recording—MLA

Put first the name most relevant to what you discuss in your paper (performer,
conductor, work performed). Include the recording's title, the medium for any
recording other than a CD (*LP, Audiocassette*), the name of the issuer, and the
year the work was issued.

Smetana, Bedrich. *My Country.* Czech Philharmonic Orch. Cond. Karel Anserl.
LP. Vanguard, 1975. CD.

Radiohead. "Jigsaw Falling into Place." *In Rainbows.* Radiohead, 2007. MP3 file.

85. Live Performance (Play, Concert, etc.)—MLA

All My Sons. By Arthur Miller. Dir. Calvin McLean. Center for the Performing
Arts, Normal, IL. 27 Sept. 2005. Performance.

86. Work of Art, Photograph, or Musical Composition—MLA

Cassatt, Mary. *La Toilette.* 1890. Oil on canvas. Art Institute of Chicago.

Mydans, Carl. *General Douglas MacArthur Landing at Luzon, 1945.* Gelatin
silver print. Soho Triad Fine Art Gallery, New York. 21 Oct.-28 Nov. 1999.

Italicize any musical work that has a title, such as an opera, a ballet, or a named
symphony.

Schubert, Franz. *Unfinished Symphony.* Print.

Don't underline or put in quotation marks music identified only by form, number, and key.

Schubert, Franz. Symphony no. 8 in B minor. Print.

To cite a published score, use the following format.

Schubert, Franz. *Symphony in B Minor (Unfinished)*. Ed. Martin Cusid. New
York: Norton, 1971. Print.

87. Television or Radio Program—MLA

Include at least the title of the program (in italics), the network, the local station and its city, and the date of the broadcast.

*Not for Ourselves Alone: The Story of Elizabeth Cady Stanton and Susan B.
Anthony*. By Ken Burns. Perf. Julie Harris, Ronnie Gilbert, and Sally
Kellerman. Prod. Paul Barnes and Ken Burns. PBS. WNET, New York.
8 Nov. 1999. Television.

For a series, also supply the title of the specific episode (in quotation marks) before the title of the program (italicized) and the title of the series (neither underlined nor in quotation marks).

88. Image or Photograph in a Print Publication—MLA

Give the photographer (if known), the title or caption of the image, and complete publication information, as for an article. If the image has no title, provide a brief description.

Greene, Herb. "Grace Slick." *Rolling Stone* 30 Sept. 2004: 102. Print.

89. Advertisement—MLA

American Airlines. Advertisement. ABC. 24 Aug. 2003. Television.

Canon Digital Cameras. Advertisement. *Time* 2 June 2003: 77. Print.

90. Video Game or Software—MLA

Guitar Hero III: Legends of Rock. Santa Monica: Activision, 2007. Game.

91. Nonperiodical Publications on CD, DVD, or Magnetic Tape—MLA

Citations for publications on DVD, CD-ROM, or other recording formats follow guidelines for print publications, with two additions: list the publication medium (for example, *CD*), and give the vendor's name.

Perl, Sondra. *Felt Sense: Guidelines for Composing*. Portsmouth: Boynton, 2004.
CD.

92. Materials on CD or DVD with a Print Version—MLA

"The Price Is Right." *Time* 20 Jan. 1992: 38. *Time Man of the Year*. CD-ROM. New
York: Compact, 1993.

Information for the print version ends with the article's page number, 38. The title of the CD-ROM is *Time Man of the Year*, its producer is the publisher Compact, and its copyright year is 1993. Both the title of the print publication and the title of the CD-ROM are italicized.

93. Materials on CD or DVD with No Print Version—MLA

"Artificial Intelligence." *Encarta 2003*. Redmond: Microsoft, 2003. CD-ROM.

Encarta 2003 is a CD-ROM encyclopedia with no print version. "Artificial Intelligence" is the title of an article in *Encarta 2003*.

94. Book in Digital Format—MLA

Many books are now available for downloading from the Internet in digital format, to be read on special players.

Gilbert, Elizabeth. *Eat, Pray, Love*. New York: Viking, 2007. Kindle Edition.

95. PowerPoint or Similar Presentation—MLA

Delyser, Ariel. "Political Movements in the Philippines." University of Denver.
7 Apr. 2006. PowerPoint.

96. Work in More Than One Publication Medium—MLA

Shamoon, Linda, et al., eds. *Coming of Age: The Advanced Writing Curriculum*.
Coming of Age Course Descriptions. Portsmouth: Boynton, 2000. Print,
CD-ROM.

This book and CD-ROM come together. Each has its own title, but the publication information—Portsmouth: Boynton, 2000—applies to both.

34c What are MLA guidelines for content or bibliographic notes?

In MLA style, footnotes or endnotes serve two specific purposes: (1) You can use them for ideas and information that do not fit into your paper but are still worth relating; and (2) you can use them for bibliographic information that would intrude if you were to include it in your text. See 35a for advice about formatting notes.

TEXT OF PAPER

Eudora Welty's literary biography, *One Writer's Beginnings*, shows us how both the inner world of self and the outer world of family and place form a writer's imagination.[1]

CONTENT NOTE—MLA

1. Welty, who valued her privacy, resisted investigation of her life. However, at the age of seventy-four, she chose to present her own autobiographical reflections in a series of lectures at Harvard University.

TEXT OF PAPER

Barbara Randolph believes that enthusiasm is contagious (65).[1] Many psychologists have found that panic, fear, and rage spread more quickly in crowds than positive emotions do, however.

BIBLIOGRAPHIC NOTE—MLA

1. Others who agree with Randolph include Thurman 21, 84, 155; Kelley 421-25; and Brookes 65-76.

For more help with your writing, grammar, and research, go to **www.mycomplab.com**

A Student's MLA-Style Research Paper

35a What are MLA format guidelines for research papers?

Check whether your instructor has special instructions for the final draft of your research paper. If there are no special instructions, you can use the MLA STYLE guidelines here. The student paper in 35b was prepared according to MLA guidelines.

■ General formatting instructions—MLA

Use 8½-by-11-inch white paper. Double-space throughout. Use a one-inch margin on the left, right, top, and bottom. Don't justify the type.

Drop down ½ inch from the top edge of the paper to the name-and-page-number line described below. Then drop down another 1/2 inch to the first line, whether that is a heading, a title, or a line of the text of your paper. For an example, see page 249.

Paragraph indents in the body of the paper and indents in Notes and Works Cited are 1/2 inch or about five characters. The indent in Microsoft Word is a hanging indent of 0.5″ for "first line." The indent for a set-off quotation (pp. 213–214) is 1 inch or about ten characters.

■ Order of parts—MLA

Use this order for the parts of your paper: body of the paper; endnotes, if any (headed "Notes," without quotation marks); Works Cited list; attachments, if any (such as questionnaires, data sheets, or any other material your instructor tells you to include). Number all pages consecutively.

■ Name-and-page-number line for all pages—MLA

Use a name-and-page-number line on every page of your paper, including the first, unless your instructor requires otherwise. Drop down ½ inch from the top edge of the sheet of paper. Type your last name, then a one-character space and the page number. Align the typed line about an inch from the right edge of the paper. Many writers take advantage of the word processing function that inserts last name and page numbers as a header.

■ First page—MLA

Use a name-and-page number line. MLA doesn't require a cover page but understands that some instructors do, in which case you should follow your instructor's prescribed format.

If your instructor does not require a cover page, use a four-line heading at the top of the first page. Drop down 1 inch from the top edge of the paper. Start each line at the left margin, and include the following information.

Your name (first line)

Your instructor's name (second line)

Your course name and section (third line)

The date you hand in your paper (fourth line)

For the submission date, use either day-month-year form (26 November 2005) or month-day-year style (November 26, 2005).

On the line below this heading, center the title of your paper. Don't underline the title or enclose it in quotation marks. On the line below the title, start your paper.

Capitalization Alerts: (1) Use a capital letter for the first word of your title and the first word of a subtitle, if you use one. Start every NOUN, PRONOUN, VERB, ADVERB, ADJECTIVE, and SUBORDINATING CONJUNCTION with a capital letter. Capitalize the last word of your title, no matter what part of speech it is. In a hyphenated compound word (two or more words used together to express one idea), capitalize every word that you would normally capitalize: Father-in-Law.

(2) Don't capitalize an article (*a, an, the*) unless one of the preceding capitalization rules applies to it. Don't capitalize any PREPOSITIONS, no matter how many letters they contain. Don't capitalize COORDINATING CONJUNCTIONS. Don't capitalize the word *to* used in an INFINITIVE. ●

■ Notes—MLA

If you use a note in your paper (p. 245), try to structure the sentence so that the note number falls at the end. The ideal place for a note number, which appears slightly raised above the line of words, is after the sentence-ending punctuation. Don't leave a space before the number. Word processing programs have commands for inserting "references" such as notes, and you'll want to choose endnotes rather than footnotes. If you use the references feature to insert a note, the program will generally open a box in which you type the words of your note. The program then saves all your notes together, in order.

Your notes should come on a separate page after the last page of the body of your paper and before the Works Cited list. You may have to cut and paste your notes file into the proper position. Center the word *Notes* at the top of the page, using the same 1-inch margin; don't underline it or enclose it in quotation marks.

Number the notes consecutively throughout the paper, except for notes accompanying tables or figures. Place table or figure notes below the table or illustration. Instead of note numbers, use raised lowercase letters: a, b, c.

■ Works Cited list—MLA

The Works Cited list starts on a new page that has the same name-and-page-number heading as the previous pages. One inch below the top edge of the paper, center the words "Works Cited." Don't underline them or put them in quotation marks.

One double space after the Works Cited heading, start the first entry in your list at the left margin. If an entry takes more than one line, indent each subsequent line after the first five characters (or ½ inch). Use no extra spacing between entries.

35b A student's MLA-style research paper

MLA style doesn't require an outline before a research paper. Nevertheless, many instructors want students to submit them. Most instructors prefer the standard traditional outline format that we discuss in 8h. Unless you're told otherwise, use that format.

Some instructors prefer what they consider a more contemporary outline format. Never use it unless it's explicitly assigned. It differs because it outlines the content of the INTRODUCTORY and CONCLUDING PARAGRAPHS, and full wording of the THESIS STATEMENT is placed in the outline of the introductory paragraph. We show an example of this type in the topic outline of Andrei Gurov's paper below.

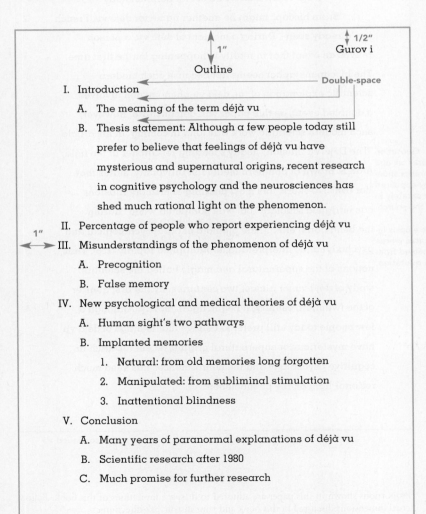

Gurov i

Outline

I. Introduction

    A. The meaning of the term déjà vu

    B. Thesis statement: Although a few people today still prefer to believe that feelings of déjà vu have mysterious and supernatural origins, recent research in cognitive psychology and the neurosciences has shed much rational light on the phenomenon.

II. Percentage of people who report experiencing déjà vu

III. Misunderstandings of the phenomenon of déjà vu

    A. Precognition

    B. False memory

IV. New psychological and medical theories of déjà vu

    A. Human sight's two pathways

    B. Implanted memories

        1. Natural: from old memories long forgotten

        2. Manipulated: from subliminal stimulation

        3. Inattentional blindness

V. Conclusion

    A. Many years of paranormal explanations of déjà vu

    B. Scientific research after 1980

    C. Much promise for further research

MLA

↑ ½"

↑ 1"
↓

Use 1/2-inch   Gurov 1   1
top margin,
1-inch bottom
and side
margins;
double-space
throughout.

Andrei Gurov

Professor Ryan

English 101, Section A4

12 December 2007

Put identifying
information in
upper left corner.

Center title.   Déjà Vu: At Last a Subject for Serious Study

"Brain hiccup" might be another name for *déjà vu*, French   2

for "already seen." During a moment of déjà vu, a person

relives an event that in reality is happening for the first time.

The hiccup metaphor seems apt because each modern

scientific explanation of the déjà vu phenomenon involves

a doubled event, as this paper will demonstrate. However,

such modern scientific work was long in coming. In his article

Quotation "The Déjà Vu Illusion," today's leading researcher in the field,

marks around

phrases show Alan S. Brown at Southern Methodist University, states that

they appeared "for over 170 years, this most puzzling of memory illusions

separately in

the source. has intrigued scholars" but was hampered when "during

The ellipsis in-the behaviorist era . . . the plethora of parapsychological and

dicates words

omitted from psychodynamic interpretations" multiplied rapidly (256). Thus,   3

a quotation. notions of the supernatural and magic halted the scientific

study of déjà vu for almost two centuries. By the first quarter

of the twentieth century, it began again slowly. Although a   4

few people today still prefer to believe that feelings of déjà vu

have mysterious or supernatural origins, recent research in

cognitive psychology and the neurosciences has shed much

rational light on the phenomenon.

continued >>

(Proportions shown in this paper are adjusted to fit space limitations of this book. Follow
actual dimensions discussed in this book and your instructor's directions.)

MLA

COMMENTARY

1 **Computer tip.** Following MLA style, Andrei uses his last name and the page number as a header (meaning "at the top" of his pages) throughout the paper. He doesn't use a footer (meaning "at the bottom" of his pages). To do this, he accesses the "header and footer" option in the "View" choice on the toolbar in his Microsoft Word word processing program and inserts the proper information so that it will appear automatically on each page.

2 **Introductory strategy.** Andrei hopes to attract his readers' interest by making up the unusual phrase "brain hiccups," which ties into the dual visual processing that he describes later in his paper. He also refers briefly to the paranormal and immediately discredits it by quoting the leading modern researcher into déjà vu, Alan S. Brown.

3 **PROCESS NOTE:** I use a quotation from Brown's journal article "The Déjà Vu Illusion," so I include the page number in parentheses.

4 **Thesis statement.** The last sentence of Andrei's introductory paragraph is his THESIS STATEMENT. He had drafted two preliminary thesis statements. The thesis statement is a bridge from his introduction to the rest of his paper and helps his readers anticipate the main message of his paper. All of his topic sentences have to tie into his thesis statement.

MLA

Gurov 2

Some people report never having experienced déjà vu, and the percentages vary for the number of people who report having lived through at least one episode of it. In 2004, Brown reports that of the subjects he has interviewed, an average of 66 percent say that they have had one or more déjà vu experiences during their lives (*Experience* 33). However, in early 2005 in "Strangely Familiar," Uwe Wolfradt reports that "various studies indicate that from 50 to 90 percent of the people [studied] can recall having had at least one such déjà vu incident in their lives."

Perhaps part of the reason for this variation in the range of percentages stems from a general misunderstanding of the phrase *déjà vu*, even by some of the earlier scientific researchers twenty or more years ago. Indeed, in today's society, people throw around the term *déjà vu* without much thought. For example, it is fairly common for someone to see or hear about an event and then say, "Wow. This is déjà vu. I had a dream that this exact same thing happened." However, dreaming about an event ahead of time is a different phenomenon known as *precognition*, which relates to the paranormal experience of extrasensory perception. To date, precognition has never been scientifically demonstrated. As Johnson explains about dreams, however,

> . . . there is usually very little "data," evidence, or documentation to confirm that a Precognition has taken place. If a person learns about some disaster and THEN [author's emphasis] tells people that he/she has foreseen it the day before, that may or may not

continued >>

5 **Summarizing and citing a source by an author of two different sources used in this paper.** Andrei summarizes the percentage information that Brown gives in his book *The Déjà Vu Experience.* Then Andrei cites his source with a shortened title and page number. He includes a title because he has been drawing on two of Brown's writings for this paper—one book and one journal article that he accesses online—and he knows that he needs to make a clear distinction between them whenever he cites them.

6 **The writer inserting words to fit a quotation into the writer's sentence.** Nothing is wrong with Uwe Wolfradt's sentence, but Andrei needs to add the word *studied* to make the meaning clear within his research paper. To do this in proper MLA form, Andrei put his added word in brackets to indicate that he is adding the word—that is, the word is not in the original text by Uwe Wolfradt.

7 **Figuring out a page number from an online source.** Andrei found the article "Strangely Familiar" by Uwe Wolfradt online using Google Scholar at http://www.googlescholar.com. Even though the citation for the article on the opening screen page says that the page spread is pages 32–37, and Andrei might feel quite safe in assuming that his information is on the first page—namely, page 32—he can't be sure, so he can't include a page number.

8 **PROCESS NOTE:** I kept being distracted about using the word *déjà vu* as a term or as the name of an experience. As I was drafting, I purposely overlooked the problem, but I circled each use so that I could tackle the issue on my final draft.

9 **PROCESS NOTE:** I'm fairly certain that my instructor will know that this quotation is not from a source, but it's rather one I made up from everyday speech.

10 **No capital letter to start block-indented quotation.** Andrei took this quotation from the middle of a sentence in the source, so he can't start it with a capital letter. The ellipsis indicates he omitted words to make the quotation fit stylistically.

11 **How "[author's emphasis]" is used.** Whenever a source uses a typographical technique of emphasis—such as italics or all capital letters—the writer who quotes that source is required to indicate that the emphasis belongs to the source, not to the writer. In MLA style, "[author's emphasis]" is required so that the reader won't think the emphasis has been added by the writer of the paper.

MLA

Gurov 3

be true, because there is usually not corroborative   12
confirmation of what the person claims.

Thus, precognition, a phenomenon talked about frequently but one that has never held up under scientific scrutiny, is definitely not the same as déjà vu.

False memory is another phenomenon mislabeled *déjà vu*. It happens when people are convinced that certain events took place in their lives, even though the events never happened. This occurs when people have strong memories of many unrelated occurrences that suddenly come together into a whole that's very close to the current experience. It seems like a déjà vu experience. This occurs from the

> converging elements of many different but related
> experiences. When this abstract representation,
> which has emerged strictly from the melding
> together of strongly associated elements, happens
> to correspond to the present experience, a déjà vu
> may be the outcome. (Brown, *Experience* 160).   13

To illustrate lab-induced false memory, Brown in *The Déjà Vu*   14
Experience cites investigations in which subjects are shown lists of words related to sleep; however, the word *sleep* itself is not on the list. In recalling the list of words, most subjects insist that the word *sleep* was indeed on the list, which means that the memory of a word that was never there is false memory. This is exactly what happens when well-intentioned eyewitnesses believe they recall certain criminal acts even though, in fact, they never saw or experienced the events at all (159).

In the last twenty years especially, new theories have come to the fore as a result of rigorous work from psychological and medical points of view. In *Experience,* Brown surveys the   15

Introductory phrase smoothly leads into direct quotation.

Put only page number in parentheses when author is named in text.

continued >>

12 **MLA style for a block-indent quotation.** MLA style requires that when a quotation takes up more than four lines in a research paper that it be set off in a block. A block indent calls for all lines to be indented ten spaces from the left margin. The quotation's end punctuation, such as a period, is placed before the source information. Following the end punctuation, the source information is given in parentheses. Because Andrei's online source did not provide page, paragraphs, or screen numbers, he could not include a parenthetical citation after the quotation.

13 PROCESS NOTE: I want to use Brown in two different ways in this paragraph because I've drawn on Brown as a major reference throughout my paper. I don't want to only use quotations or only summaries. Here I use a quotation but don't call attention to the source. I place all source information in parentheses after the end of the quotation. I include a shortened version of the title of the source because I've used two different sources by the same author to write this paper.

14 **MLA treatment of titles.** MLA style requires that the first time a title is used in the writer's sentence (outside of a parenthetical citation), the title must be given in full, although the subtitle can be omitted. In subsequent references, a shortened form of the title can be used.

15 PROCESS NOTE: I now need to write a paragraph of transition from what was *not* déjà vu to what was. My plan is to write about two types of phenomena that aren't déjà vu, and then write about three types of phenomena that are. I checked my outline to make sure I was adhering to my plan.

MLA

Gurov 4

literature and concludes that this relatively young field of
investigation is dividing itself into four categories: (1) dual
processing, (2) memory, (3) neurological, and (4) attentional. This   16
paper briefly discusses the first and second as each relates to
the third. Next, I discuss the fourth as it relates to the second.

Brain-based studies of the human sense of sight are one
heavily researched theory of déjà vu that has been partially
explained in the last two decades. Such studies focus on the
dual pathways by which the sight of an event reaches the

**Put author
and page
number in
parentheses
when author is
not named in
the sentence.**

brain (Glenn; Carey F1). For example, the left hemisphere   17
processes information from the right eye and the right
hemisphere processes information from the left eye. The brain
is incapable of storing data with respect to time and is only
able to "see" events in relation to others. Each eye interprets
data separately, at the same precise time. According to
research, the human brain can perceive two visual stimuli at
one instant as long as they are "seen" less than 25 milliseconds   18
apart. Since the human brain is capable of interpreting both
signals within this time, when events are perceived normally,
they are seen and recognized by the brain as one single event

**Paragraph
summarizes
several pages
of source
material, as
parenthetical
citation
shows.**

(Weiten 69, 97-99, 211).

Occasionally, however, the neurological impulses that   19
carry data from each eye to the brain are delayed. As Johnson
explains, the person might be fatigued or have had his or her
attention seriously distracted (as when crossing the street at a
dangerous intersection). As a result, one signal may reach the
brain in under 25 milliseconds, while the other signal is slowed
and reaches the brain slightly more than 25 milliseconds later.
Even a few milliseconds' delay makes the second incoming
signal arrive late—and, without fail, the brain interprets the

continued >>

MLA

16 **PROCESS NOTE:** Every time I type the word *attentional* (using Microsoft Word) into my paper, a red wavy line pops up under it, which means a misspelling. However, because the word is spelled that way consistently in all my sources, I've just ignored the red wavy line and added the word, with confidence, to my personal dictionary provided by the Microsoft Word program.

17 **Two sources for one piece of information.** When two sources contain the same information, MLA style permits the citing of both sources. Each source is given with its page number; don't provide a page number if you're using a one-page source or an online source with no page numbers. A semicolon divides the sources.

18 **Words used in a nonliteral way.** The words *see* and *seen* here do not carry their literal meaning related to conscious sight. Rather, they refer to subconscious sight. Therefore, they belong in quotation marks.

19 **PROCESS NOTE:** Earlier in the paper, I devoted two paragraphs to each of two non-déjà vu topics. Now, I'm giving more attention to each of the three types of legitimate déjà vu phenomena that I've chosen to discuss (dual pathways of sight, implanted memories, and inattentional blindness). This paragraph is the second I'm writing about dual pathways of sight.

MLA

stimuli as two separate events rather than one event. The person thus has the sensation of having seen the event before because the brain has recognized the milliseconds-later event as a memory.

Implanted memories are another well-researched [20] explanation for the déjà vu phenomenon. Examples of implanted memories originate in both the natural and the lab-induced experiences of people. For instance, perhaps a person walks into the kitchen of a new friend for the first time and, although the person has never been there before, the person feels certain that he or she has. With hypnosis and other techniques, researchers could uncover that the cupboards are almost exactly like those that the person had forgotten were in the kitchen of the person's grandparents' house and that the scent of baking apple pie is identical to the smell the person loved when walking into the grandparents' home during holidays (Carey F1).

Thomas McHugh, a researcher at MIT, believes he has even discovered the specific "memory circuit" in the brain that is the source of this kind of déjà vu (Lemonick). This circuit allows people to complete memories with just a single cue. For example, you can remember much about a football game you saw even if someone just mentions the two teams involved. Sometimes, however, the circuit "misfires," and it signals that a new memory is actually part of the pattern of an old one.

Wolfradt describes a lab-induced experiment in which [21] psychologist Larry L. Jacoby in 1989 manipulated a group of subjects so that he could implant a memory that would lead to a déjà vu experience for each of them. He arranged for his subjects to assemble in a room equipped with a screen in front. He flashed on the screen one word so quickly that no one was

continued >>

20 **PROCESS NOTE:** I'm now starting to write about the second of the three types of déjà vu that I'm covering in this paper. I'm intentionally using the word *another* in my topic sentence to bridge from dual pathways of sight to implanted memories. Because there are so many concepts and examples of them in this paper, I'm trying to be very clear in my transitions.

21 **PROCESS NOTE:** Specific examples are very important to me as I write this paper. It's far too easy for me to write on and on about theory and concepts. As I'm writing this paper, I find myself often cutting generalizations to make room for details. When I've read my sophomore and junior friends' papers from when they were freshmen, I'm surprised to see how few specifics and concrete details they put in their freshman composition papers—and their grades and the comments they got reflect this fact.

MLA

Gurov 6

consciously aware they had seen the word. Jacoby was certain, however, that the visual centers of the brain of each subject had indeed "seen" the word. Later, when he flashed the word leaving it on the screen long enough for the subjects to consciously see it, everyone indicated they had seen the word somewhere before. All the subjects were firmly convinced that the first time they had seen the word, it absolutely was not on the screen at the front of the room they were in. Some became annoyed at being asked over and over. Since Jacoby's work, lab-induced memory research has become very popular in psychology. In fact, it has been given its own name: *priming*.

Inattention, or what some researchers call "inattentional blindness," is also an extensively researched explanation for the déjà vu experience. Sometimes people can see objects without any impediment right before them but still not process the objects because they're paying attention to something else (Brown, *Experience* 181). The distraction might be daydreaming, a sudden lowering of energy, or simply being drawn to another object in the environment. As David Glenn explains in "The Tease of Memory":

22

> Imagine that you drive through an unfamiliar town but pay little attention because you're talking on a cellphone [sic]. If you then drive back down the same streets a few moments later, this time focusing on the landscape, you might be prone to experience déjà vu. During your second pass, the visual information is consciously processed in the hippocampus [of the brain] but feels falsely "old"

23

continued >>

MLA

22 **PROCESS NOTE:** When I wrote my first draft, I felt that my discussion of implanted memories was pretty weak. I did some further research and was happy to find enough information to write this additional paragraph in my second draft. It is, to me, a dramatic demonstration of laboratory-manipulated implanted memory.

23 **Using [sic].** This quotation spells "cell phone" as one word. Therefore, Andrei uses [sic] to tell his readers that he knows this is a misspelling.

MLA

Gurov 7

because the images from your earlier drive still linger in your short term memory.   24

The busy lifestyle today would seem to lead to many distractions of perception and thus to frequent experiences of déjà vu; however, these are no more frequently reported than any other causes reported concerning déjà vu.

One compelling laboratory experiment studying   25 inattention is described by Carey in "Déjà Vu: If It All Seems Familiar, There May Be a Reason." He recounts a test with many college students from Duke University in Durham, North Carolina. The students were asked to look at a group of photographs of the campus of Southern Methodist University in Dallas, Texas, that were flashed before them at a very quick speed. A small black or white cross was superimposed on each photograph, and the students were instructed to find the cross and focus on it (F6). Brown in *Experience* explains that the researchers assumed that the quick speed at which the photographs had been shown would result in no one's having noticed the background scenes. A week's time passed, and the same students were shown the pictures again, this time without the crosses. Almost all insisted that they had been to the college campus shown in the photos, which was physically impossible for that many students since they lived in Durham, North Carolina, and the college in the photographs was in Dallas, Texas (182-83). This means that the scenes in the photographs did indeed register in the visual memories of the students in spite of the quick speed and the distraction of looking only for the crosses.

continued >>

24 **PROCESS NOTE:** Here's how I wasted a day of researching for this paper. I know it's not unusual for freshmen to go off the topic and waste their time, so I am trying to stay very conscious of what I am doing so that I can learn what NOT to do in the future. What happened was that I was becoming aware that psychologists have named many phenomena that are closely related to déjà vu, each somewhat different from it and from each other. For example, Brown in *Experience* names over twenty relatives of déjà vu, while other sources name as few as eight. This captured my interest, but once I got into writing up the information, I began to realize that I was going off my topic. I'll list here some that had potential but that, in the end, I never used in my paper:

- **Déjà eprouvé:** A sense that this act has already been attempted and didn't work out.

- **Déjà senti:** A mental feeling that one is *feeling* something again. It is limited to feeling, and does not include a sense of being in a place.

- **Déjà visité:** The knowledge of a large place, such as an entire village, but knowing still that one has never been there.

- **Jamais vu:** This is the opposite of déjà vu. Even though one knows something has happened before, the experience feels completely unfamiliar.

- **Presque vu:** This is the sense of almost, but not quite, remembering something—as in "it's on the tip of my tongue."

25 **PROCESS NOTE:** To stay on the topic, I needed a third type of déjà vu—for which I used inattentional blindness—to drive home my thesis statement.

MLA

Gurov 8

The worlds of psychology and neurology have learned
much since the age of paranormal interpretations of déjà vu
experiences, starting around 1935. That is when rational
science energetically began its disciplined investigations of
brain-based origins of the déjà vu phenomenon. Concepts
such as dual processing of sight, implanted memories, and
inattentional blindness, among other theories, have gone far in
opening the door to the possibilities of many more inventive
theories to explain incidents of déjà vu. The leading researcher
in the field today, Alan S. Brown, is among the strongest voices
urging a vast expansion of investigations into this still
relatively unexplored phenomenon. He is optimistic this will
happen, given his whimsical remark to Carlin Flora of
Psychology Today: "We are always fascinated when the
brain goes haywire."

26

Concluding paragraph summarizes paper.

continued >>

26 **PROCESS NOTE:** In my second draft, I decided to check whether all my topic sentences tied together with each other. I remembered that neither the introductory nor the concluding paragraphs have topic sentences. Here's a list of my thesis and topic sentences.

THESIS STATEMENT: Although a few people today still prefer to believe that feelings of déjà vu have mysterious or supernatural origins, recent research in cognitive psychology and the neurosciences has shed much rational light on the phenomenon.

- Some people report never having experienced déjà vu, and the percentages vary for the number of people who report having lived through at least one episode of it.

- Perhaps part of the reason for this variation in the range of percentages stems from a general misunderstanding of the phrase *déjà vu,* even by some of the earlier scientific researchers twenty or more years ago.

- False memory is another phenomenon mislabeled *déjà vu.*

- In the last twenty years especially, new theories have come to the fore as a result of rigorous work from psychological and medical points of view.

- Brain-based studies of the human sense of sight are one heavily researched theory of déjà vu that has been partially explained in the last two decades.

- Occasionally, however, the neurological impulses that carry data from each eye to the brain are delayed.

- Implanted memories are another well-researched explanation for the déjà vu phenomenon.

- Wolfradt describes a lab-induced experiment in which psychologist Larry L. Jacoby in 1989 manipulated a group of subjects so that he could implant a memory that would lead to a déjà vu experience for each of them.

- Inattention, or what some researchers call "inattentional blindness," is also an extensively researched explanation for the déjà vu experience.

- One compelling laboratory experiment studying inattention is described by Carey in "Déjà Vu: If It All Seems Familiar, There May Be a Reason."

MLA

Gurov 9

Works Cited   27

Works Cited begins on a new page.

Brown, Alan S. *The Déjà Vu Experience: Essays in Cognitive*   28
    Psychology. New York: Psychology, 2004. Print.

--- . "The Déjà Vu Illusion." *Current Directions in Psychological*
    Science 13.6 (2004): 256-59. Print.

Double-space throughout.

Carey, Benedict. "Déjà Vu: If It All Seems Familiar, There May
    Be a Reason." *New York Times* 14 Sept. 2004: F1+.
    LexisNexis. Web. 11 Nov. 2007.   29

List sources in alphabetical order.

Flora, Carlin. "Giving Déjà Vu Its Due." *Psychology Today*
    Mar.-Apr. 2005: 27. *Academic Search Premier.* Web.   30
    7 Nov. 2007.

Glenn, David. "The Tease of Memory." *Chronicle of Higher*
    Education 23 July 2004: A12. Print.

Johnson, C. "A Theory on the Déjà Vu Phenomenon." 8 Dec.
    2001. Web. 20 Nov. 2007.

Lemonick, Michael D. "Explaining Déjà Vu." *Time* 20 Aug. 2007.
    Academic Search Premier. Web. 5 Dec. 2007.

Thompson, Rebecca G., et al. "Persistent Déjà Vu: A Disorder of
    Memory." *International Journal of Geriatric Psychiatry*
    19.9 (2004): 906-07. Print.

Weiten, Wayne. *Psychology: Themes and Variations.* Belmont:
    Wadsworth, 2005. Print.

Wolfradt, Uwe. "Strangely Familiar." *Scientific American Mind*
    16.1 (2005): 32-37. *Academic Search Elite.* Web. 7 Nov. 2007.

27 **Working versus final bibliography.** In keeping with MLA style, Andrei developed a working bibliography using those sources referred to in drafts of his research paper. His bibliography contained over twice the number of sources in his final Works Cited. He dropped sources he considered less authoritative and ones that were not specifically targeted to the subjects that he chose to discuss related to déjà vu.

28 **Balance of source types.** Andrei's final list of Works Cited contains ten works, five from online databases and five from print sources—a proportion that is typical of today's college-level research papers.

29 **What is LexisNexis?** LexisNexis is an online database, available to students through their college library, that contains a large number of research and other scholarly collections, including the LexisNexis Academic and Library Solutions. Originally a document service for law students and lawyers, it now includes areas of study such as government, business, and environmental issues.

30 **What is Academic Search Premier?** Academic Search Premier is a widely used online database in English studies and the humanities. It's available to students through their college library and gives access to over one hundred reference databases, thousands of online journals, lists of book titles at some libraries, linking services, and much more.

36

APA In-Text Citations

36a   What is APA documentation style?

APA

The American Psychological Association (APA) sponsors the **APA style**, a DOCUMENTATION* system widely used in the social sciences. APA style has two equally important features that need to appear in research papers.

1. Within the body of your paper, use IN-TEXT CITATIONS, in parentheses, to acknowledge your SOURCES. Sections 36b and 36c explain the proper way to provide in-text citations.

2. At the end of the paper, provide a list of the sources you used—and only those sources. Title this list, which contains complete bibliographic information about each source, "References." Chapter 37 provides examples.

See Chapter 38 for a sample student paper in APA style.

36b   What are APA in-text parenthetical citations?

APA style requires parenthetical in-text citations that identify a source by the author's name and the copyright year. If there is no author, use a shortened version of the title. In addition, APA style requires page numbers only for DIRECT QUOTATIONS but recommends using them also for PARAPHRASES and SUMMARIES. Some instructors expect you to give page references for paraphrases and summaries and others don't, so find out your instructor's preference to avoid any problems in properly crediting your sources. Separate the parts of a parenthetical citation with commas. End punctuation always follows the citation unless it's a long quotation set in block style.

Put page numbers in parentheses, using the abbreviation *p.* before a single page number and *pp.* when the material you're citing falls on more than one page. For a direct quotation from an electronic source that numbers paragraphs, give the paragraph number (or numbers). Handle paragraph numbers as you do page numbers, but use *para.* or ¶ (the symbol for paragraph) rather than *p.* or *pp.*

APA style recommends that if you refer to a work more than once in a paragraph, you give the author's name and the date at the first mention and then

---

*Words printed in SMALL CAPITAL LETTERS are discussed elsewhere in the text and are defined in the Terms Glossary at the back of the book.

use only the name after that. An exception is when you're citing two or more works by the same author. In that case, each citation must include the date to identify which work you're citing. When two or more of your sources have the same last name, keep them clear by using both first and last names in the text or first initial(s) and last names in parentheses.

36c   What are APA guidelines for in-text citations?

In this section, you'll find examples showing how to cite various kinds of sources in the body of your research paper. The directory at the beginning of this tab corresponds to the numbered examples in this section.

1. Paraphrased or Summarized Source—APA

People from the Mediterranean prefer an elbow-to-shoulder distance from each other (Morris, 1977). [Author name and date cited in parentheses.]

Desmond Morris (1977) notes that people from the Mediterranean prefer an elbow-to-shoulder distance from each other. [Author name cited in text; date cited in parentheses.]

2. Source of a Short Quotation—APA

A report of reductions in SAD-related "depression in 87 percent of patients" (Binkley, 1990, p. 203) reverses the findings of earlier studies. [Author name, date, and page reference cited in parentheses.]

Binkley (1990) reports reductions in SAD-related "depression in 87 percent of patients" (p. 203). [Author name cited in text, followed by the date cited in parentheses incorporated into the words introducing the quotation; page number in parentheses immediately following the quotation.]

3. Source of a Long Quotation—APA

When you use a quotation of forty or more words, set it off in block style indented ½ inch or five spaces from the left margin. Don't use quotation marks. Place the parenthetical reference one space after the end punctuation of the quotation's last sentence.

Jet lag, with its characteristic fatigue and irregular sleep patterns, is a common problem among those who fly great distances to different time zones:

Jet lag syndrome is the inability of the internal body rhythm to rapidly resynchronize after sudden shifts in the timing. For a variety of reasons, the system attempts to maintain stability and resist temporal change. Consequently, complete adjustment can often be delayed for several days—sometimes for a week— after arrival at one's destination. (Bonner, 1991, p. 72) [Author name, date, and page reference cited in parentheses following the end punctuation.]

4. One Author—APA

One of his questions is, "What binds together a Mormon banker in Utah with his brother or other coreligionists in Illinois or Massachusetts?" (Coles, 1993, p. 2).

In a parenthetical reference in APA style, a comma and a space separate a name from a year and a year from a page reference.

5. Two Authors—APA

If a work has two authors, give both names in each citation.

One report describes 2,123 occurrences (Krait & Cooper, 2003).

The results that Krait and Cooper (2003) report would not support the conclusions Davis and Sherman (1999) draw in their review of the literature.

When you write a parenthetical in-text citation naming two (or more) authors, use an ampersand (&) between the final two names, but write out the word *and* for any reference in your own sentence.

6. Three, Four, or Five Authors—APA

For three, four, or five authors, use all of the authors' last names in the first reference. In all subsequent references, use only the first author's last name followed by *et al.* (meaning "and others"). No period follows *et*, but one always follows *al.*

FIRST REFERENCE

In one study, only 30% of the survey population could name the most commonly spoken languages in five Middle Eastern countries (Ludwig, Rodriquez, Novak, & Ehlers, 2008).

SUBSEQUENT REFERENCE

Ludwig et al. (2008) found that most Americans could identify the language spoken in Saudi Arabia.

7. Six or More Authors—APA

For six or more authors, name the first author followed by *et al.* in all in-text references, including the first.

These injuries can lead to an inability to perform athletically, in addition to initiating degenerative changes at the joint level (Mandelbaum et al., 2005).

8. Author(s) with Two or More Works in the Same Year—APA

If you use more than one source written in the same year by the same author(s), alphabetize the works by title for the REFERENCES list, and assign letters in alphabetical order to each work: (2007a), (2007b), (2007c). Use the year-letter combination in parenthetical references. Note that a citation of two or more such works lists the year extensions in alphabetical order.

> Most recently, Torrevillas (2007c) draws new conclusions from the results of eight experiments conducted with experienced readers (Torrevillas, 2007a, 2007b).

9. Two or More Authors with the Same Last Name—APA

Include first initials for every in-text citation of authors who share a last name. Use the initials appearing in the References list. (In the second example, a parenthetical citation, the name order is alphabetical, as explained in item 12.)

> R. A. Smith (2008) and C. Smith (1999) both confirm these results.

> These results have been confirmed independently (C. Smith, 1999; R. A. Smith, 2008).

10. Group or Corporate Author—APA

If you use a source in which the "author" is a corporation, agency, or group, an in-text reference gives that name as author. Use the full name in each citation, unless an abbreviated version of the name is likely to be familiar to your audience. In that case, use the full name and give its abbreviation at the first citation; then, use the abbreviation for subsequent citations.

> This exploration will continue into the 21st century (National Aeronautics and Space Administration [NASA], 1996). [In subsequent citations, use the abbreviated form alone.]

11. Work Listed by Title—APA

If no author is named, use a shortened form of the title for in-text citations. Ignoring *A, An,* or *The,* make the first word the one by which you alphabetize the title in your References list. The following example refers to an article fully titled "Are You a Day or Night Person?"

> Scientists group people as "larks" or "owls" on the basis of whether individuals are more efficient in the morning or at night ("Are You," 1989).

12. Two or More Sources in One Reference—APA

If more than one source has contributed to an idea or opinion in your paper, cite the sources alphabetically by author in one set of parentheses; separate each source of information with a semicolon, as in the following example.

> Conceptions of personal space vary among cultures (Morris, 1977; Worchel & Cooper, 1983).

13. Personal Communication, Including E-Mail and Other Nonretrievable Sources—APA

Telephone calls, personal letters, interviews, and e-mail messages are "personal communications" that your readers can't access or retrieve. Acknowledge personal communications in parenthetical references, but never include them in your References list at the end of your research paper.

> Recalling his first summer at camp, one person said, "The proximity of 12 other kids made me—an only child with older, quiet parents—frantic for eight weeks" (A. Weiss, personal communication, January 12, 2006).

14. Other Retrievable Online Sources—APA

When you quote, paraphrase, or summarize an online source that is available to others, cite the author (if any) or title and the date as you would for a print source, and include the work in your References list.

> It is possible that similarity in personality is important in having a happy marriage (Luo & Clonen, 2005, p. 324).

15. Online Sources with No Page Numbers—APA

If an online source doesn't provide page numbers, use the paragraph number, if available, preceded by the abbreviation *para*. It is rare, however, to number paragraphs. If you can't find a page or paragraph number, cite a heading if possible.

> (Migueis, 2002, Introduction)

16. Source Lines for Graphics and Table Data—APA

If you use a graphic from another source or create a table using data from another source, provide a note at the bottom of the table or graphic, crediting the original author and the copyright holder. Here are examples of two source notes, one for a graphic using data from an article, the other for a graphic reprinted from a book.

GRAPHIC USING DATA FROM AN ARTICLE—APA

Note. The data in columns 1 and 2 are from "Advance Organizers in Advisory Reports: Selective Reading, Recall, and Perception" by L. Lagerwerf et al., 2008, *Written Communication, 25*(1), p. 68. Copyright 2008 by Sage Publications. Adapted with permission of the author.

GRAPHIC FROM A BOOK—APA

Note. From *The Road to Reality: A Complete Guide to the Laws of the Universe* (p. 270), by R. Penrose, 2005, New York, NY: Alfred Knopf. Copyright 2004 by R. Penrose. Reprinted with permission of the publisher.

36d What are APA guidelines for writing an abstract?

As the APA *Publication Manual* (2010) explains, "an abstract is a brief, comprehensive summary" (p. 25) of a longer piece of writing. The APA estimates that an abstract should be no longer than about 120 words. Your instructor may require that you include an abstract at the start of a paper; if you're not sure, ask. Make the abstract accurate, objective, and exact. For an example of an abstract, see the student paper in 38b.

36e What are APA guidelines for content notes?

Content notes in APA-style papers add relevant information that cannot be worked effectively into a text discussion. Use consecutive arabic numerals for note numbers, both within your paper and on any separate page following the last text page of your paper. Try to arrange your sentence so that the note number falls at the end. Use a numeral raised slightly above the line of words and immediately after the final punctuation mark. See page 297 for instructions on formatting the Footnotes page.

For more help with your writing, grammar, and research, go to **www.mycomplab.com**

mycomp**lab**

APA References List

The **References** list at the end of your research paper provides complete bibliographic information for readers who may want to access the SOURCES you drew on to write your paper.

Include in the References list all the sources you quote, paraphrase, or summarize in your paper so that readers can find the same sources with reasonable effort. Never include in your References list any source that's not generally available to other people (see item 13 in 36c).

37a What are APA guidelines for a references list?

An APA References list needs to meet specific requirements in terms of its title, placement, contents and format, spacing, arrangement, type and order of elements included for each kind of entry, punctuation, capitalization, and so on. Quick Reference 37.1 provides details.

Quick Reference 37.1 ■ ■ ■ ■ ■ ■ ■

Guidelines for an APA-style References list

TITLE
The title is "References," centered, without quotation marks, italics, or underlining.

PLACEMENT OF LIST
Start a new page numbered sequentially with the rest of the paper, immediately after the body of the paper (38a).

CONTENTS AND FORMAT
Include all quoted, paraphrased, or summarized sources in your paper that are not personal communications, unless your instructor tells you to include all the references you have consulted, not just those you have to credit. Start each entry on a new line, and double-space all lines. APA recommends that student papers use a *hanging indent* style: The first line of each entry begins flush left at the margin, and all other lines are indented. The hanging indent makes source names and dates more prominent. Type the first line of each entry full width, and indent subsequent lines five spaces or ½ inch. The easiest way to do this is by using the word processor's ruler bar.

continued >>

Quick Reference 37.1 (continued)

Shuter, R. (1977). A field study of nonverbal communication in Germany, Italy, and the United States. *Communication Monographs, 44,* 298–305.

SPACING AFTER PUNCTUATION
APA calls for one space after commas, periods, question marks, and colons.

ARRANGEMENT OF ENTRIES
Alphabetize by the author's last name. If no author is named, alphabetize by the first significant word (ignore *A, An,* or *The*) in the title of the work.

AUTHORS' NAMES
Use last names, first initials, and middle initials, if any. Reverse the order for all authors' names, and use an ampersand (&) before the last author's name: Mills, J. F., & Holahan, R. H.

Give names in the order in which they appear on the work (on the title page of a book or under the title of an article or other printed work). Use a comma between each author's last name and first initial and after each complete name except the last. Use a period after the last author's name.

DATES
Date information follows the name information and is enclosed in parentheses. Place a period followed by one space after the closing parenthesis.

For books, articles in journals that have volume numbers, and many other print and nonprint sources, the year of publication or production is the date to use. For articles from most general-circulation magazines and newspapers, use the year followed by a comma and then the exact date that appears on the issue (month and day for daily and weekly publications, month alone for monthly and bimonthly publications, and season for quarterly publications). Capitalize any words in dates and use no abbreviations.

CAPITALIZATION OF TITLES
For book, article, and chapter titles, capitalize the first word, the first word after a colon between a title and subtitle, and any proper nouns. For names of journals and proceedings of meetings, capitalize the first word; all NOUNS, VERBS, ADVERBS, and ADJECTIVES; and any other words four or more letters long.

SPECIAL TREATMENT OF TITLES
Use no special treatment for titles of shorter works (poems, short stories, essays, articles, Web pages). Italicize titles of longer works (books, newspapers, journals, or Web sites). If an italic typeface is unavailable, underline the title and the end punctuation using one unbroken line.

Do not drop any words (such as *A, An,* or *The*) from the titles of periodicals such as newspapers, magazines, and journals.

continued >>

Quick Reference 37.1 (continued)

PUBLISHERS
Use a shortened version of the publisher's name except for an association, corporation, or university press. Drop *Co., Inc., Publishers,* and the like, but retain *Books* or *Press.*

PLACE OF PUBLICATION
For US publishers, give the city and add the state (use the two-letter postal abbreviations listed in most dictionaries) for all US cities. For publishers in other countries, give city and country spelled out. However, if the state or country is part of the publisher's name, omit it after the name of the city.

ABBREVIATIONS OF MONTHS
Do not abbreviate the names of months in any context.

PAGE NUMBERS
Use all digits, omitting none. For references to books and newspapers only, use *p.* and *pp.* before page numbers. List all discontinuous pages, with numbers separated by commas: pp. 32, 44–45, 47–49, 53.

REFERENCES ENTRIES: BOOKS
Citations for books have four main parts: author, date, title, and publication information (place of publication and publisher). Each part ends with a period.

AUTHOR DATE TITLE
Wood, P. (2003). *Diversity: The invention of a concept.*

PUBLICATION INFORMATION
San Francisco, CA: Encounter Books.

REFERENCES ENTRIES: ARTICLES
Citations for periodical articles contain four major parts: author, date, title of article, and publication information (usually, the periodical title, volume number, and page numbers). Each part ends with a period.

AUTHOR DATE ARTICLE TITLE
Wood, W., Witt, M.G., & Tam, L. (2005). Changing circumstances, disrupting

PERIODICAL TITLE VOLUME NUMBER PAGE RANGE
habits. *Journal of Personality and Social Psychology, 88,* 918–933.

continued >>

APA

Quick Reference 37.1   (continued)

REFERENCES ENTRIES: ELECTRONIC AND ONLINE SOURCES

When citing electronic or online sources, include the name(s) of author(s) the same way as for books and journals. Always include the publication date in parentheses after the author(s)' name(s), followed by a period. Titles of books, periodicals, and whole Web sites should be italicized; titles of articles or pages in a Web site should not use italics.

You then include retrieval information for the electronic source. For articles with DOI (Digital Object Identifier) numbers, this is simply the letters "doi" followed by a colon, then the number. Figure 37.1 (page 281) shows how to find publication information in a journal article with a DOI. Figure 37.1a shows how the source is listed in a database. Figure 37.1b shows the actual page of the article itself. We illustrate this below and in example 39. If the site does not list a DOI, search for one at <http://www.cross ref.org/guestquery/>.

For nearly all other references, retrieval information begins with the words "Retrieved from," sometimes followed by the date you actually retrieved it, then the URL and, occasionally, additional information, such as database names. We provide more detailed information about documenting electronic resources beginning on page 288.

In the meantime, however, here are three examples of electronic source entries. The first is for an article that does not have a DOI number. Because it is for a permanent version of the article, you don't include a date in your "retrieved from" statement.

AUTHOR   DATE   ARTICLE TITLE

Overbye, D. (2005, June 28). Remembrance of things future: The mystery

                                              ONLINE
            NEWSPAPER TITLE   RETRIEVAL INFORMATION

of time. *The New York Times*. Retrieved from http://www.nytimes.com

Notice that the only punctuation in the URL is part of the address. Do not add a period after a URL.

continued >>

Quick Reference 37.1 (continued)

The second example is for an electronic article that has a DOI number. Note that this is for the article in Figure 37.1.

AUTHOR   DATE   ARTICLE TITLE
Agliata, A.K., Tantelff-Dunn, S., & Renk, K. (2007). Interpretation of teasing

PUBLICATION INFORMATION
during early adolescence. *Journal of Clinical Psychology, 63*(1), 23–30.

DOI
doi: 10.1002/jclp.20302

A third example is for an article from a Web site. This example has no author.

ARTICLE TITLE   DATE
Think again: Men and women share cognitive skills. (2006).

PUBLICATION INFORMATION   RETRIEVAL INFORMATION
American Psychological Association. Retrieved from

URL
http://www.psychologymatters.org/thinkagain.html

37b What are APA guidelines for sources in a References list?

The directory at the beginning of this tab corresponds to the numbered examples in this section. For quick help deciding which example you should follow, see the decision flowchart in Figure 37.2 (page 282). However, you can find other examples in the *Publication Manual of the American Psychological Association* (6th edition) or at the APA Web site, http://www.apastyle.org.

Note that all entries use the hanging indent style: the first line of an entry is flush to the left margin, and all other lines in the entry are indented five spaces or ½ inch.

PRINT REFERENCES—BOOKS

1. Book by One Author—APA

Bradway, B. (2002). *Pink houses and family taverns*. Bloomington: Indiana University Press.

APA

A

ARTICLE TITLE ———
AUTHORS ———
PUBLICATION INFORMATION ———
DATE ———
DOI ———

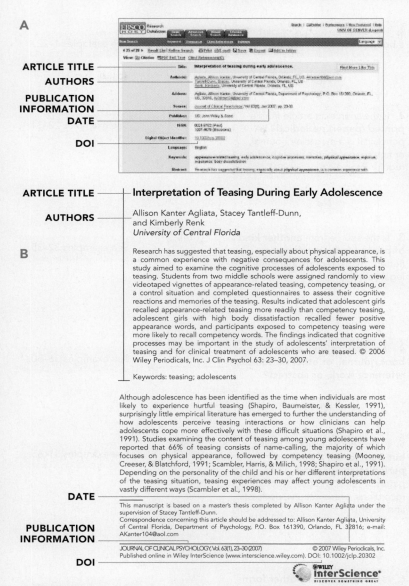

B

ARTICLE TITLE ——— **Interpretation of Teasing During Early Adolescence**

AUTHORS ———
Allison Kanter Agliata, Stacey Tantleff-Dunn, and Kimberly Renk
University of Central Florida

Research has suggested that teasing, especially about physical appearance, is a common experience with negative consequences for adolescents. This study aimed to examine the cognitive processes of adolescents exposed to teasing. Students from two middle schools were assigned randomly to view videotaped vignettes of appearance-related teasing, competency teasing, or a control situation and completed questionnaires to assess their cognitive reactions and memories of the teasing. Results indicated that adolescent girls recalled appearance-related teasing more readily than competency teasing, adolescent girls with high body dissatisfaction recalled fewer positive appearance words, and participants exposed to competency teasing were more likely to recall competency words. The findings indicated that cognitive processes may be important in the study of adolescents' interpretation of teasing and for clinical treatment of adolescents who are teased. © 2006 Wiley Periodicals, Inc. J Clin Psychol 63: 23–30, 2007.

Keywords: teasing; adolescents

Although adolescence has been identified as the time when individuals are most likely to experience hurtful teasing (Shapiro, Baumeister, & Kessler, 1991), surprisingly little empirical literature has emerged to further the understanding of how adolescents perceive teasing interactions or how clinicians can help adolescents cope more effectively with these difficult situations (Shapiro et al., 1991). Studies examining the content of teasing among young adolescents have reported that 66% of teasing consists of name-calling, the majority of which focuses on physical appearance, followed by competency teasing (Mooney, Creeser, & Blatchford, 1991; Scambler, Harris, & Milich, 1998; Shapiro et al., 1991). Depending on the personality of the child and his or her different interpretations of the teasing situation, teasing experiences may affect young adolescents in vastly different ways (Scambler et al., 1998).

DATE ———
This manuscript is based on a master's thesis completed by Allison Kanter Agliata under the supervision of Stacey Tantleff-Dunn.
Correspondence concerning this article should be addressed to: Allison Kanter Agliata, University of Central Florida, Department of Psychology, P.O. Box 161390, Orlando, FL 32816; e-mail: AKanter104@aol.com

PUBLICATION INFORMATION ———
JOURNAL OF CLINICAL PSYCHOLOGY, Vol. 63(1), 23–30 (2007)   © 2007 Wiley Periodicals, Inc.
Published online in Wiley InterScience (www.interscience.wiley.com). DOI: 10.1002/jclp.20302

DOI ———

WILEY InterScience°
DISCOVER SOMETHING GREAT

Figure 37.1 Publication information in a journal article with a DOI

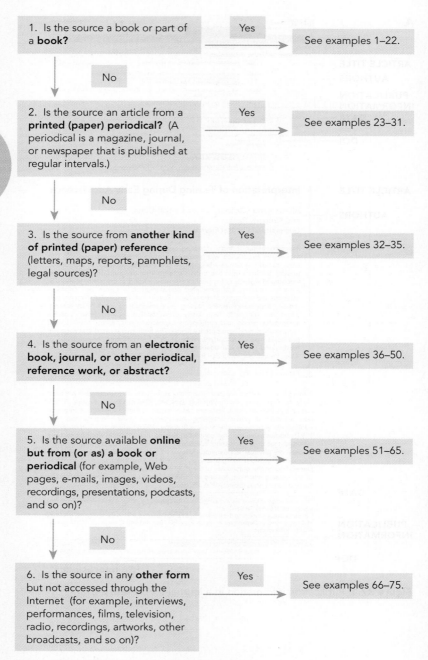

1. Is the source a book or part of a **book?** — Yes → See examples 1–22.

No ↓

2. Is the source an article from a **printed (paper) periodical?** (A periodical is a magazine, journal, or newspaper that is published at regular intervals.) — Yes → See examples 23–31.

No ↓

3. Is the source from **another kind of printed (paper) reference** (letters, maps, reports, pamphlets, legal sources)? — Yes → See examples 32–35.

No ↓

4. Is the source from an **electronic book, journal, or other periodical, reference work, or abstract?** — Yes → See examples 36–50.

No ↓

5. Is the source available **online but from (or as) a book or periodical** (for example, Web pages, e-mails, images, videos, recordings, presentations, podcasts, and so on)? — Yes → See examples 51–65.

No ↓

6. Is the source in any **other form** but not accessed through the Internet (for example, interviews, performances, films, television, radio, recordings, artworks, other broadcasts, and so on)? — Yes → See examples 66–75.

Figure 37.2 APA References visual directory

2. Book by Two Authors—APA

Edin, K., & Kefalas, M. (2005). *Promises I can keep: Why poor women put motherhood before marriage.* Berkeley: University of California Press.

3. Book by Three or More Authors—APA

Lynam, J. K., Ndiritu, C. G., & Mbabu, A. N. (2004). *Transformation of agricultural research systems in Africa: Lessons from Kenya.* East Lansing: Michigan State University Press.

For a book by three to seven authors, include all the authors' names. For a book by more than seven authors, use only the first six names, then insert three ellipses, then add the last author's name.

4. Two or More Books by the Same Author(s)—APA

Jenkins, H. (1992). *Textual poachers: Television fans and participatory culture.* New York, NY: Routledge.

Jenkins, H. (2006). *Convergence culture: Where old and new media collide.* New York: New York University Press.

References by the same author are arranged chronologically, with the earlier date of publication listed first.

5. Book by a Group or Corporate Author—APA

American Psychological Association. (2001). *Publication manual of the American Psychological Association* (5th ed.). Washington, DC: Author.

Boston Women's Health Collective. (1998). *Our bodies, ourselves for the new century.* New York, NY: Simon & Schuster.

Cite the full name of the corporate author first. If the author is also the publisher, use the word *Author* as the name of the publisher.

6. Book with No Author Named—APA

The Chicago manual of style (15th ed.). (2003). Chicago, IL: University of Chicago Press.

Ignoring *The*, this would be alphabetized under *Chicago*, the first important word in the title.

7. Book with an Author and an Editor—APA

Brontë, E. (2002). *Wuthering heights* (R. J. Dunn, Ed.). New York, NY: Norton.

8. Translation—APA

Kundera, M. (1999). *The unbearable lightness of being* (M. H. Heim, Trans.). New York, NY: HarperPerennial. (Original work published 1984)

9. Work in Several Volumes or Parts—APA

Chrisley, R. (Ed.). (2000). *Artificial intelligence: Critical concepts* (Vols. 1–4). London, England: Routledge.

10. One Selection in an Anthology or an Edited Book—APA

Trujillo, L. (2004). Balancing act. In R. Moreno & M. H. Mulligan (Eds.), *Borderline personalities: A new generation of Latinas dish on sex, sass, and cultural shifting* (pp. 61–72). New York, NY: HarperCollins.

Give the author of the selection first. The word *In* introduces the larger work from which the selection is taken. To refer to an anthology, see the Chaudhuri citation in example 11.

11. Selection in a Work Already Listed in References—APA

Bond, R. (2004). The night train at Deoli. In A. Chaudhuri (Ed.), *The Vintage book of modern Indian literature* (pp. 415–418). New York, NY: Vintage Books.

Chaudhuri, A. (Ed.). (2004). *The Vintage book of modern Indian literature.* New York, NY: Vintage Books.

Provide full information for the already cited anthology (first example), along with information about the individual selection. Put entries in alphabetical order.

12. Signed Article in a Reference Book—APA

Burnbam, J. C. (1996). Freud, Sigmund. In B. B. Wolman (Ed.), *The encyclopedia of psychiatry, psychology, and psychoanalysis* (p. 220). New York, NY: Holt.

13. Unsigned Article in a Reference Book—APA

Ireland. (2002). In *The new encyclopaedia Britannica: Macropaedia* (15th ed., Vol. 21, pp. 997–1018). Chicago, IL: Encyclopaedia Britannica.

14. Second or Later Edition—APA

Gibaldi, J. (2003). *MLA handbook for writers of research papers* (6th ed.). New York, NY: Modern Language Association.

Any edition number appears on the title page.

15. Anthology or Edited Book—APA

Purdy, J. L., & Ruppert, J. (Eds.). (2001). *Nothing but the truth: An anthology of Native American literature.* Upper Saddle River, NJ: Prentice Hall.

16. Introduction, Preface, Foreword, or Afterword—APA

Hesse, D. (2004). Foreword. In D. Smit, *The end of composition studies* (pp. ix–xiii). Carbondale: Southern Illinois University Press.

If you're citing an introduction, preface, foreword, or afterword, give its author's name first. After the year, give the name of the part cited. If the writer of the material you're citing isn't the author of the book, use the word *In* and the author's name before the title of the book.

17. Unpublished Dissertation or Essay—APA

Stuart, G.A. (2006). *Exploring the Harry Potter book series: A study of adolescent reading motivation.* Unpublished doctoral dissertation, Utah State University.

18. Reprint of an Older Book—APA

O'Brien, F. (1998). *At Swim-Two-Birds.* Normal, IL: Dalkey Archive Press. (Original work published 1939)

You can find republishing information on the copyright page.

19. Book in a Series—APA

Goldman, D. J. (1995). *Women writers and World War I.* New York, NY: Macmillan.

Give the title of the book but not of the whole series.

20. Book with a Title Within a Title—APA

Lumiansky, R. M., & Baker, H. (Eds.). (1968). *Critical approaches to six major English works:* Beowulf *through* Paradise Lost. Philadelphia, PA: University of Pennsylvania Press.

Never italicize a title within a title, even though it would appear in italic typeface if it were by itself.

21. Government Publication—APA

U.S. Congress. House Subcommittee on Health and Environment of the Committee on Commerce. (1999). *The nursing home resident protection amendments of 1999* (99-0266-P). Washington, DC: U.S. Government Printing Office.

U.S. Senate Special Committee on Aging. (1998). *The risk of malnutrition in nursing homes* (98-0150-P). Washington, DC: U.S. Government Printing Office.

Use the complete name of a government agency as author when no specific person is named.

22. Published Proceedings of a Conference—APA

Rocha, L., Yaeger, L., Bedau, M., Floreano, D., Goldstone, R. & Vespignani, A. (Eds.). (2006, June). *Artificial Life X: Proceedings of the Tenth International Conference on the Simulation and Synthesis of Living Systems.* Bloomington, IN. Cambridge: MIT Press.

When citing a specific department or other university facility, put the name of the university first.

PRINT REFERENCES—PERIODICALS

23. Article in a Journal with Continuous Pagination—APA

Tyson, P. (1998). The psychology of women. *Journal of the American Psychoanalytic Association, 46*, 361–364.

Give the volume number, italicized after the journal title.

24. Article in a Journal That Pages Each Issue Separately—APA

Adler-Kassner, L., & Estrem, H. (2003). Rethinking research writing: Public literacy in the composition classroom. *WPA: Writing Program Administration, 26*(3), 119–131.

Give the volume number, italicized with the journal title, followed by the issue number in parentheses (not italicized), and the page number(s).

25. Signed Article in a Weekly or Biweekly Periodical—APA

Brink, S. (2005, March 28). Eat this now! *U.S. News & World Report,* 56–58.

26. Signed Article in a Monthly or Bimonthly Periodical—APA

Fallows, J. (2008, January/February). The $1.4 trillion question. *The Atlantic, 301*(1), 36–48.

Give the year and month(s) for a periodical published every month or every other month. Insert the volume number, italicized with the periodical title. Put the issue number in parentheses; do not italicize it.

27. Unsigned Article in a Periodical—APA

The price is wrong. (2003, August 2). *The Economist, 368,* 58–59.

28. Signed Article in a Daily Newspaper—APA

Green, P. (2008, January 31). The slow life picks up speed. *The New York Times,* p. D1.

Use the abbreviation *p.* (or *pp.* for more than one page) for newspapers.

29. Unsigned Article in a Daily Newspaper—APA

Oscars ready plans to deal with strike. (2008, January 31). *The Denver Post*, p. B3.

30. Editorial, Letter to the Editor, or Review—APA

Primary considerations. (2008, January 27). [Editorial]. *The Washington Post*, p. B6.

Finanger, E. (2008, February). [Letter to the editor]. *Outside*, 14.

Shenk, D. (2003, Spring). Toolmaker, brain builder [Review of the book *Beyond Big Blue: Building the computer that defeated the world chess champion*]. *The American Scholar*, 72, 150–152.

Do not use the abbreviations *p.* or *pp.* for magazines or journals. Give year, month, and day for a periodical published every week or every two weeks.

31. Article in a Looseleaf Collection of Reprinted Articles—APA

Hayden, T. (2002). The age of robots. In E. Goldstein (Ed.), *Applied Science 2002. SIRS 2002*, Article 66. (Reprinted from *U.S. News & World Report*, pp. 44–50, 2001, April 23).

OTHER PRINT REFERENCES
32. Published and Unpublished Letters—APA

Williams, W. C. (1935). Letter to his son. In L. Grunwald & S. J. Adler (Eds.), *Letters of the century: America 1900–1999* (pp. 225–226). New York, NY: Dial Press.

In the APA system, unpublished letters are considered personal communications inaccessible to general readers, so they do not appear in the References list. They are cited only in the body of the paper (see example 66).

33. Map or Chart—APA

Colorado Front Range Mountain Bike Topo Map [Map]. (2001). Nederland, CO: Latitude 40.

34. Report or Pamphlet—APA

National Commission on Writing in America's Schools and Colleges. (2003). *The neglected "R": The need for a writing revolution* [Report]. New York, NY: College Board.

35. Legal Source—APA

Brown v. Board of Educ., 347 U.S. 483 (1954).

Include the name of the case, the number of the case, the name of the court deciding the case (if other than the US Supreme Court), and the year of the decision.

ELECTRONIC AND ONLINE SOURCES

In general, APA recommends giving the same information, in the same order, as you would for a print source: author name(s), date of publication, title, and publication information (title, volume, issue, pages). Then you add as much retrieval information as others will need to locate the source. This retrieval information may include a DOI number (see example 39) or it may consist of a "Retrieved from" statement along with a URL. If the document being cited is unstable, you may also need to include the date you retrieved the information.

- **DOI (Direct Object Identifier):** These numerical codes are sometimes assigned to online journal articles and are typically located on the first page of the online article or included in the database. The DOI for an article will be the same even if the article appears on many different Web sites. As a result, you don't use a URL or a "retrieved from" statement if a source contains a DOI. Include the number after the publication information.

- **URL:** If no DOI has been assigned, include the homepage URL. Include a complete URL only if you think readers will need it to retrieve the source. If a URL must be divided on two or more lines, only break the address before slashes or punctuation marks (except within "http://").

- **Databases:** A retrieval line is not needed for materials located on widely available databases like library subscription services. If, however, the source is difficult to locate, include the name of the database in the retrieval line.

- **Retrieval date:** Include the date you retrieved the information only if the item is likely to be changed in the future (such as a prepublication version of an article, a Web page, or a Wiki).

- **Nonretrievable sources:** Don't include personal communications such as e-mail messages in your References list; instead, cite it in the text with a parenthetical notation saying it's a personal communication. (Also see example 66.) If you have a scholarly reason to cite a message from a newsgroup, forum, or electronic mailing list that is available in an electronic archive, then see example 52 or 53.

ELECTRONIC BOOKS

36. Entire Electronic Book—APA

Adams, H. (1918). *The education of Henry Adams.* New York, NY: Houghton Mifflin. Retrieved from http://www.columbia.edu/acis/bartleby/159/index/html

Provide information about the print version, if available. The retrieval statement gives the specific URL of the work.

37. Chapter from Electronic Book—APA

Gembris, H. (2006). The development of musical abilities. In R. Colwell (Ed). *MENC handbook of musical cognition and development*. New York, NY: Oxford University Press (pp.124–164). Retrieved from http://site.ebrary .com.bianca.penlib.du.edu/

38. Thesis or Dissertation—APA

Stuart, G. A. (2006). *Exploring the Harry Potter book series: A study of adolescent reading motivation*. Retrieved from ProQuest Digital Dissertations. (AAT 3246355)

The number in parentheses at the end is the accession number.

ELECTRONIC JOURNALS

39. Article with DOI Assigned—APA

Gurung, R., & Vespia, K. (2007). Looking good, teaching well? Linking liking, looks, and learning. *Teaching of Psychology, 34*, 5-10. doi: 10.1207/ s15328023top3401_2

40. Article with No DOI Assigned—APA

Pollard, R. (2002). Evidence of a reduced home field advantage when a team moves to a new stadium. *Journal of Sports Sciences 20*, 969–974. Retrieved from http://0-find.galegroup.com.bianca.penlib.du.edu:80/itx /start.do?prodId=AONE

No retrieval date is included because the final version of the article is being referenced.

41. In-press Article—APA

In-press means that an article has been accepted for publication but has not yet been published in its final form. Therefore, there is no publication date, and the retrieved from statement includes a date.

George, S. (In press). How accurately should we estimate the anatomical source of exhaled nitric oxide? *Journal of Applied Physiology*. doi:10.1152/japplphysiol.00111.2008. Retrieved from http:// jap.physiology .org/papbyrecent.shtml

APA

OTHER ELECTRONIC PERIODICALS

42. Newspaper Article—APA

Wilson, J. (2005, March 5). EPA fights waste site near river. *Los Angeles Times*. Retrieved from http://www.latimes.com

43. Online Magazine Content Not Found in Print Version—APA

Shulman, M. (2008, January 23). 12 diseases that altered history. [Online exclusive]. *U.S. News and World Report*. Retrieved from http://health .usnews.com/articles/health/

44. Web Page or Article on Web Site—APA

Think again: Men and women share cognitive skills. (2006). *American Psychological Association*. Retrieved from http://www.psychology matters.org/thinkagain.html

ELECTRONIC REFERENCE MATERIALS

45. Online Encyclopedia—APA

Turing test. (2008). In *Encyclopædia Britannica*. Retrieved from http:// www.britannica.com/bps/topic/609757/Turing-test

46. Online Dictionary—APA

Asparagus. (n.d.). *Merriam-Webster's online dictionary*. Retrieved from http://dictionary.reference.com/browse/asparagus

47. Online Handbook—APA

Gembris, H. (2006). The development of musical abilities. In R. Colwell (Ed). *MENC handbook of musical cognition and development*. New York, NY: Oxford University Press (pp. 124–164). Retrieved from http://0-site .ebrary.com.bianca.penlib.du.edu/lib/udenver/Doc?id= 10160594

48. Wiki—APA

Machine learning. (n.d.) Retrieved January 5, 2008, from Artificial Intelligence Wiki: http://www.ifi.unizh.ch/ailab/aiwiki/aiw.cgi

N.d. means "no date."

The date of retrieval is included because the document being cited is unstable.

ELECTRONIC ABSTRACTS
49. Abstract from a Secondary Source—APA

Walther, J.B., Van Der Heide, B., Kim, S., Westerman, D., & Tong, S. (2008). The role of friends' appearance and behavior on evaluations of individuals on Facebook: Are we known by the company we keep? *Human Communication Research, 34,* 28–49. Abstract retrieved from PsycINFO database.

50. Abstract Submitted for Meeting or Poster Session—APA

Wang, H. (2007). Dust storms originating in the northern hemisphere of Mars. AGU 2007 Fall Meeting. Abstract retrieved from http://www.agu.org /meetings/fm07/?content=program

OTHER ELECTRONIC REFERENCES
51. Personal or Professional Web Site—APA

Hesse, Doug. (2008, November). Home page. Retrieved November 21, 2008, from http://http://portfolio.du.edu/dhesse

Association for the Advancement of Artificial Intelligence. (2008, March). Retrieved March 17, 2008, from http://www.aaai.org

Because material on a Web site may change, use a "retrieved from" date.

52. Message on a Newsgroup, Online Forum, or Discussion Group—APA

Boyle, F. (2002, October 11). Psyche: Cemi field theory: The hard problem made easy [Msg 1]. Retrieved from news://sci.psychology.consciousness

53. Message on an Electronic Mailing List (Listserv)—APA

Haswell, R. (2005, October 17). A new graphic/text interface [Electronic mailing list message]. Retrieved from the Writing Program Administrators electronic mailing list: http://lists.asu.edu/archives/wpa-l.html

APA advises using *electronic mailing list,* as Listserv is the name of specific software.

54. Course Home Page—APA

St. Germain, S. (2003, Summer). Myths and fairytales: From *Inanna* to *Edward Scissorhands.* Retrieved February 20, 2005, from http://www.public.iastate .edu/~sgermain/531.homepage.html

55. Blog (Web log) Post—APA

McLemee, S. (2008, January 1). To whom it may concern [Web log post]. Retrieved from http://www.artsjournal.com/quickstudy/

APA

56. Video Web log Post—APA

Wesch, M. (2007, January 31). *Web 2.0 . . . the machine is us/ing us.* [Video file]. Retrieved from http://www.youtube.com/watch?v=6gmP4nk0EOE

Also see example 59 for online television programs or movies.

57. Online Digital Recording—APA

Komunyakaa, Y. (2005). My father's love letters [Digital recording]. Retrieved from http://www.poets.org/poems/poems.cfm?prmID=2065

58. Audio Podcast—APA

Business marketing with podcast: What marketing professionals should know (2005, October 13). *Podblaze* [Audio podcast]. Retrieved from http://business.podblaze.com/

59. Online Television Program—APA

Bender, J. (Director/Producer). (2008, January 30). The beginning of the end [Television series episode]. In *Lost.* Retrieved from http://dynamic .abc.go.com

If producers or directors can be identified, list them in the author position. Include the episode title, if any, and the title of the series. If it is a one-time program, list only the title.

60. Online Advertisement—APA

Samsung. (2005, November). [Advertisement]. Retrieved from http://rollingstone.com

61. Computer Software or Video Game—APA

Guitar hero III: Legends of rock. (2007). [Video game]. Santa Monica, CA: Activision.

Provide an author name, if available. Standard software (Microsoft Word) and program languages (C++) don't need to be given in the References list.

62. Brochure—APA

U.S. Department of Agriculture. (2007). *Organic foods and labels* [Brochure]. Retrieved from http://www.ams.usda.gov/nop/Consumers/brochure.html

63. Policy Brief—APA

Haskins, R., Paxson, C., & Donahue, E. (2006). *Fighting obesity in the public schools*. Retrieved from http://www.brookings.edu/~/media/Files /rc/papers/2006/spring_childrenfamilies_haskins/20060314foc.pdf

64. Presentation Slides—APA

Alaska Conservation Solutions. (2006). *Montana global warming* [PowerPoint slides]. Retrieved from http://www.alaskaconservationsolutions.com/acs /presentations.html

65. Graphs, Maps, Other Images—APA

New York Times Online. (2005, September 24). *Hurricane Rita* [Interactive map]. Retrieved from http://www.nytimes.com/packages/html/national /20050923_RITA_GRAPHIC/index.html

OTHER NONPRINT REFERENCES

66. Interview—APA

In APA style, a personal interview is not included in the References list. Cite the interview in the text as a personal communication.

Randi Friedman (personal communication, June 30, 2007) endorses this view.

67. Lecture, Speech, or Address—APA

Kennedy, J. F. (1960, September 12). Speech to the Greater Houston Ministerial Association, Rice Hotel, Houston, TX.

68. Film, Videotape, or DVD—APA

Capra, F. (Director/Producer). (1934). *It happened one night* [Motion picture]. United States: Columbia Pictures.

Madden, J. (Director), Parfitt, D., Gigliotti, D., Weinstein, H., Zwick, E., & Norman, M. (Producers). (2003). *Shakespeare in love* [DVD]. (Original motion picture released 1998)

69. Recording—APA

Smetana, B. (1975). *My country* [Recorded by the Czech Philharmonic Orchestra with K. Anserl conducting]. [Record]. London, England: Vanguard Records.

Radiohead. (2007). Jigsaw falling into place. On *Rainbows* [MP3]. Radiohead.

APA

70. Live Performance—APA

Miller, A. (Author), & McLean, C. (Director). (2005, September 27). *All my sons* [Theatrical performance]. Center for the Performing Arts, Normal, IL.

71. Work of Art, Photograph, or Musical Composition—APA

Cassatt, M. (1891). *La toilette* [Artwork]. Chicago, IL: Art Institute of Chicago.

Mydans, C. (1999, October 21–November 28). *General Douglas MacArthur landing at Luzon, 1945* [Photograph]. New York, NY: Soho Triad Fine Art Gallery.

Schubert, F. (1822). *Unfinished symphony* [Musical composition].

72. Radio or Television Broadcast—APA

Burns, K. (Writer/Producer), & Barnes, P. (Producer). (1999, November 8). *Not for ourselves alone: The story of Elizabeth Cady Stanton and Susan B. Anthony* [Television broadcast]. New York, NY and Washington, DC: Public Broadcasting Service.

If you're citing a television series produced by and seen on only one station, cite its call letters.

73. Information Service—APA

Chiang, L. H. (1993). *Beyond the language: Native Americans' nonverbal communication.* (ERIC Document Reproduction Service No. ED368540)

74. Advertisement—APA

Swim at home. (2005). [Advertisement]. *The American Scholar 74*(2), 2.

75. Image—APA

If you're reproducing an image in your paper, follow the guidelines for graphics in item 16 in 37c. Include the citation in the body of your paper. If you're only referring to an image, cite the photographer or illustrator (if known), the title (or a brief description of the image), and source information.

Arthur Miller in 1961. (2005). [Photograph]. *The American Scholar 74*(2), 123.

38

A Student's APA-Style Research Paper

38a What are APA format guidelines for research papers?

Ask whether your instructor has instructions for preparing a final draft. If not, you can use the APA guidelines here. For an illustration of these guidelines, see the student paper in 38b.

■ General instructions—APA

Use 8½-by-11-inch white paper. The APA *Publication Manual* recommends double-spacing for a final manuscript of a student research paper. Set at least a 1-inch margin on the left (slightly more if you submit your paper in a binder), and leave no less than 1 inch on the right and at the bottom.

Leave ½ inch from the top edge of the paper to the title-and-page-number line (also known as a running head). Leave another ½ inch (or 1 inch from the top edge of the paper) before the next line on the page, whether that's a heading (such as "Abstract" or "Notes") or a line of your paper.

Use indents of ½ inch for the first line of all paragraphs, except in an abstract, the first line of which isn't indented. Do not justify the right margin. Indent footnotes ½ inch.

■ Order of parts—APA

Number all pages consecutively. Use this order for the parts of your paper:

1. Title page
2. Abstract (if required)
3. Body of the paper
4. References
5. Appendixes, if any
6. Footnotes, if any

APA

7. Attachments, if any (questionnaires, data sheets, or other material your instructor asks you to include)

■ Title-and-page-number line (running head) for all pages—APA

Use a title-and-page-number line on all pages of your paper. Leaving a margin of ½ inch from the top edge of the paper, type the title (use a shortened version if necessary) one inch from the left edge of the paper. Type the page number one inch from the right edge of the paper. The "header" tool on a word processing program will help you create the title-and-page-number line easily.

■ Title page—APA

Use a separate title page. On it, begin the title-and-page-number line (described above) with the words "Running head:" (lower case). Use the numeral 1 for this first page. Then center the complete title vertically and horizontally on the page. Use two or more double-spaced lines if the title is long. Do not italicize or underline the title or enclose it in quotation marks. On the next line, center your name, and below that center the course title and section, your professor's name, and the date.

Alerts: (1) Use the guidelines here for capitalizing the title of your own paper and for capitalizing titles you mention in the body of your paper (but not in the REFERENCES list; see Quick Reference 37.1 on pp. 276–280).

(2) Use a capital letter for the first word of your title and for the first word of a subtitle, if any. Start every NOUN, PRONOUN, VERB, ADVERB, and ADJECTIVE with a capital letter. Capitalize each main word in a hyphenated compound word (two or more words used together to express one idea): *Father-in-Law, Self-Consciousness.*

(3) Do not capitalize ARTICLES (*a, an, the*) unless one of the other capitalization rules applies to them. Do not capitalize PREPOSITIONS and CONJUNCTIONS unless they're four or more letters long. Do not capitalize the word *to* used in an INFINITIVE. ●

■ Abstract—APA

See 36d for advice about the abstract of your paper. Type the abstract on a separate page, using the numeral 2 in the title-and-page-number line. Center the word *Abstract* 1 inch from the top of the paper. Do not italicize or underline it or enclose it in quotation marks. Double-space below this title, and then start your abstract, double-spacing it. Do not indent the first line.

■ Set-off quotations—APA

Set off (display in block style) quotations of forty words or more. See 36c for a detailed explanation and example.

If you're quoting part of a paragraph or one complete paragraph, do not indent the first line more than ½ inch. But if you quote two or more paragraphs, indent the first line of the second and subsequent paragraphs 1 inch.

■ References list—APA

Start a new page for your References list immediately after the end of the body of your paper. Use a title-and-page-number line. Drop down 1 inch from the top of the paper and center the word *References*. Don't italicize or underline it or put it in quotation marks. Double-space below it. Start the first line of each entry at the left margin, and indent any subsequent lines five spaces or ½ inch from the left margin. Use this "hanging indent" style unless your instructor prefers a different one. Double-space within each entry and between entries.

■ Notes—APA

Put any notes on a separate page after the last page of your References list and any Appendixes. Use a title-and-page-number line. Then center the word *Footnotes* one inch from the top of the paper. Do not italicize or underline it or put it in quotation marks.

On the next line, indent ½ inch and begin the note. Raise the note number slightly (you can use the superscript feature in your word processing program), and then start the words of your note, leaving no space after the number. If the note is more than one typed line, do not indent any line after the first. Double-space throughout.

38b A student's APA-style research paper

Shawn Hickson wrote the following research paper in response to an assignment that asked students to use psychological research to analyze the effects of behaviors.

APA

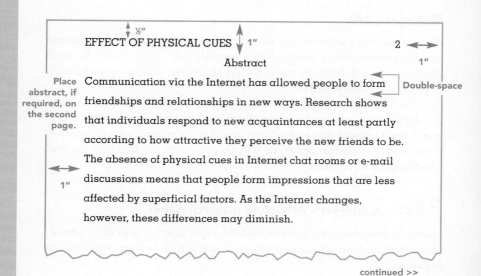

Running head: EFFECT OF PHYSICAL CUES   ½"   1

1"

Use the first
page for the
title page.

The Effect of Physical Cues on New Relationships

Shawn Hickson

General Psychology 131

Professor M. Staley

May 10, 2005

Center
the
title,
student
name,
course,
instructor,
and date on
the page.
Use double
spacing.

EFFECT OF PHYSICAL CUES   ½" ↓ 1"   2

1"

Abstract

Place
abstract, if
required, on
the second
page.

Communication via the Internet has allowed people to form
friendships and relationships in new ways. Research shows
that individuals respond to new acquaintances at least partly
according to how attractive they perceive the new friends to be.
The absence of physical cues in Internet chat rooms or e-mail
discussions means that people form impressions that are less
affected by superficial factors. As the Internet changes,
however, these differences may diminish.

Double-space

1"

continued >>

EFFECT OF PHYSICAL CUES   3

The Effect of Physical Cues on New Relationships

Over the past 20 years, the Internet has enabled people to
meet others from around the world with a few simple
keystrokes. Occasionally, these interactions extend beyond
the confines of chat rooms and e-mail discussions, so that
individuals arrange to meet in person. Of course, people have
learned to be cautious because others online can easily
misrepresent themselves and their intentions. Nonetheless,
lasting friendships, romances, and even marriages have
resulted from first interactions that have happened online.
Surprisingly, research shows that compared to people who
meet face to face, those who meet on the Internet develop a
greater liking for each other (McKenna, Green, & Gleason,
2003). This result is an example of a larger phenomenon: The
presence or absence of physical characteristics during first
meetings can influence how people respond to each other.

Judging People by Appearances

It can be troubling to know that something as shallow as
someone's physical attractiveness can affect how people treat
that person. However, the truth is that even if people do not
mean to judge others based on their appearance, they tend to
do so. Dion, Berscheid, and Walster (1972) showed research
participants pictures of stereotypically attractive and
unattractive individuals and then asked them to judge the
people in the photographs according to several personality
traits. The researchers found that the more attractive a person
was judged to be, the more desirable traits that person was
judged to have. For example, people might believe that
beautiful women are smarter or that handsome men are more
clever. Several studies found that individuals assume that

APA STYLE:
1-inch
margins;
double space
throughout

INTRODUCTION

APA-STYLE
IN-TEXT
CITA-
TION:
Doesn't
require
page
numbers
for a
paraphrase
or summary;
check whether
your instructor
prefers that
you include
them

THESIS
STATEMENT:
Gives paper's
focus

FIRST
HEADING

PARA-
GRAPH 2:
Provides
background
information

APA-STYLE
INTEGRATED
CITATION:
Author names
cited in
text; date
cited in
parentheses

APA

continued >>

EFFECT OF PHYSICAL CUES   4

attractive people will agree with them more often than those who are unattractive; they assume that the attractive person will be more like them (Miyake & Zuckerman, 1993).

PARA-
GRAPH 3:
Provides
further
examples
of thesis

Even when people are young, appearance colors how others perceive them. Studies of preschoolers show that both peers and teachers treat children differently based on their physical appearances. Both expect attractive children to be more active socially, and teachers believe that attractive children have more academic potential (Kachel, 1996). Perhaps more astounding, some controversial research shows that children's physical appearances may affect how their very own parents treat them (Bakalar, 2005).

PARA-
GRAPH 4:
Provides
information
and bridges
to next
paragraph

Attractiveness has a different importance for men and women. While both sexes value physical appearance in brief relationships, men tend to view it as vital in long-term relationships. In contrast, women tend to regard other qualities more highly, especially financial stability and high social status (Singh, 2004).

PARA-
GRAPH 5:
Summarizes
research
findings

However, for men and women alike, physical cues at the first meeting can shape not only impressions but also behaviors. Snyder, Tanke, and Berscheid (1977) showed male participants a picture of either an attractive or an unattractive female and then asked the men to rate her personality traits. Results of this initial rating were very similar to those obtained by Dion et al. (1972). Snyder's group next took the study one step further. Each male participant then had a phone conversation with a female participant who he thought was the female from the picture. In these conversations, men treated their phone partners as if they possessed the characteristics they believed went along with the photograph.

continued >>

EFFECT OF PHYSICAL CUES   5

However, the men obviously knew nothing about the women; they assigned the women traits simply on the basis of a photograph. Even more interesting, women responded in a manner that was consistent with the images that were being projected onto them. Attractive women who were treated like they were unattractive actually behaved as if they were, and vice versa. What happened was a clear example of a self-fulfilling prophecy (Snyder et al., 1977). Judgments based on appearance clouded other realities.

Meeting on the Internet

Meeting people online, especially through e-mail or in a chat room, obviously differs from meeting them face to face because there are no physical cues, only other people's words. Do people meeting in that environment engage one another differently? A study conducted by McKenna et al. (2003) suggests that they do. McKenna and colleagues divided participants into two groups: an experimental group and a control group. All participants had two separate conversations, one in person and the other online. Both conversations took place with the same person. Those in the control group knew this, but those in the experimental group believed they were talking with two different people. Participants in both groups then rated the quality of the interactions on three factors: (a) the quality of the conversations, (b) the degree to which they felt they had gotten to know the other person, and (c) how well they liked the other person in general. For the control groups, the ratings were similar in all categories, for both in-person and online conversations. However, differences emerged with the participants who thought they had been interacting with two different people, not the same person: They

Side notes:

Replaces names with et *al.* because this is second reference to same work with multiple authors

SECOND HEADING

PARA-GRAPH 6: Explains research on Internet meetings

Creates clarity by using letters in parentheses to identify factors

continued >>

EFFECT OF PHYSICAL CUES   6

consistently rated the Internet partner higher in all three
categories.

PARA-
GRAPH 7:
Interprets
findings
summa-
rized
in pre-
vious
para-
graph

        One probable explanation for this occurrence is that
Internet interactions do away with traditional physical
judgments. Attractiveness, extreme shyness, speech
impediments, and many other superficial factors can hinder
people from expressing their true selves and accepting others
who are deficient in one area or another (McKenna et al., 2003).
Because early judgments determine how two people will
interact, a physical meeting makes it harder for some
individuals to become comfortable and disclose at the same
level as they would in a situation where physical cues don't
matter.

PARA-
GRAPH 8:
Explains
interests of
people
meeting
online

        By the time people engage in online romantic
relationships, according to researcher Malin Sveningsson
(2002), they have already established a written relationship
based on common interests. They know each other on a basis
other than physical characteristics. Most people who enter chat

APA-STYLE
IN-TEXT
CITATION:
Requires
page
number for
direct
quotation;
uses *p.* not
page

rooms do so with the hope of making "contact with people,
getting into a rewarding discussion, or just small-talking and
having a good time in general" (p. 49). Those who meet on
Internet chat sites or listservs nearly always come together
over a shared interest. A chat room frequenter named Richard
explained his reasons for taking part in online conversations:

Shawn uses
brackets in
quotation to
show she
(not the
speaker)
has altered
wording
to improve
clarity

"When you enter a place like that, you just want somebody to
talk to . . . so you actively [look] for people who [have] something
to say. And all the time you [make] comments just to find
someone who [has] something to tell" (p. 50). Women and men
are nearly equal in their use of the Internet for purposes of
community. The Cyber Dialogue group found that about 27%

continued >>

APA

EFFECT OF PHYSICAL CUES   7

of women and 31% of men first went to the Internet to "join an
online community" and that 85% of women and 82% of men
came to believe that "the Internet community is an important
part" of their lives (Hawfield & Lyons, 1998). It appears, then,
that the primary motivation for both is not physical but rather
communicative.

Uses statistics to illustrate example

    Attractiveness is hardly the only physical quality by
which men and women judge others. Broad features of identity
such as race, gender, and ethnicity can also trigger uninformed
responses. Researcher Lisa Nakamura (2002) found that when a
person's race is revealed on the Internet, he or she can be just
as subject to prejudicial assumptions as if the reality had been
revealed face to face. Because of this, some people online
deliberately try to mask their race or gender. They want others
to judge them by what they say and think rather than by how
they look, especially in a first encounter.

PARA-GRAPH 9: Gives other factors that influence relationships

    Whether Internet communication will continue to support
first meetings that occur purely in writing is uncertain. With
the increased use of digital images and audio, the Internet has
begun to provide more and more physical cues. Participants in
chat rooms tend to request images earlier as a sign of interest.
People can post false photographs or videos, of course, but
deception complicates any desired face-to-face meeting later
on. Further, the sound of a person's voice shapes others'
perceptions. When voice communication over the Internet
becomes more prevalent, it is likely that our stereotypical
notions will return. Dr. Clifford Nass of Stanford University has
predicted that when voice becomes a part of online interaction,
people will "apply gender stereotypes" (Eisenberg, 2000, para.
6). Nass says that people tend to interpret the female voice as

PARA-GRAPH 10: Explains how increased use of images and sounds changes nature of online meetings

APA-STYLE IN-TEXT CITATION: Includes paragraph or screen nmber for direct quotation from online source without numbered pages

continued >>

EFFECT OF PHYSICAL CUES 8

being "less accurate," with deeper male voices projecting authority. Some voices are perceived as more attractive than others, too.

Conclusion

CONCLUSION: Summarizes main points and looks to the future

Research on Internet relationships suggests that communication without visual cues can increase people's acceptance of one another. In face-to-face meetings, people form impressions based solely on physical appearance, impressions that both influence the way they treat others and the way those people respond. People who are treated well, for example, tend to take on positive characteristics. Because Internet conversations rely more heavily on the quality of communication than on superficial factors, meeting online allows people to suspend judgments based on appearance. This advantage may disappear as images and sounds increasingly accompany online meetings. Perhaps society would be healthier if people judged others not by their looks but by their character as expressed in words and ideas; however, the current tendency to treat stereotypically attractive and unattractive people differently shows the remoteness of that ideal.

continued >>

EFFECT OF PHYSICAL CUES   9

References

Bakalar, N. (2005, May 3). Ugly children may get parental short shrift. *The New York Times*, p. F7.

Dion, K., Berscheid, E., & Walster, E. (1972). What is beautiful is good. *Journal of Personality and Social Psychology, 24*, 285–290.

Eisenberg, A. (2000, October 12). Mars and Venus on the Net: Gender stereotypes prevail. *New York Times*. Retrieved from http://www.nytimes.com

Hawfield, K., & Lyons, E. (1998). Conventional wisdom about women and Internet use: Refuting traditional perceptions. Retrieved from http://elab.vanderbilt.edu/research/papers /html/studentprojects/women/conventional_wisdom.html

Kachel, J. (1996, March). Good looks count during childhood. *Brown University Child and Adolescent Newsletter, 12*. Retrieved from http://www.childresearch.net/RESOURCE /NEWS/index.html

McKenna, K. Y., Green, A. S., & Gleason, M. E. (2003). Relationship formation on the Internet: What's the big attraction? *Journal of Social Issues, 58*, 9–31.

Miyake, K., & Zuckerman, M. (1993). Beyond personality impressions. *Journal of Personality, 61*, 411–436.

Nakamura, L. (2002). *Cybertypes: Race, ethnicity, and identity on the Internet*. New York, NY: Routledge.

Singh, D. (2004). Mating strategies of young women: Role of physical attractiveness. *Journal of Sex Research, 41*, 43–54. doi: 10.1080/00224490409552212

Begins References on new page

Double-spaces through-out

Lists References in alphabetical order by author

Provides a source that appears only on the Web

APA

continued >>

EFFECT OF PHYSICAL CUES   10

Snyder, M., Tanke, E. D., & Berscheid, E. (1977). Social perception
        and interpersonal behavior: On the self-fulfilling nature
        of social stereotypes. *Journal of Personality and Social
        Psychology, 35,* 656–666.

Sveningsson, M. (2002). Cyberlove: Creating romantic
        relationships on the Net. In J. Fornäs, K. Klein, M.
        Ladendorf, J. Sundén, & M. Sveningsson (Eds.), *Digital
        borderlands: Cultural studies of identity and interactivity
        on the Internet* (pp. 48–78). New York, NY: Lang.

APA

Provides
source
infor-
mation
for a
chapter
in a book

39

CM-Style Documentation

39a   What is CM-style documentation?

The Chicago Manual of Style (CM) endorses two styles of documentation. One **CM style** is an author-date style, similar to the APA STYLE of IN-TEXT CITATIONS (Ch. 36), that includes a list of SOURCES usually titled "Works Cited" or "References."

The other CM style uses a **bibliographic note system**. This system gives information about each source in two places: (1) in a *footnote* (at the bottom of a page) or an *endnote* (in a separate page following your paper) and, (2) if required, in a BIBLIOGRAPHY that begins on a separate page. We present this style here because it's often used in such humanities courses as art, music, history, philosophy, and sometimes English. Within the bibliographic note system, there are two substyles: "full" and "abbreviated."

■ The full bibliographic note system in CM style

The CM full bibliographic note system requires you to give complete information, in a footnote or an endnote, the first time you cite a source. Because you're giving full information, you don't need to include a bibliography page. If you cite a source a second time, you provide shortened information that includes the last name(s) of the author(s) and the key words in the work's title. The following example uses the full bibliographic note system.

TEXT

Ulrich points out that both Europeans and Native Americans told war stories, but with different details and different emphases.[3]

FULL FOOTNOTE (SAME PAGE) OR ENDNOTE
(SEPARATE PAGE FOLLOWING TEXT)

3. Laurel Thatcher Ulrich, *The Age of Homespun: Objects and Stories in the Creation of an American Myth* (New York: Knopf, 2001), 269.

SECOND CITATION OF THIS SOURCE

6. Ulrich, *Age of Homespun*, 285.

■ The abbreviated bibliographic note system, plus bibliography, in CM style

In the abbreviated bibliographic note system, even your first endnote or footnote provides only brief information about the source. You provide complete information in a bibliography, which appears as a separate page at the end of the paper. Following is an example of using the full bibliographic note system.

TEXT

Ulrich points out that both Europeans and Native Americans told war stories, but with different details and different emphases.[3]

ABBREVIATED FOOTNOTE (SAME PAGE) OR ENDNOTE
(SEPARATE PAGE FOLLOWING TEXT)

3. Ulrich, *Age of Homespun,* 269.

BIBLIOGRAPHY (SEPARATE PAGE AT END OF THE PAPER)

Ulrich, Laurel Thatcher. *The Age of Homespun: Objects and Stories in the Creation of an American Myth.* New York: Knopf, 2001.

Alert: Ask your instructor which style he or she prefers. Remember that CM style requires a separate bibliography only when you use the abbreviated notes style. ●

Quick Reference 39.1 provides guidelines for compiling CM-style bibliographic notes.

Quick Reference 39.1

Guidelines for compiling CM-style bibliographic notes

TITLE AND PLACEMENT OF NOTES
If you're using endnotes, place them all on a separate page, before your bibliography. Center the heading "Notes," without using italics, underlining, or quotation marks, an inch from the top of the page. If you're using footnotes, place them at the bottom of the page on which the source needs to be credited. Never use a title above a note at the foot of the page. CM generally uses blank space (not a line) to divide the footnote(s) from the body text.

TITLE AND PLACEMENT OF BIBLIOGRAPHY
The abbreviated notes style requires a bibliography, which begins on a separate page at the end of the paper, following the endnotes page. An inch from the top of the page, center the heading "References" or "Works Cited" (either is acceptable in CM style). Don't underline the heading or put it in quotation marks.

continued >>

Quick Reference 39.1   (continued)

FORMAT FOR ENDNOTES AND FOOTNOTES
Include an endnote or a footnote every time you use a source. Number notes sequentially throughout your paper whether you're using endnotes or footnotes. Use superscript (raised) arabic numerals for the footnote or endnote numbers in your paper. Position note numbers after any punctuation mark except the dash. The best position is at the end of a sentence, unless that position would be so far from the source material that it would be confusing. Don't use raised numbers in the endnote or footnote itself. Place the number, followed by a period, on the same line as the content of the note. Single-space both within each note and between notes. Indent each note's first line three-tenths of an inch (0.3″ tab), which equals about three characters, but place subsequent lines flush left at the margin.

SPACING AFTER PUNCTUATION
A single space follows all punctuation, including the period.

AUTHORS' NAMES
In endnotes and footnotes, give the name in standard (first-name-first) order, with names and initials as given in the original source. Use the word *and* before the last author's name if your source has more than one author.

    In the bibliography, invert the name: last name, first name. If a work has two or more authors, invert only the first author's name. If your source has up to ten authors, give all the authors' names. If your source has eleven or more authors, list only the first seven and use *et al.* for the rest.

CAPITALIZATION OF SOURCE TITLES
Capitalize the first and last words and all major words.

SPECIAL TREATMENT OF TITLES
Use italics for titles of long works, and use quotation marks around the titles of shorter works. Omit *A, An,* and *The* from the titles of newspapers and periodicals. For an unfamiliar newspaper title, list the city (and state, in parentheses, if the city isn't well known): *Newark (NJ) Star-Ledger,* for example. Use postal abbreviations for states.

PUBLICATION INFORMATION
Enclose publication information in parentheses. Use a COLON and one space after the city of publication. Give complete publishers' names or abbreviate them according to standard abbreviations in *Books in Print.* Omit *Co., Inc.,* and so on. Spell out *University* or abbreviate to *Univ.* Never use *U* alone. Spell out *Press;* never use *P* alone. Don't abbreviate publication months.

continued >>

CM

CM

Quick Reference 39.1 (continued)

PAGE NUMBERS
For inclusive page numbers, give the full second number for 2 through 99. For 100 and beyond, give the full second number only if a shortened version would be ambiguous: 243–47, 202–6, 300–304. List all discontinuous page numbers. (See "First Endnote or Footnote: Book" toward the end of this box.) Use a comma to separate parenthetical publication information from the page numbers that follow it. Use the abbreviations *p.* and *pp.* with page numbers only for material from newspapers, for material from journals that do not use volume numbers, and to avoid ambiguity.

CONTENT NOTES
Try to avoid using content notes. If you must use them, use footnotes, not endnotes, with symbols rather than numbers: an asterisk (*) for the first note on that page and a dagger (†) for a second note on that page.

FIRST ENDNOTE OR FOOTNOTE: BOOK
For books, include the author, title, publication information, and page numbers when applicable.

1. Eudora Welty, *One Writer's Beginnings* (Cambridge, MA: Harvard University Press, 1984), 25–26, 30, 43–51, 208.

FIRST ENDNOTE OR FOOTNOTE: ARTICLE
For articles, include the author, article title, journal title, volume number, year, and page numbers.

1. D. D. Cochran, W. Daniel Hale, and Christine P. Hissam, "Personal Space Requirements in Indoor versus Outdoor Locations," *Journal of Psychology* 117 (1984): 132–33.

SECOND MENTION IN ENDNOTES OR FOOTNOTES
Second (or later) citations of the same source can be brief. See 39b, item 4, for an explanation.

39b What are CM guidelines for bibliographic notes?

The following directory corresponds to the sample bibliographic note forms that follow it. In a few cases, we give sample Bibliography forms as well. If you need a model that isn't here, consult *The Chicago Manual of Style,* 15th ed. (Chicago: University of Chicago Press, 2003).

DIRECTORY: CM STYLE FOR FOOTNOTES AND ENDNOTES

CM

BOOKS AND PARTS OF BOOKS

1. Book by One Author—CM
Footnote or Endnote

1. Becky Bradway, *Pink Houses and Family Taverns* (Bloomington, IN: Indiana University Press, 2001).

Bibliography

Bradway, Becky. *Pink Houses and Family Taverns.* Bloomington, IN: Indiana
    University Press, 2001.

The format for the bibliography is the reverse of the format for the note, in which first lines indent. In bibliographic form, the first line is placed flush left to the margin and the second and other lines are indented three-tenths to one-half inch (0.3″ to 0.5″ tab). Notice also where periods replace commas and where parentheses are omitted.

2. Book by Two or Three Authors—CM
Footnote or Endnote

1. Edward E. Gordon and Elaine H. Gordon, *Literacy in America: Historic Journey and Contemporary Solutions* (Westport, CT: Praeger, 2003).

2. John K. Lynam, Cyrus G. Ndiritu, and Adiel N. Mbabu, *Transformation of Agricultural Research Systems in Africa: Lessons from Kenya* (East Lansing: Michigan State University Press, 2004), 41.

Bibliography

Lynam, John K., Cyrus G. Ndiritu, and Adiel N. Mbabu. *Transformation of
    Agricultural Research Systems in Africa: Lessons from Kenya.* East
    Lansing: Michigan State University Press, 2004.

In a bibliography entry, invert only the name of the first author listed.

3. Book by More Than Three Authors—CM

1. Wendy Saul and others, *Beyond the Science Fair: Creating a Kids' Inquiry Conference* (Portsmouth, NH: Heinemann, 2005), 72.

4. Multiple Citations of a Single Source—CM

For subsequent references to a work you've already named, use a shortened citation. Give the last name of the author, the title of the work, and the page number, all separated by commas. Shorten the title if it is longer than four words. This example shows the form for a subsequent reference to the work fully described in item 1.

1. Bradway, *Pink Houses*, 25.

If there are more than three authors for a source, use only the name of the first author followed by *et al.* The following example shows the shortened citation for the work in item 3.

2. Saul et al., *Beyond the Science Fair*, 72.

If you cite two or more authors with the same last name, include first names or initials in each note.

3. Eudora Welty, *One Writer's Beginnings*, 25.

4. Paul Welty, *Human Expression*, 129.

If you cite the same source as the source immediately preceding, you may use *Ibid.*, followed by a comma and the page number, instead of repeating the author's name and the title.

5. Ibid., 152.

5. Book by a Group or Corporate Author—CM

1. American Psychological Association, *Publication Manual of the American Psychological Association*, 5th ed. (Washington, DC: American Psychological Association, 2001).

2. Boston Women's Health Collective, *Our Bodies, Ourselves for the New Century* (New York: Simon & Schuster, 1998).

If a work issued by an organization has no author listed on the title page, give the name of the organization as the author of the work. The organization may also be the publisher of the work.

6. Book with No Author Named—CM

1. *The Chicago Manual of Style*, 15th ed. (Chicago: University of Chicago Press, 2003).

Begin the citation with the name of the book.

7. Book with an Author and an Editor—CM

1. Emily Brontë, *Wuthering Heights*, ed. Richard J. Dunn (New York: Norton, 2002).

In this position, the abbreviation *ed.* stands for "edited by," not "editor." Therefore, *ed.* is correct whether a work has one or more than one editor. (Also see items 10 and 16.)

8. Translation—CM

1. Milan Kundera, *The Unbearable Lightness of Being*, trans. Michael Henry Heim (New York: HarperPerennial Library, 1999).

The abbreviation *trans.* stands for "translated by," not "translator."

9. Work in Several Volumes or Parts—CM

The following notes show ways to give bibliographic information for a specific place in one volume of a multivolume work. Use whichever you prefer, staying consistent throughout a paper.

1. Ernest Jones, *The Last Phase*, vol. 3 of *The Life and Work of Sigmund Freud* (New York: Basic Books, 1957), 97.

1. Ernest Jones, *The Life and Work of Sigmund Freud*, vol. 3, *The Last Phase* (New York: Basic Books, 1957), 97.

If you're citing an entire work in two or more volumes, use the form shown below.

2. Ronald Chrisley, ed., *Artificial Intelligence: Critical Concepts*, 4 vols. (London: Routledge, 2000).

10. One Selection from an Anthology or an Edited Book—CM

1. Laura Trujillo, "Balancing Act," in *Border-Line Personalities: A New Generation of Latinas Dish on Sex, Sass, and Cultural Shifting*, ed. Robyn Moreno and Michelle Herrera Mulligan (New York: Harper, 2004), 61–72.

11. More Than One Selection from an Anthology or an Edited Book—CM

If you cite more than one selection from the same anthology or edited book, give complete bibliographical information in each citation.

12. Signed Article in a Reference Book—CM

1. John C. Burnbam, "Freud, Sigmund," in *The Encyclopedia of Psychiatry, Psychology, and Psychoanalysis*, ed. Benjamin B. Wolman (New York: Henry Holt, 1996), 220.

13. Unsigned Article in a Reference Book—CM

1. *Encyclopaedia Britannica*, 15th ed., s.v. "Ireland."

The abbreviation *s.v.* stands for *sub verbo,* meaning "under the word." Capitalize the heading of the entry only if it is a proper noun. Omit publication information except for the edition number.

14. Second or Later Edition—CM

1. Anthony F. Janson, *History of Art,* 6th ed. (New York: Abrams, 2001).

Here the abbreviation *ed.* stands for "edition." Give the copyright date for the edition you're citing.

15. Anthology or Edited Book—CM

1. Eduardo del Rio, ed. *The Prentice Hall Anthology of Latino Literature* (Upper Saddle River, NJ: Prentice Hall, 2002).

Here the abbreviation *ed.* stands for "editor." For a source with two or more editors, use the plural *eds.*

16. Introduction, Preface, Foreword, or Afterword—CM

1. Elizabeth Fox-Genovese, foreword to *Southern Mothers,* ed. Nagueyalti Warren and Sally Wolff (Baton Rouge: Louisiana State University Press, 1999).

If the author of the book is different from the author of the cited part, give the name of the book's author or editor after the title of the book, preceded by the word *by* or *ed.* (for "edited by").

17. Unpublished Dissertation or Essay—CM

1. Gina Anne Stuart, "Exploring the Harry Potter Book Series: A Study of Adolescent Reading Motivation" (PhD diss., Utah State University, 2006), 21.

List the author's name first, then the title in quotation marks (not italicized), a descriptive label (such as *PhD diss.* or *master's thesis),* the degree-granting institution, the date, and the page numbers you're citing.

18. Reprint of an Older Book—CM

1. Marian Anderson, *My Lord, What a Morning* (1956; repr., Urbana: University of Illinois Press, 2002).

Republishing information is located on the copyright page. List the original date of publication first, followed by the publication information for the reprint.

19. Book in a Series—CM

1. Dorothy J. Goldman, *Women Writers and World War I,* Literature and Society Series (New York: Macmillan, 1995).

If the series numbers its volumes and the volume number isn't part of the title, you would include the volume number after the series title. Separate the volume number from the series title with a comma.

20. Book with a Title Within a Title—CM

1. Aljean Harmetz, *The Making of "The Wizard of Oz"* (New York: Hyperion, 1998).

If the name of a work that's usually italicized appears in an italicized title, put quotation marks around it. If the name of a work that's usually in quotation marks appears in an italicized title, keep it in quotation marks.

21. Government Publication—CM

1. House Committee on Resources, *Coastal Heritage Trail Route in New Jersey*, 106th Cong., 1st sess., 1999, H. Rep. 16.

If a government department, bureau, agency, or committee produces a document, cite that group as the author. In a bibliography entry, the author is often identified as *U.S. Congress,* followed by either *House* or *Senate* and the committee or subcommittee, if any, before the title of the document.

22. Published Proceedings of a Conference—CM

1. Anne Dobyns, "Civil Disobedience and the Ethical Appeal of Self-Representation," in *Rhetorical Democracy: Discursive Practices of Civic Engagement*, ed. Gerald A. Hauser and Amy Grim (Mahwah, NJ: Erlbaum, 2003), 131–36.

Treat published conference proceedings as you would a chapter in a book.

23. Secondary Source from a Book—CM

When you quote one person's words, having found them in another person's work, give information as fully as you can about both sources. CM style recommends, however, that original sources be consulted and cited whenever practical.

1. Mary Wollstonecraft, *A Vindication of the Rights of Woman* (1792), 90, quoted in Caroline Shrodes, Harry Finestone, and Michael Shugrue, *The Conscious Reader*, 4th ed. (New York: Macmillan, 1988), 282.

2. Caroline Shrodes, Harry Finestone, and Michael Shugrue, *The Conscious Reader*, 4th ed. (New York: Macmillan, 1988), 282, quoting Mary Wollstonecraft, *A Vindication of the Rights of Woman* (1792), 90.

PERIODICALS—PRINT

24. Signed Article in a Daily Newspaper—CM

1. Penelope Green, "The Slow Life Picks Up Speed," *New York Times*, January 31, 2008, national edition, sec. D.

Because many newspapers print more than one edition a day and reposition the same articles on different pages, CM style recommends that you omit page numbers from note entries. When applicable, identify the specific edition (such as *Southeastern edition* or *final edition*). For a paper that specifies sections, use *sec.* before the section's letter or number or use *section* for a section's name (such as *Weekend section*). If a paper gives column titles, you may use the title (not italicized or in quotation marks) in addition to or in place of the article title. Separate all items with commas.

25. Editorial, Letter to the Editor, or Review—CM

1. "Primary Considerations," editorial, *Washington Post*, January 27, 2008, sec. B.

2. Emily Finanger, letter to the editor, *Outside*, February 2008, 14.

3. David Shenk, "Toolmaker, Brain Builder," review of *Beyond Big Blue: Building the Computer That Defeated the World Chess Champion*, by Feng-Hsiung Hsu, *American Scholar* 72 (Spring 2003): 150–52.

Before page numbers, use a comma for popular magazines and a colon for journals.

26. Unsigned Article in a Daily Newspaper—CM

1. "Oscars Ready Plans to Deal with Strike," *Denver Post*, January 31, 2008, sec. B.

27. Signed Article in a Weekly or Biweekly Magazine or Newspaper—CM

1. Christine Gorman, "How to Age Gracefully," *Time*, June 6, 2005, 73–74.

For general-readership weekly and biweekly magazines and newspapers, give the month, day, and year of publication. Separate page numbers from the year with a comma.

28. Signed Article in a Monthly or Bimonthly Periodical—CM

1. James Fallows, "The $1.4 Trillion Question," *The Atlantic*, January/February 2008, 36–48.

For general-readership monthly and bimonthly magazines, give the month and year of publication. Separate page numbers from the year with a comma.

29. Unsigned Article in a Periodical—CM

1. "The Price Is Wrong," *Economist*, August 2, 2003, 58–59.

30. Article in a Collection of Reprinted Articles—CM

1. Thomas Hayden, "The Age of Robots," in *Applied Science*, Social Issues Resources Series (Boca Raton, FL: Social Issues Resources, 2002).

Cite only the publication actually consulted, not the original source. If you use a bibliography, cite its location in both the reprinted publication you consulted and the publication where the article first appeared.

31. Article in a Journal with Continuous Pagination—CM

1. Phyllis Tyson, "The Psychology of Women Continued," *Journal of the American Psychoanalytic Association* 46 (1998): 361–63.

32. Article in a Journal That Pages Each Issue Separately—CM

1. Linda Adler-Kassner and Heidi Estrem, "Rethinking Research Writing: Public Literacy in the Composition Classroom," *WPA: Writing Program Administration* 26, no. 3 (2003): 119–31.

The issue number of a journal is required only if each issue of the journal starts with page 1. In this example, the volume number is 26 and the issue number, abbreviated *no.,* is 3.

INTERNET SOURCES

If there is a print version of the source (as in item 35), provide information about that source. Also include information about how to find the electronic version. CM style does not generally recommend including access dates, nor does it use angle brackets around URLs. Following are examples of a few common types of electronic sources. For additional types, consult *The Chicago Manual of Style*.

33. Online Book—CM

1. Kate Chopin, *The Awakening* (Washington, DC: PBS, 1998), http://www.pbs.org/katechopin/library/awakening.

Include the author's name, the title, and access information—in this case, the name of the organization that sponsors the site—and the URL.

34. Article from a Periodical Available Only Online—CM

1. Jody Shipka, "This Was (NOT!!) an Easy Assignment," *Computers and Composition Online*, fall 2007, http://www.bgsu.edu/cconline/not_easy/.

Include the author, title of the article, title of the publication, volume and issue number (if given), publication date, and URL.

35. Article Accessed Through a Database—CM

1. Gail Dutton, "Greener Pigs," *Popular Science* 255, no. 5 (November 1999): 38–39, http://proquest.umi.com (accessed September 2, 2007).

Include the author, title of the article, title of the publication, volume and issue numbers (if given) of the original publication, the original publication date, and the URL of the database through which you accessed the article. Include an access date. Insert the access date in parentheses after the URL, followed by a period.

36. Source from an Internet Site—CM

1. Association for the Advancement of Artificial Intelligence, "AI Overview," Association for the Advancement of Artificial Intelligence, http://www.aaai.org/AITopics/html/overview.html (accessed January 22, 2008).

Provide the author's name, the title of the Web page, the title or owner of the site, and the URL. When no specific author is listed, you may use the owner of the site as the author, as in the example. Include an access date if your source is likely to be updated frequently, as is often the case with Internet sites.

37. Electronic Mailing List—CM

1. T. Caruso, e-mail to Calls for Papers mailing list, June 30, 2002, http://www.cfp.english.upenn.edu/archive/2002-09/0041.html.

38. E-Mail Message—CM

1. Eliana Pessin, e-mail message to Georgia Dobyns, November 11, 2007.

39. Weblog Entry—CM

1. Scott McLemee, "To Whom It May Concern," Weblog posting to *Quick Study*, January 1, 2008, http://www.artsjournal.com/quickstudy/ (accessed May 14, 2008).

40. Online Video or Podcast—CM

1. Michael Wesch, *Web 2.0 . . . The Machine is Us/ing Us*, video posted January 31, 2007 (accessed July 7, 2007).

Wesch is the director and producer of this video.

OTHER SOURCES

41. Speech or Conference Presentation—CM

1. Peter Leslie Mortensen, "Meet the Press: Reading News Coverage of Research on Writing" (paper presented at the annual meeting of the Modern Language Association, Washington, DC, December 29, 2005).

42. Personal Interview—CM

1. Randi Friedman, interview by author, August 30, 2008, Austin, TX.

For an unpublished interview, give the name of the interviewee and the interviewer, the date of the interview, and the location of the interview. CM style recommends that you incorporate this information into the text, making a note unnecessary.

43. Published and Unpublished Letters—CM

1. William Carlos Williams to his son, 13 March 1935, in *Letters of the Century: America 1900–1999*, ed. Lisa Grunwald and Stephen J. Adler (New York: Dial, 1999), 225–26.

2. Theodore Brown, letter to author, December 7, 2005.

For an unpublished letter, give the name of the writer, the name of the recipient, and the date the letter was written.

44. Film, Videotape, or DVD—CM

1. Marc Norman and Tom Stoppard, *Shakespeare in Love*, DVD (1998; New York: Miramax Films/Universal Pictures, 2003).

The note begins with the authors of the screenplay. If the point of the note was about the director or the producers, then the title would appear first and the abbreviations *dir.* and/or *prod.* ("directed by," "produced by") would follow a comma after the title, along with the relevant names.

45. Recording—CM

1. Bedrich Smetana, *My Country*, Czech Philharmonic, Karel Anserl, Vanguard SV-9/10.

Bedrich Smetana is the composer, and Karel Anserl is the conductor.

2. Bruce Springsteen, "Lonesome Day," on *The Rising*, Sony CD B000069 HKH.

46. Computer Software—CM

1. Guitar Hero III: Legends of Rock, 2007. Activision, Santa Monica.

2. Dreamweaver, Ver. MX, Macromedia, San Francisco, CA.

Place the version or release number, abbreviated *Ver.* or *Rel.*, directly after the name of the software. Then, list the company that owns the rights to the software, followed by that company's location.

For more help with your
writing, grammar, and research,
go to **www.mycomplab.com**

40

CSE-Style Documentation

40a   What is CSE-style documentation?

The Council of Science Editors, or CSE, produces a manual called *Scientific Style and Format* to guide publications in the mathematics, the life sciences, and the physical sciences. The information in this chapter adheres to the style guidelines in the seventh edition of that manual. For up-to-date information about any changes, go to the organization's Web site at http://www.councilscienceeditors.org.

CSE has two components: (1) citations within the text (called "in-text references") tied to (2) a bibliography ("end references") at the end of the text. However, CSE offers three different options for in-text references: the citation-sequence system, the name-year system, and the citation-name system. In this chapter we explain the citation-name system, which the CSE most strongly endorses.

In the citation-name system, the in-text references use numbers to refer to end references that are arranged alphabetically. In other words, first complete the list of end references, arranging them alphabetically by author. Then, number each reference; for example, if you were documenting references by Schmidt, Gonzalez, Adams, and Zurowski, in your end references, they would be arranged:

1. Adams . . .

2. Gonzalez . . .

3. Schmidt . . .

4. Zurowski . . .

Finally, use superscript (raised) numbers for source citations in your sentences that correspond to the numbered author names in the end references. (Numbers in parentheses are also acceptable.)

IN-TEXT REFERENCES—CITATION-NAME

Sybesma[2] insists that this behavior occurs periodically, but Crowder[1] claims never to have observed it.

END REFERENCES—CITATION-NAME

1. Crowder W. Seashore life between the tides. New York: Dodd, Mead; 1931. New York: Dover Reprint; 1975. 372 p.

2. Sybesma C. An introduction to biophysics. New York: Academic; 1977. 648 p.

Quick Reference 40.1 gives guidelines for compiling a References list. Especially pay attention to the arrangement of entries in a citation-name system.

When you're citing more than one reference at a time, list each source number in numeric order, followed by a comma with no space. Use a hyphen to show the range of numbers in a continuous sequence, and put all in superscript: [2,5-7,8]

Quick Reference 40.1   ■ ■ ■ ■ ■ ■ ■

Guidelines for compiling a CSE-style Cited References list

TITLE
Use "Cited References" or "References" as the title (no underlining, no italics, no quotation marks).

PLACEMENT OF LIST
Begin the list on a separate page at the end of the research paper. Number the page sequentially with the rest of the paper.

CONTENT AND FORMAT OF CITED REFERENCES
Include all sources that you quote, paraphrase, or summarize in your paper. Center the title one inch from the top of the page. Start each entry on a new line. Put the number, followed by a period and a space, at the regular left margin. If an entry takes more than one line, indent the second and all other lines under the first word, not the number. Single-space each entry and double-space between entries.

SPACING AFTER PUNCTUATION
CSE style specifies no space after date, issue number, or volume number of a periodical, as shown in the models in 40b.

continued >>

Quick Reference 40.1 (continued)

ARRANGEMENT OF ENTRIES

Sequence the entries in alphabetical order by author, then title, etc. Number the entries. Put the number, followed by a period and a space, at the regular left margin.

AUTHORS' NAMES

Reverse the order of each author's name, giving the last name first. For book citations, you can give first names or use only the initials of first and (when available) middle names; for journal citations, use only initials. However, CSE style recommends you use only initials. Don't use a period or a space between first and middle initials. Use a comma to separate the names of multiple authors identified by initials; however, if you use full first names, use a semicolon. Don't use *and* or *&* with authors' names. Place a period after the last author's name.

TREATMENT OF TITLES

Never underline titles or enclose them in quotation marks. Capitalize a title's first word and any proper nouns. Don't capitalize the first word of a subtitle unless it's a proper noun. Capitalize the titles of academic journals. If the title of a periodical is one word, give it in full; otherwise, abbreviate the title according to recommendations established by the *American National Standard for Abbreviations of Titles of Periodicals*. Capitalize a newspaper title's major words, giving the full title but omitting *A, An,* or *The* at the beginning.

PLACE OF PUBLICATION

Use a COLON after the city of publication. If the city name could be unfamiliar to readers, add in parentheses the postal abbreviation for the US state or Canadian province. If the location of a foreign city will be unfamiliar to readers, add in parentheses the country name, abbreviating it according to International Organization for Standardization (ISO) standards. Find ISO abbreviations at http://un.org/Depts/cartographic/english/geoinfo/geoname.pdf.

PUBLISHER

Give the name of the publisher, without periods after initials, and use a semicolon after the publisher's name. Omit *The* at the beginning or *Co., Inc., Ltd.,* or *Press* at the end. However, for a university press, abbreviate *University* and *Press* as *Univ* and *Pr,* respectively, without periods.

PUBLICATION MONTH

Abbreviate all month names longer than three letters to their first three letters, but do not add a period.

continued >>

Quick Reference 40.1   (continued)

INCLUSIVE PAGE NUMBERS
Shorten the second number as much as possible, making sure that the number isn't ambiguous. For example, use 233–4 for 233 to 234; 233–44 for 233 to 244; and 233–304, not 233–04, for 233 to 304.

DISCONTINUOUS PAGE NUMBERS
Give the numbers of all discontinuous pages, separating successive numbers or ranges with a comma: 54–7, 60–6.

TOTAL PAGE NUMBERS
When citing an entire book, the last information unit gives the total number of book pages, followed by the abbreviation *p* and a period.

FORMAT FOR CITED REFERENCES ENTRIES: BOOKS
Citations for books usually list author(s), title, publication information, and pages (either total pages when citing an entire work or inclusive pages when citing part of a book). Each unit of information ends with a period.

1. Primrose SB, Twyman RM, Old RW. Principles of gene manipulation. London: Blackwell; 2002. 390 p.

FORMAT FOR CITED REFERENCES ENTRIES: ARTICLES
Citations for articles usually list author(s), article title, and journal name and publication information, each section followed by a period. Abbreviate a journal's name only if it's standard in your scientific discipline. For example, *Exp Neurol* is the abbreviated form for *Experimental Neurology.* In the following example, the volume number is 184, and the issue number, in parentheses, is 1. Notice the lack of a space after the semicolon, before the parentheses, and after the colon.

1. Ginis I, Rao MS. Toward cell replacement therapy: promises and caveats. Exp Neurol 2003;184(1):61–77.

40b What are CSE guidelines for sources in a list of references?

The directory that follows corresponds to the sample references that follow it. If you need a model not included in this book, consult *Scientific Style and Format,* 7th ed. (2006).

DIRECTORY: CSE STYLE FOR A CITED REFERENCES LIST

CSE

BOOKS AND PARTS OF BOOKS

1. Book by One Author—CSE

1. Hawking SW. Black holes and baby universes and other essays. New York: Bantam; 1993. 320 p.

Use one space but no punctuation between an author's last name and the initial of the first name. Don't put punctuation or a space between first and middle initials (*Hawking SW*). Do, however, use the hyphen in a hyphenated first and middle name (for example, *Gille J-C* represents *Jean-Claude Gille* in the next item).

2. Book by More Than One Author—CSE

1. Wegzyn S, Gille J-C, Vidal P. Developmental systems: at the crossroads of system theory, computer science, and genetic engineering. New York: Springer-Verlag; 1990. 595 p.

3. Book by a Group or Corporate Author—CSE

1. Chemical Rubber Company. Handbook of laboratory safety. 3rd ed. Boca Raton (FL): CRC; 1990. 1352 p.

4. Anthology or Edited Book—CSE

1. Heerrmann B, Hummel S, editors. Ancient DNA: recovery and analysis of genetic material from paleontological, archeological, museum, medical, and forensic specimens. New York: Springer-Verlag; 1994. 1020 p.

5. One Selection or Chapter in an Anthology or Edited Book—CSE

1. Basov NG, Feoktistov LP, Senatsky YV. Laser driver for inertial confinement fusion. In: Bureckner KA, editor. Research trends in physics: inertial confinement fusion. New York: American Institute of Physics; 1992. p. 24–37.

6. Translation—CSE

1. Magris C. A different sea. Spurr MS, translator. London: Harvill; 1993. 194 p. Translation of: Un mare differente.

7. Reprint of an Older Book—CSE

1. Carson R. The sea around us. New York: Oxford Univ Pr; 1951. New York: Oxford Univ Pr; 1991. 288 p.

8. All Volumes of a Multivolume Work—CSE

1. Crane FL, Moore DJ, Low HE, editors. Oxidoreduction at the plasma membrane: relation to growth and transport. Boca Raton (FL): CRC; 1991. 2 vol.

9. Unpublished Dissertation or Thesis—CSE

1. Baykul MC. Using ballistic electron emission microscopy to investigate the metal-vacuum interface [dissertation]. Orem (UT): Polytechnic Univ Pr; 1993. 111 p. Available from: UMI Dissertation Express, http://tls.il.proquest.com/hp/Products/DisExpress.html, Document 9332714.

10. Published Article from Conference Proceedings—CSE

1. Tsang CP, Bellgard MI. Sequence generation using a network of Boltzmann machines. In: Tsang CP, editor. Proceedings of the 4th Australian Joint

Conference on Artificial Intelligence; 1990 Nov 8–11; Perth, AUS. Singapore: World Scientific; 1990. p. 224–33.

PRINT ARTICLES FROM JOURNALS AND PERIODICALS

11. Article in a Journal—CSE

1. Ginis I, Rao MS. Toward cell replacement therapy: promises and caveats. Exp Neurol 2003;184(1):61–77.

Give both the volume number and the issue number (here, *184* is the volume number and *1* is the issue number). Note that there is no space between the year and the volume, the volume and the issue, or the issue and the pages.

12. Journal Article on Discontinuous Pages—CSE

1. Richards FM. The protein folding problem. Sci Am 1991;246(1):54–7, 60–6.

13. Article with No Identifiable Author—CSE

1. Cruelty to animals linked to murders of humans. AWIQ 1993 Aug;42(3):16.

14. Article with Author Affiliation—CSE

1. DeMoll E, Auffenberg T (Department of Microbiology, University of Kentucky). Purine metabolism in *Methanococcus vannielii*. J Bacteriol 1993;175:5754–61.

15. Entire Issue of a Journal—CSE

1. Whales in a modern world: a symposium held in London, November 1988. Mamm Rev 1990 Jan;20(9).

The date of the symposium, November 1988, is part of the title of this issue.

16. Signed Newspaper Article—CSE

1. Kilborn PT. A health threat baffling for its lack of a pattern. New York Times 2003 Jun 22;Sect. A:14.

Sect. stands for *section.* Note that there is no space between the date and the section.

17. Unsigned Newspaper Article—CSE

1. Supercomputing center to lead security effort. Pantagraph (Bloomington, IL) 2003 Jul 4;Sect. A:7.

18. Editorial or Review—CSE

CSE allows "notes" after the page number(s) that will help readers understand the nature of the reference.

CSE

1. Leshner AI. "Glocal" science advocacy. Science 2008;319(5865):877. Editorial.

2. Myer A. Genomes evolve, but how? Nature 2008;451(7180):771. Review of Lynch M, The Origins of Genome Architecture.

ELECTRONIC SOURCES ON THE INTERNET

In general, CSE style requires that you cite electronic sources by including the author's name, if available; the work's title; the type of medium, in brackets, such as [*Internet*] or [*electronic mail on the Internet*]; the title of the publication if there's a print version or, if not, the place of publication and the publishing organization; the date the original was published or placed on the Internet; the date you accessed the publication, preceded by the word *cited* enclosed in brackets; and the address of the source, if from the Internet or a database. Omit end punctuation after an Internet address.

19. Books on the Internet—CSE

1. Colwell R, editor. MENC handbook of musical cognition and development [Internet]. New York (NY): Oxford Univ Pr; c2006 [cited 2008 Feb 4]. Available from: http://site.ebrary.com.bianca.penlib.du.edu/

20. Articles with Print Versions on the Internet—CSE

1. Pollard R. Evidence of a reduced home field advantage when a team moves to a new stadium. Journal of Sports Sciences [Internet]. 2002. [cited 2007 Nov 5]; 20(12):969–974. Available from: http://0-find.galegroup.com.bianca .penlib.du.edu:80/itx/start.do?prodId=AONE

21. Articles Available Only on the Internet—CSE

1. Overbye D. Remembrance of things future: the mystery of time. The New York Times on the Web [Internet]. 2005 Jun 28 [cited 2005 Dec 11]. Available from: http://www.nytimes.com/2005/06/28/science/28time.html

22. Web Pages—CSE

Begin with author, if available; otherwise, begin with title.

1. Think again: men and women share cognitive skills [Internet]. Washington, DC: American Psychological Association; 2006 [cited 2007 Jan 17]. Available from: http://www.psychologymatters.org/thinkagain.html

1. Welcome to AAAI [Internet]. Menlo Park (CA): Association for the Advancement of Artificial Intelligence. c2008 [cited 2008 Mar 17]. Available from: http://www.aaai.org

23. Videos or Podcasts—CSE

1. Wesch M. Web 2.0 . . . the machine is us/ing us [video on the Internet]. 2007
   Jan 31 [cited 2007 Dec 14]. Available from: http://www.youtube.com/
   watch?v=6gmP4nk0EOE

OTHER SOURCES
24. Map—CSE

1. Russia and post-Soviet republics [political map]. Moscow: Mapping
   Production Association; 1992. Conical equidistant projection; 40×48 in.;
   color, scale 1:8,000,000.

25. Unpublished Letter—CSE

1. Darwin C. [Letter to Mr. Clerke, 1861]. Located at: University of Iowa Library,
   Iowa City.

26. Video Recording—CSE

1. Nova—The elegant universe [DVD]. Boston: WGBH; 2004. 2 DVDs: 180 min,
   sound, color.

27. Slide Set—CSE

1. Human parasitology [slides]. Chicago: American Society of Clinical
   Pathologists; 1990. Color. Accompanied by: 1 guide.

28. Presentation Slides—CSE

1. Beaudoin E. Fruit fly larvae [PowerPoint slides]. Denver, CO: University
   of Denver; 2007 Oct 17. 49 slides.

For more help with your writing, grammar, and research,
go to **www.mycomplab.com**

mycomplab

41

Parts of Speech and Parts of Sentences

PARTS OF SPEECH

Knowing the parts of speech gives you a basic vocabulary not only for identifying words but also for understanding how language works. To identify a word's part of speech, see how the word functions in the sentence you're analyzing. Often the same word functions differently in different sentences.

We ate **fish**. [*Fish* is a NOUN.* It represents a thing.]

We **fish** on weekends. [*Fish* is a VERB. It represents an action.]

41a   What is a noun?

A **noun** represents a person, place, thing, or idea: *student, college, textbook, education*. Quick Reference 41.1 (p. 332) lists types of nouns.

ESOL TIPs: (1) Speakers of languages other than English find it helpful to know whether nouns are count nouns or noncount nouns. We cover this topic in Chapter 69.

(2) Nouns often appear with words that tell how much, how many, whose, which one, and similar information. These words include ARTICLES (*a, an, the*), ADJECTIVES, and other DETERMINERS, which we discuss in Chapters 69–71.

(3) Words with the SUFFIXES (word endings) *-ance, -ence, -ment, -ness,* and *-ty* are usually nouns. We discuss the spelling of suffixes in 56b. ●

41b   What is a pronoun?

A **pronoun** stands for or refers to a noun. The word or words a pronoun replaces are called its **antecedents** (44a). Quick Reference 41.2 (p. 333) lists types of pronouns.

Sonya is an architect. [noun]

She is an architect. [pronoun]

---

*Words printed in SMALL CAPITAL LETTERS are discussed elsewhere in the text and are defined in the Terms Glossary at the back of the book.

Quick Reference 41.1 ■ ■ ■ ■ ■ ■ ■

Types of nouns

PROPER	names of specific people, places, or things (first letter is always capitalized)	*Faith Hill, Will Smith, Paris, Buick*
COMMON	general groups, places, people, or things	*singer, city, automobile*
CONCRETE	things experienced through the senses: sight, hearing, taste, smell, and touch	*landscape, pizza, thunder*
ABSTRACT	things not knowable through the senses	*freedom, shyness*
COLLECTIVE	groups	*family, team*
NONCOUNT	"uncountable" things	*beef, dirt*
COUNT	countable items (singular or plural)	*lake (lakes), minute (minutes)*

Note: Some nouns fit into more than one category. For example, *family* is both a common noun and a collective noun.

The interior designer needs to consult **her**. [The pronoun *her* refers to its antecedent, which is *Sonya* in the first sentence and *she* in the second sentence.]

🌐 **ESOL TIP:** Pronouns and nouns are closely linked in function. We therefore discuss them together in Chapters 69, 70, 72, and 73. ●

41c What is a verb?

Verbs are of two types: main verbs and AUXILIARY VERBS (Ch. 74). **Main verbs** express action, occurrence, or state of being (Ch. 42).

> I **dance**. [action]
>
> The audience **became** silent. [occurrence]
>
> Your dancing **was** excellent. [state of being]

🚫 **Alert:** When you're not sure if a word is a verb, try putting it into a different TENSE. If the sentence still makes sense, the word is a verb. (For help with verb tenses, see 42e.)

Quick Reference 41.2

Types of pronouns

PERSONAL *I, you, they, her, its, ours,* and others	refers to people or things	I saw **her** take a book to **them**.
RELATIVE *who, which, that*	introduces certain NOUN CLAUSES and ADJECTIVE CLAUSES	The book **that** I lost was valuable.
INTERROGATIVE *who, whose, what, which,* and others	introduces a question	**Who** called?
DEMONSTRATIVE *this, these, that, those*	points out the antecedent	Whose books are **these**?
REFLEXIVE, INTENSIVE *myself, themselves,* and other *-self* or *-selves* words	refers to or intensifies the antecedent	They claim to support **themselves.** I **myself** doubt it.
RECIPROCAL *each other, one another*	refers to individual parts of a plural antecedent	We respect **each other**.
INDEFINITE *all, anyone, each,* and others	refers to nonspecific persons or things	**Everyone** is welcome here.

NO He is a **changed** person. He is a **will change** person. [The sentence does not make sense when the verb *will change* is substituted, so *changed* is not functioning as a verb.]

YES The store **changed** owners. The store **will change** owners. [Because the sentence still makes sense when the verb *will change* is substituted, *changed* is functioning as a verb.] ●

Auxiliary and modal auxiliary verbs, as well as many aspects of using verbs, are covered in detail in Chapter 38. In addition, Chapter 74 offers information about verbs of particular use to multilingual writers of English.

41d What is a verbal?

Verbals are verb parts that function as nouns, adjectives, or ADVERBS. Quick Reference 41.3 (p. 334) lists types of verbals.

Quick Reference 41.3

■ ■ ■ ■ ■ ■ ■

Types of verbals and functions they perform

INFINITIVE *to* + SIMPLE FORM of verb	1. NOUN: represents an action, state, or condition	**To eat** soon is our goal.
	2. ADJECTIVE or ADVERB: describes or modifies	Still, we have nothing **to eat**.
PAST PARTICIPLE *-ed* form of REGULAR VERB or equivalent for IRREGULAR VERB	ADJECTIVE: describes or modifies	**Boiled, filtered** water is usually safe to drink.
PRESENT PARTICIPLE *-ing* form of verb	1. ADJECTIVE: describes or modifies	**Running** water may not be safe.
	2. NOUN: represents an action, state, or condition*	**Drinking** contaminated water is dangerous.

*A present participle functioning as a noun is called a **gerund**.

🌐 **ESOL TIPS:** The word *to* has several functions, each of which is discussed in Chapter 46. (1) As part of the INFINITIVE *to eat,* the word *to* modifies (limits) the PRONOUN *nothing*.

He has nothing **to eat**.

(2) *To* can be part of a MODAL AUXILIARY VERB, such as *have to,* which means "must" (74b).

He **has to eat** something.

(3) *To* is also a preposition that must be followed by a noun, pronoun, or gerund OBJECT—in this example, the word *eating* (73a).

He is **accustomed to eating** at noon.

(4) Infinitives and gerunds often challenge multilingual writers of English. We discuss them in detail in Chapter 73. ●

41e　What is an adjective?

Adjectives modify—describe or limit—nouns, pronouns, and word groups that function as nouns.

I saw a **green** and **leafy** tree. [*Green* and *leafy* modify the noun *tree*.]

Descriptive adjectives, such as *green* and *leafy*, can show levels of intensity: *green, greener, greenest; leafy, more leafy, most leafy* (45e). **Proper adjectives** emerge from PROPER NOUNS: *American, Victorian.* In addition, words with these suffixes (word endings) are usually adjectives: *-ful, -ish, -less,* and *-like.* (For more about suffixes, see 56b.)

Determiners, sometimes called *limiting adjectives* because they "limit" nouns, tell whether a noun is general (**a** *tree*) or specific (**the** *tree*). Determiners also tell which one (**this** *tree*), how many (**twelve** *trees*), whose (**our** *tree*), and similar information. Quick Reference 41.4 lists types of determiners.

Quick Reference 41.4

Types of determiners

ARTICLES *a, an, the*	**A** reporter working on **an** assignment is using **the** telephone.
DEMONSTRATIVE *this, these, that, those*	**Those** students rent **that** house.
INDEFINITE *any, each, few, other, some,* and others	**Few** films today have complex plots.
INTERROGATIVE *what, which, whose*	**What** answer did you give?
NUMERICAL *one, first, two, second,* and others	The **fifth** question was tricky.
POSSESSIVE *my, your, their,* and others	**My** dog is older than **your** cat.
RELATIVE *what, which, whose, whatever,* and others	He is the instructor **whose** course I enjoyed.

🌐 **ESOL Tip:** To provide more help for multilingual writers, we discuss articles extensively in Chapter 70. ●

41f What is an adverb?

An **adverb** modifies—describes or limits—verbs, adjectives, other adverbs, and CLAUSES.

Chefs plan meals **carefully**. [*Carefully* modifies the verb *plan*.]

Vegetables provide **very** important vitamins. [*Very* modifies the adjective *important.*]

Those potato chips are **too** heavily salted. [*Too* modifies the adverb *heavily.*]

Fortunately, people realize that salt can do harm. [*Fortunately* modifies the entire sentence.]

Descriptive adverbs show levels of intensity, usually by adding *more* (or *less*) and *most* (or *least*): *more happily, least clearly.* Many descriptive adverbs are formed by adding *-ly* to adjectives: *sadly, loudly, normally.* But many adverbs don't end in *-ly: very, always, not, yesterday,* and *well* are a few. Also, some adjectives look like adverbs but are really adjectives: *brotherly, lovely.* (For more about adverbs, see Chapter 45.)

Relative adverbs introduce adjective clauses with words such as *where, why,* and *when.*

Conjunctive adverbs modify by creating logical connections in meaning to express relationships as shown in Quick Reference 41.5.

Quick Reference 41.5

Conjunctive adverbs and relationships they express

Relationship	Adverbs
ADDITION	*also, furthermore, moreover, besides*
CONTRAST	*however, still, nevertheless, conversely, nonetheless, instead, otherwise*
COMPARISON	*similarly, likewise*
RESULT OR SUMMARY	*therefore, thus, consequently, accordingly, hence, then*
TIME	*next, then, meanwhile, finally, subsequently*
EMPHASIS	*indeed, certainly*

41g What is a preposition?

Prepositions are common words that hold sentences together by showing relationships: *The professor walked **into** the classroom **before** the students.* Some common prepositions are *on, in, at, by, for, during, before, after, over, above, under, underneath, below,* and *behind.*

Prepositions combine with other words to form PREPOSITIONAL PHRASES. These phrases often express relationships in time or space: *in April, under the orange umbrella.*

🌐 **ESOL Tip:** Prepositions play an important role in PHRASAL VERBS, which multilingual writers need to study closely. We discuss them in more detail in Chapter 72. ●

41h   What is a conjunction?

A **conjunction** connects words, phrases, or clauses. **Coordinating conjunctions**, which express the types of relationships listed in Quick Reference 41.6, join two or more grammatically equivalent structures.

Quick Reference 41.6 ∎∎∎∎∎∎∎

Coordinating conjunctions and relationships they express

Relationship	Coordinating Conjunction
ADDITION	*and*
CONTRAST	*but, yet*
REASON OR CAUSE	*for*
RESULT OR EFFECT	*so*
CHOICE	*or*
NEGATIVE CHOICE	*nor*

We hike **and** camp every summer. [*And* joins two verbs.]

I love the outdoors, **but** my family does not. [*But* joins two INDEPENDENT CLAUSES.]

Correlative conjunctions function in pairs to join equivalent grammatical structures. They include *both . . . and, either . . . or, neither . . . nor, not only . . . but (also), whether . . . or,* and *not . . . so much as.*

Not only students **but also** businesspeople should study a second language.

Subordinating conjunctions introduce DEPENDENT CLAUSES. They tell us that the dependent clauses are grammatically less important than any independent clause in the same sentence.

Because it snowed, the school superintendent canceled all classes. [The important part is that the superintendent canceled classes.]

Quick Reference 41.7 shows the various relationships subordinating conjunctions express.

Subordinating conjunctions and relationships they express

Relationship	Subordinating Conjunction
TIME	*after, before, once, since, until, when, whenever, while*
REASON OR CAUSE	*as, because, since*
RESULT OR EFFECT	*in order that, so, so that, that*
CONDITION	*if, even if, provided that, unless*
CONTRAST	*although, even though, though, whereas*
LOCATION	*where, wherever*
CHOICE	*rather than, than, whether*

41i What is an interjection?

An **interjection** is a word or group of words showing surprise or strong emotion. When it stands alone, punctuate an interjection with an exclamation point: *Hooray!* As part of a sentence, set off an interjection with a comma or commas: *Hooray, you got the promotion.* Use interjections sparingly, if at all, in ACADEMIC WRITING.

PARTS OF SENTENCES

When you're aware of the parts of sentences, you have one tool for understanding the art of writing.

41j What are subjects and predicates?

A sentence consists of two basic parts: a **subject** and a **predicate**.

A **simple subject** is the word (or words) that acts, is described, or is acted on: *The **telephone** rang.* A **complete subject** is the subject and all its MODIFIERS: ***The red telephone** rang.*

The **simple predicate** consists of the verb: *The telephone **rang**.* The **complete predicate** is the verb and all its modifiers: *The telephone **rang loudly**.* Quick Reference 41.8 explains three subject and predicate sentence patterns.

ESOL Tip: Never repeat a SUBJECT with its PERSONAL PRONOUN in the same clause.

NO   **My grandfather he** lived to be eighty-seven.

YES   **My grandfather** lived to be eighty-seven.

Quick Reference 41.8

Sentence patterns: subjects and predicates

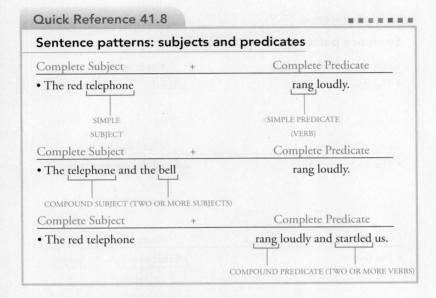

Complete Subject	+	Complete Predicate
• The red telephone		rang loudly.

SIMPLE SUBJECT

SIMPLE PREDICATE (VERB)

Complete Subject	+	Complete Predicate
• The telephone and the bell		rang loudly.

COMPOUND SUBJECT (TWO OR MORE SUBJECTS)

Complete Subject	+	Complete Predicate
• The red telephone		rang loudly and startled us.

COMPOUND PREDICATE (TWO OR MORE VERBS)

41k What are direct and indirect objects?

A **direct object** completes the meaning of TRANSITIVE VERBS. To find a direct object, ask *whom?* or *what?* about the verb: *Keisha bought* [what?] *a sweater*. To find an **indirect object**, ask *to whom? for whom? to what?* or *for what?* about the verb: *Keisha bought* [for whom?] *me a sweater*. Quick Reference 41.9 (p. 340) illustrates direct and indirect objects.

 ESOL Tips: (1) In sentences with indirect objects that follow the word *to* or *for*, always put the direct object before the indirect object.

NO   Will you please give **to** John this letter?

YES   Will you please give this letter **to** John?

(2) When a pronoun works as an indirect object, some verbs that go with the pronoun require *to* or *for* before the pronoun.

NO   Please explain **me** the rule. [*Explain* requires *to* before the pronoun *me*, which functions as an indirect object.]

YES   Please explain the rule **to me**.

(3) Even if a verb doesn't require *to* before an indirect object, you may use *to* if you wish. Make sure, however, that if you do use *to*, you put the direct object before the indirect object.

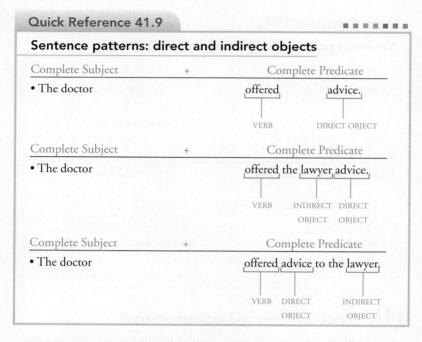

Quick Reference 41.9

Sentence patterns: direct and indirect objects

Complete Subject	+	Complete Predicate
• The doctor		offered advice.
		VERB DIRECT OBJECT

Complete Subject	+	Complete Predicate
• The doctor		offered the lawyer advice.
		VERB INDIRECT DIRECT
		OBJECT OBJECT

Complete Subject	+	Complete Predicate
• The doctor		offered advice to the lawyer.
		VERB DIRECT INDIRECT
		OBJECT OBJECT

NO   Please give **to me** that book. [*Give* does not require *to* before the pronoun *me*, which functions as an indirect object.]

YES   Please give that book **to me**.

(4) When both the direct object and the indirect object are pronouns, put the direct object first and use *to* with the indirect object.

NO   He gave **me it**. [The indirect object *me* should not go before the direct object *it*.]

YES   He gave **it to me**. [The direct object *it* goes first; *to* is used with the indirect object *me*.] ●

41I   What are complements, modifiers, and appositives?

■ Recognizing complements

A **complement** renames or describes a subject or an object. It appears in the predicate of a sentence. A **subject complement** is a noun, a pronoun, or an adjective that follows a LINKING VERB. An **object complement** is a noun or an adjective that follows a DIRECT OBJECT. We illustrate subject and object complements in Quick Reference 41.10.

Quick Box 41.10

Sentence patterns: complements

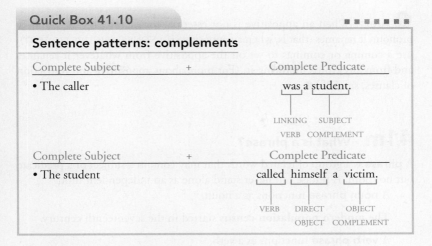

Complete Subject	+	Complete Predicate
• The caller		was a student.

LINKING   SUBJECT
VERB   COMPLEMENT

Complete Subject	+	Complete Predicate
• The student		called himself a victim.

VERB   DIRECT   OBJECT
OBJECT   COMPLEMENT

■ Recognizing modifiers

A **modifier** is a word or words that function the same way as an adjective or adverb. Modifiers can appear anywhere in a sentence.

The **large red** telephone rang. [The adjectives *large* and *red* modify the noun *telephone*.]

The lawyer answered **quickly**. [The adverb *quickly* modifies the verb *answered*.]

The person **on the telephone** was **extremely** upset. [The prepositional phrase *on the telephone* modifies the noun *person;* the adverb *extremely* modifies the adjective *upset*.]

Therefore, the lawyer spoke gently. [The adverb *therefore* modifies the INDEPENDENT CLAUSE *the lawyer spoke gently*.]

Because the lawyer's voice was calm, the caller felt reassured. [*Because the lawyer's voice was calm* is a single ADVERB CLAUSE; it modifies the independent clause *the caller felt reassured*.]

■ Recognizing appositives

An **appositive** is a word or group of words that renames the noun or pronoun that comes before it.

The student's story, **a tale of broken promises**, was complicated. [*A tale of broken promises* is an appositive that renames the noun *story*.]

The lawyer consulted an expert, **her law professor**. [*Her law professor* is an appositive that renames the noun *expert*.]

Alert: When an appositive is not essential for identifying the noun or pronoun it renames (that is, when an appositive is a NONRESTRICTIVE ELEMENT), use a comma or commas to set off the appositive from whatever it renames and from any words following it. (For more about appositives and restriction of clauses, see 57f.) ●

41m What is a phrase?

A **phrase** is a group of related words that may contain a subject or a predicate but not both. A phrase can never stand alone as an independent unit.

A **noun phrase** functions as a noun.

The modern population census started in the seventeenth century.

A **verb phrase** functions as a verb.

Two military censuses **are mentioned** in the Bible.

A **prepositional phrase**, which starts with a PREPOSITION and contains a noun or pronoun, functions as a modifier.

William the Conqueror conducted a census **of landowners in newly conquered England in 1086.** [three prepositional phrases in a row, beginning with *of, in, in*]

An **absolute phrase** is a word group that contains a noun or pronoun and a PARTICIPLE. It modifies the entire sentence.

Censuses being the fashion, Quebec and Nova Scotia took sixteen counts between 1665 and 1754.

A **verbal phrase** is a word group that contains a VERBAL.

In 1624, Virginia began **to count** its citizens in a census. [infinitive phrase = direct object]

Going from door to door, census takers interview millions of people. [participial phrase = adjective modifying *census takers*]

Amazed by some people's answers, the census takers always listen carefully. [participial phrase = adjective modifying *census takers*]

The way that a verbal phrase functions tells you the difference between a gerund phrase and a present-tense participial phrase. Although both types of phrases use the *-ing* form of a verb, a **gerund phrase** functions only as a *noun,* while a **present-tense participial phrase** functions only as a *modifier.*

Including each person in the census was important. [*Including each person* functions as a noun, so it is a gerund phrase.]

Including each person in the census, Abby spent many hours on the crowded city block. [*Including each person* functions as a present-tense participial phrase, so it is an adjective.]

41n What is a clause?

A **clause** is a group of words that contains both a subject and a predicate.

■ Recognizing independent clauses

An **independent clause**, also known as a **main clause**, can stand alone as a sentence, as shown in Quick Reference 41.11.

Quick Reference 41.11	■ ■ ■ ■ ■ ■ ■

Sentence patterns: independent clauses	
Complete Subject +	Complete Predicate
• The telephone	rang.

■ Recognizing dependent clauses

A **dependent clause**, also known as a **subordinate clause**, contains a subject and a predicate, but it cannot stand alone as a sentence because it contains a SUBORDINATING CONJUNCTION (see Quick Reference 41.7). Therefore, you need always to join a dependent clause to an independent clause.

Some dependent clauses start with *subordinating conjunctions*. Such clauses are called **adverb clauses**. They function as adverbs, usually answering one of these questions about the independent clause: *How? Why? When? Under what circumstances?*

If the bond issue passes, the city will install sewers. [The adverb clause modifies the verb *will install*, explaining under what circumstances.]

They are drawing up plans **as quickly as they can**. [The adverb clause modifies the verb *are drawing up*, explaining how.]

The homeowners feel happier **because they know the flooding will soon be better controlled**. [The adverb clause modifies the entire independent clause, explaining why.]

🛈 **Alert:** When an adverb clause comes before its independent clause, the clauses are usually separated by a comma (57b). ●

Adjective clauses are also dependent clauses and are sometimes called **relative clauses.** These clauses start with RELATIVE PRONOUNS (*who, whom, which, whose,* and *that*) or occasionally with RELATIVE ADVERBS such as *when* or *where.*

The car **that Jack bought** is practical. [The adjective clause describes the noun *car.*]

The day **when I can buy my own car** is getting closer. [The adjective clause modifies the noun *day.*]

Quick Reference 41.12 illustrates adverb and adjective clauses.

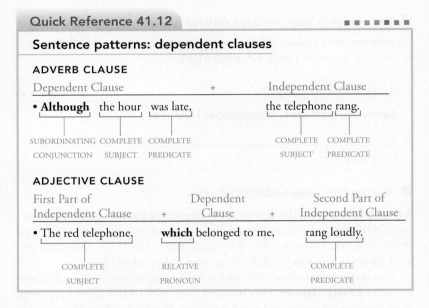

Quick Reference 41.12

Sentence patterns: dependent clauses

ADVERB CLAUSE

| Dependent Clause | + | Independent Clause |

• **Although** the hour was late, the telephone rang.

SUBORDINATING COMPLETE COMPLETE   COMPLETE COMPLETE
CONJUNCTION SUBJECT PREDICATE   SUBJECT PREDICATE

ADJECTIVE CLAUSE

First Part of Independent Clause + Dependent Clause + Second Part of Independent Clause

• The red telephone, **which** belonged to me, rang loudly.

COMPLETE SUBJECT   RELATIVE PRONOUN   COMPLETE PREDICATE

Noun clauses usually begin with *that, who,* or *which,* but they can also start with *whoever, whichever, when, where, whether, why, what,* or *how.*

Promises are not always dependable. [noun]

What politicians promise is not always dependable. [noun clause]

Often voters do not know **the truth**. [noun]

Often voters do not know **that the truth is being manipulated**. [noun clause]

Because noun clauses and adjective clauses start with similar words, they're sometimes confused with each other. A noun clause is a subject, an object, or a COMPLEMENT; an adjective clause *modifies* a subject, object, or complement.

Politicians understand **whom they must please**. [The noun clause *whom they must please* is an object.]

Politicians **who make promises** sometimes fail to keep them. [The adjective clause *who make promises* modifies the noun *politicians*.]

Alert: A noun clause functioning as a subject takes a *singular* verb: *What most politicians try to do is* [not *are*] *serve the public. What most politicians need is* [not *are*] *new careers.*

41o What are sentence types?

A **sentence** can be simple, compound, complex, or compound-complex.

A **simple sentence** is composed of a single independent clause with no dependent clauses.

Charlie Chaplin was born in London on April 16, 1889.

As a mime, he was famous for his character the Little Tramp.

A **compound sentence** is composed of two or more independent clauses joined by a comma and a COORDINATING CONJUNCTION or just a semicolon.

Chaplin's father died early, **and** his mother spent time in mental hospitals.

Many people enjoy Chaplin's films; they laugh at his characters.

A **complex sentence** consists of one independent clause along with one or more dependent clauses.

When Chaplin was performing with a troupe that was touring the United States, he was hired by Mack Sennett, who owned the Keystone Comedies. [This sentence contains a dependent clause starting with *When*, a dependent clause starting with *that*, an independent clause starting with *he*, and a dependent clause starting with *who*.]

A **compound-complex sentence** joins a compound sentence with a complex sentence.

Once studios could no longer afford him, Chaplin cofounded United Artists, and then he was able to produce and distribute his own films. [This sentence contains a dependent clause starting with *Once*, an independent clause starting with *Chaplin*, and an independent clause starting with *then*.]

42

Verbs

42a How do verbs function?

A **verb** expresses an action (*Many people **overeat** on Thanksgiving*), an occurrence (*Mother's Day **fell** early this year*), or a state of being (*Memorial Day **is** tomorrow*). Verbs also convey other information.

PERSON
: First person (the speaker: *I dance*), second person (the one spoken to: *you dance*), or third person (the one spoken about: *the pop star dances*).

NUMBER
: Singular (one) or plural (more than one).

TENSE
: Past (*we **danced***), present (*we **dance***), or future (*we **will dance***); see 42e.

MOOD
: Moods are indicative (*we dance*), imperative (commands and polite requests: *Dance*), or subjunctive (speculation, wishes: *if we were dancing*); see 42f.

VOICE
: Active voice or passive voice; see 42g.

Types of verbs vary as listed in Quick Reference 42.1.

42b What are the forms of main verbs?

The **simple form** expresses an action, occurrence, or state of being in the present (*I laugh*) or, with an AUXILIARY VERB, in the future (*I will laugh*).

The **past-tense form** represents an action, occurrence, or state completed in the past (*I laughed*). Regular verbs add *-ed* or *-d* to the simple form. Irregular verbs vary as listed in Quick Reference 42.2 (pp. 348–349).

The **past participle** uses the same form as the past tense for regular verbs. Irregular verbs vary (see Quick Reference 42.2). To function as a verb, a past participle must combine with one or more auxiliary verbs: *I have laughed*. Used alone, past participles function as ADJECTIVES: *crumbled cookies*.

The **present participle** is formed by adding *-ing* to the simple form (*laughing*). To function as a verb, a present participle must combine with one or more auxiliary verbs (*I was laughing*). Used alone, present participles function as NOUNS (*Laughing is healthy*) or as adjectives (*my laughing friends*).

The **infinitive** uses the simple form, usually but not always following *to* (*I started to laugh*). The infinitive functions as a noun or an adjective, not as a verb.

Quick Reference 42.1

Types of verbs

MAIN VERB	The word in a PREDICATE that says something about the SUBJECT: *She **danced** for the group.*
AUXILIARY VERB	A verb that combines with a main verb to convey information about TENSE, MOOD, or VOICE (42c). The verbs *be, do,* and *have* can be auxiliary verbs or main verbs. The verbs *can, could, may, might, should, would, must,* and others are MODAL AUXILIARY VERBS (Ch. 47). They add shades of meaning such as ability or possibility to verbs: *She **might dance** again.*
LINKING VERB	A verb that links a subject to a **complement**, a word or words that rename or describe the subject: *She **was** happy dancing. Be* is the most common linking verb; sometimes sense verbs (*smell, taste*) or verbs of perception (*seem, feel*) function as linking verbs. (For a sentence pattern with a linking verb, see Quick Reference 41.10.)
TRANSITIVE VERB	A verb followed by a DIRECT OBJECT that completes the verb's message: *They **sent** her a fan letter.* (For sentence patterns with objects, see Quick Reference 41.9.)
INTRANSITIVE VERB	A verb that does not require a direct object: *Yesterday she **danced**.*

■ Using regular verbs

Most verbs in English are regular. **Regular verbs** form the past tense and past participle by adding *-ed* or *-d* to the simple form: *enter, entered, entered; smile, smiled, smiled.*

❶ Alert: Speakers sometimes skip over or swallow the *-ed* sound in the past tense. If you do not pronounce this sound, you may forget to add it when you write: *The birthday cake was **supposed** [not suppose] to be ready by now.* ●

■ Using irregular verbs

More than two hundred English verbs are *irregular,* meaning that they form their past tense and past participle in unusual ways. You can look in a dictionary for the principal parts of any verb, but memorizing the most common **irregular verbs,** listed in Quick Reference 42.2, can save you time.

■ Using the -s form of verbs

The -s form of a verb is used only in the third-person singular of the present tense. The -s ending attaches to the simple form (*laugh, laughs*).

Quick Reference 42.2

Common irregular verbs

Simple Form	Past Tense	Past Participle
awake	awoke *or* awaked	awaked *or* awoken
be	was, were	been
become	became	become
begin	began	begun
break	broke	broken
bring	brought	brought
build	built	built
buy	bought	bought
catch	caught	caught
choose	chose	chosen
cost	cost	cost
deal	dealt	dealt
dive	dived *or* dove	dived
do	did	done
drink	drank	drunk
drive	drove	driven
eat	ate	eaten
fall	fell	fallen
fight	fought	fought
find	found	found
freeze	froze	frozen
get	got	got *or* gotten
give	gave	given
go	went	gone
grow	grew	grown
have	had	had
hear	heard	heard

continued >>

Quick Reference 42.2 (continued)

Simple Form	Past Tense	Past Particle
keep	kept	kept
know	knew	known
lay	laid	laid
lead	led	led
lie	lay	lain
lose	lost	lost
make	made	made
read	read	read
ring	rang	rung
run	ran	run
say	said	said
see	saw	seen
send	sent	sent
sing	sang	sung
sink	sank	sunk
sit	sat	sat
sleep	slept	slept
speak	spoke	spoken
stand	stood	stood
steal	stole	stolen
swim	swam	swum
take	took	taken
teach	taught	taught
throw	threw	thrown
wear	wore	worn
write	wrote	written

Alert: Only the verbs *be* and *have* have irregular forms for the third-person singular of the present tense: *is* and *has*. They are the standard third-person singular forms to use in EDITED AMERICAN ENGLISH.

NO   Jasper be studying hard because he have to win a scholarship.

YES   Jasper **is** studying hard because he **has** to win a scholarship. ●

42c What are auxiliary verbs?

Auxiliary verbs, also called **helping verbs**, combine with MAIN VERBS to make VERB PHRASES.

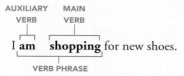

I **am** **shopping** for new shoes.

Clothing prices **have** [auxiliary verb] **soared** [main verb] recently. [*Have soared* is a verb phrase.]

Leather shoes **can** [auxiliary verb] **be** [main verb] expensive. [*Can be* is a verb phrase.]

Modal auxiliary verbs include *can, could, may, might, must, shall, should, will, would,* and others. Modals communicate meanings of ability, permission, obligation, advisability, necessity, or possibility.

ESOL Tip: Modal auxiliary verbs can challenge multilingual writers, so we discuss them in detail in Chapter 74. ●

Three frequently used irregular auxiliary verbs are *be, do,* and *have.* They vary in form more than most other irregular verbs.

FORMS OF *BE, DO,* AND *HAVE*

	Be	Do	Have
SIMPLE FORM	be	do	have
PAST TENSE	was, were	did	had
PAST PARTICIPLE	been	done	had
-S FORM	is	does	has
PRESENT PARTICIPLE	being	doing	having

ESOL Tips: (1) Write with edited American English forms of *be.*

The gym **is** a busy place. [edited American English, meaning "it is always that way"]

The gym **is filling** with young athletes. [edited American English, meaning "it is happening right now"]

(2) If you use an auxiliary verb with a main verb, the auxiliary verb often changes to an *-s* form. This means that it agrees with a third-person singular subject, and the main verb doesn't change:

Does the gym **close** [*not* closes] at midnight? ●

42d Should I use *lie* or *lay*?

Many people confuse the forms of the irregular verbs *lie* and *lay* because the word *lay* is both the PAST-TENSE FORM of *lie* and the SIMPLE FORM of *lay*. Use *lie* ("to recline") and *lay* ("to place something down") with care. *Lie* is intransitive, so a direct object can *never* follow it. *Lay* is transitive, so a direct object *must* follow it.

FORMS OF *LIE* AND *LAY*

	Lie	Lay
SIMPLE FORM	lie	lay
PAST TENSE	lay	laid
PAST PARTICIPLE	lain	laid
-S FORM	lies	lays
PRESENT PARTICIPLE	lying	laying

The hikers are ~~laying~~ *lying* down to rest.

The hikers ~~laid~~ *lay* down to rest.

The hikers took off their gear and ~~lay~~ *laid* it on the rocks.

42e What are verb tenses?

The **tenses** of a verb express time. To do this, main verbs change form and combine with auxiliary verbs. **Simple tenses** divide time into the past, the present, and the future. **Progressive forms** show ongoing actions or conditions.

SIMPLE TENSES

		Progressive Forms
PRESENT	I talk.	I am talking.
PAST	I talked.	I was talking.
FUTURE	I will talk.	I will be talking.

PERFECT TENSES

		Progressive Forms
PRESENT PERFECT	I have talked.	I have been talking.
PAST PERFECT	I had talked.	I had been talking.
FUTURE PERFECT	I will have talked.	I will have been talking.

■ Using the simple present tense

The simple **present tense** describes (1) what is happening now, (2) what is true at the moment, (3) what is generally or consistently true, or (4) what event will take place at a fixed time in the future.

> The tourists **are** on vacation. [happening now]
>
> They **enjoy** the sunshine. [true at the moment]
>
> Ocean voyages **make** them seasick. [consistently true]
>
> A cruise **is** an expensive vacation. [generally true]
>
> Their ship **departs** at midnight. [fixed-time future event]

! **Alert:** Use the present tense to discuss action that takes place in a work of literature.

> In *Romeo and Juliet,* Juliet's father **wants** Juliet to marry Paris.
>
> Shakespeare's play **depicts** the tragedy of ill-fated love. ●

● **ESOL Tip:** Use the simple present in a DEPENDENT CLAUSE, even if it refers to the future. In a dependent clause that begins with *if, when, before, after, until,* or *as soon as,* use the simple present in that clause; use *will* with the verb in the INDEPENDENT CLAUSE.

> **NO**   After they **will arrive**, the meeting **will begin**.
>
> **YES**   After they **arrive**, the meeting **will** begin. ●

■ Using tense sequence accurately

The sequence of verb tenses in your sentence communicates time relationships. Accurate sequence becomes an issue only when your sentence contains both an independent clause and a dependent clause. Quick Reference 42.3 (pp. 353–354) shows how the **tense sequence** communicates when something is happening, has happened, or will happen.

42f What are indicative, imperative, and subjunctive moods?

Mood conveys an attitude toward the action in a sentence. The **indicative mood** expresses statements about real things (*The door **opened***) or highly likely ones (*She **seemed** lost*). Questions about real events and facts are also expressed in the indicative (***Do** you **need** help?*).

The **imperative mood** expresses commands and direct requests (*Please **shut** the door. **Watch** out!*). If the subject is omitted in an imperative sentence, the subject is understood to be *you.*

Quick Reference 42.3

■ ■ ■ ■ ■ ■ ■

Sequence of verb tenses with independent and dependent clauses

Tense in the Independent Clause	Tense to Use in the Dependent Clause
PRESENT	Use *present tense* to show same-time action: I **avoid** shellfish because I *am allergic* to it. Use *past tense* to show earlier action: I **am sure** that I *deposited* the check. Use *present perfect tense* to show (1) a period of time extending from some point in the past to the present or (2) an indefinite time in the past: They **say** that they *have lived* in Canada since 1979. I **believe** that I *have seen* this movie before. Use *future tense* for action to come: The book **is** open because I *will be reading* it later.
PAST	Use *past perfect tense* to show earlier action: The sprinter **knew** that she *had broken* the record. Use *present tense* to state a general truth: Columbus **determined** that the world *is* round.
PRESENT PERFECT OR PAST PERFECT	Use *past tense:* The bread **has become** moldy since I *purchased* it. Sugar prices **had** already **declined** when artificial sweeteners first *appeared*.
FUTURE	Use *present tense* to show action happening at the same time: You **will be** rich if you *win* the prize. Use *past tense* to show earlier action: You **will have** a good chance of winning if you *remembered* to send in your entry form.
FUTURE	Use *present perfect tense* to show future action occurring sooner than the action of the verb in the independent clause: The river **will flood** again next year unless we *have built* a better dam by then.

continued >>

Tense in the Independence Clause	Tense to Use in the Dependent Clause
FUTURE PERFECT	Use *present tense* or *past perfect tense:*
	Dr. Chang **will have delivered** five thousand babies by the time she *retires*.
	Dr. Chang **will have delivered** five thousand babies by the time she *has retired*.

The **subjunctive mood** expresses conditions that are not literally true or do not currently exist, such as wishes, recommendations, demands, indirect requests, and speculations: *If I **were** you, I **would** ask for directions.*

■ Using the subjunctive with *if, as if, as though,* and *unless* clauses

Many CLAUSES introduced by *if, as if, as though,* and *unless* require the subjunctive, but some don't. Use the subjunctive only when such clauses describe a speculation or condition contrary to fact.

INDICATIVE   If she **leaves** late, I **will drive** her to the party. [fact, not speculation]

SUBJUNCTIVE   If she **were** [*not* was] **going to leave** late, I **would drive** her to the party. [speculation]

SUBJUNCTIVE   If it **were** [*not* was] **raining**, some people **would stay** home. [condition contrary to fact—it is not raining]

■ Using the subjunctive in *that* clauses

When *that* clauses express wishes, indirect requests, recommendations, and demands, use the subjunctive.

I wish **that** this party **were** [*not* was] scheduled for tomorrow. [wish]

I requested **that** the birthday cake **be ready** [*not* is ready *or* will be ready] at noon. [request]

42g   What is "voice" in verbs?

Voice indicates how the subject relates to the action of the verb. In the **active voice**, the subject performs the action. In the **passive voice**, the subject is acted upon.

ACTIVE   **Svetlana considers** clams a delicacy. [The subject, *Svetlana*, performs the action: she *considers*.]

PASSIVE   **Clams are considered** a delicacy by Svetlana. [The subject, *clams*, is acted on—they *are considered*—by Svetlana.]

The active voice—which is usually more direct, concise, and dramatic than the passive voice—emphasizes the doer of an action. The passive voice, however, may be appropriate when who or what did the action is unknown or unimportant.

The lock **was broken** sometime last night. [The doer of the action is unknown.]

The formula **was discovered** years ago. [The doer of the action is unimportant.]

⬤ **ESOL Tip:** The passive voice works only with TRANSITIVE VERBS. Many English verbs are not transitive, so if you're not certain, look up the verb in a dictionary. ⬤

The passive voice is appropriate when the action itself is more important than the performer of the action. For example, if your point is to emphasize the discovery of oxygen rather than the person who discovered it, the passive voice is an appropriate choice.

ACTIVE VOICE   **Joseph Priestley discovered** oxygen in 1774.

PASSIVE VOICE   **Oxygen was discovered** in 1774.

Do not use the passive voice to make your writing seem "lofty" or to hide who has done an action.

NO   An experiment **was conducted by me** to demonstrate the existence of carbon. [pointless passive that is trying to sound lofty]

YES   I **conducted** an experiment to demonstrate the existence of carbon.

For more help with your writing, grammar, and research,
go to **www.mycomplab.com**

mycomp**lab** ▐

43

■ ■ ■ ■ ■ ■ ■ ■

Subject-Verb Agreement

43a What is subject-verb agreement?

Subject-verb agreement means that SUBJECTS and their VERBS need to match in **number** (singular or plural) and **person** (42a). **Singular** subjects require singular verbs, **plural** subjects require plural verbs, and third-person singular subjects require the -*s* form of present-tense verbs and AUXILIARIES.

Problems can arise with the letter *s* at the end of words. The diagram in Quick Reference 43.1 shows how the -*s* ending works in most cases. The -*s* or -*es* can take only one path at a time, going either to a noun subject (at the top) or to a verb (at the bottom).

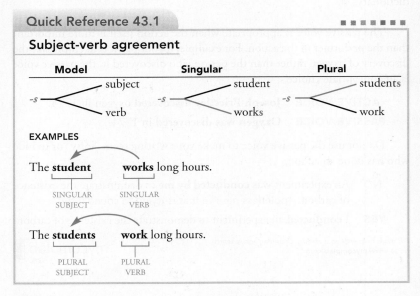

Quick Reference 43.1   ■ ■ ■ ■ ■ ■ ■

Subject-verb agreement

Model	Singular	Plural
subject	student	students
-*s*	-*s*	-*s*
verb	works	work

EXAMPLES

The **student** **works** long hours.

SINGULAR SUBJECT — SINGULAR VERB

The **students** **work** long hours.

PLURAL SUBJECT — PLURAL VERB

🌐 **ESOL Tip:** Several spoken versions of English, including British Cockney, Caribbean Creole, and African American Vernacular, don't observe the rules of agreement. For example, instead of *She **doesn't** eat potatoes,* which is correct EDITED AMERICAN ENGLISH, speakers of such English variants may say, *She **don't never** eat potatoes.* For ACADEMIC WRITING, use the correct edited American English forms. ●

43b Can I ignore words between a subject and its verb?

You can ignore words between a subject and verb. Such words do not influence subject-verb agreement.

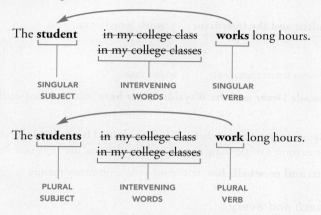

| The **student** | in my college class | **works** long hours. |
| in my college classes | |

| SINGULAR | INTERVENING | SINGULAR |
| SUBJECT | WORDS | VERB |

| The **students** | in my college class | **work** long hours. |
| in my college classes | |

| PLURAL | INTERVENING | PLURAL |
| SUBJECT | WORDS | VERB |

NO The **winners** in the state competition **goes** to the national finals. [*Winners* is the subject, so the verb must agree with it. *In the state competition* is a PREPOSITIONAL PHRASE that comes before the verb, and it does not alter subject-verb agreement.]

YES The **winners** in the state competition **go** to the national finals.

Whenever you need to locate the subject of a sentence, first look over your sentence and eliminate any PHRASES that start with PREPOSITIONS. What remains usually makes the subject stand out more obviously.

NO The **moon**, as well as Venus, **are** visible in the night sky. [*Moon* is the subject, so the verb needs to agree with it. *Are* does not agree with *moon*. The writer forgot to ignore the prepositional phrase *as well as Venus*.]

YES The **moon**, as well as Venus, **is** visible in the night sky.

■ Using *one of the*

A construction that starts with the words *one of the* takes a singular verb to agree with the word *one*. (This is not true of the construction *one of the . . . who*; see 43g.)

43c How do verbs work when subjects are connected by *and*?

When two or more subjects are joined by *and*, they become plural as a group. The group requires a plural verb.

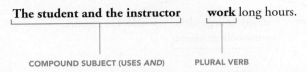

The student and the instructor   **work** long hours.

COMPOUND SUBJECT (USES *AND*)   PLURAL VERB

The Cascade Diner and the Wayside Diner have [*not* has] fried catfish today.

The only exception occurs when subjects are joined by *and* and the subjects combine to form a single thing or person. In such cases, use a singular verb.

Spaghetti and meatballs has [*not* have] a place on many menus.

■ Using *each* and *every*

Each and *every* are singular PRONOUNS and require singular verbs. Even when *each* or *every* comes before subjects joined by *and*, use a singular verb.

Each human hand and foot **leaves** a distinctive print. [*Each*, a singular pronoun, requires *leaves*, a singular verb.]

43d How do verbs work when subjects are connected by *or*?

When subjects are joined with *or, nor, either . . . or, neither . . . nor,* or *not only . . . but (also)*, the verb agrees with the subject nearest it. Ignore everything before the final subject.

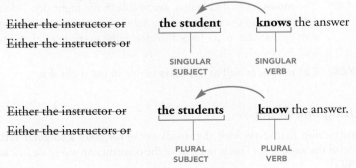

~~Either the instructor or~~
~~Either the instructors or~~   **the student**   **knows** the answer

                                SINGULAR   SINGULAR
                                SUBJECT   VERB

~~Either the instructor or~~
~~Either the instructors or~~   **the students**   **know** the answer.

                                PLURAL   PLURAL
                                SUBJECT   VERB

43e How do verbs work with indefinite pronouns?

Indefinite pronouns refer to nonspecific people or things. They are usually singular, so they usually take singular verbs.

COMMON INDEFINITE PRONOUNS

another	each	everything	nothing
anybody	either	neither	somebody
anyone	every	nobody	someone
anything	everyone	no one	something

> Whenever **anyone says** anything, **nothing is** done.
>
> **Everything** about these roads **is** [*not* are] dangerous.
>
> **Each** of the roads **has** [*not* have] to be resurfaced.

A few indefinite pronouns—*none, some, more, most, any,* and *all*—can be either singular or plural, depending on the meaning of the sentence.

> **Some** of our streams **are** polluted; **some** pollution **is** reversible, but **all** pollution **is** a threat to the balance of nature. [The first *some* refers to the plural *streams,* so the plural verb *are* agrees with it; the second *some* and *all* refer to the singular word *pollution,* so the singular verb *is* agrees with them.]

43f How do verbs work with *who, which,* and *that?*

When a CLAUSE starts with *who, which,* or *that,* the verb agrees with the noun or pronoun to which *who, which,* or *that* refers (its ANTECEDENT).

> The scientist will share the income from her new patent with the graduate students **who work** with her. [*Who* refers to the plural *students,* and *work* is a plural verb.]
>
> David Pappas is the student **who works** in the science lab. [*Who* refers to the singular *student,* and *works* is a singular verb.]

43g How do verbs work with *one of the . . . who?*

In the PHRASE *one of the . . . who,* the verb agrees with what comes before *who*—which is always a plural word. Therefore, the verb is always plural. The same rule applies to the phrase *one of the . . . that* and *one of the . . . which.*

> Tracy is **one of the students who talk** [*not* talks] in class. [*Who* refers to the plural *students* and requires the plural verb *talk.*]

However, if the phrase includes the word *only,* as in *the only one of the . . . who,* the verb has to agree with *only one,* which is always singular. Therefore, the verb is always singular.

> Tracy is **the only one** of the students **who talks** [*not* talk] in class. [*Who* refers to the singular *only one* and requires the singular verb *talks.*]

43h How do verbs work in other complicated cases of subject-verb agreement?

■ Finding the subject in inverted word order

Inverted word order changes the usual order in a sentence: *The mayor walked in* is standard word order. *In walked the mayor* is inverted word order. (Most questions use inverted word order: *Is the mayor here?*) In inverted word order, you want the verb to agree with the subject that comes after the verb, not before it.

> Across the street **stand** [*not* stands] the protesters. [The subject is *protesters,* and *stand* agrees with it.]

■ Finding the subject with an expletive construction

Expletive constructions—phrases introduced by such expressions as *there is, it is,* and *there were*—put the verb before the subject. Therefore, you want to look beyond the verb to find the subject, and be sure they agree in number.

> There **are** nine **planets** in our solar system. [The subject is *planets,* which is plural, so the verb is *are,* which is also plural.]

■ Agreeing with the subject, not the subject complement

A SUBJECT COMPLEMENT is a NOUN or an ADJECTIVE that follows a LINKING VERB. This means that you want your verb to agree with the subject that comes before it, not after it.

> **NO** The worst **part** of owning a car **are** the bills. [The subject is the singular noun *part,* which requires the singular verb *is. Bills* is a subject complement, so it isn't involved in the subject-verb agreement.]

> **YES** The worst **part** of owning a car **is** the bills. [Now singular *part* agrees with singular *is.*]

> **YES** **Bills are** the worst part of owning a car. [The sentence is rewritten to make the plural noun *bills* the subject, so the plural verb *are* is correct.]

■ Making verbs agree with collective nouns

A **collective noun** names a group of people or things, such as *family, group, audience, class,* or *number.* When the group acts as one unit, use a singular verb. When the members of the group act individually, use a plural verb.

> The senior **class has** [*not* have] 793 people in it. [Here, *class* operates as one unit, so the singular verb *has* agrees with it.]
>
> The senior **class were** [*not* was] **fitted** for their graduation robes today. [Here, *class* means the people in the class acting as individual members within the group, so the plural verb phrase *were fitted* agrees with it.]

🛇 **Alert:** Notice that the pronouns also agree with the nouns to which they refer (*it* agrees with *class, their* agrees with *class*). ●

■ Making verbs agree with subjects that specify amounts

Use a singular verb with a subject that specifies an amount of money, time, weight, or distance considered as one unit.

> **Ninety cents is** the current bus fare.
>
> **Two miles passes** quickly for a serious jogger.

In contrast, when a subject refers to units of measurement, each of which is considered individually rather than as a unit, use a plural verb.

> **Eighteen inches are** marked off on that ruler.
>
> **Fifty percent** of these peaches **are** rotten.

■ Making verbs agree with singular subjects in plural form

A singular subject can look like a plural word, but it remains singular. It needs a singular verb, despite its plural appearance. Often but not always, such words end in *-s* or *-ics.* Some examples are *ethics, economics, mathematics, physics,* and *statistics* when used to refer to a course of study. Other subjects that look like plurals but are really singulars include *news* and *measles.*

> **Statistics is** a requirement for science majors. [Here, *statistics* refers to a course of study, so the singular verb *is* agrees with it.]
>
> **Statistics show** that a recession is coming. [Here, *statistics* refers to items of data, so the plural verb *show* agrees with it.]

In some cases, the sentence's meaning determines whether a subject ending in *-s* needs a singular or plural verb. For example, *series* and *means* have the same form in singular and plural.

Six new television **series are** beginning this week. [Here, *six* determines that *television series* is plural, so the plural verb *are* is correct.]

A **series** of disasters **is** delaying our production. [Here, *series* is a single unit, so the singular verb *is* is correct.]

■ Using singular verbs with titles, terms, and plural words representing a single unit

The title of a work or a series of words used as a term is a single unit. Therefore, use a singular verb, even when the title or term contains plural words.

Cats **was** [*not* were] a popular musical. [*Cats,* a plural word, is a title; it therefore calls for the singular verb *was.*]

"Protective reaction strikes" is a euphemism for bombing. [The entire expression *"protective reaction strikes"* acts as a single unit; it therefore calls for the singular verb *is.*]

Used alone, the word *states* is always plural. However, the name *United States* refers to a single country, so it takes a singular verb.

The United States has [*not* have] a large television industry.

For more help with your
writing, grammar, and research,
go to **www.mycomplab.com**

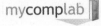

44

Pronouns: Agreement, Reference, and Case

PRONOUN-ANTECEDENT AGREEMENT

44a   What is pronoun-antecedent agreement?

Pronoun-antecedent agreement means that a PRONOUN must match the grammatical form of the word or words it refers to (the pronoun's ANTECEDENT). For example, if an antecedent is third-person singular, the pronoun that refers to it needs to be third-person singular, too (see Quick Reference 44.1).

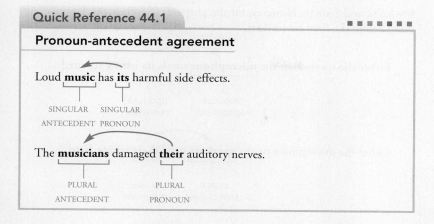

Quick Reference 44.1

Pronoun-antecedent agreement

Loud **music** has **its** harmful side effects.

SINGULAR   SINGULAR
ANTECEDENT PRONOUN

The **musicians** damaged **their** auditory nerves.

PLURAL   PLURAL
ANTECEDENT   PRONOUN

44b How do pronouns work when *and* connects antecedents?

Two or more antecedents joined by *and* require a plural pronoun, even if each antecedent is itself singular.

> **The United States and Canada** maintain **their** border as the world's longest open frontier.

> **The Cascade Diner and the Wayside Diner** closed for New Year's Eve to give **their** employees the night off.

One exception occurs when *each* or *every* comes before singular NOUNS joined by *and*. In such cases, a singular pronoun is correct.

> **Every car and truck** that comes through the border station has **its** [not their] contents inspected. [Each car and truck is separate.]

Another exception occurs when singular nouns joined by *and* refer to a single person or thing. In such cases, a singular pronoun is correct.

> Our **guide and translator** told us to watch out for traffic as **she** [not they] helped us off the tour bus. [The guide is the same person as the translator.]

44c How do pronouns work when *or* connects antecedents?

Some antecedents are joined by the word *or* or *nor*. In addition, CORRELATIVE CONJUNCTIONS such as *either . . . or* and *not only . . . but (also)* can join antecedents. These antecedents can mix masculine and feminine as well as

SINGULAR and PLURAL. However, for the purposes of agreement, ignore everything before the final antecedent.

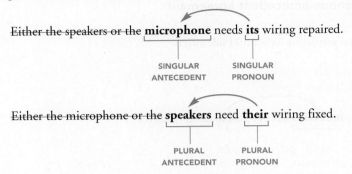

Either the speakers or the **microphone** needs **its** wiring repaired.

SINGULAR ANTECEDENT — SINGULAR PRONOUN

Either the microphone or the **speakers** need **their** wiring fixed.

PLURAL ANTECEDENT — PLURAL PRONOUN

44d How do pronouns work when their antecedents are indefinite pronouns?

INDEFINITE PRONOUNS are pronouns that refer to no particular person, thing, or idea (43e). They are general or generic and take on definite meanings according to the sentence they're in.

Indefinite pronouns are usually singular: ***Anyone*** *who knows the answer should raise* ***his or her*** *hand.* Some indefinite pronouns can be either singular or plural (*none, some, more, most, any, all*), depending on the meaning of the sentence.

None fear that **they** will fail. [All the people in the group expect to succeed; the plural pronoun *they* reflects this meaning.]

None fears that **he or she** will fail. [No individual expects to fail; the pair of singular pronouns *he or she* reflects this meaning.]

The indefinite pronouns *each* and *every* are singular, no matter what words follow.

                                            his or her
Each of the students handed in ~~their~~ final term paper.
                                          ^
                                              his or her
Every student in my classes is studying ~~their~~ hardest.
                                            ^

Be especially careful about agreement when you use the words *this* (singular) and *these* (plural): ***This*** *kind of hard work has* ***its*** *advantages.* ***These*** *kinds of difficult jobs have* ***their*** *advantages.*

⚠ **Alert:** The expression *he or she* operates as a single unit and therefore calls for a singular antecedent. Generally, however, try to avoid this awkward expression by switching to plural forms. ●

44e How do pronouns work when antecedents are collective nouns?

A COLLECTIVE NOUN names a group of people or things, such as *family, group, audience, class,* or *number* (43h). When the group acts as one unit, a singular pronoun can refer to it. However, when the members of the group act individually, a plural pronoun should be used.

> The **audience** cheered as **it** rose to applaud. [The singular pronoun *it* conveys that the audience is acting as one unit.]

> The **audience** put on **their** coats and walked to the exits. [The plural pronoun *their* conveys that the members of the audience are acting as many separate individuals.]

PRONOUN REFERENCE

If a word or words are replaced by, or stand for, a pronoun, that pronoun needs to refer precisely to what it replaces or stands for.

44f How can I avoid unclear pronoun reference?

In sentences that contain more than one logical antecedent, meaning can get muddled.

UNCLEAR PRONOUN REFERENCE	In 1911, Roald Amundsen reached the South Pole just thirty-five days before Robert F. Scott arrived. **He** [*Amundsen or Scott?*] had told people that he was going to sail north to the Arctic, but then **he** [*Amundsen or Scott?*] turned south for the Antarctic. On the journey back from the South Pole, **he** [*Amundsen or Scott?*] and **his** [*Amundsen's or Scott's?*] party froze to death just a few miles from safety.
REVISED	In 1911, Roald Amundsen discovered the South Pole just thirty-five days before Robert F. Scott arrived. Amundsen had told people that he was going to sail north to the Arctic, but then he turned south for the Antarctic. On the journey home, Scott and his party froze to death just a few miles from safety.

In addition, when too much material comes between a pronoun and the word or words the pronoun refers to, readers often lose track of the meaning.

Alfred Wegener, a German meteorologist and professor of geophysics at the University of Graz, was the first to suggest that all the continents on earth were originally part of one large landmass. According to his theory, the supercontinent broke up long ago and the fragments drifted apart. Slowly, these fragments formed the pattern of landmasses and oceans that we know today. Although they do so slowly over centuries, the landmasses are continuing to move. ~~He~~ *Wegener* named this supercontinent Pangaea.

[Although *he* can refer only to *Wegener*, the material about his theory and about landmass patterns takes up three sentences, so using the name *Wegener* again, rather than using *he*, jogs the reader's memory and makes comprehension easier.]

44g How do pronouns work with *it, that, this,* and *which*?

Too often writers use the words *it, that, this,* and *which* carelessly, making it difficult for readers to understand what's being referred to.

> **NO** Comets usually fly by the earth at 100,000 mph, whereas asteroids sometimes collide with the earth. **This** interests scientists. [This could refer to the speed of comets, comets flying by the earth, or asteroids colliding with the earth.]

> **YES** Comets usually fly by the earth at 100,000 mph, whereas asteroids sometimes collide with the earth. **This difference** interests scientists.

In ACADEMIC WRITING, avoid imprecise statements such as "It said on the news . . ." or "In Washington, they say . . ."

> **NO** In California, **they say** that no one feels a minor earthquake. [Who is *they*?]

> **YES** **Residents of California say** that no one feels a minor earthquake.

44h When should I use *you* for direct address?

Reserve *you* for **direct address**, writing that speaks directly to the reader. Avoid using *you* in generalizations referring to people, situations, or occurrences.

> **NO** Prison uprisings often happen when you allow overcrowding. [The reader did not allow the overcrowding.]

> **YES** Prison uprisings often happen when prisons are overcrowded.

44i When should I use *who, which,* and *that*?

Who refers to people and animals mentioned by name.

> **Theodore Roosevelt, who** served as the twenty-sixth US president, inspired the creation of the stuffed animal called the teddy bear.

> **Lassie, who** was known for her intelligence and courage, was actually played by a series of male collies.

Which and *that* refer to animals, things, and sometimes anonymous or collective groups of people. Quick Reference 44.2 shows how to choose between *that* and *which*. (For help in using commas with *that* and *which*, see 57f.)

Quick Reference 44.2 ∎∎∎∎∎∎∎

Choosing between *that* and *which*

In informal writing, you can use either *that* or *which* in a restrictive clause (a clause that is essential to the sentence's meaning), as long as you do so consistently in each piece of writing. However, in academic writing, your instructor and peers usually expect you to use *that*.

> The zoos **that most children like** display newborn and baby animals. [The point of this sentence is to identify the kind of zoos that children like. Therefore, the clause *that most children like* is essential to the meaning of the sentence; if you remove it, the meaning changes substantially.]

Use *which* in a **nonrestrictive clause** (a clause that isn't essential to the sentence's meaning).

> Zoos, **which most children like**, attract more visitors if they display newborn and baby animals. [This sentence concerns what attracts more visitors to zoos. The clause *which most children like* is not essential to the meaning of the sentence; if you remove it, the meaning of the sentence doesn't change substantially.]

PRONOUN CASE

44j What is pronoun case?

Case applies in different ways to pronouns and to nouns. For pronouns, case refers to three pronoun forms: **subjective** (pronoun SUBJECTS), **objective** (pronoun OBJECTS), and **possessive** (pronouns that are possessive). For nouns, case refers to only one noun form: possessive. (For using apostrophes in the possessive case, see Chapter 60.)

44k   What are personal pronouns?

Personal pronouns refer to persons or things. Quick Reference 44.3 shows the case forms of personal pronouns (subjective, objective, and possessive) in both the singular and the plural.

Quick Reference 44.3   ■ ■ ■ ■ ■ ■ ■

Case forms of personal pronouns

	Subjective	Objective	Possessive
SINGULAR	I, you, he, she, it	me, you, him, her, it	mine, yours, his, hers, its
PLURAL	we, you, they	us, you, them	ours, yours, theirs

Most questions about pronoun case concern *who/whom* and *whoever/whomever*. For a full discussion, see 44p.

44l   How can I select the correct case?

When you're unsure whether to use the SUBJECTIVE CASE or the OBJECTIVE CASE, try the three-step test shown in Quick Reference 44.4.

44m   Which case is correct when *and* connects pronouns?

When *and* connects more than one noun, one pronoun, or a noun and a pronoun, it forms a compound subject or a compound object. Compounding doesn't affect pronoun case—use the same case for all the pronouns.

COMPOUND PRONOUN SUBJECT   **He and I** saw the solar eclipse.

COMPOUND PRONOUN OBJECT   That eclipse astonished **him and me**.

Whenever you're unsure of whether to use pronouns in the subjective or objective case, use the QA case test in Quick Reference 44.4 to get the answer.

She and I [not Her and me, She and me, or Her and I] learned about the moon.

The instructor taught **her and me** [not she and I, her and I, or she and me] about the moon.

🚫 **Alert:** In PREPOSITIONAL PHRASES, pronouns are always in the objective case.

Quick Reference 44.4

Using the "QA case test"

These examples use pronouns. The test also works with nouns.

Step 1   Write the sentence twice, once using the subjective case and once using the objective case. Then cross out enough words to isolate the element you're questioning.

~~Janet and~~ me learned about the moon.

~~Janet and~~ I learned about the moon.

Step 2   Omit the crossed-out words and read both sentences aloud to see which one sounds right.

Me learned about the moon. [No, this doesn't sound right.]

I learned about the moon. [This sounds right.]

Step 3   Select the correct version and restore what you crossed out.

Janet and I learned about the moon.

NO   Mrs. Parks gave an assignment to Sam and I. [The prepositional phrase starts with *to*, so the subjective-case *I* is wrong.]

YES   Mrs. Parks gave an assignment to **Sam and me**. [The prepositional phrase starts with *to*, so the objective-case *me* is correct.]

Be careful when a pronoun object follows the preposition *between*.

NO   Mrs. Parks divided the work between **he and I**. [The prepositional phrase starts with *between*, so the subjective-case *I* is wrong.]

YES   Mrs. Parks divided the work between **him and me**. [The prepositional phrase starts with *between*, so the objective-case *me* is correct.]●

44n   How can I match case in appositives?

You can match case in APPOSITIVES by putting pronouns and nouns in the same case. Whenever you're unsure of whether to use the subjective or objective case, use the QA case test in Quick Reference 44.4 to get the answer.

We [*not* Us] tennis players practice hard. [Here the pronoun *we*, which is in the subjective case, comes before the noun *tennis players*.]

The winners, **she and I** [*not* her and me], advanced to the finals. [Here the pronouns *she* and *I*, which are in the subjective case, come after the noun *winners*.]

The coach tells **us** [*not* we] tennis players to practice hard. [Here the pronoun *us*, which is in the objective case, comes before the noun *tennis players*.]

The crowd cheered the winners, **her and me** [*not* she and I]. [Here the pronouns *her* and *me*, which are in the objective case, come after the noun *winners*.]

44o How does the subjective case work after linking verbs?

A pronoun that comes after a LINKING VERB either renames the SUBJECT or shows possession. In such cases, always use a pronoun in the subjective case.

The contest winner was **I** [*not* me]. [*I* renames the subject, which is the noun *contest winner*, so the subjective-case *I* is correct.]

The prize was **mine.** [*Mine* shows possession, so the possessive-case *mine* is correct.]

44p When should I use *who, whoever, whom,* and *whomever*?

The pronouns *who* and *whoever* are in the subjective case. The pronouns *whom* and *whomever* are in the objective case.

Informal spoken English tends to blur distinctions between *who* and *whom*, so with these words some people can't rely entirely on what "sounds right." Whenever you're unsure of whether to use the subjective-case *who* and *whoever* or the objective-case *whom* and *whomever*, use a variation of the QA case test in Quick Reference 44.4. For *who* and *whoever*, substitute *he, she,* or *they*. For *whom* and *whomever*, substitute *him, her,* or *them*. Doing so, you get the following results:

My father tells the story to **whoever/whomever** he meets.

My father tells the story to **he/him**. [By temporarily substituting the subjective-case *he* and the objective-case *him* for *whoever/whomever*, you see that *him* is correct. Therefore, the objective-case *whomever* is correct.]

Sometimes you will need to add a word to make the test work. In this example, you add the word *if*.

I wondered **who/whom** would vote for her.

I wondered **if he/him** would vote for her. [The subjective-case *who* is correct because the sentence works when you substitute *if he* for *who/whom*. In contrast, the objective-case *whom* is wrong because the sentence doesn't work when you substitute *if him* for *who/whom*.]

At other times you will need to invert the word order to make the test work.

Babies **who/whom** mothers cuddle grow faster and are happier.

Mothers cuddle **they/them**. [By inverting the word order of the phrase *who/whom mothers cuddle* (*mothers cuddle who/whom*) and substituting *they/them* for *who/whom*, you can see that *them* is correct. Therefore, the objective-case *whom* is correct.]

When *who* or *whom* comes at the beginning or end of a question, use *who* if the question is about the subject and *whom* if the question is about the OBJECT. To determine which case to use, recast the question into a statement, substituting *he* or *him* (or *she* or *her*).

Who watched the space shuttle liftoff? [*He* (not *Him*) *watched the space shuttle liftoff* would be correct, so the subjective-case *Who* is called for.]

Ted admires **whom**? [*Ted admires him* (not *he*) would be correct, so the objective-case *whom* is called for.]

Whom does Ted admire? [*Ted admires him* (not *he*) would be correct, so the objective-case *whom* is called for.]

To **whom** does Ted speak about becoming an astronaut? [*Ted speaks to them* (not *they*) would be correct, so the objective-case *whom* is called for.]

44q What case should I use after *than* and *as*?

When a pronoun follows *than* or *as,* choose the pronoun case according to the meaning you want to convey. The following two sentences convey very different messages simply because of the use of *me* or *I* after *than.*

SENTENCE 1 My sister loved that dog more than **me**.

SENTENCE 2 My sister loved that dog more than **I**.

Sentence 1 means "My sister loved that dog more than she loved me" because the pronoun *me* is in the objective case. Sentence 2 means "My sister loved that dog more than I loved it" because the pronoun *I* is in the subjective case.

To make sure that your sentences using *than* or *as* deliver the message you intend, mentally fill in the implied words.

44r What case should I use with infinitives and *-ing* words?

When you use INFINITIVES, make sure that your pronouns are in the objective case. This rule holds whether the pronoun is the subject or the object of the infinitive.

Our tennis coach expects **me** *to serve*. [*Me* is the subject of the infinitive *to serve*.]

Our tennis coach expects him *to beat* me. [*Me* is the object of the infinitive *to beat*.]

With *-ing* words, the POSSESSIVE CASE can change a sentence's meaning entirely. For example, the following two sentences convey very different messages simply because of the change in case of the noun *man*. The same distinction applies to both nouns and pronouns.

SENTENCE 1 The detective noticed the **man** staggering. [objective case]

SENTENCE 2 The detective noticed the **man's** staggering. [possessive case]

Sentence 1 means that the detective noticed the *man*. In contrast, sentence 2 means that the detective noticed the *staggering*. The same differences exist for the following two sentences, which use pronouns.

SENTENCE 3 The detective noticed **him** staggering. [objective case]

SENTENCE 4 The detective noticed **his** staggering. [possessive case]

44s What case should I use for *-self* pronouns?

Pronouns that end in *-self* (singular) or *-selves* (plural) usually refer to the subject of the sentence. They have a limited number of case forms.

FIRST PERSON myself; ourselves

SECOND PERSON yourself; yourselves

THIRD PERSON himself, herself, itself; themselves

-Self pronouns are called **reflexive pronouns** when they are the object of a verb or preposition or when they otherwise complete the meaning of a verb.

She freed **herself** from a difficult situation.

They allowed **themselves** another break from work.

He is not **himself** today.

Their new business can't possibly pay for **itself**.

Never use a reflexive pronoun in place of a subject or an object.

NO The detective and **myself** had a long talk. He wanted my partner and **myself** to help him. [The reflexive pronoun *myself* cannot serve as a subject or an object; it can only reflect back on a subject or object.]

YES The detective and **I** had a long talk. He wanted my partner and **me** to help him.

-Self pronouns are called **intensive pronouns** when they provide emphasis by intensifying the meaning of a nearby word: *The detective felt that his* ***career itself*** *was at risk.*

For more help with your writing, grammar, and research, go to **www.mycomplab.com**

45

▪ ▪ ▪ ▪ ▪   ▪ ▪

Adjectives and Adverbs

45a What are the differences between adjectives and adverbs?

Both **adjectives** and **adverbs** are MODIFIERS. Modifiers describe other words. The key to distinguishing between adjectives and adverbs is understanding that they modify very different parts of speech.

WHAT ADJECTIVES MODIFY

NOUNS	The *busy* **lawyer** rested.
PRONOUNS	**She** felt *tired*.

WHAT ADVERBS MODIFY

VERBS	The lawyer **spoke** *quickly*.
ADVERBS	The lawyer spoke *very* quickly.
ADJECTIVES	The lawyer was *extremely* busy.
INDEPENDENT CLAUSES	*Undoubtedly,* **the lawyer needed a rest.**

Many adverbs end in *-ly* (*run* ***swiftly***), but some do not (*run* ***often***). Also, some adjectives end in *-ly* (***friendly*** *dog*). Therefore, never depend entirely on an *-ly* ending to identify a word as an adverb.

45b What is wrong with double negatives?

A **double negative** is nonstandard. STANDARD ENGLISH requires only one negative (for example, *no, not, never, none, nothing,* or *hardly*) in a sentence.

NO   The union members did **not** have **no** money in the reserve fund. [Two negatives, *not* and *no*, are used in the same sentence, contrary to the rules of standard English.]

YES   The union members did **not** have **any** money in the reserve fund. [Only one negative, *not*, is in this sentence.]

YES   The union members had **no** money in the reserve fund. [Only one negative, *no*, is in this sentence.]

45c Do adjectives or adverbs come after linking verbs?

LINKING VERBS use adjectives as COMPLEMENTS. In contrast, ACTION VERBS use adverbs.

> Anne **looks** *happy*. [Here *looks* functions as a linking verb, so the adjective *happy* is correct.]

> Anne **looks** *happily* at the sunset. [Here *looks* functions as an action verb, so the adverb *happily* is correct.]

■ Using *bad* and *badly*

Never substitute *bad* (an adjective) for *badly* (an adverb). These words are often misused with linking verbs such as *feel, grow, smell, sound,* and *taste*.

> **NO** The student **felt** *badly*. [Here *felt* functions as a linking verb, so the adverb *badly* is wrong.]

> **YES** The student **felt** *bad*. [Here *felt* functions as a linking verb, so the adjective *bad* is correct.]

■ Using *good* and *well*

Good is always an adjective. *Well* is an adjective only when it is referring to health; otherwise, *well* is an adverb.

> You look **well**. [This means "You look to be in fine health." *Well* functions as an adjective.]

> You write **well**. [This means "You write skillfully." *Well* functions as an adverb.]

45d What are correct comparative and superlative forms?

When comparisons use adjectives and adverbs, the forms of the adjectives and adverbs are either regular or irregular.

■ Regular forms of adjectives and adverbs

Regular adjectives and adverbs show comparisons in two ways. They add either an *-er* ending or the word *more* or *less* to form the **comparative**, used for comparing two things. They add either an *-est* ending or the word *most* or *least* to form the **superlative**, used for comparing three or more things.

Positive [1]	Comparative [2]	Superlative [3+]
green	greener	greenest
happy	happier	happiest
selfish	less selfish	least selfish
beautiful	more beautiful	most beautiful

[1]   That tree is **green**.

[2]   That tree is **greener** than this tree.

[3+]   That tree is the **greenest** tree on the block.

The number of syllables in the adjective or adverb usually determines whether you choose *-er* or *more*. Similarly, the number of syllables determines whether you choose *-est* or *most*.

- Add *-er* and *-est* to one-syllable adjectives and adverbs: *large, larger, largest* (adjective); *far, farther, farthest* (adverb).

- Use *more* and *most* for adverbs with two or more syllables: for example, *easily, more easily, most easily*.

- Use either the *-er* and *-est* endings or *more* and *most* for two-syllable adjectives. The only way to know which forms are correct is to check the dictionary. The forms vary greatly.

- Add *more* and *most* to adjectives and adverbs with three or more syllables: *protective, more protective* [*not* "protectiver"], *most protective* [*not* "protectivest"].

Alert: Never use *more* or *most* together with the *-er* or *-est* ending. For example, *more louder* and *most happiest* are incorrect forms. ●

■ **Irregular forms of adjectives and adverbs**

A few adjectives and adverbs have irregular forms in the comparative and superlative.

Positive [1]	Comparative [2]	Superlative [3+]
good [adjective]	better	best
well [adverb]	better	best
well [adjective]		
bad [adjective]	worse	worst
badly [adverb]	worse	worst
many	more	most
much	more	most
some	more	most
little	less	least

[1]   The Millers had **little** trouble finding jobs.

[2]   The Millers had **less** trouble finding jobs than the Smiths did.

[3+]   The Millers had the **least** trouble finding jobs of everyone.

Alert: Do not use *less* and *fewer* interchangeably. Use *less* when referring to NONCOUNT NOUNS and *fewer* when referring to numbers and COUNT NOUNS: *They consumed **fewer calories** by using **less sugar**.* ●

45e Why should I avoid using too many nouns as modifiers?

Sometimes NOUNS function as modifiers of other nouns, as in *truck driver, train track,* and *sound system.* Problems arise when modifying nouns pile up. This makes it difficult for your reader to tell which nouns are being modified and which nouns are doing the modifying. You can use several strategies to revise a long string of nouns.

SENTENCE REWRITTEN

NO   I asked my adviser to write **two college recommendation letters**.

YES   I asked my adviser to write **letters of recommendation** to **two colleges**.

NOUN REVISED TO POSSESSIVE CASE

NO   Some students might take the **US Navy engineering training examination**.

YES   Some students might take the **US Navy's examination** for **engineering training**.

NOUN REVISED TO PREPOSITIONAL PHRASE

NO   Our **student adviser training program** has won awards for excellence.

YES   Our **training program for student advisers** has won awards for excellence. [Notice here that this revision also requires the plural *advisers.* Plural nouns are generally changed to singular when used as modifiers.]

ESOL Tips: (1) Never add *-s* to an adjective, even when it modifies a plural noun.

NO   The instructor taught us **hards lessons**.

YES   The instructor taught us **hard lessons**.

(2) Never put an adverb between a VERB and a DIRECT OBJECT.

NO   He drank **quietly** the cola.

YES   He **quietly** drank the cola.

YES   He drank the cola **quietly**. ●

46

Sentence Fragments

46a What is a sentence fragment?

A **sentence fragment** is an error because it looks like a sentence but isn't one. It wants to give the impression that it's a sentence by starting with a capital letter and ending with a period (or question mark or exclamation point). But it's only an imitation of the real thing. A fragment is not a whole sentence. Watch out for errors like these.

When winter comes early. [fragment]

Whales in the Arctic Ocean. [fragment]

Stranded in the Arctic Ocean. [fragment]

46b How can I recognize fragments?

You'll find it easier to recognize fragments once you can recognize complete sentences. Get to know the basic pattern of an INDEPENDENT CLAUSE* (41n). Then, when you read your own writing, ask yourself the questions in Quick Reference 46.1 (p. 378). If any answer is yes, you're looking at a sentence fragment. To eliminate the fragment, follow the advice in 46c, 46d, or 46e.

46c How can I correct a fragment that starts with a subordinating word?

Start by recognizing SUBORDINATING CONJUNCTIONS (41h). Then you can choose between two methods to correct a fragment that starts with a subordinating conjunction. You can join the fragment to an existing independent clause, or you can delete the subordinating conjunction.

FRAGMENT   **Because** the ship had to cut a path through the ice.

CORRECT   Because the ship had to cut a path through the ice, the rescue effort took time. [fragment corrected by joining it to an existing independent clause]

CORRECT   The ship had to cut a path through the ice. [fragment corrected by deleting the subordinating conjunction]

---

*Words printed in SMALL CAPITAL LETTERS are discussed elsewhere in the text and are defined in the Terms Glossary at the back of the book.

> ## Quick Reference 46.1 ■ ■ ■ ■ ■ ■ ■
>
> ### How to identify sentence fragments
>
> If any answer here is yes, you have a sentence fragment.
>
> - Is a word group that starts with a subordinating conjunction not joined to a complete sentence?
>
>   FRAGMENT **When** winter comes early.
>
>   CORRECT **When winter comes early,** ice sometimes traps whales in the Arctic Ocean.
>
> - Does a word group lack a VERB without being joined to a complete sentence?
>
>   FRAGMENT Whales in the Arctic Ocean.
>
>   CORRECT Whales **live** in the Arctic Ocean.
>
> - Does a word group lack a SUBJECT without being joined to a complete sentence?
>
>   FRAGMENT Trapped in the Arctic Ocean.
>
>   CORRECT **Many whales** were trapped in the Arctic Ocean.

Some fragments start with the subordinating words *who* or *which*. You can either join such fragments to an existing independent clause or rewrite the idea into its own independent clause.

FRAGMENT The ship's noisy motor worried the **scientists. Who feared the whales would panic.**

CORRECT The ship's noisy motor worried the **scientists, who feared the whales would panic**. [fragment corrected by joining it to an existing independent clause]

CORRECT The ship's noisy motor worried the **scientists. They feared the whales would panic**. [fragment corrected by rewriting it into its own independent clause]

46d How can I correct a phrase fragment?

Start by recognizing a PHRASE (41m). A phrase that begins with a capital letter and ends with a period (or question mark or exclamation point) is a fragment. In the following examples, the phrase fragments are in bold type and each comment in brackets identifies the type of phrase.

The crew played classical music. **To calm the whales.** [infinitive phrase fragment]

The crew chose classical music. **Hoping for success.** [-*ing* participle phrase fragment]

The whales began to panic. **Trapped by the ice.** [past participle phrase fragment]

The ship moved slowly. **Toward the whales.** [prepositional phrase fragment]

An enormously powerful icebreaker. The ship arrived to free the whales. [appositive phrase fragment]

You can choose between two methods to correct a fragment that is a phrase not joined to an independent clause. You can join it to an existing independent clause, or you can rewrite it into its own independent clause.

FRAGMENTS JOINED TO AN EXISTING INDEPENDENT CLAUSE

The crew played classical music **to calm the whales**.

The crew chose classical music, **hoping for success**.

The whales began to panic, **trapped by the ice**.

The ship moved slowly **toward the whales**.

An enormously powerful icebreaker, the ship arrived to free the whales.

FRAGMENTS REWRITTEN INTO AN INDEPENDENT CLAUSE

The major concern was how **to calm the whales**.

The crew, **hoping for success,** put classical music on the ship's sound system.

No one knew whether whales **trapped by the ice** would cooperate with a rescue attempt.

The ship moved quietly and slowly **toward the whales**.

An enormously powerful icebreaker arrived to free the whales.

46e How can I correct a fragment that is a part of a compound predicate?

In a complete sentence, a **compound predicate** contains two or more verbs connected by a COORDINATING CONJUNCTION (*and, but, for, or, nor, yet, so*). The boldface type in the next example shows a fragment that is half of a compound predicate. You can choose between two methods to correct this kind of fragment. You can join it to an existing independent clause, or you can rewrite the sentence without a compound predicate.

FRAGMENT   The ship reached the whales. **And led them to freedom.**

CORRECT   The ship reached the whales **and led them to freedom**. [fragment corrected by joining it to an existing independent clause]

CORRECT The crew cheered as the whales swam to freedom.
[fragment corrected by rewriting it without a compound predicate]

46f What are intentional fragments?

Professional writers sometimes intentionally use fragments for emphasis and effect. The ability to judge the difference between acceptable and unacceptable sentence fragments comes from much exposure to the works of skilled writers. Be aware that most educators consider sentence fragments errors. A few teachers occasionally allow well-placed intentional fragments after a student has shown the consistent ability to write well-constructed complete sentences.

For more help with your
writing, grammar, and research,
go to **www.mycomplab.com**

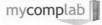

47

Comma Splices and Run-On Sentences

47a What are comma splices and run-on sentences?

Comma splices and run-on sentences are errors that look almost alike. They incorrectly join two INDEPENDENT CLAUSES. A **comma splice** is created when only a comma separates independent clauses. A **run-on sentence** is created when no punctuation at all separates independent clauses (see Quick Reference 47.1).

COMMA SPLICE The hurricane **intensified, it** turned toward land.

RUN-ON SENTENCE The hurricane **intensified it** turned toward land.

Alert: Occasionally, experienced writers use a comma to join short, contrasting independent clauses: *Mosquitoes do not **bite**, they* stab. Your teacher may consider this punctuation an error, so check before you use it. ●

Quick Reference 47.1

■ ■ ■ ■ ■ ■ ■

How to identify and correct comma splices and run-on sentences

1. Watch out for a second independent clause that starts with a PRONOUN.

COMMA SPLICE	Thomas Edison was a productive **inventor, he held** more than 1,300 American and foreign patents.
RUN-ON SENTENCE	Thomas Edison was a productive **inventor he held** more than 1,300 American and foreign patents.
CORRECT	Thomas Edison was a productive **inventor. He held** more than 1,300 American and foreign patents.

2. Watch out for a CONJUNCTIVE ADVERB that joins two sentences.

COMMA SPLICE	Thomas Edison was a brilliant **scientist, however,** he spent only three months in school.
RUN-ON SENTENCE	Thomas Edison was a brilliant **scientist however,** he spent only three months in school.
CORRECT	Thomas Edison was a brilliant **scientist; however,** he spent only three months in school.

3. Watch out for a TRANSITIONAL EXPRESSION that joins two sentences.

COMMA SPLICE	Thomas Edison invented the **microphone, in addi-tion, he created** a superior storage battery.
RUN-ON SENTENCE	Thomas Edison invented the **microphone in addition, he created** a superior storage battery.
CORRECT	Thomas Edison invented the **microphone. In addi-tion, he created** a superior storage battery.

4. Watch out when a second independent clause explains or gives an example of the information in the first independent clause.

COMMA SPLICE	Thomas Edison was the genius behind **many inven-tions, among** the best known are the phonograph and the incandescent lamp.
RUN-ON SENTENCE	Thomas Edison was the genius behind **many inven-tions among** the best known are the phonograph and the incandescent lamp.
CORRECT	Thomas Edison was the genius behind many **inventions. Among** the best known are the phonograph and the incandescent lamp.

47b   How can I correct comma splices and run-on sentences?

To correct comma splices and run-on sentences, you can use punctuation or a coordinating conjunction, or you can revise one of the two incorrectly joined sentences into a DEPENDENT CLAUSE.

Using punctuation

You can use a period or a semicolon to separate independent clauses in a comma splice or run-on sentence.

COMMA SPLICE	A shark's skeleton is all **cartilage, the shark** does not have a bone in its body.
RUN-ON SENTENCE	A shark's skeleton is all **cartilage the shark** does not have a bone in its body.
CORRECT	A shark's skeleton is all **cartilage. The shark** does not have a bone in its body.

Using a coordinating conjunction

If the ideas in your independent clauses relate closely in meaning and are grammatically equivalent, you can connect them with a comma followed by a coordinating conjunction (*and, but, for, or, nor, yet, so*).

COMMA SPLICE	Every living creature gives off a weak electrical charge in **water, special pores** on a shark's skin can detect these signals.
RUN-ON SENTENCE	Every living creature gives off a weak electrical charge in **water special pores** on a shark's skin can detect these signals.
CORRECT	Every living creature gives off a weak electrical charge in **water, *and* special pores** on a shark's skin can detect these signals.

Revising an independent clause into a dependent clause

If one of two independent clauses expresses information that can be logically subordinated to the other independent clause, start it with a subordinating word and join it correctly to the independent clause.

COMMA SPLICE	Costa Rica's Cocos Island harbors more sharks than anywhere else on **earth, it is** paradise to underwater filmmakers.

RUN-ON SENTENCE	Costa Rica's Cocos Island harbors more sharks than anywhere else on **earth it is** paradise to underwater filmmakers.
CORRECT	***Because*** Costa Rica's Cocos Island harbors more sharks than anywhere else on **earth, it is** paradise to underwater filmmakers. [*Because* makes the first clause dependent.]
COMMA SPLICE	Some sharks have large, triangular **teeth, these** teeth can tear flesh.
RUN-ON SENTENCE	Some sharks have large, triangular **teeth these** teeth can tear flesh.
CORRECT	Some sharks have large, triangular **teeth *that*** can tear flesh. [*That* makes the second clause dependent.]

When a conjunctive adverb (such as *however, therefore, also, next, then, thus, furthermore,* or *nevertheless*) or a transitional expression (such as *for example* or *for instance*) falls between spliced or run-on independent clauses, you need to use a period or a semicolon to correct the error.

COMMA SPLICE	Some sharks cannot **bite, for example,** the basking shark can only filter plankton through its small mouth.
RUN-ON SENTENCE	Some sharks cannot **bite for example,** the basking shark can only filter plankton through its small mouth.
CORRECT	Some sharks cannot **bite. For example,** the basking shark can only filter plankton through its small mouth.
CORRECT	Some sharks cannot **bite; for example,** the basking shark can only filter plankton through its small mouth.

48

Problems with Sentence Shifts

A correct sentence doesn't "shift." **Shifts** are grammatical changes that lead to errors because they're mismatched grammatical forms. To avoid writing sentence shifts, be consistent in using the grammatical forms covered in 48a–48d.

48a How can I be consistent in person and number?

Person tells who or what is acting or being acted on. **First person** (*I, we*) focuses attention on the writer or speaker: *I see a field of fireflies.* **Second person** (*you*) focuses attention on the reader or listener: *You see a shower of sparks.* **Third person** focuses attention on the action of someone or something else: *The physicist sees a cloud of cosmic dust.* Don't shift person unless a particular context makes it necessary.

> **NO**   I enjoy reading financial forecasts, but **you** wonder which will be correct. [The first person *I* shifts to the second person *you*.]
>
> **YES**   I enjoy reading financial forecasts, but **I** wonder which will be correct.

! **Alert:** NOUNS and many PRONOUNS are always in the third person. ●

Number refers to SINGULAR (one) or PLURAL (more than one). Don't mix singular and plural unless your meaning calls for it.

> **NO**   Because **people** are living longer, **an employee** now retires later. [The plural *people* shifts to the singular *employee*.]
>
> **YES**   Because **people** are living longer, **employees** now retire later.

! **Alerts:** (1) Watch out for shifts from nouns (always in the third person) to the second-person pronoun *you*.

By the year 2020, **most people** will live longer, and ~~you~~ *they* will have to work longer, too.

(2) Watch out for shifts between singular and plural in the third person.

The longer ~~a people stays~~ *people stay* in the workforce, the more competition they will face from younger job seekers. ●

48b How can I be consistent in subject, voice, and mood?

A shift in SUBJECT within or between sentences shows that your writing is drifting out of focus. To be consistent in subject, VOICE, and MOOD, avoid changing these aspects within sentences and paragraphs. For example, don't switch between the ACTIVE VOICE and the PASSIVE VOICE.

SHIFT IN SUBJECT AND VOICE	**People complain** about sugary, high-fat foods, but *donuts* by the millions **are eaten** for breakfast every day. [The subject shifts from *people* to *donuts,* and the verb voice shifts from active *complain* to passive *are eaten.*]
CORRECT	**People complain** about sugary, high-fat foods, but **they eat** donuts by the millions for breakfast every day.

Similarly, within the same sentence, avoid combining statements or questions (INDICATIVE MOOD), commands (IMPERATIVE MOOD), or conditional statements (SUBJUNCTIVE MOOD).

SHIFT IN MOOD	Breakfast is the most important meal, if we often weren't too busy to eat it. [The first clause is indicative, but the second shifts to subjunctive.]
CORRECT	Breakfast is the most important meal, but we're often too busy to eat it.

48c How can I be consistent in verb tense?

To be consistent in verb TENSE, remain in the same tense unless a shift is necessary to show time passing (see Quick Reference 42.3).

SHIFT IN VERB TENSE	The campaign to clean up the movies **began** in the late 1940s when civic and religious groups **try** to ban sex and violence from films. [The tense shifts from past *began* to present *try,* even though the action of both verbs occurred in the past.]
CORRECT	The campaign to clean up the movies **began** in the late 1940s when civic and religious groups **tried** to ban sex and violence from films. [Both verbs are in the past tense.]

48d How can I be consistent in direct and indirect discourse?

Because the grammatical patterns of direct discourse and indirect discourse differ, writers should not shift between the two. **Direct discourse** repeats someone's words exactly, with quotation marks enclosing them. **Indirect discourse** reports, rather than repeats exactly, someone's words without using quotation marks.

SHIFT BETWEEN DIRECT AND INDIRECT DISCOURSE	He asked did we enjoy the movie. [The verb *asked* is direct discourse, but *did we enjoy the movie* are the person's exact words]
CORRECT	He asked, "Did you enjoy the movie?" [The quotation marks indicate this is direct discourse.]
CORRECT	He asked whether we had enjoyed the movie. [This statement indicates that the content of the man's question is being *reported*, not quoted.]

48e What happens in sentences with mixed parts?

A sentence with mixed parts starts in one direction but confusingly goes off in a different direction. To revise such errors, think through exactly what you want to say.

■ Avoiding mixed clauses

In a sentence containing a DEPENDENT CLAUSE and an INDEPENDENT CLAUSE, the clauses are clear when they carry meaning in one direction, not two directions.

MIXED CLAUSES	Because television's early transmissions in the late 1940s included **news, programs** were popular. [The dependent clause talks about news, but the independent clause goes off in another direction by talking about the popularity of programs in general.]
CORRECT	Television's early transmissions in the late 1940s included **news programs, which** were popular. [The focus is now on news programs throughout.]

■ Avoiding mixed constructions

If a group of words contains a PHRASE and only part of an independent clause, it forms a **mixed construction** that makes no sense.

MIXED CONSTRUCTION	**By doubling the time allotment** to thirty minutes **increased** the prestige of news programs. [This sentence starts with the prepositional phrase *By doubling the time allotment*, but what follows does not make sense because there is no subject to go with the verb *increased*.]

CORRECT	**Doubling** the time allotment to thirty minutes **increased** the prestige of news programs. [Dropping the preposition *By* allows the sentence to make sense.]
CORRECT	**By doubling the time allotment** to thirty minutes, **network executives increased** the prestige of news programs. [Inserting a logical subject, *network executives*, allows the sentence to make sense.]

▣ Avoiding faulty predication

Faulty predication results when the subject and PREDICATE of a sentence don't make sense together. You can correct the error by revising one part or the other so that they work together.

FAULTY PREDICATION	The purpose of television was invented to entertain. [The subject of the sentence is *purpose*. The predicate is *was invented to entertain*. Together, they don't make sense.]
CORRECT	**Television** was invented to entertain. [Revising the subject and keeping the original predicate *was invented to entertain* allows the sentence to make sense.]
CORRECT	The purpose of television **was to entertain.** [Revising the predicate and keeping the original subject *the purpose of television* allows the sentence to make sense.]

48f   How do elliptical constructions and comparisons work?

An **elliptical construction** deliberately leaves out, rather than repeats, one or more words that appear earlier in a sentence. An elliptical sentence is correct only when it has omitted exactly the same words as have been used previously in the same sentence.

In 1920s Chicago, cornetist Manuel Perez ~~was leading~~ led one outstanding jazz
group, Tommy and Jimmy Dorsey another.

[The singular verb *was leading* cannot take the place of *were leading* in the second part of the sentence. *Led* works because it goes with both the singular *Perez* and the plural *Tommy and Jimmy Dorsey*.]

in

The period of the big jazz dance bands began ^ and lasted through World

War II.

[*Began* needs to be followed by *in*, because *through* doesn't work after both *began* and *lasted*.]

In writing a comparison, you can omit words as long as the reader can clearly tell what the missing words are.

than low achievers do

High achievers make better business executives.
                                              ^

[*Better* implies a comparison, but none is stated, so the revision corrects the problem.]

they value

Most stockholders value high achievers more than ^ risk takers.

[Before the revision, who values whom isn't clear. The revised sentence is clear. An alternative revision, with a different meaning, would be *Most stockholders value high achievers more than risk takers do*.]

from that of a high achiever

A risk taker's ability to manage long-term growth is very different.
                                                                  ^

[Different from what? Both items must be expressed for the comparison to work.]

 Alert: When you write *as much as, as . . . as . . . than* (for example, *as pretty as, if not prettier than*), and similar comparisons, be sure to state the second *as*.

as

High achievers value success as much, if not more than, high salary. ●
                                    ^

■ ■ ■ ■ **49** ■ ■

Misplaced Modifiers

A MODIFIER describes or limits other words, PHRASES, or CLAUSES. A modifier itself can be a word, phrase, or clause. When you write, place modifiers carefully so that your intended meaning is clear.

49a How can I correct misplaced modifiers?

The correct placement for a modifier is almost always next to the word that it modifies. If you place a modifier elsewhere in a sentence, you are misplacing the modifier, which confuses the meaning of the sentence.

MISPLACED MODIFIER	Nicholas Cugnot built the first self-propelled vehicle, determined to travel without horses. [The modifier *determined to travel without horses* is meant to describe *Nicholas Cugnot*. But because it's placed next to *vehicle*, the sentence says the *vehicle* was the entity determined to travel without horses.]
CORRECT	Determined to travel without horses, Nicholas Cugnot built the first self-propelled vehicle.

ADVERBS such as *only, just, almost, hardly, scarcely,* and *simply* always limit the word that comes immediately after them. Place them with care because they can strongly affect the meaning of your sentence. For example, notice how various positions of *only* influence the meaning of the sentence *Professional coaches say that high salaries motivate players.*

Only professional coaches say that high salaries motivate players. [No one else says that.]

Professional coaches **only** say that high salaries motivate players. [The coaches don't believe it.]

Professional coaches say that **only** high salaries motivate players. [The coaches think nothing else works.]

Professional coaches say that high salaries motivate **only** players. [No one else is motivated by high salaries.]

49b How can I correct squinting modifiers?

A **squinting modifier** appears to apply to what comes before it as well as to what comes after it. The writer needs to revise so that the modifier applies in only one direction—that is, to only one word, phrase, or clause.

SQUINTING MODIFIER	While Karl Benz watched, the vehicle he had built **noisily** announced its arrival. [Was the car built noisily? Or was its arrival announced noisily?]
CORRECT	While Karl Benz watched, the vehicle he had built announced its arrival **noisily**. [Now we know that it was the arrival that was announced noisily.]

49c   How can I correct split infinitives?

A **split infinitive** occurs when a modifier of more than one word separates *to* from the verb that completes the infinitive. (*To conclude* is an infinitive. *To without a doubt conclude* is a split infinitive.)

SPLIT
INFINITIVE

Orson Welles's radio drama *War of the Worlds* managed **to, *on October 30, 1938,* convince** listeners that they were hearing an invasion by Martians.

CORRECT

On October 30, 1938, Orson Welles's radio drama *War of the Worlds* managed **to convince** listeners that they were hearing an invasion by Martians.

49d   How can I keep modifiers from disrupting a sentence?

Avoid writing complex descriptive phrases or clauses that separate the SUBJECT and VERB of a sentence. Such modifiers make a sentence overly complicated, disturbing its smooth flow.

~~The invention of the automobile,~~ If we consider the complete history of people working independently in different countries, the invention of the automobile should probably be credited to Nicholas Cugnot in 1769.

Also, interrupting a VERB PHRASE with modifiers makes a sentence lurch instead of flow. Observe the general rule to put modifiers next to the word they modify.

Karl Benz has ~~by most automobile historians~~ been given credit by most automobile historians for the invention of the automobile.

49e   How can I correct dangling modifiers?

A **dangling modifier** is an introductory phrase that hangs (that is, it dangles) helplessly because the NOUN it modifies isn't the intended subject. Introductory phrases attach their meaning to the first noun after the phrase—indeed, that noun is the sentence's subject. If some other word falls in that position, the result is confusing (or even humorous).

DANGLING
MODIFIER

Reading Faulkner's short story "A Rose for Emily," the ending surprised us. [*The ending* did not read the story.]

CORRECT	Reading Faulkner's short story "A Rose for Emily," **we were surprised** by the ending.
CORRECT	**We read** Faulkner's short story "A Rose for Emily" **and were surprised** by the ending.
DANGLING MODIFIER	When courting Emily, the townspeople gossiped about Homer Baron. [*The townspeople* were not courting Emily, and they were not gossiping about Homer so much as about Emily.]
CORRECT	**When** Homer Baron **was courting Emily**, the townspeople gossiped about her.

For more help with your
writing, grammar, and research,
go to **www.mycomplab.com**

Conciseness

Conciseness is desirable because it makes writing direct and to the point. **Wordiness** uses empty or unnecessary words and PHRASES that contribute nothing to meaning.

50a How can I write concisely?

You can write concisely by deleting all words not necessary for delivering your message clearly. Get rid of the unneeded words listed in Quick Reference 50.1 (p. 392) and similar expressions.

50b How can I avoid redundant writing?

Redundant writing is repetitious writing, which is undesirable because it duplicates a message already stated but in different words. Unlike intentional repetition (see 52d), which can create a powerful rhythmic effect, unintentional repetition is simply sloppy writing.

Quick Reference 50.1

■ ■ ■ ■ ■ ■ ■

Deleting unneeded words

Empty Words	Wordy Examples Revised
as a matter of fact	~~As a matter of fact, m~~any marriages end in divorce. *(M)*
at the present time	The bill is being debated ~~at the present time~~. *(now)*
because of the fact that, in light of the fact that, due to the fact that	Because ~~of the fact that~~ a special exhibit is scheduled, the museum is open late each day.
factor	The project's final cost was ~~an~~ essential ~~factor~~ to consider.
that exists	The crime rate ~~that exists~~ is unacceptable.
for the purpose of	A work crew arrived ~~for the purpose of~~ ~~fix~~ing the pothole. *(to)*
in a very real sense	~~In a very real sense, d~~rainage problems caused the flooding. *(D)*
in the case of	~~In the case of~~ the proposed~~,~~ tax residents ~~were angry.~~ *(T)* *(angered)*
in the event that	~~In the event that~~ you are late, I will buy our tickets. *(If)*
it seems that	~~It seems that~~ the union struck over wages. *(T)*
manner	The hikers looked at the snake ~~in a fearful manner.~~ *(fearfully.)*
nature	The review was ~~of a~~ markedly sarcastic ~~nature.~~
the point that I am trying to make	~~The point that I am trying to make is that~~ ~~n~~ews reporters often invade people's privacy. *(N)*
what I mean to say	~~What I mean to say is that~~ I expect a bonus.
type of, kind of	Gordon took a relaxing ~~type of~~ vacation.

A   people

~~People~~ anesthetized ~~for surgery~~ can remain semiconscious during surgery but nevertheless feel no pain.

[*Surgery* is used twice unnecessarily. The word *anesthetized* carries the concept of surgery. The revision is not redundant.]

Completing

~~Bringing~~ the project ~~to final completion~~ three weeks early, the new man-

              respect.

ager earned our ~~respectful regard.~~

[*Completing* carries the idea of *final*. Also, *regard* implies *respect*. The revisions are not redundant.]

rectangular

The package, ~~rectangular in shape,~~ lay on the counter.

[*Rectangular* includes the concept of *shape*. The revision is not redundant.]

50c How can I avoid wordy sentence structures?

Two sentence structures most frequently lead to wordiness. They are expletive constructions and use of the passive voice.

Avoiding expletive constructions

An EXPLETIVE CONSTRUCTION places *it* or *there* and a form of *be* before the subject of the sentence. To make such sentences more concise, revise them to eliminate the expletive.

            S   need

~~It is necessary for~~ students to fill out both registration forms.

                      T   offers three majors

~~There are three majors offered by~~ the computer science department.

Using the passive voice appropriately

The PASSIVE VOICE is generally less lively and concise than the ACTIVE VOICE (42g). Unless your meaning justifies using the passive voice, write in the active voice.

PASSIVE Volunteer work was done by the students for credit in sociology. [Here the passive voice is unnecessary. *The students*, who are doing the action of volunteer work, need to be the subject of this sentence.]

ACTIVE The students did volunteer work for credit in sociology.

ACTIVE Volunteer work earned the students credit in sociology. [Here, *volunteer work* performs the action of the verb *earned*, so *volunteer work* is the subject of the sentence.]

50d How can combining sentence elements help me be concise?

Sometimes you can combine sentences to save words. Look at your sentences two at a time to see if a group of words in one sentence can be included in another sentence.

~~The Titanic was discovered~~ seventy-three years after being sunk by an iceberg. ~~The liner~~ was located under the water by a team of French and American scientists.

[editing marks: "s" above "discovered"; ", t" and "Titanic" inserted after "berg"]

Sometimes you can shorten longer structures to become a phrase or even a single word.

The *Titanic,* ~~which was~~ a huge ocean liner, sank in 1911.

The scientists who discovered the *Titanic* held a memorial service for the passengers and crew ~~members who had died.~~

[editing marks: "dead" inserted before "passengers"]

~~Loaded with luxuries, the~~ liner was thought to be unsinkable.

[editing marks: "luxury" inserted]

50e How do action verbs improve conciseness?

Action verbs are strong verbs. Weak verbs, especially forms of *be* and *have,* usually lead to wordy sentences.

WEAK VERB	The plan before the city council **has to do with** tax rebates.
STRONG VERB	The plan before the city council **proposes** tax rebates.

⚠️ **Alert:** When you revise, look for phrase patterns such as *be aware of* and *be capable of* and revise them to be more concise. Often such phrases are better stated with one-word verbs: for example, *I envy* [not *am envious of*] *your self-confidence.* Here are a few more examples: Use *appreciate* in place of *be appreciative of, illustrate* in place of *be illustrative of,* and *support* in place of *be supportive of.* ●

When you revise to use strong VERBS, look for NOUNS built from verbs. Turning nouns that end with *-ance, -ment,* and *-tion* into verbs allows you to write more concisely.

NO The **accumulation** of old newspapers went on for more than thirty years.

YES The old newspapers **accumulated** for more than thirty years.

For more help with your writing, grammar, and research, go to **www.mycomplab.com**

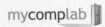

Coordination and Subordination

Coordination and *subordination* are sentence structures that help writers communicate relationships between ideas. Neither structure is superior on its own, but the emphasis that you want your sentence to deliver usually influences your choice of structures. Many experienced writers use both to achieve variety in their writing styles.

TWO IDEAS The sky turned brighter. The wind calmed down.

COORDINATED VERSION The sky turned brighter, **and** the wind calmed down [Here, the word *and* gives *the sky* and *the wind* equal emphasis.]

SUBORDINATED VERSIONS When the sky turned brighter, the wind calmed down. [Here, *the wind* is the subject of the INDEPENDENT CLAUSE, so it's the main focus of the sentence.]

As the wind calmed down, the sky turned brighter. [Here, *the sky* is the subject of the independent clause, so it's the main focus of the sentence.]

51a How does coordination show that ideas are equivalent?

Coordination gives you a grammatical written strategy to show that ideas are equal or balanced. A COMPOUND SENTENCE has independent clauses joined either by a semicolon or by a COORDINATING CONJUNCTION (*and, but, for, or, nor, yet, so*).

> The sky turned brighter, **and** the wind calmed down.
>
> The sky turned brighter; the wind calmed down.

⚠ **Alert:** Unless you use a semicolon, use a comma before a coordinating conjunction that joins two independent clauses (57c). ●

51b How can I avoid problems with coordination?

Two problems can occur when you write using coordination. First, you create an illogical sentence if you join unrelated or nonequivalent ideas with a coordinating conjunction.

> **NO**   Computers came into common use in the 1970s, and they sometimes make costly errors. [The statement in each independent clause is true, but the ideas aren't logically connected, so they can't be coordinated.]
>
> **YES** Computers came into common use in the 1970s, and now they are indispensable business tools.

Second, if you overuse coordination, you write unfocused material by stringing more than two or three sentences together with coordinating conjunctions (*and, but, for, or, nor, yet, so*).

> **NO**   Dinosaurs could have disappeared for many reasons, **and** one theory holds that the climate suddenly became cold, **and** another suggests that a sudden shower of meteors and asteroids hit the earth, **so** the impact created a huge dust cloud that caused a false winter. The winter lasted for years, **and** the dinosaurs died.
>
> **YES** Dinosaurs could have disappeared for many reasons. One theory holds that the climate suddenly became cold, **and** another suggests that a sudden shower of meteors and asteroids hit the earth. The impact created a huge dust cloud that caused a false winter. The winter lasted for years, killing the dinosaurs.

51c   How does subordination work to express nonequivalent ideas?

Subordination gives you a grammatical written strategy to show that one idea in a two-idea sentence is more important than the other idea. The more important idea goes in an independent clause; the less important idea goes in a DEPENDENT CLAUSE, also called a SUBORDINATE CLAUSE—which is why this form is called subordination. The idea you choose to subordinate in a sentence with two ideas depends on the emphasis you want to deliver.

> **NO**   In 1888, two cowboys had to fight a dangerous Colorado snowstorm. They were looking for cattle. They came to a canyon. They saw outlines of buildings through the snow. Survival then seemed certain. [No idea is emphasized more than any other, with only a singsong effect emerging from the writing.]

> **YES**   In 1888, two cowboys had to fight a dangerous Colorado snowstorm **while** they were looking for cattle. **When** they came to a canyon, they saw outlines of buildings through the snow. Survival then seemed certain. [The two underlined clauses get the emphasis because they are independent clauses; the others have been turned into dependent clauses.]

To subordinate ideas successfully, you need a SUBORDINATING CONJUNCTION to start the dependent clause. Subordinating conjunctions (see Quick Reference 51.1) start ADVERB CLAUSES. RELATIVE PRONOUNS, such as *who, which,* and *that* (41b), and RELATIVE ADVERBS, such as *where, why,* and *when* (41f), start ADJECTIVE CLAUSES.

51d   How can I avoid problems with subordination?

Two problems can occur when you write using subordination. First, you create an illogical sentence when the subordinating conjunction doesn't communicate a sensible relationship between the independent clause and the dependent clause. (For the relationships subordinating conjunctions express, see Quick Reference 41.7.)

> **NO**   **Because** Beethoven was deaf when he wrote them, his final symphonies were masterpieces. [*Because* is illogical. The masterpieces were not the result of Beethoven's being deaf.]

> **YES**   **Although** Beethoven was deaf when he wrote them, his final symphonies were masterpieces. [*Although* is logical. It suggests that Beethoven wrote musical masterpieces despite being deaf.]

Subordination patterns

SENTENCES WITH ADVERB CLAUSES

ADVERB CLAUSE AT BEGINNING

After the sky grew dark, the wind died suddenly.

ADVERB CLAUSE AT END

Birds stopped singing, **as they do during an eclipse.**

The stores closed **before the storm began.**

SENTENCES WITH ADJECTIVE CLAUSES

RESTRICTIVE ADJECTIVE CLAUSE* AT END

Weather forecasts warned of a storm **that might bring a thirty-inch snowfall.**

NONRESTRICTIVE ADJECTIVE CLAUSE* AT END

Spring is the season for tornadoes, **which may develop wind speeds over 220 miles per hour.**

RESTRICTIVE ADJECTIVE CLAUSE* BETWEEN PARTS OF THE INDEPENDENT CLAUSE

Anyone **who lives through a tornado** remembers the experience.

NONRESTRICTIVE ADJECTIVE CLAUSE* BETWEEN PARTS OF THE INDEPENDENT CLAUSE

The sky, **which had been clear,** turned greenish black.

*To understand RESTRICTIVE (essential) and NONRESTRICTIVE (nonessential) CLAUSES, see Quick Reference 40.2 and 57f.

Second, if you overuse subordination, your readers lose track of your message because you crowd too many ideas together.

NO A new technique for eye surgery, **which** is supposed to correct nearsightedness, **which** previously could be corrected only by glasses, has been developed, **although** many doctors do not approve of the new technique **because** it can create unstable vision.

YES A new technique for eye surgery, which is supposed to correct nearsightedness, has been developed. Previously, nearsightedness could be corrected only by glasses. However, many doctors do not approve of the new technique because it can create unstable vision. [In this revision, one long sentence is broken into three sentences, making the relationships among ideas clearer.]

For more help with your writing, grammar, and research, go to **www.mycomplab.com**

52

Sentence Style

To develop your writing style, experiment with the techniques described in this chapter: parallelism, sentence variety, and sentence emphasis.

52a What is parallelism?

When words, PHRASES, or CLAUSES within a sentence grammatically match, the result is **parallelism**. Parallelism serves to emphasize information or ideas. Also, balance and rhythm in parallel structures add style and grace to your writing.

PARALLEL WORDS	Recommended exercise includes **running**, **swimming**, and **cycling.**
PARALLEL PHRASES	Exercise helps people **maintain healthy bodies** and **handle mental pressures**.
PARALLEL CLAUSES	Many people exercise **because they want to look healthy, because they need to increase stamina,** and **because they hope to live longer.**

52b How can I avoid faulty parallelism?

You can avoid faulty parallelism by checking that you always use the same grammatical form for words, phrases, or clauses.

NO	The strikers had tried **shouting**, **threats**, and **pleading**. [The list incorrectly mixes -*ing* forms and a plural.]
YES	The strikers had tried **shouting**, **threatening**, and **pleading**. [The three words are all in -*ing* form.]

YES   The strikers had tried **shouts**, **threats**, and **pleas**. [The three words are all plural nouns.]

NO   The strikers **read** the offer, **were discussing** it, and the unanimous **decision was to reject** it. [Two of the three items incorrectly mix verb forms, and the third item switches to the PASSIVE VOICE.]

YES   The strikers **read** the offer, **discussed** it, and unanimously **decided** to reject it. [All three items are in the past tense.]

52c How should I use parallelism with conjunctions?

Words, phrases, or clauses joined with COORDINATING CONJUNCTIONS (*and, but, for, or, nor, yet, so*) usually deliver their message most clearly and concisely when written in parallel form.

> You come to understand what to expect when you **tease** a cat, or **toss** a pebble in a pool, or **touch** a hot stove.
>
> —Ann E. Berthoff, *Forming, Thinking, and Writing*

Similarly, use parallel forms when you link sentence elements with CORRELATIVE CONJUNCTIONS (such as *either . . . or* and *not only . . . but also*).

> Differing expectations for marriage can lead **not only** to disappointment **but also** to anger.
>
> —Norman Du Bois, student

52d How does parallelism strengthen my message?

Parallelism—which calls for deliberate but controlled repetition of word forms, word groups, and sounds—creates a rhythm that strengthens and intensifies a sentence's message.

> You can fool some of the people all of the time and all of the people some of the time, but you cannot fool all of the people all of the time.
>
> —Abraham Lincoln

Another technique for creating parallel structures to intensify ideas is to write balanced sentences. **Balanced sentences** consist of two short independent clauses that compare or contrast.

> **By night**, the litter and desperation disappeared as the city's glittering lights came on; **by day**, the filth and despair reappeared as the sun rose.
>
> —Jennifer Kirk, student

52e   What is sentence variety?

Writers use sentence variety when they vary the length and structure of their sentences in relation to each other.

■ Revising strings of short sentences

Sometimes you can plan several short sentences in a row to create impact. Be careful, however, to avoid strings of short sentences that don't establish relationships among ideas; they tend to make reading dull.

> **NO**   There is a problem. It is widely known as sick-building syndrome. It comes from indoor air pollution. It causes the suffering of office workers. They have trouble breathing. The workers develop rashes that are painful. Their heads ache badly. Their eyes burn.

> **YES**   Widely known as sick-building syndrome, indoor air pollution causes office workers to suffer. They have trouble breathing. They have painful rashes. Their heads ache. Their eyes burn. [Many revisions are possible. This one begins with a long sentence that introduces the interaction of indoor air pollution and its victims. Then a series of short sentences emphasizes each problem the victims suffer. The revised version is also more concise, reducing forty-two words to twenty-seven.]

■ Revising for a mix of sentence lengths

You can emphasize one idea among many others by expressing that idea in a sentence noticeably different in length or structure from the sentences surrounding it. The "yes" example above illustrates the graceful impact of one long sentence among many shorter ones. Here's an example of one short sentence among longer ones.

> Today is one of those excellent January partly cloudies in which light chooses an unexpected landscape to trick out in gilt, and then shadow sweeps it away. **You know you are alive.** You take huge steps, trying to feel the planet's roundness arc between your feet.
>
> —Annie Dillard, *Pilgrim at Tinker Creek*

52f   How does the subject of a sentence affect emphasis?

Because the SUBJECT of a sentence establishes the sentence's focus, always choose for the sentence's subject what you want to emphasize. Each of the following sentences contains the same information, but changing the subject (and VERB, as needed) affects each sentence's meaning and emphasis.

Our study showed that 25 percent of college students' time is spent eating or sleeping. [Focus is on the study.]

College students eat or sleep 25 percent of the time, according to our study. [Focus is on the students.]

Eating or sleeping occupies 25 percent of college students' time, according to our study. [Focus is on eating and sleeping.]

Twenty-five percent of college students' time is spent eating or sleeping, according to our study. [Focus is on the percentage of time.]

52g How does adding modifiers affect writing style?

You can add richness and variety to your writing with MODIFIERS. You can expand a sentence with modifiers depending on the focus you want to achieve.

BASIC SENTENCE	The river rose.
ADJECTIVE	The **swollen** river rose.
ADVERB	The river rose **dangerously**.
PREPOSITIONAL PHRASE	**In April**, the river rose **above its banks**.
PARTICIPIAL PHRASE	**Swelled by melting snow**, the river rose, **flooding the farmland**.
ABSOLUTE PHRASE	**Trees swirling away in the current**, the river rose.
ADVERB CLAUSE	**Because the snows had been heavy that winter**, the river rose.
ADJECTIVE CLAUSE	The river, **which runs through vital farmland**, rose.

52h How does inverting standard word order affect writing style?

Standard word order in English sentences places the subject before the verb: *The mayor* [subject] *walked* [verb] *into the room.*

Because standard word order is common, variations from it create emphasis. **Inverted word order**, which places the verb before the subject, when used sparingly, produces emphasis.

STANDARD	The mayor walked into the room.
INVERTED	Into the room walked the mayor.

53

Usage Glossary

This usage glossary explains the customary manner of using particular words and PHRASES. "Customary manner," however, is not as firm in practice as the term implies. Usage standards change. If you think a word's usage might differ from what you read here, consult a dictionary published more recently than this book.

As used here, *informal* and *colloquial* indicate that words or phrases occur commonly in speech but should be avoided in ACADEMIC WRITING. *Nonstandard* indicates that words or phrases should not be used in either standard spoken English or writing.

All grammatical terms mentioned here are defined in the Terms Glossary at the back of the book. Also consult the commonly confused words listed in Quick Reference 56.1.

a, an   Use *a* before words that begin with a consonant (*a dog, a grade, a hole*) or a consonant sound (*a one-day sale, a European*). Use *an* before words or acronyms that begin with a vowel sound or a silent *h* (*an owl, an hour, an MRI*). American English uses *a,* not *an,* before words starting with a pronounced *h: a* [not *an*] *historical event.*

accept, except   The verb *accept* means "agree to, receive." As a preposition, *except* means "leaving out." As a verb, *except* means "exclude, leave out."

The workers were ready to **accept** [verb] management's offer **except** [preposition] for one detail: They wanted the no-smoking rule **excepted** [verb] from the contract.

advice, advise   *Advice,* a noun, means "recommendation." *Advise,* a verb, means "recommend, give advice."

I **advise** [verb] you to follow your car mechanic's **advice** [noun].

affect, effect   As a verb, *affect* means "cause a change in, influence." (*Affect* also functions as a noun in the discipline of psychology.) As a noun, *effect* means "result or conclusion"; as a verb, it means "bring about."

Loud music **affects** people's hearing for life, so some bands have **effected** changes to lower the volume. Many fans, however, don't care about the harmful **effects** of high decibel levels.

aggravate, irritate *Aggravate* is used colloquially to mean "irritate." In formal writing, use *aggravate* to mean "intensify, make worse." Use *irritate* to mean "annoy, make impatient."

> The coach was **irritated** by her assistant's impatience, which **aggravated** the team's inability to concentrate.

ain't *Ain't* is a nonstandard contraction. Use *am not, is not,* or *are not* instead.

all right *All right* should be written as two words, never one (not *alright*).

allusion, illusion An *allusion* is an indirect reference to something. An *illusion* is a false impression or idea.

> The applicant's casual **allusions** to many European tourist attractions created the **illusion** that he had seen them himself.

a lot *A lot* is informal for *a great deal* or *a great many;* avoid it in academic writing. Write it as two words (not *alot*) when you do use it.

a.m., p.m. These abbreviations may also be written as A.M., P.M. Use them only with numbers, not as substitutes for *morning, afternoon,* or *evening.*

> We will arrive **in the afternoon** [not in the p.m.], and we have to leave no later than **8:00 a.m.**

among, amongst, between Use *among* for three or more items and *between* for two items. American English prefers *among* to *amongst.*

> My three roommates discussed **among** [not between or amongst] themselves the choice **between** staying in school and getting full-time jobs.

amount, number Use *amount* for uncountable things (*wealth, work, corn, happiness*). Use *number* for countable items.

> The **amount** of rice to cook depends on the **number** of dinner guests.

an See *a, an.*

and/or This term is appropriate in business and legal writing when either or both of two items can apply: *The process is quicker if you have a wireless connection and/or a fax machine.* In the humanities, writers usually express the alternatives in words: *This process is quicker if you have a wireless connection, a fax machine, or both.*

anyplace *Anyplace* is informal. Use *any place* or *anywhere* instead.

anyways, anywheres *Anyways* and *anywheres* are nonstandard. Use *anyway* and *anywhere* instead.

apt, likely, liable *Apt* and *likely* are used interchangeably. Strictly, *apt* indicates a tendency or inclination. *Likely* indicates a reasonable expectation or greater certainty than *apt. Liable* denotes legal responsibility or implies unpleasant consequences.

Alan is **apt** to leave early on Friday. I will **likely** go with him to the party. Maggy and Gabriel are **liable** to be angry if we do not show up.

as, as if, as though, like   Use *as, as if,* or *as though,* but not *like,* to introduce clauses.

This hamburger tastes good, **as** [not like] a hamburger should. It tastes **as if** [or as though but not like] it were barbequed over charcoal.

Both *as* and *like* can function as prepositions in comparisons. Use *as* to indicate equivalence between two nouns or pronouns. Use *like* to indicate similarity but not equivalence.

Beryl acted **as** [not like] the moderator in our panel.

Mexico, **like** [not as] Argentina, belongs to the United Nations.

assure, ensure, insure   *Assure* means "promise, convince." *Ensure* and *insure* both mean "make certain or secure," but *insure* is reserved for financial or legal certainty, as in insurance.

The agent **assured** me that he could **insure** my roller blades but that only I could **ensure** that my elbows and knees would outlast the skates.

as to   *As to* is nonstandard. Use *about* instead.

awful, awfully   Do not use *awful* or *awfully* in place of *terribly, extremely,* or *very.*

a while, awhile   As two words, *a while* (an article and a noun) can function as a subject or object. As one word, *awhile* is an adverb; it modifies verbs. In a prepositional phrase, the correct form is *a while: for a while, in a while, after a while.*

The seals basked **awhile** in the sun after they had played for **a while** in the sea.

backup, back up   As a noun, *backup* is a copy of electronic data. *Backup* can also be used as an adjective to mean "alternative." *Back up* is a verb phrase.

Many people recommend that you **back up** even your **backup** files and protect all your **backups** from heat.

bad, badly   *Bad* is an adjective; use it after linking verbs. (Remember that verbs like *feel* and *smell* can function as either linking verbs or action verbs.) *Badly* is an adverb and is nonstandard after linking verbs (45d).

Farmers feel **bad** because a **bad** drought has **badly** damaged the crops.

beside, besides   *Beside* is a preposition meaning "next to, by the side of."

She stood **beside** the new car, insisting that she would drive.

As a preposition, *besides* means "other than, in addition to."

No one **besides** her had a driver's license.

As an adverb, *besides* means "also, moreover."

Besides, she owned the car.

better, had better   Used in place of *had better, better* is informal.

We **had better** [*not* We better] be careful.

between   See *among, amongst, between.*

bring, take   Use *bring* to indicate movement from a distant place to a near place or to the speaker. Use *take* to indicate movement from a near place or from the speaker to a distant place.

If you **bring** a leash to my house, you can **take** the dog to the vet.

but, however, yet   Use *but, however,* or *yet* alone, not in combination with each other.

The economy is strong, **but** [*not* but yet *or* but however] unemployment is high.

can, may   *Can* signifies ability or capacity; *may* requests or grants permission. In negations, however, *can* is acceptable in place of *may.*

When you **can** get here on time, you **may** be excused early.

can't hardly, can't scarcely   These double negatives are nonstandard (45b).

censor, censure   The verb *censor* means "delete objectionable material, judge." The verb *censure* means "condemn or reprimand officially."

The town council **censured** the mayor for trying to **censor** a report.

chairman, chairperson, chair   Many writers and speakers prefer the gender-neutral terms *chairperson* and *chair* to *chairman; chair* is more common than *chairperson.*

complement, compliment   Each term functions as both a noun and a verb. As a noun, *complement* means "something that goes well with or completes." As a noun, *compliment* means "praise, flattery." As a verb, *complement* means "bring to perfection, go well with; complete." As a verb, *compliment* means "praise, flatter."

The president's **compliment** was a fine **complement** to our celebration.

When the president **complimented** us, her praise **complemented** our joy.

comprise, include   See *include, comprise.*

conscience, conscious   The noun *conscience* means "a sense of right and wrong." The adjective *conscious* means "aware or awake."

To live happily, be **conscious** of what your **conscience** tells you.

continual(ly), continuous(ly)   *Continual* means "occurring again and again." *Continuous* means "occurring without interruption."

Intravenous fluids were given **continuously** for three days after surgery, so nurses were **continually** hooking up new bottles of saline solution.

could care less *Could care less* is nonstandard; use *couldn't care less* instead.

could of *Could of* is nonstandard; use *could have* instead.

couple, a couple of These terms are informal. Use *a few* or *several* instead.

Rest for **a few** [not a couple or a couple of] minutes.

criteria, criterion A *criterion* is "a standard of judgment." *Criteria* is the plural form of *criterion*.

Although charisma is an important **criterion** for political candidates to meet, voters must also consider other **criteria**.

data This is the plural of *datum,* a rarely used word. Informally, *data* is commonly used as a singular noun requiring a singular verb. In academic or professional writing, it is more acceptable to treat *data* as plural.

The researchers' **data** suggest that some people become addicted to e-mail.

different from, different than *Different from* is preferred for formal writing, although *different than* is common in speech.

Please advise the council if your research produces data **different from** past results.

don't *Don't* is a contraction for *do not* but not for *does not* (use *doesn't*).

She **doesn't** [not She don't] like crowds.

effect See *affect, effect.*

elicit, illicit The verb *elicit* means "draw forth or bring out." The adjective *illicit* means "illegal."

The government's **illicit** conduct **elicited** mass protest.

emigrate (from), immigrate (to) *Emigrate* means "leave one country to live in another." *Immigrate* means "enter a country to live there."

My great-grandmother **emigrated** from the Ukraine in 1890. After a brief stay in Germany, she **immigrated** to Canada in 1892.

ensure See *assure, ensure, insure.*

etc. *Etc.* is the abbreviation for the Latin *et cetera,* meaning "and the rest." For writing in the humanities, avoid using *etc.* outside parentheses. Acceptable substitutes are *and the like, and so on,* and *and so forth.*

everyday, every day The adjective *everyday* means "daily." *Every day* is an adjective-noun combination that can function as a subject or an object.

Being late for work has become an **everyday** occurrence. **Every day** that I am late brings me closer to being fired.

everywheres Nonstandard for *everywhere*.

except See *accept, except*.

explicit, implicit *Explicit* means "directly stated or expressed." *Implicit* means "implied, suggested."

> The warning on cigarette packs is **explicit**: "Smoking is dangerous to health." The **implicit** message is "Don't smoke."

fewer, less Use *fewer* for anything that can be counted (with count nouns): *fewer dollars, fewer fleas, fewer haircuts*. Use *less* with collective or other noncount nouns: *less money, less scratching, less hair*.

finalize Academic audiences prefer *complete* or *make final* instead of *finalize*.

> After intense negotiations, the two nations **completed** [not finalized] a treaty.

former, latter When two items are referred to, *former* signifies the first one and *latter* signifies the second. Avoid using *former* and *latter* in a context with more than two items.

> Brazil and Ecuador are South American countries. Portuguese is the most common language in the **former**, Spanish in the **latter**.

go, say *Go* is nonstandard when used for forms of *say*.

> After he stepped on my hand, he **said** [not he goes], "Your hand was in my way."

gone, went *Gone* is the past participle of *go*; *went* is the past tense of *go*.

> They **went** [not gone] to the concert after Ira **had gone** [not had went] home.

good and This phrase is an informal intensifier; omit it from writing.

> They were **exhausted** [not good and tired].

good, well *Good* is an adjective. Using it as an adverb is nonstandard. *Well* is the equivalent adverb.

> **Good** maintenance helps cars run **well**.

hardly See *can't hardly, can't scarcely*.

have, of Use *have*, not *of*, after such verbs as *could, should, would, might*, and *must*.

> You **should have** [not should of] called first.

have got, have to, have got to Avoid using *have got* when *have* alone delivers your meaning.

> I **have** [not have got] two more sources to read.

Avoid using *have to* or *have got to* for *must*.

> I **must** [not have got to] finish this assignment today.

he/she, s/he, his, her   To avoid sexist language, use *he or she* or *his or her*. A less wordy solution is to use plural pronouns and antecedents.

> Every mourner bowed **his or her** head [not his head *or* their head].

> The **mourners** bowed **their** heads.

hopefully   An adverb meaning "with hope, in a hopeful manner," *hopefully* can modify a verb, an adjective, or another adverb: *They waited hopefully for the plane to land. Hopefully* is commonly used as a sentence modifier with the meaning "I hope," but you should avoid this usage in academic writing.

> **I hope** [not Hopefully] the plane will land safely.

humanity, humankind, humans, mankind   To avoid sexist language, use *humanity, humankind,* or *humans* instead of *mankind*.

> Some people think computers have influenced **humanity** more than any other twentieth-century invention.

i.e.   This abbreviation refers to the Latin term *id est*. In formal writing, use the English translation *that is*.

if, whether   At the start of a noun clause, use either *if* or *whether*.

> I don't know **if** [or whether] I want to dance with you.

In conditional clauses, use *whether* (or *whether or not*) when alternatives are expressed or implied.

> I will dance with you **whether or not** I like the music. I will dance with you **whether** the next song is fast or slow.

In a conditional clause that does not express or imply alternatives, use *if*.

> **If** you promise not to step on my feet, I will dance with you.

illicit   See *elicit, illicit*.

illusion   See *allusion, illusion*.

immigrate   See *emigrate, immigrate*.

imply, infer   *Imply* means "hint at or suggest." *Infer* means "draw a conclusion." A writer or speaker implies; a reader or listener infers.

> When the governor **implied** that she would not seek reelection, reporters **inferred** that she was planning to run for vice president.

include, comprise   The verb *include* means "contain or regard as part of a whole." The verb *comprise* means "to be composed of."

inside of, outside of   These phrases are nonstandard when used to mean *inside* or *outside*.

She waited **outside** [*not* outside of] the dormitory.

In time references, avoid using *inside of* to mean "in less than."

I changed clothes **in less than** [*not* inside of] ten minutes.

insure　See *assure, ensure, insure.*

irregardless　*Irregardless* is nonstandard. Use *regardless* instead.

is when, is where　Avoid these constructions in giving definitions.

Defensive driving **requires that** [*not* is when] drivers stay alert.

its, it's　*Its* is a personal pronoun in the possessive case. *It's* is a contraction of *it is.*

The dog buried **its** bone.

It's a hot day.

kind, sort　Use *this* or *that* with these singular nouns; use *these* or *those* with the plural nouns *kinds* and *sorts.* Also, do not use *a* or *an* after *kind of* or *sort of.*

Drink **these kinds of** fluids [*not* this kind of fluids] on **this sort of** [*not* this sort of a] day.

kind of, sort of　These phrases are colloquial adverbs. In formal writing, use *somewhat* instead.

The campers were **somewhat** [*not* kind of] dehydrated after the hike.

lay, lie　*Lay* (*laid, laid, laying*) means "place or put something, usually on something else" and needs a direct object. *Lie* (*lay, lain, lying*), meaning "recline," does not take a direct object (41k). Substituting *lay* for *lie* is nonstandard.

Lay [*not* Lie] the blanket down, and then **lay** the babies on it so they can **lie** [*not* lay] in the shade.

leave, let　*Leave* means "depart"; *let* means "allow, permit." *Leave* is nonstandard for *let.*

Let [*not* Leave] me use your car tonight.

less　See *fewer, less.*

lie　See *lay, lie.*

like　See *as, as if, as though, like.*

likely　See *apt, likely, liable.*

lots, lots of, a lot of　These are colloquial usages. Use *many, much,* or *a great deal* instead.

mankind　See *humanity, humankind, humans, mankind.*

may　See *can, may.*

maybe, may be   *Maybe* is an adverb; *may be* is a verb phrase.

Maybe [adverb] we can win, but our team **may be** [verb phrase] too tired.

may of, might of   *May of* and *might of* are nonstandard. Use *may have* and *might have* instead.

media   This word is the plural of *medium,* yet colloquial usage now pairs it with a singular verb.

The **media** saturates us with information about every fire.

morale, moral   *Morale* is a noun meaning "a mental state relating to courage, confidence, or enthusiasm." As a noun, *moral* means an "ethical lesson implied or taught by a story or event"; as an adjective, *moral* means "ethical."

One **moral** to draw from corporate downsizings is that overstressed employees suffer from low **morale**. Unhappy employees with otherwise high **moral** standards may steal from their employers.

most   *Most* is nonstandard for *almost: Almost* [not *Most*] *all the dancers agree. Most* is correct as the superlative form of an adjective (*some, more, most*): *Most dancers agree.* It also makes the superlative form of adverbs and some adjectives: *most suddenly, most important.*

Ms.   *Ms.* is a women's title free of reference to marital status, equivalent to *Mr.* for men. For a woman who does not use *Dr.* or another title, use *Ms.* unless she requests *Miss* or *Mrs.*

must of   *Must of* is nonstandard. Use *must have* instead.

nowheres   Nonstandard for *nowhere.*

number   See *amount, number.*

of   Use *have* instead of *of* after the following verbs: *could, may, might, must, should,* and *would.*

OK, O.K., okay   All three forms are acceptable in informal writing. In academic writing, try to express meaning more specifically.

The weather was **suitable** [not OK] for the picnic.

outside of   See *inside of, outside of.*

pixel, pixelation, pixilated   Pixel, a relatively new word created from "picture/pix" and "element," is the name for a small dot on a video screen. Pixelation (with an *e,* as in pixel) is a noun meaning "a film technique that makes people appear to move faster than they are." Pixilated (with an *i*), a verb unrelated to pixels, derives from pixie, meaning "a mischievous elf," and now describes someone who is slightly drunk.

plus *Plus* is nonstandard as a substitute for *and, also, in addition,* or *moreover.*

The band will give three concerts in Hungary, **and** [not plus] it will tour Poland for a month. **Also** [not Plus], it may perform once in Vienna.

precede, proceed *Precede* means "go before." *Proceed* means "advance, go on; undertake; carry on."

Preceded by elephants and tigers, the clowns **proceeded** into the tent.

pretty *Pretty* is an informal qualifying word; in academic writing, use *rather, quite, somewhat,* or *very.*

The flu epidemic was **quite** [not pretty] severe.

principal, principle *Principle* means "a basic truth or rule." As a noun, *principal* means "chief person; main or original amount"; as an adjective, *principal* means "most important."

During the assembly, the **principal** said, "A **principal** value in this society is the **principle** of free speech."

proceed See *precede, proceed.*

quotation, quote *Quotation* is a noun; *quote* is a verb. Do not use *quote* as a noun.

The newspaper **quoted** the attorney general, and the **quotations** [not quotes] quickly showed up in public health messages.

raise, rise *Raise* (*raised, raised, raising*) means "lift" and needs a direct object. *Rise* (*rose, risen, rising*) means "go upward" and does not take a direct object (41k). Using these verbs interchangeably is nonstandard.

If the citizens **rise** [not raise] up in protest, they may **raise** the flag of liberty.

real, really *Real* is nonstandard as an intensifier, and *really* is almost always unnecessary; leave it out.

reason is because This phrase is redundant; use *reason is that* instead.

One **reason** we moved **is that** [not is because] we changed jobs.

regardless See *irregardless.*

respective, respectively The adjective *respective* relates the noun it modifies to two or more individual persons or things. The adverb *respectively* refers to a second set of items in a sequence established by a preceding set of items.

After the fire drill, Dr. Pan and Dr. Moll returned to their **respective** offices [that is, each to his or her office] on the second and third floors, **respectively**. [Dr. Pan has an office on the second floor; Dr. Moll has an office on the third floor.]

right   *Right* is a colloquial intensifier; use *quite, very, extremely,* or a similar word for most purposes.

You did **very** [not right] well on the quiz.

rise   See *raise, rise.*

scarcely   See *can't hardly, can't scarcely.*

seen   The past participle of *see* (*see, saw, seen, seeing*), *seen* is a nonstandard substitute for the past-tense form, *saw.* As a verb, *seen* must be used with an auxiliary verb.

Last night, I **saw** [not seen] the show that you **had seen** in Florida.

set, sit   *Set* (*set, set, setting*) means "put in place, position, put down" and must have a direct object. *Sit* (*sat, sat, sitting*) means "be seated" and does not take a direct object (41k). Using these verbs interchangeably is nonstandard.

Susan **set** [not sat] the sandwiches beside the salad, made Spot **sit** [not set] down, and then **sat** [not set] on the sofa.

should of   *Should of* is nonstandard. Use *should have* instead.

sit   See *set, sit.*

sometime, sometimes, some time   The adverb *sometime* means "at an unspecified time." The adverb *sometimes* means "now and then." *Some time* is an adjective-noun combination meaning "an amount or span of time."

Sometime next year we have to take qualifying exams. I **sometimes** worry about finding **some time** to study for them.

sort of   See *kind of, sort of.*

such   *Such* is an informal intensifier; avoid it in academic writing unless it precedes a noun introducing a *that* clause.

The play got **terrible** [not such terrible] reviews. It was **such** a dull drama **that** it closed after one performance.

supposed to, used to   The final *d* is essential in both phrases.

We were **supposed to** [not suppose to] leave early. I **used to** [not use to] wake up as soon as the alarm rang.

sure   *Sure* is nonstandard as a substitute for *surely* or *certainly.*

I was **certainly** [not sure] surprised at the results.

sure and, try and   Both phrases are nonstandard. Use *sure to* and *try to* instead.

than, then   *Than* indicates comparison; *then* relates to time.

Please put on your gloves, and **then** put on your hat. It is colder outside **than** inside.

that there, them there, this here, these here   These phrases are nonstandard. Use *that, them, this,* and *these,* respectively.

that, which   Use *that* with restrictive (essential) clauses only. *Which* can be used with both restrictive and nonrestrictive clauses; many writers, however, use *which* only for nonrestrictive clauses and *that* for all restrictive clauses (40g, 40i).

> The house **that** [*or* which] Jack built is on Beanstalk Street, **which** [*not* that] runs past the reservoir.

their, there, they're   *Their* is a possessive. *There* means "in that place" or is part of an expletive construction (39h). *They're* is a contraction of *they are.*

> **They're** going to **their** accounting class in the building **there** behind the library. **There** are twelve sections of Accounting 101.

theirself, theirselves, themself   These are nonstandard. Use *themselves* instead.

them   Use *them* as an object pronoun only. Do not use *them* in place of the adjective *these* or *those.*

> Buy **those** [*not* them] strawberries.

then   See *than, then.*

till, until   Both are acceptable; except in expressive writing, avoid the contracted form *'til.*

to, too, two   *To* is a preposition. *Too* is an adverb meaning "also; more than enough." *Two* is the number.

> When you go **to** Chicago, visit the Art Institute. Go **to** Harry Caray's for dinner, **too.** It won't be **too** expensive because **two** people can share an entrée.

try and, sure and   See *sure and, try and.*

type   *Type* is nonstandard when used to mean *type of.*

> Use that **type of** [*not* type] glue on plastic.

unique   *Unique* is an absolute adjective; do not combine it with *more, most,* or other qualifiers.

> Solar heating is **uncommon** [*not* somewhat unique] in the Northeast. A **unique** [*not* very unique] heating system in one Vermont home uses hydrogen for fuel.

used to   See *supposed to, used to.*

utilize   Academic writers prefer *use* to *utilize.*

> The team **used** [*not* utilized] all its players to win the game.

way, ways   When referring to distance, use *way* rather than *ways.*

> He is a long **way** [*not* ways] from home.

well   See *good, well.*

where   *Where* is nonstandard when used for *that* as a subordinating conjunction.

> I read **that** [not where] Bill Gates is the richest man alive.

> **Where** is your house? [*not* Where is your house at?]

whether   See *if, whether.*

which   See *that, which.*

who, whom   Use *who* as a subject or a subject complement. Use *whom* as an object (40p).

who's, whose   *Who's* is a contraction of *who is. Whose* is a possessive pronoun.

> **Who's** willing to drive? **Whose** truck should we take?

would of   *Would of* is nonstandard. Use *would have* instead.

your, you're   *Your* is a possessive. *You're* is the contraction of *you are.*

> **You're** generous to volunteer **your** time at the elementary school.

For more help with your
writing, grammar, and research,
go to **www.mycomplab.com**

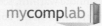

Word Meanings and Word Impact

54a   How can I learn about words and their meanings?

A good recently published dictionary tells you about the meaning and use of words. Three fine dictionaries are *Webster's New World Dictionary, Merriam-Webster's Collegiate Dictionary,* and the *American Heritage Dictionary of the English Language.* For students whose native language is not English, we recommend the *American Heritage English as a Second Language Dictionary.* Each dictionary's introductory pages describe the types of information found in word entries.

54b   How can I choose exact words?

Exact words are words that are precise and accurate for the context in which you use them. Your **diction**, the official term for the use of exact words, affects the clarity and impact of your messages. To use good diction in your writing, you want to be aware of the distinctions between denotation and connotation, as well as between general and specific words.

Distinguishing between denotation and connotation

Denotation is a word's explicit dictionary meaning—its definition. Interestingly, subtle shades of meaning differentiate words with the same general definitions. For example, would you use *famous* or *notorious* to describe a person well known for praiseworthy achievements? *Famous* is correct because it means "much talked about" and "renowned." *Notorious* means "unfavorably known or talked about." George Washington is famous; Osama bin Laden is notorious.

Connotation refers to ideas that a word implies. Connotations convey the associations and emotional overtones we bring to a word from our experiences. For example, the word *home* may evoke more emotion than its denotation, "a dwelling place," or its synonym *house*. For some people, *home* may connote warmth, security, and the love of family. For others, however, *home* may carry unpleasant connotations, such as abusive experiences or the impersonal atmosphere of an institution to house the elderly.

Using specific and concrete language

Specific words identify individual items in a group (*Jeep, Honda*). General words relate to an overall group (*car*). Concrete words identify persons and things that can be perceived by the senses—seen, heard, tasted, felt, smelled (*black padded vinyl dashboard*). Abstract words denote qualities, concepts, relationships, acts, conditions, and ideas (*transportation*).

Specific and concrete words bring life to general and abstract words. As you write, try to supply specific, concrete details and EXAMPLES to illustrate generalizations and abstractions. At the same time, keep in mind that most good writing combines general and specific with abstract and concrete.

GENERAL   SPECIFIC   SPECIFIC   SPECIFIC
My **car**, a **220-horsepower Maxi Armo**, accelerates **from 0 to 50**
SPECIFIC   SPECIFIC   SPECIFIC
miles per hour in **6 seconds** but gets only **18 miles per gallon**.
SPECIFIC   GENERAL
In contrast, the **Gavin Motors' Bobcat** gets **very good** gas mileage,
SPECIFIC   GENERAL   SPECIFIC   SPECIFIC
about **35 mpg** in **highway driving** and **30 mpg** in **stop-and-go traffic**.

54c   How can I increase my vocabulary?

All people have an **active vocabulary**, the words that come to mind easily. Everyone also has a **passive vocabulary**, the words people don't use actively yet recognize and understand. The larger your vocabulary, the more you understand what you read and hear—and the more skillfully you can speak and write.

Choosing What Words to Learn

- Move words in your passive vocabulary into your active one. Because you're already familiar with the words you know passively, you can push them into your active vocabulary rather quickly.

- Underline or circle unfamiliar words as you read them and then write them on index cards to study.

- Use context clues to figure out definitions.

- Use **prefixes**, syllables added to the front of a word that modify its meaning (for example, *intend* and *pretend*).

- Use **suffixes**, syllables added to the end of a word that modify its meaning (for example, *excitable* means "able to be excited" and *excitement* means "the state of being excited").

- Listen closely to speakers who know the language well. When you hear a new word, jot it down to look up later in the dictionary.

- Look up the words in a dictionary and then write them on index cards to study.

Studying New Vocabulary Words

- Select eight to ten words to study each week.

- Write each new word and its meaning on an index card, in a notebook, or on a computer list.

- Set aside time each day to study your selected words. (Carry your cards, notebook, or computer printout to study in spare moments.)

- Try **mnemonics**—memory-jogging techniques—to help you memorize words. (For example, *desert*, spelled with one *s*, is filled with *sand*; in contrast, *dessert*, spelled with two *s*'s, could stand for *strawberry shortcake*, a favorite end-of-the-meal treat.)

- Push yourself to actively use your newly learned vocabulary words in writing and conversation.

54d What is suitable language for writing?

■ Using appropriate language

When you use **appropriate language**, your word choice suits your AUDIENCE and PURPOSE. For example, profane and obscene words don't belong in ACADEMIC WRITING. Similarly, technical medical terms don't belong in a magazine for the general public.

■ Being aware of levels of formality

The **levels of formality** in English include informal, semiformal, and formal. The level you choose depends on your audience and purpose. Informal language can be suitable for a letter or an e-mail message to a friend. In contrast, formal language is suitable for speeches at, or writings for, ceremonial occasions or for official invitations to events such as weddings. Semiformal writing uses standard vocabulary (for example, *learn,* not *wise up*) and conventional sentence structure. The level of formality you choose affects the style and tone of your writing; see 10c.

■ Using edited American English

Edited American English conforms to established rules of grammar, sentence structure, punctuation, and spelling. Academic writing uses edited American English—the forms of written language that we use in this handbook.

Almost everyone has read English that varies from the standard, especially in advertisements. As a writer, never think that because you see SENTENCE FRAGMENTS and slang in print, you can use them in academic writing. In addition, many people speak or have heard nonedited American English typical of various groups of people. These language forms, often based on a long history of combining diverse languages, serve legitimately to unify a group and often to promote solidarity and comradeship. Even though such language forms serve important purposes for many people, they're rarely acceptable in academic writing.

■ Using slang, colloquialisms, and regionalisms

Slang consists of new words (*phat* meaning "very good") or existing words that have new meanings (*sick* meaning "awesome"). Slang is appropriate only in very informal situations.

Colloquial language is characteristic of casual conversation and informal writing: *The student flunked* [instead of *failed*] *chemistry.* **Regional language** (also called **dialect**) is specific to a particular geographic area: *They have nary a cent.* Slang, colloquial, and regional language are not substandard or illiterate, but they're usually not appropriate for academic writing or situations.

54e   What is figurative language?

Figurative language consists of words that carry other meanings along with their literal meaning. There are various kinds of figurative language.

Analogy compares similar traits shared by dissimilar things. You can develop an analogy in one, several, or many sentences.

> A **cheetah sprinting across the dry plains** after its prey, the **base runner dashed** for home plate, cleats kicking up dust.

Irony uses words to suggest the opposite of their usual sense.

> Told that a minor repair to her home would cost $2,000 and take two weeks, she said, "**Oh, how nice!**"

Metaphor compares otherwise dissimilar things. A metaphor doesn't use the word *like* or *as* to make a comparison.

> Rush-hour **traffic** in the city **bled out through major arteries** to the suburbs.

Avoid **mixed metaphors**, the combining of two or more inconsistent images in one sentence or expression.

> The violence of the hurricane reminded me of a train ride. [A train ride is not violent, stormy, or destructive.]

Personification involves assigning a human trait to something not human. (Be careful to avoid mixed metaphors.)

> The **book begged** to be read.

Overstatement (also called **hyperbole**) uses deliberate exaggeration for emphasis.

> If this paper is late, **the professor will kill me**.

Simile compares dissimilar things using the word *like* or *as*.

> Langston Hughes observes that a deferred dream dries up "**like a raisin in the sun**."

Understatement emphasizes by using deliberate restraint.

> **It feels warm** when the temperature reaches 105 degrees.

54f   What is a cliché?

A **cliché** is an overused, worn-out expression. Clichés are once-clever phrases that have grown trite from overuse: *dead as a doornail, gentle as a lamb, straight as an arrow.* Such clichés are *similes* (comparisons using *like* or *as*) that have become corny. Sometimes a cliché is an action or idea, such as "living happily ever after." Rephrase a cliché or delete it.

> **NO** Needing to travel five hundred miles before dark, we left **at the crack of dawn**.

> **YES** Needing to travel five hundred miles before dark, we left **at dawn**.

54g What is the effect of tone in writing?

TONE relates not so much to *what* you say as to *how* you say it. You want to control your choice of words so that they work with your message, not against it (2b). Words carry messages beyond their literal meanings. For example, if you were to write a chatty, informal message to your superiors about safety hazards in your workplace, you would communicate both that you don't take the hazards seriously and that you have little respect for your superiors. Similarly, when you report bad news, jokes are in bad taste. In academic writing, you want to convey a reasonable tone in both content and choice of words. Avoid the misuses of word choice discussed below.

■ Avoiding slanted language

When you feel strongly about a topic, you might slip into using SLANTED LANGUAGE (13g). Such language is biased or emotionally loaded. It doesn't persuade your readers to agree with you. Rather, it ruins your credibility in the reader's mind. For example, suppose you're arguing against the reelection of your senator. If you write "Our senator is a deceitful, crooked thug," you're using slanted language. Less loaded language would be "Our senator has lied to the public and taken bribes" (assuming that your statements are true).

■ Avoiding pretentious language

Pretentious language draws attention to itself with big, unusual words and overly complex sentence structures. Such overblown language obscures your message and damages your credibility with your readers.

> **NO** The **raison d'être** for my **matriculation** at this **institution of higher learning** is the **acquisition** of an education.

> **YES** My reason for being in college is to get an education.

■ Avoiding jargon

Jargon is common in every field—the professions, academic disciplines, business, and sports—because each field has its own specialized vocabulary. Specialized language, including jargon, allows people who share technical vocabularies to understand each other quickly. When your readers are members of the general public, however, you can't assume that they will know what you mean. Therefore, if you absolutely can't avoid a specialized term when writing for such an audience, define it in simpler terms.

■ Avoiding euphemisms

Euphemisms attempt to avoid unpleasant truths by substituting "tactful" words for more direct, perhaps harsh-sounding words. When the truth is "Our leader tells many lies," you don't want to be overly indirect by writing "Our leader has a wonderfully vivid imagination." Of course, a euphemism is not only acceptable but also expected in certain social situations. When offering condolences, for example, you may use *passed away* instead of *died*.

For more help with your
writing, grammar, and research,
go to **www.mycomplab.com**

Using Inclusive Language

55a   What is gender in the English language?

Gender is a grammatical classification reflecting masculinity or femininity. Many languages assign gender (a masculine, feminine, or neuter identity) to a large variety of words. In English, only a few words have gender-specific meanings, all based on actual physical identity: *she, it, him, her, his, hers, its, man, boy, woman, girl, prince, princess.* These words deliver gender information along with other meanings.

55b   What is gender-neutral language?

Using **gender-neutral language**, sometimes called *nonsexist language,* means choosing words that don't carry a message of masculinity or femininity. **Sexist language** unfairly discriminates against both sexes. For example, it inaccurately assumes that all nurses and homemakers are female (calling them *she*) and all physicians and car mechanics are male (calling them *he*).

When you write, turn any gender-specific words you have used into gender-neutral words. For example, use *police officer* instead of *policeman, people* or *humans* instead of *mankind, representative* instead of *congressman,* and *salesperson* instead of *salesman* or *saleswoman.* Also eliminate your use of masculine PRONOUNS in instances where gender is unknown or irrelevant. Revise the sexist sentence *Every* **man** *must plan for* **his** *future* to **People** *must plan for* **their** *futures.* Follow the guidelines in Quick Reference 55.1.

Quick Reference 55.1

■ ■ ■ ■ ■ ■ ■

Avoiding sexist language

Avoid using masculine pronouns to refer to both men and women.

* Use a pair of pronouns.

  A doctor has little time to read outside his ^or her^ specialty.

* Use the plural.

  ~~A~~ successful doctor~~s~~ know~~s~~ that ~~he has~~ ^they have^ to work hard.

* Omit gender-specific pronouns.

  Everyone hopes ~~that he will~~ ^to^ win the scholarship.

* Avoid stereotyping jobs and roles by gender.

  supervisor [*not* foreman]

  businessperson, business executive [*not* businessman]

  poet, actor [*not* poetess, actress]

* Avoid expressions that exclude one sex.

  person [*not* man]

  humanity, people [*not* mankind]

  the average person [*not* the common man]

  superstitions [*not* old wives' tales]

* Avoid demeaning and patronizing labels.

  nurse [*not* male nurse]

  professional, executive, manager [*not* career girl]

  My assistant will help you *or* Ida Morea will help you [*not* My girl will help you].

Some writers avoid sexist pronouns by using a *he or she* construction rather than only *he* or only *she*. Revising the pronouns into the plural is preferred whenever possible. If you do choose to use *he or she,* remember that it is a singular expression. Be careful not to use too many *he or she* constructions in a given context.

Most writers today use gender-neutral language to avoid demeaning stereotypes such as *Women are bad drivers* or *Men can't cook.* In ACADEMIC WRITING, treat both sexes equally. For example, if you describe a woman by her looks, clothes, age, or marital status, describe a man the same way in the same context. If you use the first name of one person in a partnership, use the first name of the other—and if you use a title for one, such as *Mr., Dr.,* or *Mrs.,* use a title for both.

> **NO**   Mr. Nathaniel Wallace and his wife Lisa are both lawyers.
>
> **YES**   Nathaniel and Lisa Wallace are both lawyers.
>
> **YES**   Mr. and Mrs. Wallace are both lawyers.

For more help with your writing, grammar, and research, go to **www.mycomplab.com**

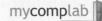

Spelling

You might be surprised to learn that good spellers don't know how to spell every word they want to use. What they do know is to check if they are not sure of a word's spelling. If your inner voice questions a spelling, do what good spellers do—check your dictionary.

But how do you look up a word when you don't know how to spell it? If you know the first few letters, find them and then browse for the word. If you do not know the first few letters, think of a synonym and look it up in a thesaurus.

56a   How are plurals spelled?

- **Adding -s or -es:** Plurals of most words are formed by adding -*s*, including words that end in "hard" *ch* (sounding like *k*): *leg, legs; shoe, shoes; stomach, stomachs.* Words ending in *s, sh, x, z,* or "soft" *ch* (as in *beach*) are formed by adding *-es* to the singular: *lens, lenses; wish, wishes; tax, taxes; coach, coaches.*

- **Words ending in *o*:** Add *-s* if the *o* is preceded by a vowel: *radio, radios; cameo, cameos.* Add *-es* if the *o* is preceded by a consonant: *potato, potatoes.* A few words can be made plural either way: *cargo, volcano, tornado, zero.*
- **Words ending in *f* or *fe*:** Some *f* and *fe* words are made plural by adding *-s: belief, beliefs.* Others require changing *f* or *fe* to *ves: life, lives; leaf, leaves.* For words ending in *ff* or *ffe*, simply add *-s: staff, staffs; giraffe, giraffes.*
- **Compound words:** For most compound words, add *-s* or *-es* at the end of the last word: *checkbooks, player-coaches.* In a few cases, the first word is made plural: *sister-in-law, sisters-in-law; attorney general, attorneys general.* (For guidelines on hyphenating compound words, see Quick Reference 64.3.)
- **Internal changes and endings other than *-s*:** A few words change internally or add endings other than *-s* to become plural: *foot, feet; man, men; mouse, mice; crisis, crises; child, children.*
- **Foreign words:** Some foreign words retain their original plurals; others take standard *-s* or *-es* English plurals. The best advice is to check your dictionary. In general, though, many Latin words ending in *um* form the plural by changing *um* to *a: curriculum, curricula; datum, data; medium, media; stratum, strata.* Latin words that end in *us* usually form the plural by changing *us* to *i: alumnus, alumni; syllabus, syllabi.* Greek words that end in *on* usually form the plural by changing *on* to *a: criterion, criteria; phenomenon, phenomena.*
- **One-form words:** Some words have the same form in both the singular and the plural: *deer, elk, fish, quail.*

56b How are suffixes spelled?

A SUFFIX is an ending added to a word to change the word's meaning or its grammatical function. For example, adding the suffix *-able* to the verb *depend* creates the adjective *dependable.*

- **Words ending in *y*:** If the letter before the final *y* is a consonant, change the *y* to *i* and add the suffix: *fry, fried.* If, however, the suffix begins with an *i*, keep the *y: fry, frying.* If the letter before the *y* is a vowel, keep the final *y: employ, employed, employing.* These rules do not apply to irregular verbs (see Quick Reference 42.2).
- **Words ending in *e*:** Drop a final *e* when the suffix begins with a vowel unless this would cause confusion: *be + ing* does not become *bing*, but *require*,

requiring; like, liking. Keep the final *e* when the suffix begins with a consonant: *require, requirement; like, likely.* Exceptions include *argument, judgment,* and *truly.*

- **Words that double a final letter:** If the final letter is a consonant, double it only if it passes all three of these tests: (1) Its last two letters are a vowel followed by a consonant. (2) It has one syllable or is accented on the last syllable. (3) The suffix begins with a vowel: *drop, dropped; begin, beginning; forget, forgettable.*
- **Words ending in *cede, ceed,* or *sede*:** Only one word in the English language ends in *sede: supersede.* Three words end in *ceed: exceed, proceed, succeed.* All other words with endings that sound like "seed" end in *cede: concede, intercede, precede.*
- **Adding *-ally* and *-ly*:** The suffixes *-ally* and *-ly* turn ADJECTIVES into ADVERBS. For all words ending in *ic* except *public,* add *-ally: logically, statistically.* Otherwise, add *-ly: quickly, sharply.*

56c What is the *ie, ei* rule?

The old rhyme for *ie* and *ei* is usually true:

I before *e* [believe, field, grief],
Except after *c* [ceiling, conceit],
Or when sounded like "ay"
As in *neighbor* and *weigh* [eight, vein].

Unfortunately, many exceptions exist (sorry!), so you need to memorize them.

ie   conscience, financier, science, species
ei   either, neither, leisure, seize, counterfeit, foreign, forfeit, sleight (*as in* sleight of hand), weird

56d How are homonyms and other frequently confused words spelled?

Words that sound exactly like others (*to, too, two; no, know*) are called **homonyms.** They, along with words that sound almost alike (*accept, except; morning, mourning*), can lead to spelling errors that mark a writer as ignorant or careless. Quick Reference 56.1 lists some of these words. Also refer to Chapter 53.

Quick Reference 56.1 ■ ■ ■ ■ ■ ■ ■

Homonyms and other commonly confused words

ALL READY	fully prepared
ALREADY	by this time
ALL TOGETHER	all in one place
ALTOGETHER	thoroughly
ASCENT	the act of rising or climbing
ASSENT	consent [NOUN, VERB]
BARE	nude, unadorned
BEAR	carry [VERB]; an animal [NOUN]
BUY	purchase
BY	next to, through the agency of
CAPITAL	major city; money
CAPITOL	government building
COUNCIL	governing body
COUNSEL	advice [NOUN]; advise [VERB]
DESERT	abandon [VERB]; dry, usually sandy area [NOUN]
DESSERT	final, sweet course in a meal
DEVICE	a plan; an implement
DEVISE	create
DIE	lose life (dying) [VERB]; one of a pair of dice [NOUN]
DYE	change the color of something (dyeing)
DOMINANT	commanding, controlling
DOMINATE	control
EMINENT	prominent
IMMANENT	living within; inherent
IMMINENT	about to happen
ENSURE	guarantee, protect
INSURE	buy or give insurance
FORMALLY	conventionally, with ceremony
FORMERLY	previously
FORTH	forward
FOURTH	number four in a series
GORILLA	animal in the ape family
GUERRILLA	soldier conducting surprise attacks

continued >>

Quick Reference 56.1 (continued)

HOLE	opening
WHOLE	complete [ADJECTIVE]; an entire thing [NOUN]
ITS	POSSESSIVE form of *it*
IT'S	CONTRACTION for *it is*
LEAD	heavy metal substance [NOUN]; guide [VERB]
LED	PAST TENSE of *lead*
LIGHTENING	making lighter
LIGHTNING	storm-related electricity
LOOSE	unbound, not tightly fastened
LOSE	misplace
MAY BE	might be [VERB]
MAYBE	perhaps [ADVERB]
PASSED	PAST TENSE of *pass*
PAST	at an earlier time
PATIENCE	forbearance
PATIENTS	people under medical care
PLAIN	simple, unadorned [ADJECTIVE]; area of level land [NOUN]
PLANE	shave wood [VERB]; aircraft [NOUN]
PRECEDE	come before
PROCEED	continue
PRESENCE	being at hand; attendance at a place or in something
PRESENTS	gifts
PRINCIPAL	foremost [ADJECTIVE]; school head [NOUN]
PRINCIPLE	moral conviction, basic truth
RAIN	water that falls to earth [NOUN]; fall like rain [VERB]
REIGN	rule
REIN	strap to guide or control an animal [NOUN]; guide or control [VERB]
RESPECTFULLY	with respect
RESPECTIVELY	in that order
RIGHT	correct; opposite of *left*
RITE	ritual
WRITE	put words on paper
SCENE	place of an action; segment of a play
SEEN	viewed

continued >>

Quick Reference 56.1 (continued)

SENSE	perception, understanding
SINCE	from that time; because
STATIONARY	standing still
STATIONERY	writing paper
THAN	in comparison with; besides
THEN	at that time; next; therefore
THEIR	POSSESSIVE form of *they*
THERE	in that place
THEY'RE	CONTRACTION for *they are*
TO	toward
TOO	also; excessively
TWO	number following *one*
WEATHER	climatic conditions
WHETHER	if
WERE	PAST TENSE of *be*
WHERE	in which place
WHICH	one of a group
WITCH	female sorcerer
WHO'S	CONTRACTION for *who is*
WHOSE	POSSESSIVE form of *who*
YORE	long past
YOUR	POSSESSIVE form of *you*
YOU'RE	CONTRACTION for *you are*

56e   What else leads to spelling errors?

"Swallowed" pronunciation—not pronouncing a letter or letters at the end of a word—can cause misspellings. For example, the *-ed* endings in *used to* and *prejudiced* are often swallowed and pronounced as *use to* and *prejudice*. If you write what you hear, your spelling will be incorrect.

In addition, some misspellings result from writing one word instead of two. The most common errors of this kind are *all right* (not *alright*) and *a lot* (not *alot*).

For more help with your writing, grammar, and research, go to www.mycomplab.com

mycomplab

57

Commas

57a When do I use commas?

The comma separates sentence parts for greater clarity. You can avoid most comma errors with these two bits of advice. (1) While you're writing or reading what you've written, don't insert a comma whenever you pause to think or take a breath before moving on. (2) If you're unsure about a comma, insert it and circle the spot. Later, when you're editing, look in this book for the rule you need to check.

For quick answers to most comma questions, see Quick Reference 57.1. If you want more information about a rule listed in the box, go to the section of this chapter shown in parentheses.

57b How do I use a comma to set off introductory words?

When a DEPENDENT CLAUSE,* PHRASE, expression, or word comes before an INDEPENDENT CLAUSE, place a comma after the introductory material.

When the topic is dieting, many people say sugar craving is their worst problem. [introductory DEPENDENT CLAUSE (in bold) followed by a comma]

Between 1544 and 1689, sugar refineries appeared in London and New York. [introductory PREPOSITIONAL PHRASE (in bold) followed by a comma]

Beginning in infancy, we develop lifelong tastes for sweet and salty foods. [introductory PARTICIPIAL PHRASE (in bold) followed by a comma]

Sweets being a temptation for many adults, parents need to know that most commercial baby foods contain sugar. [introductory ABSOLUTE PHRASE (in bold) followed by a comma]

For example, fructose comes from fruit, but it is still sugar. [introductory TRANSITIONAL EXPRESSION (in bold) followed by a comma]

Nevertheless, many people think fructose is not harmful. [introductory CONJUNCTIVE ADVERB (in bold) followed by a comma]

---

*Words printed in SMALL CAPITAL LETTERS are discussed elsewhere in the text and are defined in the Terms Glossary at the back of the book.

Quick Reference 57.1

When to use commas

COMMAS AFTER INTRODUCTORY ELEMENTS (57b)

Although most postcards cost only a dime, one recently sold for thousands of dollars. [clause]

On postcard racks, several designs are usually available. [phrase]

For example, animals are timeless favorites for postcards. [transitional expression]

However, most postcards show local landmarks. [word]

COMMAS WITH COORDINATING CONJUNCTIONS LINKING INDEPENDENT CLAUSES (57c)

Postcards are ideal for brief greetings, **and** they are sometimes miniature works of art.

COMMAS WITH ITEMS IN SERIES (57d)

Places, paintings, and people appear on postcards. [The word *and* comes between the last two items.]

The illustrations on postcards—**places, paintings, people, animals**—are chosen for their wide appeal. [The word *and* is not used between the last two items.]

COMMAS WITH COORDINATING ADJECTIVES (57e)

Some postcards feature **breathtaking, dramatic** scenes.

NO COMMAS WITH CUMULATIVE ADJECTIVES (57e)

Other postcards feature **famous historical** scenes.

COMMAS WITH NONRESTRICTIVE ELEMENTS (57f)

Four years after the first postcard appeared, the US government began to issue prestamped postcards. [Nonrestrictive element (in bold) introduces independent clause.]

The Golden Age of postcards, **which lasted from about 1900 to 1929,** yielded many especially valuable cards. [Nonrestrictive element (in bold) interrupts independent clause.]

Collectors attend postcard shows, **which are similar to baseball card shows.** [Nonrestrictive element (in bold) ends independent clause.]

continued >>

Quick Reference 57.1   (continued)

NO COMMAS WITH RESTRICTIVE ELEMENTS (57f)

Collectors **who attend these shows** may specialize in a particular kind of postcard. [restrictive clause (in bold)]

COMMAS WITH QUOTED WORDS (57g)

One collector told me, **"Attending a show is like digging for buried treasure."** [Quoted words (in bold) are at end of sentence.]

"I always expect to find a priceless postcard," he said. [Quoted words (in bold) are at start of sentence.]

"Everyone there," he joked, **"believes a million-dollar card is hidden in the next stack."** [Quoted words (in bold) are interrupted in midsentence.]

57c How do I use a comma before a coordinating conjunction?

When you link independent clauses, place a comma before a COORDINATING CONJUNCTION (*and, but, for, or, nor, yet, so*).

The sky turned black**, and** the wind blew fiercely. [A comma and *and* link two independent clauses.]

The sky began to brighten**, but** the wind continued blowing strongly. [A comma and *but* link two independent clauses.]

When commas are already part of one or both independent clauses, use a semicolon to clearly show exactly where the link between independent clauses occurs.

With temperatures below freezing, the snow did not melt**; and** people, gazing at the white landscape, wondered when they would see grass again. [Each of the two independent clauses contains one or more commas. Therefore, a semicolon with *and* does the linking of the independent clauses.]

⚠ Alerts: (1) Never put a comma *after* a coordinating conjunction that joins independent clauses.

NO   A house is renovated in two weeks **but,** an apartment takes a week.
YES   A house is renovated in two weeks**, but** an apartment takes a week.

(2) Never use a comma when a coordinating conjunction links only two words, phrases, or dependent clauses.

NO   Habitat for Humanity depends on volunteer **labor, and dona-tions** for its construction projects. [Only two words are linked by *and,* so the comma is incorrect.]

YES   Habitat for Humanity depends on volunteer **labor and dona-tions** for its construction projects.

(3) Never use a comma between independent clauses unless you also use a co-ordinating conjunction. (If you make this error, you create a COMMA SPLICE.)

NO   Five inches of snow fell in two **hours, driving** was hazardous.
YES   Five inches of snow fell in two **hours, and driving** was hazardous. ●

57d   How do I use commas with a series?

A *series,* which always calls for commas, consists of three or more elements with the same grammatical form serving the same function in a sentence. The elements in a series can be words, phrases, or clauses.

WORDS   The earliest clothing fabrics were made from natural fibers such as **cotton, silk, linen,** and **wool.**

PHRASES   Fabrics today are made **from natural fibers, from synthetic fibers,** and **from natural and synthetic fiber blends.**

CLAUSES   **Natural fibers are durable as well as absorbent, synthetic fibers resist wrinkling as well as fading,** and **blends of the two fibers offer the advantages of both.**

Although some professional writers omit the comma before a final coor-dinating conjunction in a series, most instructors prefer that you use that comma. The comma helps readers understand the sentence.

NO   Ivan wears only **natural fibers, nylon** and **thinsulate.** [In this sen-tence, *nylon and thinsulate* functions as an APPOSITIVE. However, the two substances are not natural fibers, so the sentence conveys in-correct information.]

YES   Ivan wears only **natural fibers, nylon,** and **thinsulate.** [Ivan wears clothes made from three distinct types of fabric: natural fibers, nylon, and thinsulate.]

Items in a series often appear as numbered or lettered lists within a sen-tence. In such cases, use commas or semicolons exactly as you would if the numbers or letters were not there.

Three synthetic fibers predominate in clothing manufacturing: **(1) rayon, (2) polyester,** and **(3) acrylic.**

Three popular fabrics for blouses are **(a) cotton, a natural fiber; (b) rayon, a synthetic fiber;** and **(c) ramie, a natural fiber that feels like a synthetic**.

! Alerts: (1) Never use a comma before the first item or after the last item in a series, unless another rule makes it necessary.

NO	We decorated with**, red, white,** and **blue** ribbons for the Fourth of July.
NO	We decorated with **red, white,** and **blue,** ribbons for the Fourth of July.
YES	We decorated with **red, white,** and **blue** ribbons for the Fourth of July.

(2) Never use a comma when only two items are linked by a coordinating conjunction.

NO	Everyone enjoyed **the parade,** and **the concert**.
YES	Everyone enjoyed **the parade** and **the concert**. ●

57e When do I use a comma between adjectives?

Use a comma between **coordinating adjectives** (adjectives that carry equal weight when modifying a noun) unless a coordinating conjunction (such as *and* or *but*) already links them.

In contrast, never use a comma between **cumulative adjectives**, which do not carry equal weight in modifying a noun. The role of cumulative adjectives is to build up—accumulate—meaning as they move toward the noun.

To determine whether adjectives are carrying equal weight in a sentence, use the tests in Quick Reference 57.2 (p. 434).

57f How do commas work with nonrestrictive and restrictive elements?

A **nonrestrictive element** (also called a **nonessential element**) adds information to a sentence without changing the general meaning of the basic sentence. Nonrestrictive elements can be clauses, phrases, or APPOSITIVES. Always use commas to set off nonrestrictive elements.

In contrast, a **restrictive element** (also called an **essential element**) limits the meaning of the sentence and makes it specific. Like nonrestrictive elements, restrictive elements can be clauses, phrases, or appositives. Never use commas to set off restrictive elements, because they provide essential information.

Quick Reference 57.2

Tests for coordinating and cumulative adjectives

If the answer to either of the following questions is yes, the adjectives are coordinating and need commas.

1. Can the order of the adjectives be changed without changing the sentence's meaning or creating nonsense?

   COORDINATING   The **large, restless, noisy** crowd wanted the concert to start. [The order of adjectives can be changed (*noisy, restless, large*) and the sentence still makes sense, so these are coordinating adjectives that need commas.]

   CUMULATIVE   The concert featured **several familiar backup** singers. [*Several familiar backup* cannot be changed to *backup familiar several* and make sense, so these are cumulative adjectives, which do not need commas.]

2. Can *and* be inserted between the adjectives without changing the meaning or creating nonsense?

   $\qquad\qquad\qquad\qquad$ *and* $\qquad$ *and*
   COORDINATING   The **large, restless, noisy** crowd wanted the concert to start.

   [Inserting *and* does not change the meaning of the sentence. Therefore, the adjectives are coordinating and the commas are correct.]

   $\qquad\qquad\qquad\qquad$ *and* $\qquad$ *and*
   CUMULATIVE   The concert featured **several familiar backup** singers.

   [Inserting *and* creates nonsense. Therefore, the adjectives are cumulative adjectives and do not need commas]

■ **Punctuating nonrestrictive and restrictive clauses**

Set off nonrestrictive ADJECTIVE CLAUSES with commas. Most adjective clauses begin with *who, which,* or *that.* Never put commas around restrictive clauses.

NONRESTRICTIVE CLAUSE	Farming, **which is our major source of food production,** is relentlessly affected by the weather. [The focus of the sentence is on farming being *relentlessly affected by the weather.* Therefore, *which is our major source of food production* is not essential information, so the clause is nonrestrictive and needs commas.]
RESTRICTIVE CLAUSE	Much food **that consumers buy canned or frozen** is processed. [The focus is on *food that consumers buy canned or frozen.* Therefore, *that consumers buy canned or frozen* is essential information, so the clause is restrictive and does not need commas.]

■ **Punctuating nonrestrictive and restrictive phrases**

Set off nonrestrictive phrases with commas. Never put commas around restrictive phrases.

NONRESTRICTIVE PHRASE	Farmers, **trying to enhance crop growth,** use pesticides and fertilizers. [The sentence's focus is on farmers using pesticides and fertilizers. It says that all farmers use them. Therefore, *trying to enhance crop growth* is not essential information, so the clause is nonrestrictive and needs commas.]
RESTRICTIVE PHRASE	Farmers **trying to enhance crop growth** use pesticides and fertilizers. [The lack of commas indicates that the subject *farmers* depends on *trying to enhance crop growth* for its complete meaning. The sentence says that only farmers trying to enhance crop growth use pesticides and fertilizers. Therefore, the phrase *trying to enhance crop growth* is restrictive and does not need commas.]

■ **Punctuating nonrestrictive and restrictive appositives**

An appositive renames the noun preceding it. Most appositives are nonrestrictive. Occasionally, depending on their context, appositives are restrictive. Set off nonrestrictive appositives, but not restrictive appositives, with commas.

NONRESTRICTIVE APPOSITIVE	Agricultural scientists, **a new breed of farmer,** control the farming environment. [The sentence's focus is on agricultural scientists controlling the farming environment. Therefore, the appositive *a new breed of farmer* is not essential information, so it is nonrestrictive and needs commas.]

RESTRICTIVE APPOSITIVE	The agricultural scientist **Wendy Singh** has helped develop a crop rotation system. [The lack of commas indicates that *The agricultural scientist* depends on the name *Wendy Singh* for its complete meaning. Therefore, the appositive is restrictive and does not need commas.]

57g How do I use commas with quoted words?

Use a comma to set off quoted words from explanations anywhere in the same sentence.

> The poet William Blake wrote, "Love seeketh not itself to please." [The explanatory words *The poet William Blake wrote* come before the quoted words.]
>
> "I love you," Mary told John, "but I cannot marry you." [The explanatory words *Mary told John* interrupt the quoted words.]
>
> "My love is a fever," declared William Shakespeare. [The explanatory words *declared William Shakespeare* come after the quoted words.]

However, when you use *that* to introduce a quotation, never use a comma before or after *that*. This rule holds whether you write a DIRECT QUOTATION or an INDIRECT QUOTATION.

NO Mary claims, that "our passion is strong, but we have nothing else in common." [A comma never comes before *that*.]

NO Mary claims that, "our passion is strong, but we have nothing else in common." [A comma never comes after *that*.]

YES Mary claims that "our passion is strong, but we have nothing else in common."

57h What other word groups do I set off with commas?

Additional word groups that call for a comma to set them off from the rest of a sentence include transitional expressions, conjunctive adverbs, asides, contrasts, words addressed directly to a reader or listener, and **tag questions** (such as *isn't it?* or *don't you think?*). The following examples show where in the sentence these word groups may fall. Contrasts act like appositives and always fall right after the word they contrast with.

TRANSITIONAL EXPRESSIONS

For example, California is a major food producer.

California, **for example,** is a major food producer.

California is a major food producer, **for example**.

CONJUNCTIVE ADVERBS

However, the Midwest region of the United States is the world's breadbasket.

The Midwest region of the United States, **however,** is the world's breadbasket.

The Midwest region of the United States is the world's breadbasket, **however**.

ASIDES

Most large growers, **I imagine,** hope to export food.

Most large growers hope to export food, **I imagine**.

CONTRASTS

Food, **not technology,** tops the list of US exports.

WORDS ADDRESSED DIRECTLY TO READER

All you computer majors, perhaps the future lies in soybeans rather than software.

Perhaps the future, **all you computer majors,** lies in soybeans rather than software.

Perhaps the future lies in soybeans rather than software, **all you computer majors**.

TAG QUESTIONS (VERB-PRONOUN COMBINATION THAT CAN INTERRUPT OR END A SENTENCE)

You know, **don't you,** what tag questions are?

You know what tag questions are, **don't you?**

57i How do I use commas in dates, names, places, addresses, letter format, and numbers?

■ Punctuating dates

Use a comma between the day and the month. In addition, use a comma between a day of the week and the month.

July 20, 1969   Sunday, July 20, 1969

When you use month-day-year order for dates, use a comma after the day and the year.

Everyone watched television on July 20, 1969, to see Neil Armstrong walk on the moon.

When you use day-month-year order for dates, never use commas.

Everyone watched television on 20 July 1969 to see Neil Armstrong walk on the moon.

Never use a comma between only a month and year, only a month and day, or only a season and year.

The major news story in July 1969 was the moon landing; news coverage was especially heavy on July 21. Many older people will always remember summer 1969.

■ **Punctuating names, places, and addresses**

When an abbreviated academic degree (*MD, PhD*) comes after a name, use a comma between the name and the title (67b). When a sentence continues after a name and title, also use a comma after the title.

Rosa Gonzales, MD, was the principal witness for the defense.

However, don't place a comma before or after *Jr., Sr., II,* or *2nd* (67c).

Ron Gonzales Jr. was the defendant.

Use a comma between the last and first names in an inverted name (last name first).

Troyka, David

Use a comma between a city and state. When a sentence continues after a city and state, also use a comma after the state.

Philadelphia, Pennsylvania, is home to the Liberty Bell.

When a sentence includes a complete address, use a comma to separate all of the items in the address except the ZIP code (67e). The ZIP code follows the state after a space and no comma.

I wrote to Mr. Hugh Lern, 10-01 Rule Road, Classgate, NJ 07632, for the instruction manual.

■ **Punctuating letter openings and closings**

Use a comma after the opening of an informal letter. Use a colon after the opening of a formal letter.

Dear Betty,   Dear Ms. Renshaw:

After the closing of a formal or informal letter, use a comma.

Sincerely yours,   Love,

■ Punctuating numbers

In numbers more than four digits long, put a comma after every three digits, counting from the right.

150,567,066   72,867

In four-digit numbers, a comma is optional for money, distance, amounts, and most other measurements. Be consistent in each piece of writing.

$1776 $1,776

1776 miles   1,776 miles

1776 potatoes   1,776 potatoes

Use a comma to separate the act and scene numbers in plays. In addition, use a comma to separate a page reference in any SOURCE from a line reference.

act ii, scene iv [or act 2, scene 4]

page 120, line 6

57j How can a comma prevent a misreading?

Use a comma to clarify the meaning of a sentence, even if no other rule calls for one.

NO   People who can practice many hours a day.

YES People who can, practice many hours a day.

57k How can I avoid other comma errors?

In explaining comma rules in this chapter so far, we've covered the errors associated with those rules. Here are a few more helpful tips about using commas.

1. Never put a comma in a number in an address or in a page reference.

   11263 Dean Drive   see page 1338

2. Never put a comma in years that are expressed in four figures. If the year is expressed in five or more figures, use a comma.

   1995, 2002   25,000 BCE

3. Never put a comma after *such as*.

   NO   The Wright brothers were fascinated by other vehicles, **such as,** bicycles and gliders.

   YES The Wright brothers were fascinated by other vehicles, **such as** bicycles and gliders.

4. Never put a comma before *than* in a comparison.

 NO The 1903 airplane sustained its flight longer**, than** any other engine-powered aircraft had.

 YES The 1903 airplane sustained its flight longer **than** any other engine-powered aircraft had.

5. Never put a comma before an opening parenthesis. When a comma is required, put it *after* the closing parenthesis.

 NO Because aviation enthralls many of us**, (especially children)** a popular spot to visit is Kitty Hawk's flight museum.

 YES Because aviation enthralls many of us **(especially children),** a popular spot to visit is Kitty Hawk's flight museum.

6. Never put a comma after a PREPOSITION.

 NO People expected more damage **from,** the high winds.

 YES People expected more damage **from** the high winds.

7. Never put a comma after a SUBORDINATING CONJUNCTION.

 NO **Although,** winds exceeded fifty miles an hour, little damage occurred.

 YES **Although** winds exceeded fifty miles an hour, little damage occurred.

8. Never put a comma between a SUBJECT and its VERB. (A pair of commas, however, is acceptable.)

 NO Orville and Wilbur Wright**,** made their first successful airplane flights in 1903.

 YES Orville and Wilbur Wright made their first successful airplane flights in 1903.

 YES Orville and Wilbur Wright**,** on a beach in North Carolina**,** made their first successful airplane flights in 1903.

9. Never put a comma between a verb and its OBJECT.

 NO These inventors enthusiastically tackled**,** the problems of powered flight.

 YES These inventors enthusiastically tackled the problems of powered flight.

10. Never put a comma between a verb and its COMPLEMENT.

 NO Flying has become**,** an important industry and a popular hobby.

 YES Flying has become an important industry and a popular hobby.

58

Semicolons

58a When can I use a semicolon instead of a period between independent clauses?

You can choose whether to use a **semicolon** to replace a period, but do so only between two INDEPENDENT CLAUSES that relate closely in meaning.

> The desert known as Death Valley became a US national park in 1994; it used to be a national monument.

Alert: Never use a semicolon between a DEPENDENT CLAUSE and an independent clause.

NO   Although Death Valley is a desert; its mountain peaks are covered with snow.

YES   Although Death Valley is a desert, its mountain peaks are covered with snow. ●

You can also choose to use a semicolon to replace a period between closely related sentences when the second sentence starts with either a CONJUNCTIVE ADVERB or a TRANSITIONAL EXPRESSION.

CONJUNCTIVE ADVERB

Death Valley gets little rain each year; **nevertheless,** in the spring its mountains have spectacular wildflower displays.

TRANSITIONAL EXPRESSION

Many plant roots in Death Valley burrow dozens of feet below the surface; **in contrast,** some Death Valley plant roots run only slightly below the surface.

58b When do I need to use a semicolon to replace a comma?

A semicolon replaces a comma when you use a COORDINATING CONJUNCTION to link independent clauses that already contain commas.

Because Death Valley is the hottest place in North America, some people think that no animals live there**; but** visitors, especially, are amazed to see many tiny and a few larger animals emerge at night, when the temperatures drop, to find food.

In addition, when individual items in a series (57d) contain commas, use a semicolon instead of a comma to separate the items. By doing so, you help your reader understand your meaning.

The animals in Death Valley include **spiders,** such as black widows and tarantulas**; snakes,** such as coral snakes and sidewinders**;** and **small mammals,** such as kangaroo rats, which can convert seeds into water, and trade rats, which nest around cactus.

Alert: Never use a semicolon to introduce a list of items. Use a colon instead (59a).

NO	Many animals live in Death Valley**;** spiders, snakes, and small mammals.
YES	Many animals live in Death Valley**:** spiders, snakes, and small mammals. ●

For more help with your writing, grammar, and research, go to **www.mycomplab.com**

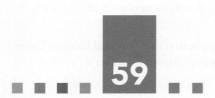

mycomplab

59

Colons

59a How do I use a colon with a list, an appositive, or a quotation?

When you introduce a list, an APPOSITIVE, or a QUOTATION with an INDEPENDENT CLAUSE, use a colon. This rule applies when the words *the following* and *as follows* end an independent clause. In contrast, when the words you use to introduce a list, an appositive, or a quotation form an incomplete sentence, never use a colon. This rule applies after the words *such as, like,* and *including.*

LISTED ITEMS

The students demanded the following**:** an expanded menu in the cafeteria, improved janitorial services, and more up-to-date textbooks.

APPOSITIVE

Museums in New York and Florida own the best-known works from Louis Tiffany's studio: those wonderful stained-glass windows. [*Stained-glass windows* is an appositive that renames *best-known works*.]

QUOTATION

The little boy in *E. T.* did say something neat: "How do you explain school to a higher intelligence?"
                                    —George F. Will, "Well, I Don't Love You, E.T."

Alert: If an incomplete sentence introduces a DIRECT QUOTATION, use a comma, not a colon (57g). ●

59b   When can I use a colon between sentences?

When a sentence serves as an introduction to a second sentence, you can choose to use a colon between the two sentences.

We will never forget the first time we made dinner at home together: He got food poisoning and was too sick to work for four days.

Alerts: (1) Never use a colon when a DIRECT OBJECT consists of a series or list of items.

NO   We bought: eggs, milk, cheese, and bread.
YES   We bought eggs, milk, cheese, and bread.

(2) Never separate a DEPENDENT CLAUSE from an independent clause with a colon. Use a comma instead.

NO   After the drought ended: water restrictions were lifted.
YES   After the drought ended, water restrictions were lifted.

(3) You can choose whether to capitalize or lowercase the first word of an independent clause following a colon. Be consistent in each piece of writing. ●

59c   What conventional formats call for colons?

BETWEEN TITLE AND SUBTITLE

Literature: An Introduction to Critical Reading

BETWEEN HOURS AND MINUTES AND MINUTES AND SECONDS

The runner passed the halfway point at 1:23:02.

BETWEEN NUMBERS IN RATIOS

a proportion of 7:1   a 3:5 ratio

AFTER WORDS IN MEMO HEADINGS

To: Dean Kristen Joy

From: Professor Daniel Black

Re: Student work-study program

AFTER FORMAL LETTER OPENINGS

Dear Ms. Carter:

BETWEEN BIBLE CHAPTERS AND VERSES

Psalm 23:1–3

Alert: In MLA STYLE, a period takes the place of the colon between chapter and verse in Bible references: *Ps. 23.1–3.* Note, too, that the name of the book in the Bible is abbreviated, followed by a period, when it appears inside parentheses. ●

For more help with your
writing, grammar, and research,
go to **www.mycomplab.com**

Apostrophes

60a   How do I use an apostrophe to show that a noun is possessive?

The **possessive case** communicates ownership (*the writer's pen*) or other relationships (*the writer's parent*). In general, to indicate possession in NOUNS, you can choose to use -*'s* (*the instructor's comments*), which calls for an apostrophe; or a PHRASE beginning with *of* (*the comments of the instructor*), which doesn't call for an apostrophe. Here are some applications of this general rule.

1. Add -*'s* to nouns not ending in *s*.

   She felt a **parent's** joy. [*Parent* is a singular noun not ending in *s*.]

They care about their **children's** education. [*Children* is a plural noun not ending in *s*.]

2. Add -'s to singular nouns ending in *s*.

   The **business's** system for handling complaints is inefficient. [*Business* is a singular noun.]

   Lee **Jones's** car insurance is expensive. [*Lee Jones* is one person—a singular noun.]

3. Add only an apostrophe to plural nouns ending in *s*.

   The **boys'** eyewitness statements helped solve the crime. [*Boys* is a plural noun, so only an apostrophe comes after the *s*.]

   Three **months'** maternity leave is in the **workers'** contract. [*Months* and *workers* are plural nouns, so only an apostrophe comes after them.]

4. Add -'s to the last word in compound words and phrases.

   His **mother-in-law's** company makes scuba gear. [The -'s comes at the end of the compound noun *mother-in-law*.]

5. Add -'s to each noun in individual possession.

   Avery's and Jimmy's houses are next to each other. [Avery and Jimmy each own a house; they do not own the houses jointly.]

6. Add -'s to only the last noun in joint or group possession.

   Lindsey and Ryan's house has a screened porch. [Lindsey and Ryan jointly own one house together, so the -'s follows only the final name.]

🛑 **Alerts:** (1) Never use an apostrophe at the end of a nonpossessive noun ending in *s*.

NO	A medical **crisis'** often involves a heart attack. [*Crisis* is a singular noun that ends in *s*, but the sentence expresses no possession.]
YES	A medical **crisis** often involves a heart attack.

(2) Never use an apostrophe with a nonpossessive plural noun.

NO	**Team's** of doctors are researching the effects of cholesterol. [*Teams* is a plural noun that ends in *s*, but the sentence expresses no possession.]
YES	**Teams** of doctors are researching the effects of cholesterol. ●

60b How do I use an apostrophe to show that an indefinite pronoun is possessive?

INDEFINITE PRONOUNS refer to general or nonspecific persons or things: *someone, somebody, anyone, anything, no one, else.* (For a complete list of types of pronouns, see Quick Reference 41.2.) To indicate possession in an indefinite pronoun, add -'s.

I need **someone's** help in studying for the test.

Are **anyone else's** notes more complete than mine are? [When one indefinite pronoun follows another (*anyone else*), the second one takes the possessive -'s.]

60c Do I ever use an apostrophe with *hers, his, its, ours, yours,* and *theirs?*

Never use an apostrophe with **possessive pronouns:** *hers, his, its, ours, yours,* and *theirs.* As possessive pronouns, they already carry possessive meaning.

NO   Because cholesterol has been widely publicized, **it's** role in heart disease is well known.

YES   Because cholesterol has been widely publicized, **its** role in heart disease is well known.

🛑 Alert: Never confuse *its*, the possessive pronoun, with the contraction *it's*, which stands for *it is*. A similar confusion arises between *you're* and *your*, *who's* and *whose*, and *they're* and *their.* ●

60d Do I ever add an apostrophe to a verb that ends in -s?

Never add an apostrophe to a VERB that ends in *s.*

NO   Cholesterol **play's** a key role in longevity.

YES   Cholesterol **plays** a key role in longevity.

60e How do I use apostrophes in contractions?

In **contractions,** an apostrophe indicates that one or more letters have been omitted from a word or a term: *can't, don't, I'm, isn't, it's, let's, they're, wasn't, weren't, we've, who's, won't, you're.*

It's [not Its] still snowing.

Alert: Many college instructors and other readers feel that contractions aren't appropriate in ACADEMIC WRITING. Indeed, the sixth edition of the *MLA Handbook* says they are "rarely acceptable in research papers" (90). ●

60f Do I use an apostrophe with letters, numerals, symbols, and terms?

Use an apostrophe before the *s* to form the plurals of single letters, numbers written as figures, symbols, and words used as terms.

LETTERS	Printing *w*'s is hard for some first graders.
NUMBERS IN FIGURES	The address includes six **2**'s.
SYMBOLS	A line of **&**'s onscreen may mean the keyboard is jammed.
WORDS USED AS TERMS	All the *for*'s were misspelled *four*.

Alert: When you use letters as letters or words as words, you can choose to underline them or put them in italics, or enclose them in quotation marks (61e). Whatever you choose, be consistent in each piece of writing. ●

For more help with your writing, grammar, and research, go to **www.mycomplab.com**

Quotation Marks

61a How do I use quotation marks with short direct quotations?

Direct quotations are exact words of prose or poetry copied from a SOURCE, either print or electronic. In MLA STYLE, a **short quotation** of prose runs four or fewer lines in your paper. A short quotation of poetry is three or fewer lines of a poem. In APA STYLE, a short quotation contains no more than forty words of prose. Whenever you write a short quotation, enclose it in quotation marks and allow it to run in with the rest of your sentence.

⚠ **Alert:** At the end of a short quotation, place the page number or the author's name and the page number (if you don't mention the author's name in the sentence that leads into the quotation) in parentheses. Put the period that ends the sentence *after the parentheses,* not before them. ●

A LONG QUOTATION needs to be *set off* or *displayed* as a whole block of words (61b).

■ Using double quotation marks (" ")

Use double quotation marks to enclose a short quotation.

> Edward T. Hall explains the practicality of close conversational distances: **"If you are interested in something, your pupils dilate; if I say something you don't like, they tend to contract"** (47). Some cultures prefer arm's length for all but the most intimate conversations.

> As W. H. Auden wittily defined personal space, **"Some thirty inches from my nose / The frontier of my person goes"** (539).

■ Using single quotation marks (' ')

The only time you can use single quotation marks in short quotations is to replace any double quotation marks that appear in the original source.

ORIGINAL SOURCE

> He has also said that he does not wish to be the arbiter for what is or is not an **"official"** intelligence.
>
> —Thomas Hoerr, "The Naturalistic Intelligence," p. 24

EXAMPLE FROM A RESEARCH PAPER

> As Thomas Hoerr reports, Gardner "does not wish to be the arbiter for what is or is not an **'official'** intelligence" (24).

⚠ **Alerts:** (1) When you quote short passages of poetry, use a slash with a space on either side of it to signal where one line ends and the next line starts in the original. (2) Capitalize and punctuate quotations of poetry exactly as in the original, even if they do not follow the rules in this book. ●

61b How do I use quotation marks with long direct quotations?

In MLA style, a **long quotation** runs five or more lines of prose or more than three lines of poetry. In APA style, a long quotation contains more than forty words of prose. A long quotation needs to start on a new line and be indented, or *displayed,* as a whole block of words, 1 inch from the left margin in MLA style (Chs. 33–35) or ½ inch from the left margin in APA style (Chs. 36–38).

Never use quotation marks to enclose indented blocks of prose or poetry. The block indentation signals that the material is a quotation. Of course, if within a long quotation some words in the original are in quotation marks, use them exactly as in the original. In the following example, the words *wrist distance* are in double quotation marks in the original source, so they are in double quotation marks in the long quotation as well.

> As Desmond Morris explains, personal space varies among cultures:
>> When you are talking to someone in the street or in any open space, reach out with your arm and see where the nearest point on his body comes. If you hail from western Europe, you will find that he is at roughly fingertip distance from you. In other words, as you reach out, your fingertips will just about make contact with his shoulder. If you come from eastern Europe, you will find you are standing at "wrist distance." If you come from the Mediterranean region you will find that you are much closer to your companion. (23)

Alert: In MLA style, at the end of a long quotation, place the page number or the author's name and the page number (only if you don't mention the author's name in the sentence that leads into the quotation) in parentheses. Put the period that ends the sentence before the parentheses, never after them. ●

61c How do I use quotation marks to indicate spoken words?

Spoken words are called DIRECT DISCOURSE. When you quote direct discourse or you want to write dialogue, use quotation marks to enclose the speaker's words. Start a new paragraph—that is, indent the first line—each time the speaker changes.

> "I don't know how you can see to drive," she said.
> "Maybe you should put on your glasses."
> "Putting on my glasses would help you to see?"
> "Not me; you," Macon said. "You're focused on the windshield instead of the road."
>
> —Ann Tyler, *The Accidental Tourist*

If the same speaker's words continue for more than one paragraph, use quotation marks at the start of each paragraph. Save your quotation marks at the end of a paragraph until you come to the final paragraph of the dialogue.

🛑 **Alert:** Never enclose INDIRECT DISCOURSE (48d) in quotation marks.

The mayor said that he was tired. [This indirect discourse needs no quotation marks. As a direct quotation, this sentence would read *The mayor said,* "*I am tired.*"]●

61d How do I use quotation marks with titles?

Use quotation marks around the titles of short published works: poems, short stories, essays, articles from periodicals, song titles, and individual episodes of a television or radio series. In contrast, use italics (or underlining) for longer works. Quick Reference 66.1 (p. 469) shows when to use quotation marks, italics or underlining, or neither.

61e How do I use quotation marks to indicate terms, language translations, and irony?

You can choose to use either quotation marks or italics (or underlining) to indicate words that are technical terms; words in another language; translated words; and words that are meant ironically. Whichever you choose, be consistent in each piece of writing.

TECHNICAL TERM — "Plagiarism"—the unacknowledged use of another person's words or ideas—is a serious offense. Plagiarism by students can result in expulsion. [Once the term has been introduced in a piece of writing, it needs no further quotation marks.]

TRANSLATED WORDS — My grandfather usually ended arguments with an old saying: *de gustibus non disputandum est* ("there is no arguing about tastes").

IRONIC WORD — The proposed "reform" is actually a tax increase.

61f When are quotation marks wrong?

Never use quotation marks around CLICHÉS, SLANG, or other language that is inappropriate in ACADEMIC WRITING. Use appropriate, alternative wording.

NO — They "eat like birds" in public and "stuff their faces" in private.

YES — They nibble in public and gorge themselves in private.

Never enclose a word in quotation marks merely to call attention to it.

NO Remember, the "customer" matters to your business.

YES Remember, the customer matters to your business.

Never enclose indirect discourse in quotation marks.

NO The College Code of Conduct points out that "plagiarism can result in expulsion." [The original words are "Grounds for expulsion include plagiarism." Here, the quotation is indirect, so quotation marks are wrong.]

YES The College Code of Conduct points out that plagiarism can result in expulsion.

Never use quotation marks around the title of your own paper, whether you place it at the top of the page or on a title page or mention it in the body of your paper. One exception exists: If the title of your paper includes another title, use quotation marks if the title is of a short work around the other title only (see Quick Reference 66.1, on p. 469).

NO "The Elderly in Nursing Homes: A Case Study"

YES The Elderly in Nursing Homes: A Case Study

NO Character Development in Shirley Jackson's Short Story The Lottery

YES Character Development in Shirley Jackson's Short Story "The Lottery"

61g How do I use quotation marks with other punctuation?

1. Put commas and periods inside closing quotation marks.

   Having enjoyed F. Scott Fitzgerald's short story **"The Freshest Boy,"** we were eager to read his longer works.

   Edward T. Hall coined the word **"proxemics."**

2. Put colons and semicolons *outside* closing quotation marks.

   We try to discover **"how close is too close":** We do not want to invade others' personal space.

   Esther DiMarzio claims that the current job market **"offers opportunities that never existed before";** others disagree.

3. Put question marks, exclamation points, and dashes inside or outside closing quotation marks, depending on their function. If a question mark, an exclamation point, or a dash punctuates the words enclosed in quotation marks, put that punctuation inside the closing quotation mark.

"Did I Hear You Call My Name?" was the winning song.

They shouted, **"We won the lottery!"**

If a question mark, an exclamation point, or a dash punctuates words not enclosed in quotation marks, put that punctuation outside the closing quotation mark.

Have you read Nikki Giovanni's poem **"Knoxville, Tennessee"**?

Edward T. Hall's coined word **"proxemics"**—a term based on the noun **"proximity"**—can now be found in dictionaries.

For more help with your writing, grammar, and research, go to **www.mycomplab.com**

62

Periods, Question Marks, and Exclamation Points

62a When should I use a period?

A period is correct after a statement, a mild command, or an **indirect question**, which reports a question that someone asks. An indirect question never calls for quotation marks. (For help in punctuating DIRECT QUESTIONS, see 62b. For help with periods in abbreviations, see Chapter 67.)

STATEMENT	Mountain climbers enjoy the outdoors.
MILD COMMAND	Pack warm clothes for the climb.
INDIRECT QUESTION	I asked whether they wanted to climb Mount Everest.

62b When should I use a question mark?

A **question mark** is correct after a direct question, a directly quoted question, a series of questions, or a polite request. A **direct question**, which asks a question outright, ends with a question mark. A **directly quoted question** calls for quotation marks and ends with a question mark *inside* the closing quotation mark. Questions in a series can be either complete or incomplete sentences. For either type, use a question mark after each.

🅐 Alert: When questions in a series are incomplete sentences, you can choose whether to capitalize the first letter of each. Whatever your choice, be consistent in each piece of writing.

DIRECT QUESTION	Have you ever wanted to climb Mount Everest**?**
DIRECTLY QUOTED QUESTION	I asked, "Do you want to climb Mount Everest**?**"
SERIES OF QUESTIONS WITH CAPITALS	The mountain climbers debated what to do: **T**urn back**? M**ove on**? R**est**?**
SERIES OF QUESTIONS WITH LOWERCASE	The mountain climbers debated what to do: **t**urn back**? m**ove on**?** rest**?** ●

To end a **polite request**, you can choose between a question mark and a period.

Would you please send me the report**.** [This version emphasizes the politeness more than the request.]

Would you please send me the report**?** [This version emphasizes the request more than the politeness.]

To convey IRONY or sarcasm, depend on words, not a question mark in parentheses, to communicate your message.

NO   Having altitude sickness is a **pleasant (?)** experience.

YES   Having altitude sickness is **as pleasant as having a terrible case of the flu.**

62c   When should I use an exclamation point?

An **exclamation point** is correct after a strong command (*Look out!*); an emphatic declaration (*Those cars are going to crash!*); or an INTERJECTION, a word that conveys surprise or other emotion (*Oh! I'm terrified of heights!*). Avoid using exclamation points in ACADEMIC WRITING. Reserve them for dialogue. Otherwise, use words with sufficient impact to communicate forceful messages.

NO   Each day in Nepal, we tried to see Mount Everest. Each day we failed**!** The summit remained shrouded**!** Clouds defeated us**!**

YES   Each day in Nepal, we tried to see Mount Everest. Each day we failed**.** The summit remained shrouded**.** Clouds defeated us**!**

To convey amazement or sarcasm, depend on words, not an exclamation point in parentheses, to communicate your strong message.

NO   At 29,035 feet **(!)**, Everest is the world's highest mountain.

YES   At **a staggering** 29,035 feet, Everest is the world's highest mountain.

■ ■ ■ ■ **63** ■ ■

Other Punctuation Marks

63a   When should I use a dash?

Dashes let you interrupt a sentence's structure to add information. They can also insert a little suspense, if the meaning calls for it. Use dashes sparingly so that you don't dilute their effect by overexposure.

You can use a dash to add information such as EXAMPLES, DEFINITIONS, APPOSITIVES, contrasts, and asides. Sometimes parentheses (63b) serve the same purposes, but they speak in a quieter voice.

Two of the strongest animals in the jungle are vegetarians—the elephant and the gorilla. [examples]

—Dick Gregory, *The Shadow That Scares Me*

Although the emphasis at the school was mainly language—speaking, reading, writing—the lessons always began with an exercise in politeness. [definition]

—Elizabeth Wong, *Fifth Chinese Daughter*

The caretakers—the helpers, nurturers, teachers, mothers—are still systematically devalued. [appositive]

—Ellen Goodman, "Just Woman's Work"

Tampering with time brought most of the house tumbling down, and it was this that made Einstein's work so important—and controversial. [contrast]

—Banesh Hoffman, "My Friend, Albert Einstein"

I live on an income well below the poverty line—although it does not seem like poverty when the redbud and dogwood are in bloom together—and when I travel I have to be careful about expenses. [aside]

—Sue Hubbell, *Beekeeper*

Alerts: (1) If the words within a pair of dashes are a complete sentence and call for a question mark or an exclamation point, place such punctuation *before* the second dash:

A first love—do you remember?—stays in the memory forever.

(2) Never use commas, semicolons, or periods next to dashes. Revise your writing to avoid these types of double punctuation. ●

63b When should I use parentheses?

Like dashes (63a), **parentheses** let you interrupt a sentence's structure to add information. Parentheses tend to deemphasize whatever they enclose; dashes tend to call attention to whatever they set off.

■ Using parentheses to add information

Parentheses can enclose the same kind of material that dashes can, such as explanations, definitions, examples, contrasts, and asides.

In division (also known as partition), a subject commonly thought of as a single unit is reduced to its separate parts. [definition]

—David Skwire, *Writing with a Thesis*

Though other cities (Dresden, for instance) had been utterly destroyed in World War II, never before had a single weapon been responsible for such destruction. [example]

—Lawrence Behrens and Leonard J. Rosen, *Writing and Reading Across the Curriculum*

The sheer decibel level of the noise around us is not enough to make us cranky, irritable, or aggressive. (It can, however, affect our mental and physical health, which is another matter.) [aside]

—Carol Tavris, *Anger: The Misunderstood Emotion*

■ Using parentheses to enclose numbers or letters

Conventional uses for parentheses include enclosing numbers or letters of listed items: *The topics to be discussed are (1) membership, (2) fund-raising, and*

(3) networking. Another conventional use occurs in business writing when parentheses sometimes enclose a number written as a figure immediately after its spelled-out version: *We shipped **fifteen (15)** cartons yesterday.*

■ Using parentheses with other punctuation

Never put a comma before an opening parenthesis, even if what precedes the parenthetical material requires a comma. Always put the comma after the closing parenthesis.

> **NO** Although different from the first film we watched**, (***The Wizard of Oz***)** *Gone with the Wind* is also worth studying.
>
> **YES** Although different from the first film we watched **(***The Wizard of Oz***),** *Gone with the Wind* is also worth studying.

If a sentence in parentheses stands on its own, rather than within another sentence, place whatever ending punctuation is called for before the closing parenthesis.

If a complete sentence in parentheses falls within another sentence, never use a period to signal the end of the parenthetical sentence. In addition, never start such a sentence in parentheses with a capital letter unless the first word is a PROPER NOUN. In contrast, if the complete sentence within parentheses calls for a question mark or an exclamation point, use it.

> **NO** Searching for his car keys **(H**e had left them in the kitchen**.)** wasted an hour.
>
> **YES** Searching for his car keys **(h**e had left them in the kitchen**)** wasted an hour.
>
> **YES** Searching for his car keys **(w**hy can't he learn to put them in the same place all the time**?)** wasted an hour.
>
> **YES** Searching for his car keys wasted an hour. **(H**e had left the keys in the kitchen**.)**

63c When should I use brackets?

Brackets enclose one or more words that a writer inserts into QUOTATIONS. As a writer, you most often use brackets to fit the wording of the quotation into the structure of your own sentence or to enclose explanatory words within quoted material in order to help your reader understand the quotation.

ORIGINAL SOURCE

For a variety of reasons, the system attempts to maintain stability and re-sist temporal change.

—Peter Bonner, "Travel Rhythms," *Sky Magazine,* p. 72

SOURCE IN A QUOTATION

In "Travel Rhythms," Bonner explains that **"maintain[ing]** stability and **resist[ing]** temporal change" are natural goals for human beings. [Brackets are used to fit the quotation's wording into the rest of the sentence structure.]

ORIGINAL SOURCE

In the future, a trip to the doctor may well involve an evaluation of such environmental components of our health.

—Winifred Gallagher, *The Power of Place,* p. 19

SOURCE IN A QUOTATION

Gallagher points out that a doctor visit may soon include "an evaluation of such environmental components **[the air we breathe and water we drink]** of our health." [Brackets indicate words inserted by the writer, not the original author, Gallagher.]

❗ **Alert:** Use the bracketed term [*sic*] when you've found an error in something you're quoting—perhaps a wrong date or an error of fact. Adding [*sic*] tells the reader, "It is this way in the original." In MLA STYLE, use regular (roman) type, not italics or underlining, for the term. When this term falls within a sentence, use brackets around it, but use parentheses when the term falls at the end of a sentence, and place punctuation after them. In APA STYLE, italicize the term *sic* between roman brackets. ●

63d When should I use ellipsis points?

Ellipsis means "omission." **Ellipsis points** consist of three spaced periods used to indicate that in copying a quotation into your writing, you've omitted some of the words in the original source. This rule applies only when the omission occurs somewhere within the material you're quoting.

■ Using ellipsis in prose quotations

Use three spaced periods (. . .) to show where you have omitted a portion of the quoted material. If ellipsis points appear in the original source, include them. Never split ellipsis points between the end of a line and the beginning of the next.

ORIGINAL SOURCE

For over a century, twins have been used to study how genes make people what they are. Because they share precisely the same genes but live in different surroundings under different influences, identical twins reared apart are helping science sort out which qualities of body and mind are shaped by our genes and which by upbringing. Researchers needn't worry about running out of subjects: according to the Twins Foundation, there are approximately 4.5 million twin individuals in the United States alone, and about 70,000 more are born each year.

—Sharon Begley, "Twins," p. 84

MLA STYLE

According to Begley, "identical twins reared apart are helping science sort out which qualities of body and mind are shaped by our genes and which by upbringing" (84). [Ellipsis points are unnecessary; quotation has been worked into a sentence.]

Begley says, "Because they share precisely the same genes . . ., identical twins reared apart are helping science sort out which qualities of body and mind are shaped by our genes and which by upbringing" (84). [Ellipsis points show that the writer has omitted words from the quoted sentence or a longer passage.]

Begley says, "Because they share precisely the same genes but live in different surroundings under different influences, identical twins reared apart are helping science . . ." (84). [Ellipsis points show that the writer has omitted words from the end of the quoted sentence or a longer passage.]

Begley says, "For over a century, twins have been used to study how genes make people what they are. . . . Researchers needn't worry about running out of subjects" (84). [Ellipsis points between sentences show that one or more sentences have been omitted from the quoted material.]

APA STYLE

Begley says, "Because they share precisely the same genes . . ., identical twins reared apart are helping science sort out which qualities of body and mind are shaped by our genes and which by upbringing" (p. 84). [Ellipsis points show that the writer has omitted words from the middle of the quoted sentence.]

Begley says, "Identical twins reared apart are helping science sort out which qualities of body and mind are shaped by our genes and which by upbringing" (p. 84). [Omission of words from the beginning of the quoted sentence doesn't require use of ellipsis points. Also, APA style permits a writer to change a lowercase letter at the start of a quotation to a capital letter.]

Begley says, "Because they share precisely the same genes but live in different surroundings under different influences, identical twins reared apart are helping science" (p. 84). [APA style does not require ellipsis points to show that words have been omitted from the end of the quoted sentence.]

Begley says, "For over a century, twins have been used to study how genes make people what they are. . . . Researchers needn't worry about running out of subjects" (p. 84). [Ellipsis points between sentences show that one or more sentences have been omitted from the quoted material.]

■ Using ellipsis in quotations from poetry

Omission of words within a line of poetry is indicated with ellipsis points exactly as for prose. Omission of an entire line or more of poetry is indicated with a row of spaced periods in MLA style.

ORIGINAL SOURCE

Fear no more the heat o' the sun
Nor the furious winter's rages;
Though thy worldly task has done,
Home art gone, and ta'en thy wages;
Golden lads and girls all must,
As chimney-sweepers, come to dust.

—William Shakespeare, *Cymbeline*

MLA STYLE

Ultimately, however, as Shakespeare reminds us, "Golden lads and girls all must / . . . come to dust." [short poetry quotation with a few words omitted]

Fear no more the heat o' the sun
Nor the furious winter's rages;
. . . .
Golden lads and girls all must
. . . come to dust. [long poetry quotation with lines and words omitted]

APA STYLE

Ultimately, however, as Shakespeare reminds us, "Golden lads and girls all must . . . come to dust." [short poetry quotation with a few words omitted]

Fear no more the heat o' the sun
Nor the furious winter's rages; . . .
Golden lads and girls all must
. . . come to dust. [long poetry quotation with lines and words omitted]

63e When should I use a slash?

When quoting three or fewer lines of poetry, use a slash to divide one line from the next. Leave a space on each side of the slash.

Consider the beginning of Anne Sexton's poem "Words": "Be careful of words, / even the miraculous ones."

To type numerical fractions that don't appear on your keyboard, use the slash to separate the numerator and denominator, leaving no space before or after the slash.

1/16   1 2/3

Avoid word combinations like *and/or* when writing in the humanities. Revise your sentence to avoid such a combination. In academic disciplines in which the use of word combinations is acceptable, separate the two words with a slash, leaving no space before or after it.

For more help with your writing, grammar, and research, go to **www.mycomplab.com**

Hyphens

64a When should I hyphenate at the end of a line?

Always set the default on your word processing program so as not to allow hyphenation. If you write laboratory reports by hand, follow the rules in Quick Reference 64.1 (p. 461).

64b When should I hyphenate prefixes and suffixes?

Prefixes and **suffixes** are syllables attached to words—prefixes at the beginning and suffixes at the end. A few prefixes and suffixes call for hyphens, but most don't (see Quick Reference 64.2, page 462).

64c When should I hyphenate compound words?

You can write a **compound word**—two or more words combined to express one concept—in one of three ways: as separate words (*night shift*), as hyphenated words (*tractor-trailer*), or as one word (*handbook*). Follow the rules in Quick Reference 64.3 (page 462).

Quick Reference 64.1

■ ■ ■ ■ ■ ■ ■

Hyphenating at the end of a line

- Never divide very short words, one-syllable words, or words pronounced as one syllable.

wealth	envy	screamed
we-alth	en-vy	scream-ed

- Never leave or carry over only one or two letters.

alive	open	covered
a-live	o-pen	cover-ed

- Divide words only between syllables. (If you're unsure about a word's syllables, look it up in a dictionary.)

pro-cess
proc-ess

- Divide between consonants, keeping pronunciation in mind.

full-ness	omit-ting	as-phalt
ful-lness	omitt-ing	asp-halt

- Divide a hyphenated word only at the hyphen, and divide a closed compound word only between complete words.

self-conscious	master-piece
self-con-scious	mas-terpiece
sister-in-law	stomach-ache
sis-ter-in-law	stom-achache

64d When should I hyphenate spelled-out numbers?

For help in deciding when to use numerals and when to spell out numbers, see Chapter 68. Quick Reference 64.4 (p. 463) shows how to hyphenate spelled-out numbers.

🛇 **Alert:** Use figures for any fraction that requires more than two words in its spelled-out form. If you can't avoid spelling out a fraction in three or more words, use a hyphen between all words in the numerator or the denominator, and use a space (but no hyphen) to separate the numerator from the denominator.

2/100 *or* two one-hundredths
33/10,000 *or* thirty-three ten-thousandths ●

Hyphenating prefixes and suffixes

Use hyphens after the prefixes *all-, ex-,* and *self-*.
> all-inclusive, self-reliant

Never use a hyphen when *self* is a root word onto which a prefix is attached.
> selfishness, selfless, selfhood

Use a hyphen to avoid a distracting string of repeated letters.
> anti-intellectual, bell-like

Use a hyphen between a prefix and the first word of a compound word.
> anti-gun control

Use a hyphen to prevent confusion in meaning or pronunciation.
> re-dress ("dress again"), un-ionize ("remove the ions")
> redress ("set right"), unionize ("form a union")

Use a hyphen when two or more prefixes apply to one root word.
> pre- and postwar eras

Use a hyphen before the suffix *-elect*.
> president-elect

Use a hyphen when a prefix comes before a number or before a word that starts with a capital letter.
> post-1950, pro-American

Hyphenating compound words

Use a hyphen for most compound modifiers that precede the noun. Never use a hyphen for compound modifiers *after* the noun.
> well-researched report; two-inch clearance [before the noun]
> report is well researched; clearance of two inches [after the noun]

Use a hyphen between compound nouns joining two units within a measure.
> light-year, kilowatt-hour, foot-pound

Never use a hyphen when a compound modifier starts with an adverb ending in *ly*.
> happily married couple

Use a hyphen for most compound modifiers in the comparative (*-er*) or superlative (*-est*) form. Never use a hyphen when the compound modifier includes *more/most* or *less/least*.
> better-fitting shoe, best-known work
> more significant factor, least welcome guest

Never use a hyphen when a compound modifier is a foreign phrase.
> post hoc fallacies

Never use a hyphen with a possessive compound modifier.
> a full week's work, eight hours' pay

For more help with your
writing, grammar, and research,
go to **www.mycomplab.com**

mycomplab

■ ■ ■   ■   ■ ■

Capitals

65a When should I capitalize a "first" word?

1. Capitalize the first word in a sentence.

   Four inches of snow fell last night.

2. If you wish, capitalize the first word of a complete sentence after a colon. When a complete sentence follows a colon, you can begin the first word with either a capital or a lowercase letter, but be consistent in each piece of writing. When the words after a colon are not a complete sentence, never capitalize.

   Only one solution occurred to her**: S**he picked up the ice cream and pushed it back into the cone. [The capital letter is acceptable after the colon because it begins a full sentence. A lowercase letter would be equally acceptable.]

   She bought four pints of ice cream**: v**anilla, chocolate, strawberry, and butterscotch swirl. [A lowercase letter is required because the words following the colon are not a full sentence.]

3. Capitalize the first word in a series of complete questions. When questions in a series are not complete sentences, you can begin the first word of each question with either a capital or a lowercase letter. Be consistent within each piece of writing.

What facial feature would most people like to change? **E**yes? **E**ars? **N**ose?

What facial feature would most people like to change? **e**yes? **e**ars? **n**ose?

4. Capitalize the first word in a list of items that are complete sentences.

Three problems caused the shortage: (1) **B**ad weather delayed delivery. (2) **P**oor scheduling created slowdowns. (3) **I**nadequate maintenance caused equipment breakdowns.

Never capitalize listed items that are not complete sentences.

The delays resulted from (1) **b**ad weather, (2) **p**oor scheduling, and (3) **e**quipment breakdowns.

5. Capitalize the first word of a complete sentence that stands alone inside parentheses. A complete sentence enclosed in parentheses may stand alone or fall within another sentence. A complete sentence that stands alone within parentheses starts with a capital letter and ends with a period, a question mark, or an exclamation point. A complete sentence that falls within another sentence does not start with a capital letter or end with a period. However, if the sentence is a question, it ends with a question mark; if it is an exclamation, it ends with an exclamation point.

I didn't know till years later that they called it the Cuban Missile Crisis. But I remember Castro. (**W**e called him Castor Oil and were awed by his beard—beards were rare in those days.) We might not have worried so much (**w**hat would the Communists want with our small New Hampshire town**?**) except that we lived 10 miles from an air base.

—Joyce Maynard, *An 18-Year-Old Looks Back on Life*

65b How should I capitalize quotations?

Capitalize the first word in a prose QUOTATION.

Encouraging students to study in other countries, Mrs. Velez says, "**Y**ou will absorb a good accent with the food."

When you interrupt quoted words, never capitalize the continued part of the quoted words.

"You will absorb a good accent," says Mrs. Velez, "**w**ith the food."

If the quoted words form part of your own sentence, never capitalize the first quoted word unless it is a PROPER NOUN. Phrases such as *writes **that**, thinks **that***, and *says **that*** usually signal this kind of quotation.

Mrs. Velez believes that "you will absorb a good accent with the food" if you study in another country.

When you quote poetry in your writing, use capital and lowercase letters exactly as they appear in the original SOURCE. (If you need help using QUOTATION MARKS, see Chapter 61.)

65c When should I capitalize nouns and adjectives?

Capitalize **proper nouns** (*Mexico, Arthur*) and **proper adjectives** (*a Mexican diplomat, the Arthurian legend*). Capitalize certain **common nouns** when you add specific names or titles to them: For example, *We visit a **lake** every summer. This summer we went to **Lake Seminole**.* See Quick Reference 65.1.

Alerts: (1) Never capitalize DETERMINERS and other words just because they accompany proper nouns or proper adjectives: *Here is a Canadian penny* [not *A Canadian penny* or *a Canadian Penny*].

(2) Be aware that some proper nouns and proper adjectives become so common that they lose their capital letters: *french fries, italics, pasteurized.* ●

Quick Reference 65.1

Capitalization guide

	Capitals	Lowercase Letters
NAMES	Mother Teresa [also when used as names: Mother, Dad, Mom, Pa]	my mother [relationship]
	Doc Holliday	the doctor [role]
TITLES	President Truman	the president
	Democrat [party member]	democrat [believer in democracy]
	Representative Harold Ford	the congressional representative
	Senator Edward M. Kennedy	the senator
	Queen Elizabeth II	the queen

continued >>

Quick Reference 65.1   (continued)

	Capitals	**Lowercase Letters**
GROUPS OF PEOPLE	Caucasian [race]	white, black [*also* White, Black]
	Korean [nationality]	
	Jew, Buddhist [religious affiliation]	
	Hispanic [ethnic group]	
ORGANIZATIONS	Congress	legislative branch of the US government
	Ohio State Supreme Court	state supreme court
	the Republican Party	the party
	National Gypsum Company	the company
	Chicago Cubs	baseball team
	American Medical Association	professional group
	Sigma Chi	fraternity
	Alcoholics Anonymous	self-help group
PLACES	Los Angeles	the city
	the South [region]	turn south [direction]
	the West Coast	the states along the western seaboard
	Main Street	the street
	Atlantic Ocean	the ocean
	the Black Hills	the hills
BUILDINGS	the Capitol [in Washington, DC]	the state capitol
	Central High School	a high school
	China West Café	a restaurant
	Highland Hospital	a hospital
SCIENTIFIC	Earth [as a planet]	the earth in the garden
	the Milky Way	the galaxy, the moon, the sun
	Streptococcus aureus	a streptococcal infection
	Gresham's law	the theory of relativity

continued >>

Quick Reference 65.1 (continued)

	Capitals	Lowercase Letters
LANGUAGES	Spanish, French, Chinese	foreign languages
SCHOOL COURSES	Chemistry 342	a chemistry course
	English 111	my English class
	Introduction to Photography	a photography class
NAMES OF SPECIFIC THINGS	the *Boston Globe*	the newspaper
	Time	the magazine
	Purdue University	the university
	Heinz ketchup	ketchup
	a Dodge Cobra	a car
SEASONS		spring, summer, fall, autumn, winter
HOLIDAYS	Passover, New Year's Day, Ramadan, Kwanzaa	
HISTORICAL EVENTS AND DOCUMENTS	World War II	the war
	the Roaring Twenties	a decade
	the Great Depression	a depression
	the Paleozoic	an era, an age
	the Reformation	the eighteenth century
	the Bill of Rights	fifth-century manuscripts
RELIGIOUS TERMS	God	a god, a goddess
	Buddhism	a religion
	the Torah, the Koran, the Bible	
LETTER PARTS	Dear Ms. Kupperman:	
	Sincerely,	
	Yours truly,	
TITLES OF PUBLISHED AND RELEASED WORKS	"The Lottery"	[Capitalize the first letter of the first and last words and all other words except ARTICLES, short PREPOSITIONS, and COORDINATING CONJUNCTIONS.]
	A History of the United States to 1877	
	Jazz on Ice	

continued >>

Quick Reference 65.1   (continued)

	Capitals	Lowercase Letters
ACRONYMS AND INITIALISMS	NATO, FBI, AFL-CIO, UCLA, DNA, CD	
COMPUTER TERMS	Microsoft Word, WordPerfect	computer software
	Netscape Navigator	a browser
	World Wide Web, the Web	
	Web site, Web page	a home page, a link
	the Internet	a computer network
PROPER ADJECTIVES	Victorian	biblical
	Midwestern	transatlantic
	Indo-European	alpine

For more help with your
writing, grammar, and research,
go to **www.mycomplab.com**

mycomplab

66

Italics (Underlining)

Most printed material is set in roman type. Type that slants to the right is called italic type. Italics and underlining mean the same thing. MLA style requires italics, not underlining, in all documents (Chs. 33–35).

HANDWRITTEN AND UNDERLINED	Great Expectations
ITALIC TYPE	*Great Expectations*

66a   How do I choose between italics and quotation marks?

Generally, use italics for titles of long works or works that contain subsections. Use quotation marks for titles of shorter works or titles of subsections within a larger work. Consult Quick Reference 66.1 for specifics.

Quick Reference 66.1 ■ ■ ■ ■ ■ ■ ■ ■

Italics, quotation marks, or nothing

	Italicize	Quotations Marks or Nothing
TITLES	*The Bell Jar* [a novel]	title of student essay
	Death of a Salesman [a play]	act 3
	Collected Works of O. Henry [a book]	"The Last Leaf" [a story in the book]
	Simon & Schuster Handbook for Writers [a book]	"Agreement" [a chapter in the book]
	The Prose Reader [a collection of essays]	"Putting in a Good Word for Guilt" [title of an essay]
	The Iliad [a book-length poem]	"Nothing Gold Can Stay" [a short poem]
	Almost Famous [a film]	
	the *Los Angeles Times** [a newspaper]	"Supreme Court Judge Steps Down" [a headline]
	Scientific American [a magazine]	"The Molecules of Life" [an article in a magazine]
	Aida [an opera]	
	Symphonie Fantastique [a long musical work]	Concerto in B-flat Minor [a musical work identified by form, number, and key]
	The Twilight Zone [a television series]	"Terror at 30,000 Feet" [an episode of the television series]
	The Best of Bob Dylan [an album or CD]	"Mr. Tambourine Man" [one cut on an album or CD]
	the USS *Intrepid* [a ship]	aircraft carrier [a class of ship]
	Voyager 2 [specific aircraft, spacecraft, satellites]	Boeing 787 [names shared by classes of aircraft, spacecraft, or satellites]
OTHER WORDS	*semper fidelis* [words in a language other than English]	burrito, chutzpah [widely understood non-English words]
	What does *our* imply? [a word referred to as such]	
	the *ABC*s; confusing *3*'s and *8*'s [letters and numerals referred to as such]	

*Even if *The* is part of the title printed on a newspaper, don't capitalize it and don't italicize it in the body of your paper. In MLA-style documentation, omit the word *The* entirely. In APA-style documentation, retain *The* as part of the title.

66b When should I use italics for emphasis?

Use italics sparingly for emphasis. Your choice of words and sentence structure normally conveys the emphasis you want to give.

> The pain from my injury was *severe*.

> The pain from my injury was so severe that I could not breathe.
> [more effective description]

For more help with your writing, grammar, and research, go to **www.mycomplab.com**

67

Abbreviations

The guidelines in this chapter apply to general writing and writing in the humanities. Guidelines in other disciplines vary. If you're in doubt about a particular abbreviation, check your college dictionary for correct capitalization, spacing, and use of periods.

Alerts: (1) When the period of an abbreviation falls at the end of a sentence, it serves also as a sentence-ending period.

(2) When a question mark or exclamation point ends a sentence, place it after the abbreviation's period. ●

67a What abbreviations can I use with times and amounts?

With exact times, use the abbreviations *a.m.* (or *A.M.*) and *p.m.* (or *P.M.*), including the periods. Use capital or lowercase letters for *a.m.* and *p.m.* as long as you are consistent in each piece of writing.

7:15 a.m.	3:47 p.m.
7:15 A.M.	3:47 P.M.

Use capital letters without periods for abbreviations for eras.

BC (meaning *before Christ*)—place after the year number: *1200 BC.*

BCE (meaning *before the Common Era*), which is a more inclusionary, contemporary form—place after the year: *1200 BCE.*

AD (Latin for *anno Domini*, which means *in the year of the Lord*)—place before the year: *AD 977.*

CE (meaning *Common Era*), a more contemporary form—place after the year: *1507 CE.*

In tables, you can abbreviate amounts and measurements (such as *in., mi., cm, km, gal., ml, lb., kg*) when you use them with exact numbers. You can also abbreviate days and months (*Mon., Jan., Aug.*).

Use the symbol *$* with exact amounts of money expressed in numerals or numerals and words.

$4.95 $34 million

As a rule, avoid symbols in the body of your writing for the humanities. Still, let common sense and a concern for clarity guide you. If you mention measurements such as temperatures once or twice in a paper, spell them out: *ninety degrees Fahrenheit, minus twenty-six degrees Celsius*. However, if you mention temperatures throughout your work, use numbers and symbols: *90°F, –26C°*.

67b   How should I use abbreviations with people's names?

Use the abbreviations *Mr., Mrs., Ms.,* and *Dr.* with either full names or last names only.

Dr. Anna Freud   Dr. Freud   Mr. Daljit Singh   Mr. Singh

When you follow a person's name with the abbreviation of a professional or academic degree, use no periods. Also, never use in the same context both a title of address before a name and an abbreviated degree after a name.

NO   **Dr.** Jill Sih, **MD**

YES   Jill Sih, **MD**

YES   **Dr.** Jill Sih

Follow the official military title abbreviations for each branch of the US armed forces (you can find the most up-to-date ones on the Internet). Today these abbreviations are almost always in all capital letters, and they use no periods.

ADM	admiral	**COL**	colonel
CPO	chief petty officer	**ENS**	ensign
CO	commanding officer	**GEN**	general

67c How do I use *Jr., Sr., II, III, 2nd,* and *3rd?*

Indicators of birth order in males never apply to females. They always follow a last name. Here are their usage rules.

1. End only the birth order indicators *Jr.* and *Sr.* with a period.

2. Never place a comma before or after any of these indicators unless another rule calls for one.

   Writing under the pseudonym James Tiptree **Jr.,** Alice B. Sheldon wrote excellent science fiction. [A period correctly follows *Jr.,* and the comma is correct here because *Jr.* falls at the end of an introductory phrase.]

   The James Tiptree **Jr.** Memorial Award pays tribute to science fiction writer Alice B. Sheldon. [A period correctly follows *Jr.,* and no comma after *Jr.* is correct because no other rule calls for one.]

   Douglas Young **III** is a physical therapist. [No period or comma is needed.]

   Douglas Young **III,** a physical therapist, specializes in complex rehabilitation programs. [Commas are correct to set off the appositive, *a physical therapist.*]

   Douglas Young **III, PT, MA** [Commas are needed between multiple titles.]

3. Never use a birth-order abbreviation with a last name only: not *Kellogg Jr.* However, you can use it if you add initials for the given name or names: *G. P. Kellogg Jr.*

67d When can I abbreviate names of countries, organizations, and government agencies?

Spell out the names of countries as a sign of respect. You can abbreviate *United States* only when it serves as an adjective (*the **US** Constitution*). Current usage doesn't require periods in the abbreviation *US,* but some disciplines still prefer them. Never abbreviate *United States* as a noun (*Constitution of the **United States***).

   When you refer to an organization throughout your document and want to use its abbreviation to save space, spell out the full name the first time you use it and then, immediately afterward, put the abbreviation in parentheses. Thereafter, you can use the abbreviation alone.

> Spain voted to continue as a member of the **North Atlantic Treaty Organization (NATO)**, to the surprise of other **NATO** members.

67e What abbreviations can I use in addresses?

You can use abbreviations for addresses such as *St.* for *Street* and *Blvd.* for *Boulevard.* You can also use abbreviations for *North* (*N.*), *South* (*S.*), *East* (*E.*), and *West* (*W.*). In the United States, use the two-letter postal abbreviations for state names in addresses: CA for California, IL for Illinois, and so on.

If you include a full address in a sentence, spell out all words in the address except the two-letter postal abbreviation. Otherwise, spell out the name of the state.

> I wrote to Mr. Hugh Lern, 10-01 Rule Road, Classgate, **NJ** 07632, for the instruction manual. Unfortunately, he had moved to Flagstaff, **Arizona**, before my letter arrived.

67f When can I use *etc.* and other Latin abbreviations?

The abbreviation *etc.* comes from the Latin term *et cetera,* which means "and the rest." When you're writing for classes in the humanities, avoid this abbreviation. Acceptable substitutes are *and the like, and so on,* and *and so forth.*

For more help with your
writing, grammar, and research,
go to **www.mycomplab.com**

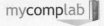

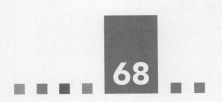

Numbers

68a When should I spell out numbers in words?

When you're writing for the humanities, and when numbers aren't the focus of your topic, use words. If, however, numbers occur frequently in your paper, spell out *one* through *nine* and use numerals for all others.

Quick Reference 68.1

Using numbers

DATES	August 6, 1941
	1732–1845
	34 BCE to AD 230
ADDRESSES	237 North Eighth Street [*or* N. 8th St.]
	Export Falls, MN 92025
TIMES	8:09 a.m., 4:00 p.m. [*but* four o'clock, *not*
	4 o'clock; 4 p.m. *or* four in the afternoon,
	not four p.m. *or* 4 in the afternoon]
CHAPTERS AND PAGES	Chapter 27, page 245
ACT, SCENE,	act 2, scene 2 (or act II, scene ii)
AND LINE	lines 75–79
SCORES	a 6–0 score
AND STATISTICS	a 5-to-3 ratio [*or* a 5:3 ratio]
	29 percent
IDENTIFICATION	93.9 on the FM dial
NUMBERS	call (212) 555-3930
MEASUREMENTS	2 feet
	67.8 miles per hour
	1.5 gallons, 3 liters
	8-by-10-inch photograph
TEMPERATURES	−5°F, 3°C, 43° Celsius
MONEY	$1.2 billion
	$3.41
	25 cents
DECIMALS	5.55
AND FRACTIONS	98.6
	3.1416
	7/8
	12 1/4
	3/4 (three-quarters *but not* 3-quarters)

❶Alert: With two-word numbers from *twenty-one* through *ninety-nine,* use a hyphen between the words. ●

If a sentence starts with a number, spell it out rather than using a numeral. Better still, revise the sentence so that the number doesn't come first.

> **ACCEPTABLE** **Three hundred seventy-five dollars** per credit is the tuition for nonresidents.

> **BETTER** The tuition for nonresidents is **$375** per credit.

Never mix spelled-out numbers and figures when they refer to the same thing. In the following example, all numbers referring to volunteers are in figures, but *four* is spelled out because it refers to days, not volunteers.

In the past ~~4~~ four days, our volunteers increased from ~~five~~ 5 to ~~eight~~ 8 to ~~seventeen~~ 17 to 233. On Saturday, ~~thirty-seven~~ 37 people who usually volunteer on weekdays joined the regular Saturday staff of ~~forty-one~~ 41 volunteers.

68b How should I write dates, addresses, times, and other numbers?

After plural numbers, use the singular form of *hundred, thousand,* and *million.* Add *-s* only when no number comes before those words.

Five hundred books were damaged in the flood.

Hundreds of books were damaged in the flood.

Quick Reference 68.1 (p. 474) shows how to write numbers in some common forms.

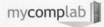

A Message from Lynn Troyka and Doug Hesse to Multilingual Writers

The process of learning to write English is like learning to play a musical instrument. Few people can play fluently without first making many errors. To advance more quickly, start by thinking about school writing in your first language. Recall how you were taught to present ideas in your written native language, especially when explaining information, giving specific details, and arguing logically about a topic. Then compare it to how writing American English works. Making yourself aware of the differences will help you learn English strategies more easily.

Most college essays and research papers in the United States are direct in tone and straightforward in structure. Typically, the THESIS STATEMENT* (the central message of the piece of writing) is at the end of the first paragraph or, in a longer piece of writing, in the second paragraph. Each paragraph that follows relates in content directly to the essay's thesis statement. In addition, each paragraph after the thesis statement needs to begin with a TOPIC SENTENCE that contains the main point of the paragraph, and then the rest of the paragraph supports the point made in the topic sentence. This support consists of RENNS (11d) that provide specific details. The final paragraph brings the content to a logical conclusion that grows out of what has come before.

Always honor your culture's writing traditions and structures, for they reflect the richness of your heritage. At the same time, try to adapt to and practice the ACADEMIC WRITING style characteristic of the United States. The *American Heritage English as a Second Language Dictionary*, which is available in paperback and hardback, can ease your way with English words and expressions. If your college library doesn't own a copy, you're permitted to ask your professor to request that the Reference Librarian purchase a few copies for students to consult.

The sixth edition of *Quick Access* offers three special features that we've designed specifically for you as a multilingual learner. Chapters 69 through 74 focus on the most challenging grammar issues that you face as you learn to write English. In other chapters throughout the book, especially Chapters 22, 28, 31, 41, and 42, "ESOL Tips" offer you more helpful hints about possible cultural references and grammar issues. Finally, our Web site at www.prenhall.com/troyka provides an "English Errors Transferred from Other Languages" chart. In this chart, you'll find information about trouble spots that commonly occur when speakers of certain first languages (Spanish, Russian, and so on) speak, read, or write in English.

As individuals, we as writing teachers greatly enjoy discovering the rich variations in the writing traditions of our students from many cultures of the

---

*Words printed in SMALL CAPITAL LETTERS are discussed elsewhere in the text and are defined in the Terms Glossary at the back of the book.

world. As US teachers, however, our responsibilities call for us to explain what you need to do as writers in the United States. If you were in one of our classes, we would say "Welcome!" and ask you to teach us about writing in your native language. Using that knowledge, we then would respectfully teach you the US approach to writing so that we could do our best to help you succeed as a writer and learner in a US college.

Lynn Quitman Troyka
Doug Hesse

69

Singulars and Plurals

69a What are count and noncount nouns?

Count nouns represent items that can be counted: *radio, fingernail, street, idea.* **Noncount nouns** represent things that cannot be counted: *knowledge, rain, traffic.*

Count nouns can be SINGULAR (*radio, street*) or PLURAL (*radios, streets*), so they may be singular or plural VERBS. Noncount nouns (see Quick Reference 69.1) are used in singular form only, so they use only singular verbs.

🚫 **Alert:** If you're not sure whether a noun is count or noncount, look it up in a learner's dictionary such as the *American Heritage English as a Second Language Dictionary.* ●

Some nouns can be count or noncount, depending on their meaning in a sentence. Most of these nouns represent things that can be meant either individually or as "wholes" made up of individual parts (see Quick Reference 69.1).

> COUNT **Two hairs** were on his collar. [individual, countable hairs]
>
> NONCOUNT **His hair** was cut very short. [all the hairs on his head considered together]

When EDITING your writing, make sure you haven't added the plural *-s* ending to any noncount nouns, which are always singular in form.

🚫 **Alert:** Use a singular verb with any noncount noun that functions as a SUBJECT in a CLAUSE. ●

Quick Reference 69.1 ■ ■ ■ ■ ■ ■ ■

Uncountable items represented by noncount nouns

- Groups of similar items making up "wholes": *clothing, equipment, furniture, luggage, mail, money*
- Abstractions: *equality, fun, health, ignorance, knowledge, peace, respect*
- Liquids: *blood, coffee, gasoline, water*
- Gases: *air, helium, oxygen, smog, smoke, steam*
- Materials: *aluminum, cloth, cotton, ice, wood*
- Food: *beef, bread, butter, macaroni, meat, cheese*
- Collections of particles or grains: *dirt, dust, hair, rice, salt, wheat*
- Languages: *Arabic, Chinese, Japanese, Spanish*
- Fields of study: *biology, computer science, history, physics, literature, math*
- Natural phenomena: *electricity, heat, moonlight, sunshine, thunder*

69b Which determiners should I use with singular and plural nouns?

DETERMINERS, including expressions of quantity, are used to tell *which, how much,* or *how many* about NOUNS. You choose the correct determiner to use with a noun depending on whether the noun is noncount or count. For count nouns, you also need to decide whether the noun is singular or plural (see Quick Reference 69.2 on p. 480).

🛑 **Alerts:** (1) *Many, most,* and *some* require *of the* before a noun that is specific but not before a noun that is a generalization.

> **Most** supervisors are well qualified. [general]
> **Most of the** supervisors **here** are well qualified. [specific]

(2) The phrases *a few* and *a little* convey the meaning "some": *I have **a few** rare books* means "I have *some* rare books." *They are worth **a little** money* means "They are worth *some* money." Without the word *a*, the meaning of *few* and *little* is "almost none": *I have **few** [or **very few**] books* means "I have *almost no* books." *They are worth [**very**] **little** money* means "They are worth *almost no* money."

(3) A phrase with *one of the* always has a plural noun as the OBJECT of the PREPOSITION *of.* The verb agrees with *one,* not with the plural noun, so it is always singular: *One of the most important inventions of the twentieth century **is** [not **are**] television* (43g). ●

| Quick Reference 69.2 | ■ ■ ■ ■ ■ ■ ■ |

Using determiners with count and noncount nouns

GROUP 1: DETERMINERS FOR SINGULAR COUNT NOUNS

With singular count nouns, use any of the determiners on the left.

a, an, the	**a** house, **an** egg; **the** house, **the** egg
one, any, some, every, each, either,	**any** book; **each** person;
neither, another, the other	**another** year
my, our, your, his, her, its, their,	**your** father; **its** cover;
nouns with *'s* or *s'*	**Connie's** car
this, that	**this** week; **that** desk
one, no, the first, the second,	**one** example; **no** reason;
and so on	**the fifth** chair

GROUP 2: DETERMINERS FOR PLURAL COUNT NOUNS

All of the following determiners can be used with plural count nouns. Plural count nouns can also be used without determiners (70b).

the	**the** bicycles; **the** rooms; **the** ideas
some, any, both, many, most, few,	**some** people; **many** jobs;
fewer, the fewest, a number of,	**all** managers
other, several, all, all the, a lot of	
my, our, your, his, her, its, their,	**our** coats; **her** books;
nouns with *'s* or *s'*	**students'** grades
these, those	**these** days; **those** computers
no; two, three, four, and so on;	**no** exceptions; **four** students;
the first, the second, the third,	**the first** month
and so on	

GROUP 3: DETERMINERS FOR NONCOUNT NOUNS

All of the following determiners can be used with noncount nouns (which are always singular). Noncount nouns can also be used without determiners (70b).

the	**the** rice; **the** electricity
some, any, much, more, most, other,	**enough** snow; **a lot of** equipment;
the other, little, less, the least,	**more** food
enough, all, all the, a lot of	
my, our, your, his, her, its, their,	**their** fame; **India's** heat;
nouns with *'s* or *s'*	**your** leadership
this, that	**this** sugar; **that** fog
no, the first, the second, the best,	**no** smoking; **the first** rainfall;
and so on	**the best** vocabulary

69c What forms are correct for nouns used as adjectives?

Some words that function as nouns can also function as ADJECTIVES. In English, adjectives don't have plural forms. If you use a noun as an adjective, don't add *-s* or *-es* to the adjective, even when the noun or PRONOUN it modifies is plural.

> Many Americans students are basketball fans.
>
> My nephew likes to look at pictures books.

For more help with your
writing, grammar, and research,
go to **www.mycomplab.com**

70

Articles

The words *a, an,* and *the* are **articles**. Articles are one type of DETERMINER. They signal that a NOUN will follow and that any MODIFIERS between the article and the noun refer to that noun (see Quick Reference 70.1 on p. 482).

> **a** chair, **the** computer

70a How should I use articles with singular count nouns?

When you use a singular COUNT NOUN (see Quick Reference 70.2 on p. 483), you need to use a determiner, as shown for Group 1 in Quick Reference 69.2. If you have to choose between *a, an,* and *the,* decide whether the noun is specific or nonspecific. A noun is specific when a reader can understand from the context exactly and specifically what the noun is referring to. Quick Reference 70.2 can help you decide when a singular count noun is specific and therefore requires *the.*

⚠ **Alerts:** (1) One common exception affects rule 3 in Quick Reference 70.2. A noun may still require *a* or *an* after the first use if one or more descriptive adjectives come between the article and the noun: *I bought a sweater today. It was a* [not *the*] ***red*** *sweater.*

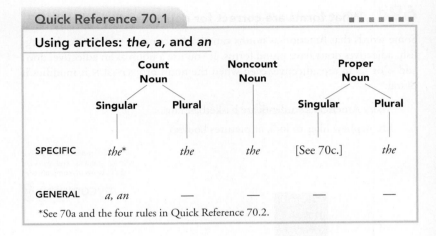

Quick Reference 70.1

Using articles: *the*, *a*, and *an*

	Count Noun		Noncount Noun	Proper Noun	
	Singular	Plural	Singular	Singular	Plural
SPECIFIC	*the**	*the*	*the*	[See 70c.]	*the*
GENERAL	*a, an*	—	—	—	—

*See 70a and the four rules in Quick Reference 70.2.

(2) *An* is used before words that begin with a vowel sound; *a* is used before words that begin with a consonant sound. Sound, not spelling, is the key. Words that begin with *h* or *u* can have either a vowel or a consonant sound; check your dictionary. Choose *a* or *an* based on the sound of the first word after the article, even if that word is not the noun.

> **an** idea, **a** good idea
> **an** umbrella, **a** useless umbrella
> **an** honor, **a** history book ●

70b How should I use articles with count and noncount nouns?

Like singular count nouns, plural count nouns and NONCOUNT NOUNS that are *specific* usually use *the* according to the rules in Quick Reference 70.2 (p. 483). When a noun has a *general* meaning, it usually does not use *the*.

■ Using articles with plural count nouns

> Geraldo planted tulips and roses this year. **The** tulips will bloom in April.

The plural count noun *tulips* is used in a general sense in the first sentence, without *the*. Therefore, the second sentence refers to them specifically as ***the** tulips*. This example is related to rule 3 in Quick Reference 70.2.

Quick Reference 70.2

Using *the* with singular count nouns

RULE 1

A noun is specific and requires *the* when it names something either unique or commonly known.

> **The** sun has risen above **the** horizon. [Because only one *sun* and one *horizon* exist, they are specific nouns.]

RULE 2

A noun is specific and requires *the* when it names something used in a representative or abstract sense.

> Benjamin Franklin favored **the** turkey as **the** national bird of the United States. [Because *turkey* and *national bird* are representative references rather than references to a particular turkey or bird, they are specific nouns in this context.]

RULE 3

A noun is specific and requires *the* when it names something that is defined elsewhere in the same sentence or in an earlier sentence.

> **The** ship *Savannah* was the first steam vessel to cross **the** Atlantic Ocean. [*Savannah* names a specific ship, and *Atlantic Ocean* identifies a specific ocean.]

> **The** carpet in my bedroom is new. [*In my bedroom* defines exactly which carpet is meant, so *carpet* is a specific noun in this context.]

> I have a computer and a fax machine in my office. **The** computer is often broken. [*Computer* is introduced in the first sentence, so it uses *a*. *Computer* has been made specific by the first sentence, so the second sentence uses *the* to refer to the same noun.]

RULE 4

A noun is specific and requires *the* when it represents something that can be inferred from the context.

> **I need an expert to fix the problem.** [If you read this sentence after the example about a computer in Rule 3, you understand that *problem* refers to the broken computer, and so *problem* is specific in this context. Here the word *the* is similar to the word *this*.]

■ Using articles with noncount nouns

Kalinda served rice and chicken to us. She flavored **the** rice with curry.

Rice is a noncount noun. By the second sentence, *rice* has become specific, so *the* is used. This example is related to rule 3 in Quick Reference 70.2.

■ Generalizing with plural and noncount nouns

Omit *the* in generalizations using plural or noncount nouns.

T
~~The~~ tulips are the flowers that grow from the bulbs.
^

Compare this sentence to a generalization with a singular count noun.

A tulip is **a** flower that grows from **a** bulb.

70c How should I use *the* with proper nouns?

Proper nouns represent specific people, places, or things. Most proper nouns do not require articles: *We visited Lake Mead* [not **the** *Lake Mead*] *with Asha and Larry.* However, certain types of proper nouns do require *the.*

> Nouns with the pattern *the . . . of . . .* : *the United States of America, the president of Mexico* [not the Mexico]
>
> Plural proper nouns: *the Johnsons, the Chicago Bulls, the United Arab Emirates*
>
> Collective proper nouns (nouns that name a group): *the Society of Friends, the AFL-CIO*
>
> Some, but not all, geographical features: *the Amazon, the Gobi Desert, the Indian Ocean*

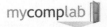

71

Word Order

71a What are standard and inverted word orders?

Standard word order is the most common sentence pattern in English. The SUBJECT comes before the VERB: *That book* [subject] *was* [verb] *heavy.*

Inverted word order, with a verb coming before the subject, is common for DIRECT QUESTIONS in English: *Was* [verb] *that book* [subject] *heavy? Were* [verb] *you* [subject] *close to it when it fell?*

A common way to form questions with MAIN VERBS other than *be* is to use inverted order with a form of the verb *do* as an AUXILIARY VERB before the subject and the SIMPLE FORM of the main verb after the subject: ***Do you want*** *me to put the book away?*

Use *do* with inverted order when a question begins with a question-forming word such as *what, why, when, where,* or *how:* ***Where does*** *the* **book** *belong?*

When a question has more than one auxiliary verb, put the subject after the first auxiliary verb: ***Would you*** *have replaced the book?*

🛑 **Alert:** Do not use inverted word order with INDIRECT QUESTIONS: *She asked where I saw the book* [not She asked where did I see the book]. ●

Verb-subject word order is also required by certain ADVERBS at the beginning of a sentence.

Only once **did she** ask my advice.

Never **have I** seen such a mess!

Verb-subject word order rules also apply to emphatic exclamations: ***Was*** *that* **book** *heavy!* ***Did she*** *ever enjoy that book!* (For advice about using word order to create emphasis in declarative sentences, see 71c.)

71b Where should I place adjectives?

In English, an ADJECTIVE ordinarily comes directly before the NOUN it modifies. Quick Reference 71.1 shows the most common order for positioning several adjectives that modify the same noun.

Quick Reference 71.1

Word order for adjectives

1. Determiner, if any: *a, an, the, my, your, Jan's, these,* and so on
2. Expressions of order, including ordinal numbers, if any: *first, second, next, last, final,* and so on
3. Expressions of quantity, including cardinal numbers, if any: *one, two, few, each, every, some,* and so on
4. Adjectives of judgment or opinion, if any: *smart, happy, interesting, sad, boring,* and so on
5. Adjectives of size or shape, if any: *big, small, short, round, rectangular,* and so on
6. Adjectives of age or condition, if any: *new, young, broken, dirty, shiny,* and so on
7. Adjectives of color, if any: *red, green, beige, turquoise,* and so on
8. Adjectives that can also be used as nouns, if any: *French, metal, Protestant, cotton,* and so on
9. The noun

1	2	3	4	5	6	7	8	9
A		few		tiny		red		ants
The	last	six					Thai	drums
My			fine		old		oak	table

71c Where should I place adverbs?

ADVERBS and adverbial PHRASES modify verbs, adjectives, other adverbs, or whole sentences. They can go in three different places in a CLAUSE: first, middle, or last. ("Middle" usually means just after the auxiliary verb, if any.) See Quick Reference 71.2.

🛈 **Alert:** If a sentence begins with a negative adverb of frequency (*never, rarely, only once, seldom*), the subject-verb word order must be inverted (71a). This creates emphasis.

Never has Nick been bitten by a dog. ●

Quick Reference 71.2

■ ■ ■ ■ ■ ■ ■

Types and positions of adverbs

ADVERBS OF MANNER
Describe how something is done. Usual position: middle or last.

> Nick **carefully** groomed the dog.

> Nick groomed the dog **carefully**.

ADVERBS OF TIME
Describe when an event occurs or how long it lasts. Usual position: first or last.

> **First,** Nick shampooed the dog.

> Nick shampooed the dog **first**.

ADVERBS OF FREQUENCY
Describe how often an event takes place. Usual position: middle to modify a verb, first to modify an entire sentence.

> Nick has **never** been bitten by a dog.

> **Occasionally,** Nick is scratched while shampooing a cat.

ADVERBS OF DEGREE OR EMPHASIS
Indicate *how much* or *to what extent* about other modifiers. Usual position: directly before the word they modify.

> Nick is **rather** quiet around animals.

> Nick wears protection **only** when examining an exotic pet. [See 49a on the placement of *only*.]

SENTENCE ADVERBS
Modify an entire sentence. They include transitional words and expressions, as well as such words as *maybe, probably, possibly, fortunately,* and *incredibly.* Usual position: first.

> **Incredibly,** Nick was once asked to groom a squirrel.

72

Prepositions

Prepositions and their OBJECTS form PREPOSITIONAL PHRASES. Such phrases often describe relationships in time or space. When prepositions are combined with certain VERBS, they are called **phrasal verbs** (72b). In some cases, phrasal verbs take on idiomatic meanings. A dictionary such as the *Longman Dictionary of Contemporary English* or the *Oxford Advanced Learner's Dictionary* is especially helpful for finding the correct preposition for certain idioms.

72a How should I use *in*, *at*, and *on* to show time and place?

To Show Time

- *in* a year or a month (*during* is also correct but less common): *in 1999, in May*
- *in* a period of time: *in a few months* (*seconds, days, years*)
- *in* a period of a day: *in the morning* (*afternoon, evening*), *in the daytime* but *at night*
- *on* a specific day: *on Friday, on my birthday, on May 12*
- *at* a specific time or period: *at noon, at 2:00, at dawn, at nightfall, at takeoff* (the time a plane leaves), *at breakfast* (the time a specific meal takes place)

To Show Place

- *in* a location surrounded by something else: *in the province of Alberta, in Utah, in downtown Bombay, in my apartment*
- *at* a specific location: *at your house, at the corner of Third Avenue and Main Street, at 376 Oak Street, at home*
- *on* a street: *on Oak Street, on Third Avenue, on the road*

72b How should I use prepositions in phrasal verbs?

Phrasal verbs are verbs that combine with prepositions to deliver their meaning. The meaning of many phrasal verbs is idiomatic, not literal; *pick on*, for example, means "annoy" or "tease" rather than anything associated with either *pick* or *on*. Also, many phrasal verbs are informal and are therefore more appropriate for conversation than for ACADEMIC WRITING. For a research paper, for example, *propose* or *suggest* is a better choice than *come up with*.

In some phrasal verbs, the verb and the preposition must always stay together, without being separated by other words: ***Look at*** *the moon* [not ***Look*** *the moon* ***at***].

In other phrasal verbs, called *separable phrasal verbs,* words can separate the verb and the preposition without interfering with meaning: *I **threw away** my homework* [or *I **threw** my homework **away**].

When a separable phrasal verb has a PRONOUN object, that object should be positioned between the verb and the preposition: *I **threw** it **away*** [not *I **threw away** it*]. Object PHRASES or CLAUSES with more than four or five words are usually positioned after the preposition: *I **threw away** the homework that was assigned last week.*

Here's a list of some common phrasal verbs. The ones that can't be separated are marked with an asterisk (*).

SELECTED PHRASAL VERBS

ask out	get along with*	look into*
break down	get back	look out for*
call back	get off*	look over
call off	go over*	make up
drop off	hand in	run across*
figure out	keep up with*	speak to*
fill out	leave out	speak with*
fill up	look after*	throw out
find out	look around*	turn down

72c How should I use prepositions with the passive voice?

VERBS used in the PASSIVE VOICE usually follow the pattern *be* + PAST PARTICIPLE + *by: The child **was frightened by** a snake.* However, many passive constructions require other prepositions instead of *by: The child **is afraid of** snakes.* Here's a list of some of these passive expressions with their prepositions. Look in a dictionary for others. (See 73a on using GERUNDS after some of these expressions.)

SELECTED VERBS AND PREPOSITIONS USED IN PASSIVE CONSTRUCTIONS

be accustomed to	be interested in
be acquainted with	be known for
be composed of	be located in
be concerned about	be made of (*or* from)
be disappointed with (*or* in)	be married to
be discriminated against	be prepared for
be done with	be satisfied with
be excited about	be tired of (*or* from)
be finished with	be worried about

72d How should I use prepositions in expressions?

Different prepositions convey great differences in meaning in many common expressions. For example, with the verb *agree,* four different prepositions create different meanings: *agree **to**, agree **about**, agree **on**,* and *agree **with**.* Check a dictionary if you're unsure of the precise differences.

Many adjectives also require certain prepositions: *afraid of, familiar with, famous for, friendly toward* (or *with*), *guilty of, patient with, proud of.*

For more help with your
writing, grammar, and research,
go to **www.mycomplab.com**

73

Gerunds and Infinitives

GERUNDS and INFINITIVES are types of verbals. **Verbals** are VERB forms that function as NOUNS or MODIFIERS. Like all nouns, gerunds and infinitives can be DIRECT OBJECTS. Some verbs call for gerund objects to follow them; other verbs must be followed by infinitive objects. Still other verbs can be followed by either gerund or infinitive objects. A few verbs change meaning depending on whether a gerund object or an infinitive object is used.

73a What verbs use a gerund, not an infinitive, object?

Certain VERBS cannot be followed by infinitives as direct objects; they require gerunds: *Yuri considered **calling** [not to call] the mayor.*

VERBS THAT USE GERUND OBJECTS

acknowledge	consist of	enjoy
admit	contemplate	escape
advise	defer from	evade
anticipate	delay	favor
appreciate	deny	finish
avoid	detest	give up
cannot help	discuss	have trouble
complain about	dislike	imagine
consider	dream about	include

insist on	practice	resist
keep (on)	put off	risk
mention	quit	suggest
mind	recall	talk about
object to	recommend	tolerate
postpone	resent	understand

■ Using a gerund after *go*

Although *go* is usually followed by an infinitive object (*We can **go to see*** [not *go seeing*] *a movie*), *go* is followed by a gerund in such phrases as *go swimming, go fishing, go shopping,* and *go driving: I will **go swimming*** [not *go to swim*] *tomorrow.*

■ Using gerunds after *be* + complement + preposition

A COMPLEMENT often follows a form of *be*. Some complements require certain PREPOSITIONS (72c).

SELECTED *BE* + COMPLEMENT + PREPOSITION EXPRESSIONS

be (get) accustomed to	be capable of
be angry about	be committed to
be bored with	be concerned about
be excited about	be tired of (*or* from)
be interested in	be (get) used to
be prepared for	be worried about
be responsible for	

> We are excited about **voting** [not to vote] in the election.
>
> They were interested in **hearing** [not to hear] the candidates' debate.

🛑 **Alert:** Always use a gerund, not an infinitive, as the object of a preposition. Be especially careful when the word *to* is functioning as a preposition in a PHRASAL VERB (72b): *We are committed to **saving*** [not *committed to save*] *the elephants.* ●

73b   What verbs use an infinitive, not a gerund, object?

Certain verbs cannot be followed by gerunds as direct objects; they can be followed by infinitives: *Three people decided **to question*** [not *decided questioning*] *the speaker.*

VERBS THAT USE INFINITIVE OBJECTS

afford to	demand to	plan to
agree to	deserve to	prepare to
aim to	expect to	pretend to
appear to	fail to	promise to
arrange to	give permission to	refuse to
ask to	hesitate to	seem to
attempt to	hope to	struggle to
be able (unable) to	intend to	tend to
be left to	know how to	threaten to
beg to	learn to	try to
care to	like to	volunteer to
claim to	manage to	wait to
consent to	mean to	want to
decide to	offer to	would like to
decline to		

■ **Using infinitives after *be* + some complements**

We are eager **to go** [*not* going] to the mountains.

I am ready **to sleep** [*not* sleeping] in a tent.

■ **Using unmarked infinitive objects**

Be careful not to overuse the word *to* in an **unmarked infinitive**, which is a verb in its SIMPLE FORM without the word *to*. Common verbs followed by unmarked infinitives are *feel, have, hear, let, listen to, look at, make* (meaning "compel"), *notice, see,* and *watch*. In the following examples, the first shows *take* as an unmarked infinitive, while the second shows *take* as a marked infinitive.

Please **let** me **take** [*not* to take] you to lunch. [*Take* is an unmarked infinitive because it's used after *let*.]

I want **to take** you to lunch. [*To take* is a marked infinitive because it's used after *want*.]

73c How does meaning change if an infinitive object or a gerund follows *stop, remember,* or *forget*?

Here are some examples of what happens when a verb is followed by either a gerund or an infinitive. Followed by a gerund, *stop* means "finish, quit": *We stopped eating* means "We finished our meal." However, followed by an infinitive, *stop* means "stop or interrupt one activity to begin another": *We stopped to eat* means "We stopped doing something [such as driving or painting the house] to eat."

Followed by a gerund, *remember* means "recall a memory": *I remember talking to you last night.* However, followed by an infinitive, *remember* means "not to forget to do something": *I must remember to talk with Isa.*

Followed by a gerund, *forget* means "do something and not recall it": *I forget having put my keys in the refrigerator.* However, followed by an infinitive, *forget* means "not do something": *If you forget to put a stamp on that letter, it will be returned.*

73d Do sense verbs change meaning with a gerund or an infinitive object?

Sense verbs such as *see, notice, hear, observe, watch, feel, listen to,* and *look at* usually don't change meaning whether a gerund or an infinitive is used as an object. *I saw the water rising* and *I saw the water rise* (unmarked infinitive—see 73b) both deliver the same message.

73e How should I choose between *-ing* and *-ed* forms of adjectives?

Deciding whether to use the *-ing* form (PRESENT PARTICIPLE) or the *-ed* form (PAST PARTICIPLE of a REGULAR VERB) as an ADJECTIVE in a specific sentence can be difficult. For example, *I am amused* and *I am amusing* are both correct in English, but their meanings are very different.

I am amused at the circus. [I experience amusement.]

I am amusing at the circus. [I cause the amusement of other people.]

To make the right choice, decide whether the modified NOUN or PRONOUN is causing or experiencing what the participle describes.

Use a present participle (*-ing*) to modify a noun or pronoun that is the cause of the action. This meaning is in the ACTIVE VOICE.

Mica explained your **interesting** plan. [The noun *plan* caused interest, so *interesting* is correct.]

I find your plan **exciting**. [The noun *plan* causes excitement, so *exciting* is correct.]

Use a past participle (*-ed* on regular verbs) to modify a noun or pronoun that experiences or receives whatever the MODIFIER describes. This meaning is in the PASSIVE VOICE.

An **interested** committee wants to hear your plan. [The noun *committee* experiences interest, so *interested* is correct.]

Excited by your plan, I called a board meeting. [The pronoun *I* experiences excitement, so *excited* is correct.]

Here's a list of some frequently used participles that can be used as adjectives. To choose the right form, decide whether the noun or pronoun *experiences* or *causes* what the participle describes.

annoyed, annoying   frightened, frightening
appalled, appalling   insulted, insulting
bored, boring   offended, offending
confused, confusing   pleased, pleasing
depressed, depressing   reassured, reassuring
disgusted, disgusting   satisfied, satisfying
fascinated, fascinating   shocked, shocking

For more help with your
writing, grammar, and research,
go to www.mycomplab.com

74

Modal Auxiliary Verbs

Modal auxiliary verbs convey meaning about ability, necessity, advice, possibility, and other conditions. These verbs include *can, could, had better, may, might, must, should, ought, will,* and *would.* Like the auxiliary verbs *be, do,* and *have,* modal auxiliary verbs help MAIN VERBS convey more information than those verbs can alone.

74a How do modal auxiliary verbs differ from *be, do,* and *have?*

Modal auxiliary verbs are always followed by the SIMPLE FORM of a main verb: *I* **might go** *tomorrow.*

One-word modal auxiliary verbs usually do not have an *-s* ending in the third-person singular: *She* **could** *go with me, you* **could** *go with me,* and *they* **could** *go with me.*

Two modals that have forms that end in *-s* are *have to* and *need to* in the third-person singular: *She* **has** *to stay; he* **needs** *to smile more.*

74b Which modal auxiliary verbs express ability, necessity, advisability, or probability?

■ Expressing ability

The modal auxiliary verb *can* means "ability in the present." The modal auxiliary verb *could* sometimes means "ability in the past." These words deliver the meaning of "able to."

> You **can work** late tonight. [This means "You are able to work late tonight."]
>
> I **could play** the piano when I was younger. [This means "I was able to play the piano when I was younger."]

The modal auxiliary verb *could* often expresses some condition that is required to be fulfilled before another condition.

> If you **could** come early, we can start on time. [This means "We can't start on time unless you come early."]
>
> I **could** have gone to bed at 10:00 if I had finished my homework. [This means "I couldn't go to bed at 10:00 because I had not finished my homework."]

Adding *not* between a modal auxiliary verb and the main verb makes the sentence negative: *I could **not** work late last night.*

■ Expressing necessity

The modal auxiliary verbs *must, have to,* and *need to* express a requirement to do something. *Must* implies only future action. *Have to* and *need to* imply action in all verb tenses.

> You **must leave** before midnight. She **has to leave** when I leave.
>
> We **needed to be** with you last night. You **will need to be** here before dark tonight.

■ Expressing advice or the notion of a good idea

The modal auxiliary verbs *should* and *ought to* mean that doing the action of the main verb in the present or future is a good idea. The PAST-TENSE FORMS are *should have* and *ought to have;* they are followed by the PAST PARTICIPLE.

> You **should call** your dentist tomorrow. I **ought to have** gone to my dentist last week.

The modal *had better* expresses the meaning of good advice or warning or threat.

> You **had better see** a doctor before your cough gets worse.

■ Expressing probability

The modal auxiliary verbs *may, might, could,* and *must* usually express probability, possibility, or likelihood.

> We **might** see a tiger in the zoo. We **could** go this afternoon.

The past-tense forms for the modal auxiliary verbs *may, might, could,* and *must* add *have* and the main verb's past participle to the modals.

> I'm hungry; I **must have neglected** to eat breakfast.

74c Which modal auxiliary verbs express preference, plan, or past habit?

■ Expressing preferences

Would rather (present tense) and *would rather have* (past tense) express a preference. In the past tense, the modal is also followed by a past participle.

> We **would rather see** a comedy than a mystery. We **would rather have seen** a movie last night.

■ Expressing a plan or obligation

A form of *be* followed by *supposed to* and the simple form of a main verb, in both present and past tense, delivers a meaning of something planned or an obligation.

> I **was supposed to meet** them at the bus stop.

The word *supposed* may be omitted with no change in meaning.

> I **was to meet** them at the bus stop.

■ Expressing past habit

The modal auxiliary verbs *used to* and *would* mean that something happened repeatedly in a time that has passed.

> I **used to hate** getting a flu shot. I **would dread** the injection for weeks beforehand.

! **Alert:** Both the modal auxiliary verbs *used to* and *would* can be used for repeated actions in the past, but the modal auxiliary verb *would* cannot be used for a situation that lasted for a period of time in the past.

used to
I ~~would~~ live in Arizona. ●
^

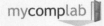

QA TERMS GLOSSARY

Words printed in SMALL CAPITAL LETTERS in your *Quick Access Reference for Writers* indicate important terms that are defined in this glossary. The parenthetical references with each definition tell you the handbook sections where each term is most fully discussed. If you can't find a term's definition in this glossary, look for the term in the Index.

absolute phrase A phrase containing a subject and a participle that modifies an entire sentence: *The semester* [subject] *being* [present participle of *be*] *over, the campus looks deserted.* (41m)

abstract noun A noun that names things not knowable through the five senses: *idea, respect.* (41a)

academic writing The writing people do for college courses and for scholarship published in print and in online journals. (8b)

action verb A verb that describes an action or occurrence done by or to the subject. (50e)

active reading Annotating reading material to make connections between prior knowledge and the author's ideas.

active voice An attribute of verbs showing that the verb's action or the condition expressed is done by the subject. The *active voice* stands in contrast with the *passive voice*, which conveys that the action or condition of the verb is done *to* the subject. (42g)

adjective A word that describes or limits (modifies) a noun, a pronoun, or a word group functioning as a noun: *silly* joke, *three* trumpets. (41e, Ch. 45)

adjective clause A dependent clause also known as a *relative clause.* An adjective clause modifies a noun or pronoun that comes before it, and it begins with a relative word (such as *who, which, that,* or *where*) that ties the clause to the noun or pronoun it modifies. Also see *clause.* (41n)

adverb A word that describes or limits (modifies) verbs, adjectives, other adverbs, phrases, or clauses: *loudly, very, nevertheless, there.* (41f, 45a)

adverb clause A dependent clause beginning with a subordinating conjunction that establishes the relationship in meaning between the adverb clause and its independent clause. An adverb clause modifies the independent clause's verb or the entire independent clause. Also see *clause, conjunction.* (41n)

agreement The concept of matching number and person between a subject and verb (Ch. 43) and between a pronoun and its antecedent (44a–44e). A pronoun that expresses gender must match its antecedent in gender. (Ch. 55)

analogy An explanation of the unfamiliar in terms of the familiar, often comparing things not usually associated with each other. Analogy is a rhetorical strategy that can be used for developing a paragraph (11f) or in sentences. Unlike a simile, which uses *like* or *as* in making a comparison, an analogy does not use such words. (54e)

analysis A process of critical thinking that divides a whole into its component parts in order to understand how the parts interrelate. Sometimes called *division,* analysis is a rhetorical strategy that can be used for developing paragraphs. (11f)

annotated bibliography Bibliography in which listed sources are accompanied by summaries or comments. (28f)

annotating Writing brief summaries or comments about a text, perhaps in the margins, on a separate page, or in a computer file. (2c)

antecedent The noun or pronoun to which a pronoun refers. (Ch. 44)

antonym A word opposite in meaning to another word.

APA style *APA* is the abbreviation for the American Psychological Association. APA style specifies the format and the form of citation and documentation used in source-based papers in many academic disciplines, especially psychology and most other social sciences. (Chs. 36–38)

appositive A word or group of words that renames the noun or noun phrase coming immediately before or after it: *my favorite month, **October***. (41l)

argument In writing, an attempt using rhetorical strategies to convince others to agree with a position about a topic open to debate. (Ch. 13)

articles Also called *determiners* or *noun markers,* articles are the words *a, an,* and *the. A* and *an* are indefinite articles; *the* is a definite article. Also see *determiner.* (Ch. 70)

assertion A sentence that makes a statement and expresses a point of view about a topic. Often used by writers in the process of developing a thesis statement. (8g)

audience The readers to whom a written document is primarily directed. (1c, 8c)

auxiliary verb Also known as a *helping verb,* an auxiliary verb is a form of *be, do, have,* or one of the modal verbs. It combines with a main verb to express tense, mood, and voice. Also see *modal auxiliary verbs.* (42c)

balanced sentences Sentences consisting of two short independent clauses that serve to compare or contrast. (52d)

bias Material that is slanted toward beliefs or attitudes and away from facts or evidence. (2b)

bibliographic note system Documentation system used by the *Chicago Manual of Style.* (39a)

bibliography A list of sources with their authorial and publication facts. (28e, 29e)

blog Shortened form of "Web log," an online journal usually updated on a fairly regular basis. (26a)

body paragraph Any of the paragraphs in an essay or other document that come between the introductory and concluding paragraphs. (11f)

book catalog Database that lists all books and bound volumes owned by a particular library. (29c)

Boolean expressions Words such as *AND, OR,* and *NOT* that researchers can use in a search engine to create keyword combinations that narrow and refine their searches. (29b)

brainstorming Listing all ideas that come to mind on a topic, and then grouping the ideas by whatever patterns emerge. (8f)

browser Software that allows people to connect to the Internet. Common examples are Microsoft Internet Explorer and Mozilla Firefox.

call number Identification number, usually according to the Dewey Decimal System, used to store and retrieve an individual book or other library material. (29c)

case The form of a noun or pronoun that shows whether it's functioning as a subject, an object, or a possessive in a particular context. In modern English, nouns change form in the possessive case only (*city* is the form for the subjective and objective cases; *city's* is the form for the possessive case). Also see *pronoun case.* (44j–44s, 60a)

case study Research that relies on the careful, detailed analysis of one person or a small group of people. (17b)

catalog Also called a *card catalog,* an extensive and methodically organized list of all books and other bound volumes in a library. Often today, a library catalog is digitized and available on a private computer system within the library and/or to students or other group members who may pay a fee for on-line access. (29a)

cause and effect The relationship between outcomes (effects) and the reasons for them (causes). Cause-and-effect analysis is one rhetorical strategy for developing paragraphs. (11f)

chronological order Also called *time order,* it is an arrangement of information sequenced according to time. Chronological order is one organizing strategy for paragraphs and longer pieces of writing. (11f)

citation Information that identifies a source referred to in a piece of writing. Also see *documentation.* (Chs. 33 and 36)

civic writing Writing done to influence public opinion or to advance causes for the public good. (8b)

claim States an issue and then takes a position on a debatable topic related to the issue. A claim is supported with evidence and reasons, moving from broad reasons to specific data and details. (13a)

classical argument An argument with a structure consisting of introduction, thesis statement, background, evidence and reasoning, response to opposing views, and conclusion. (13g)

classification A rhetorical strategy that organizes information by grouping items according to their underlying shared characteristics. (11f)

clause A group of words containing a subject and a predicate. A clause that delivers full meaning is called an *independent* (or *main) clause.* A clause that lacks full meaning by itself is called a *dependent* (or *subordinate) clause.* Also see *adjective clause, adverb clause, nonrestrictive element, noun clause, restrictive element.* (41n)

cliché An overused, worn-out phrase that has lost its capacity to communicate effectively: *soft as a kitten, lived to a ripe old age.* (54f)

climactic order Sometimes called *emphatic order,* it is an arrangement of ideas or information that moves from least important to most important. (11f)

clip art Digital artwork, often cartoon-like in appearance, that can be digitally incorporated into a variety of computer documents. (24e)

close reading The practice of reading carefully, analytically, and critically. (2c)

clustering Also called *mapping,* it is an invention technique based on thinking visually about a topic and drawing attached balloons for its increasingly specific subdivisions. (8f)

CM style *CM* is the abbreviation for *Chicago Manual* style, a form of citation and documentation used in many academic disciplines, including history and the arts. (Ch. 39)

coherence The written or spoken progression from one idea to another using transitional expressions, pronouns, selective repetition, and/or parallelism to make connections between ideas explicit. (11e)

collective noun A noun that names a group of people or things: *family, committee.* (43h)

colloquial language Casual or conversational language. (54d)

comma splice Sometimes called a *comma fault,* it is the error that occurs when a comma alone connects two independent clauses. (Ch. 47)

common noun A noun that names a general group, place, person, or thing: *dog, house.* (41a)

comparative form The form of a descriptive adjective or adverb that expresses a different degree of intensity between two things: *bluer, less blue; more easily, less easily.* Also see *positive, superlative.* (45d)

comparison and contrast A rhetorical strategy for organizing and developing paragraphs by discussing a subject's similarities (by comparing them) and differences (by contrasting them). (11f)

complement A grammatical element after a verb that completes the predicate, such as a direct object after an action verb or a noun or adjective after a linking verb. Also see *object complement, subject complement, predicate adjective, predicate nominative.* (41l, 42a)

complete predicate See *predicate.*

complete subject See *subject.*

complex sentence See *sentence types.*

compound-complex sentence See *sentence types.*

compound predicate See *predicate.*

compound sentence See *sentence types.*

compound subject See *subject.*

compound word Two or more words placed together to express one concept, such as "fuel-efficient" or "proofread." (64c)

conciseness An attribute of writing that is direct and to the point. Its opposite, which is undesirable, is *wordiness.* (Ch. 50)

concluding paragraph Final paragraph of an essay, report, or other document, usually of more than three paragraphs. (11g)

concrete noun A noun naming things that can be seen, touched, heard, smelled, or tasted: *smoke, sidewalk.* (41a)

conjunction A word that connects or otherwise establishes a relationship between two or more words, phrases, or clauses. Also see *coordinating conjunction, correlative conjunction, subordinating conjunction.* (41h)

conjunctive adverb An adverb that creates a relationship between words, such as one of addition, contrast, comparison, result, time, emphasis, and the like. (41f)

connotation Ideas implied by a word. A connotation conveys associations such as emotional overtones beyond a word's direct, explicit definition. (54b)

contraction A word in which an apostrophe takes the place of one or more omitted letters: *can't, don't, I'm, isn't, it's, let's, they're, we've, won't,* and others. (60e)

coordinating adjectives Two or more adjectives that carry equal weight in modifying a noun (**big, friendly** *dog*). The order of coordinating adjectives can be changed without changing the meaning. Also see *cumulative adjectives.* (57e)

coordinating conjunction A conjunction that joins two or more grammatically equivalent structures: *and, or, for, nor, but, so, yet.* (41h)

coordination The use of grammatically equivalent forms to show a balance in or sequence of ideas. (51a)

correlative conjunction A pair of words that joins equivalent grammatical structures: *both . . . and; either . . . or; not only . . . but also.* (41h)

count noun A noun that names items that can be counted: *radio, street, idea, fingernail.* (69a)

critical reading A parallel process to critical thinking in which the reader thinks about what he or she is reading during and after reading. (2a)

critical response Formally, an essay summarizing a source's central point or main idea and then presenting the writer's synthesized reactions in response. (7c)

critical thinking A form of thinking where you take control of your conscious thought processes through such means as judging evidence, considering assumptions, making connections, and analyzing implications. (1d)

CSE style *CSE* is the abbreviation for the Council of Science Editors. It is a form of citation and documentation used in the natural sciences. (Ch. 40)

cumulative adjectives Adjectives that build up meaning from word to word as they get closer to the noun (**familiar rock** *tunes*). The order of cumulative adjectives cannot be changed without destroying the meaning. Also see *coordinating adjectives.* (57e)

dangling modifier A modifier that attaches its meaning illogically to the rest of its sentence, either because it is closer to another noun or pronoun than to its true subject or because its true subject is not expressed in the sentence. (49e)

database An electronic collection of citations and, frequently, articles or documents on a particular subject matter or field, or about a specific body of sources. (29b)

declarative sentence A sentence that makes a statement: *Sky diving is exciting.* Also see *exclamatory sentence, imperative sentence, interrogative sentence.*

definite article See *article.*

definition A rhetorical strategy that defines or gives the meaning of terms or ideas. (11f)

deliberate repetition A writing technique that uses the conscious repetition of a word, phrase, or other element to emphasize a point or to achieve a specific effect on readers. (11e)

denotation The dictionary definition of a word. (54b)

dependent clause Also called *subordinate clause,* a subordinate clause can't stand alone as an independent grammatical unit. If it tries to, it is a sentence fragment. Also see *adjective clause, adverb clause, noun clause.* (41n)

descriptive adjective An adjective that describes the condition or properties of the noun it is modifying and (except for a very few words, such as *dead* and *unique*) has comparative and superlative forms: *flat, flatter, flattest.* (41e)

descriptive adverb An adverb that describes the condition or properties of whatever it is modifying and has comparative and superlative forms: *happily, more happily, most happily.* (41f)

descriptive writing Writing that pictures a scene as it can be imagined by the five physical senses, such as sight and sound. Often this writing is organized spatially. (11f)

determiner A word or word group, traditionally identified as an *adjective,* that limits a noun by telling "how much" or "how many" about it. Also called *expression of quantity, limiting adjective,* or *noun marker.* (41e)

diction Word choice. (54b)

direct address Words naming a person or group being spoken to: *"The solution, **my friends,** is in your hands."* (44h)

direct discourse In writing, words that repeat speech or conversation exactly. Such words are always enclosed in quotation marks. Also see *indirect discourse.* (48d, 61c)

direct object A noun, pronoun, or group of words functioning as a noun that receives the action (completes the meaning) of a transitive verb. (41k)

direct question A sentence that asks a question and ends with a question mark: *Are you going to the concert?* (62b)

direct quotation See *quotation.*

discovery draft See *drafting.*

documentation The acknowledgment of someone else's words and ideas being used in any written document by giving full and accurate information about the person whose words are used and about where those words can be found. Also see *documentation style.* (33a, 36a)

documentation style Any of various systems for providing information about the source of words, information, and ideas that a writer quotes, paraphrases, or summarizes from any source other than the writer. Documentation styles discussed in this handbook are MLA (Chs. 33–35), APA (Chs. 36–38), CM (Ch. 39), and CSE (Ch. 40).

document design The arrangement of words, images, graphics, and space on a page or screen. (24a)

double negative A nonstandard structure that uses two negative modifiers rather than one. (45b)

drafting The part of the writing process in which writers compose ideas in sentences and paragraphs. The documents produced are called *drafts.* A *discovery draft* is what some writers call an early, rough draft. (9a)

edited American English Written usage of the American English language that conforms to mainstream rules of grammar, sentence structure, punctuation, spelling, and mechanics. It is required for US academic writing. This form of English is sometimes referred to as *standard English,* but given the diversity of dialects in the United States today, the term *standard* is less descriptive than it once might have been. (54d)

editing The part of the writing process in which writers check a document for the technical correctness in edited American English of its grammar, sentence structure, punctuation, spelling, and mechanics. (10d)

elliptical construction A sentence structure that deliberately omits words that can be filled in because they repeat words already in the sentence. (48f)

emotional appeal Rhetorical strategy intended to persuade readers by appealing to their hearts more than to their minds. Its Greek name is *pathos.* (13e)

essential element See *restrictive element.*

ethical appeal Rhetorical strategy intended to reassure readers that the writer is authoritative, honest, fair, likable, and so on. Its Greek name is *ethos.* (13e)

euphemism Language that attempts to blunt certain realities by speaking of them in "nice" or "tactful" words. (54g)

evidence Facts, data, examples, and opinions of others used to support assertions and conclusions. (32c)

example Specific incident or instance provided to illustrate a point. (11f)

exclamatory sentence A sentence beginning with *What* or *How* that expresses strong feeling: *What a ridiculous statement!*

expletive construction The phrase *there is (are), there was (were), it is (was)* at the beginning of a clause, which postpones the subject: *It is Mars that we hope to reach* (a better version would be *We hope to reach Mars*). (43h)

fact Information or data widely accepted as true. (2b)

faulty predication A grammatically illogical combination of subject and predicate: *The purpose of television was invented to entertain.* (48e)

field research Primary research that involves going into real-life situations to observe, survey, interview, or be part of some activity. (28c)

figurative language Words that carry other meanings in addition to their literal meanings, sometimes by making unusual comparisons. Also see *analogy, irony, metaphor, personification, overstatement, simile, understatement.* (54e)

first person See *person.*

focused freewriting Freewriting that may start with a set topic or may build on one sentence taken from earlier freewriting. (8f)

formal outline An outline that lays out the topic levels of generalities or hierarchies and marks them with roman numerals, letters, and numbers indented in a carefully pre-scribed fashion. (8h)

freewriting Writing nonstop for a period of time to generate ideas by free association of thoughts. (8f)

future perfect progressive tense The form of the future perfect tense that de-scribes an action or condition ongoing until some specific future time: *I will have been talking.* (42e)

future perfect tense The tense indicating that an action will have been completed or a condition will have ended by a specified point in the future: *I will have talked.* (42e)

future progressive tense The form of the future tense showing that a future action will continue for some time: *I will be talking.* (42e)

future tense The form of a verb, made with the simple form and either *shall* or *will,* expressing an action yet to be taken or a con-dition not yet experienced: *I will talk.* (42e)

gender Concerning languages, the classifica-tion of words as masculine, feminine, or neuter. In English, a few pronouns show changes in gender in third-person singular: *he, him, his; she, her, hers; it, its, its.* A few nouns that define roles change form to show gender difference (*prince, princess*), but most no longer do (*actor, police officer, chairperson*). (55a)

gender-neutral language Nonsexist lan-guage. Also see *sexist language.* (55b)

gerund A present participle functioning as a noun: ***Walking*** *is good exercise.* Also see *verbal.* (41d, Quick Reference 41.3, Ch. 73)

gerund phrase A gerund, along with its modifiers and/or object(s), which functions as a subject or an object: ***Walking the dog*** *can be good exercise.* (41m)

helping verb See *auxiliary verb.*

home page The opening main page of a Web site that provides access to other pages on the site. (25d)

homonyms Words spelled differently that sound alike: *to, too, two.* (56d)

hyperbole See *overstatement.*

hyperlink Connection from one digital document to another online. (25d)

idiom A word, phrase, or other construc-tion that has a different meaning from its usual or literal meaning: *He lost his head. She hit the ceiling.* (Ch. 72)

illogical predication See *faulty predication.*

imperative mood The grammatical mood that expresses commands and direct requests, using the simple form of the verb and almost always implying but not expressing the sub-ject: *Watch out.* (42f)

imperative sentence A sentence that gives a command: *Go to the corner and buy me a newspaper.*

indefinite article See *article, determiner.*

indefinite pronoun A pronoun, such as *all, anyone, each,* and others, that refers to a non-specific person or thing. (43e, 44d)

independent clause A clause that can stand alone as an independent grammatical unit. (41n)

index List of main terms used in a text and the page(s) on which each term can be found. (29a)

indicative mood The grammatical mood of verbs used for statements about real things or highly likely ones: *I think Grace is arriv-ing today.* (42f)

indirect discourse Reported speech or con-versation that does not use the exact struc-ture of the original and so is not enclosed in quotation marks. (48d, 61c)

indirect object A noun, pronoun, or group of words functioning as a noun that tells to whom, or for whom, the action expressed by a transitive verb was done. (41k)

indirect question A sentence that reports a question and ends with a period, not a ques-tion mark: *I asked if you are going.* (62a)

indirect quotation A quotation that re-ports another person's words without quo-tation marks, except around any words repeated exactly from the source. It requires documentation of the source to avoid pla-giarism. Also see *indirect discourse.* (57g)

inference What a reader or listener under-stands to be implied but is not stated. (2b)

infinitive A verbal made of the simple form of a verb and usually, but not always, pre-ceded by the word *to.* It functions as a noun, an adjective, or an adverb. (42b, Ch. 73)

infinitive phrase An infinitive, with its modifiers and/or object, which functions as a noun, an adjective, or an adverb. (41m)

informal language Word choice that cre-ates a tone appropriate for casual writing or speaking but usually not for academic writing. (2b)

informal outline Casual outline that doesn't follow the rules of a *formal outline*. (8h)

informative writing Writing that gives information and usually explains it; also known as *expository writing*. (8b, Ch. 12)

intensive pronoun A pronoun that ends in *-self* and that intensifies its antecedent: *Vida **himself** argued against it.* Also see *reflexive pronoun*. (44s)

interjection An emotion-conveying word that is treated as a sentence, starting with a capital letter and ending with an exclamation point or a period: *Oh! Ouch!* (41i)

interrogative sentence A sentence that asks a direct question: *Did you see that?*

in-text citation Source information placed in parentheses within the body of a research paper. Also see *citation, parenthetical documentation*. (Chs. 33 and 36)

intransitive verb A verb that does not take a direct object. (Quick Reference 42.1)

introductory paragraph Opening paragraph of text that orients readers and generates interest in the paper's topic or ideas. (11b)

inverted word order In contrast to standard order, the main or auxiliary verb comes before the subject in a sentence: *In **walks** [verb] the president [subject].* Most questions and some exclamations use inverted word order: *Did [verb] you [subject] see the circus?* (43h, 52h)

irony Using words to imply the opposite of their usual meaning. (54e)

irregular verb A verb that forms the past tense and past participle in a way other than by adding *-ed* or *-d*. (42b)

jargon Specialized vocabulary of a particular field or group that a general reader is unlikely to understand. (54g)

key terms In an essay, the words central to its topic and its message.

keywords Main words in a source's title, or that the author or an editor has identified as central to that source. Sometimes keywords are called *descriptors* or *identifiers*. (29b)

levels of formality The degrees of formality of language, reflected by word choice and sentence structure. A formal level is used for ceremonial and other occasions when stylis-

tic flourishes are appropriate. A semiformal level, which is neither too formal nor too casual, is acceptable for most academic writing. (10c)

limiting adjective See *determiner*.

linking verb A main verb that links a subject with a subject complement that renames or describes the subject. Linking verbs convey a state of being, relate to the senses, or indicate a condition. (Quick Reference 42.l, 43h)

literal meaning What is stated "on the line" explicitly by words. (1d)

logical appeal Rhetorical strategy that intends to show readers that the argument depends on formal reasoning, including providing evidence and drawing conclusions from premises. Its Greek name is *logos*. (13e)

logical fallacies Flaws in reasoning that lead to illogical statements that need to be rejected in logical arguments. (13h)

long quotation A direct quotation that in an MLA-style source-based paper occupies, if it is prose, more than four lines of type, or if it is poetry, more than three lines of the poem. In an APA-style source-based paper, more than forty words of prose is considered a long quotation. Long quotations are block indented on the page. Also see *short quotation*. (61b)

main clause See *independent clause*.

main verb A verb that expresses action, occurrence, or state of being and that shows mood, tense, voice, number, and person. (41c)

mapping See *clustering*.

mechanics Conventions governing matters such as the use of capital letters, italics, abbreviations, and numbers. (Chs. 65–68)

memo Commonly shortened term for *memorandum*. A brief form of business correspondence with a format that is headed with lines for "To," "From," "Date," and "Subject" (or "Re") and uses the rest of its space for its message. (22e)

metaphor A comparison implying similarity between two things: *a mop of hair*. A metaphor does not use the words *like* or *as*, which are used in a simile to make a comparison explicit: *hair **like** a mop*. (54e)

misplaced modifier Describing or limiting words that are wrongly positioned in a sentence so that their message either is illogical or relates to the wrong word(s). (Ch. 49)

mixed construction A sentence that unintentionally changes from one grammatical structure to another incompatible grammatical structure, so that the result is garbled meaning. (48e)

mixed metaphor Inconsistent metaphors in a single expression: *You'll get into hot water skating on thin ice.* (54e)

MLA style *MLA* is the abbreviation for the Modern Language Association. It specifies the format and the form of citation and documentation in source-based papers in English and some other humanities courses. (Chs. 33–35)

modal auxiliary verb A group of auxiliary verbs that add information such as a sense of needing, wanting, or having to do something or a sense of possibility, likelihood, obligation, permission, or ability. (42c, Ch. 74)

modifier A word or group of words functioning as an adjective or adverb to describe or limit (modify) another word or word group. (41l)

mood The attribute of verbs showing a writer's attitude toward the action by the way the verbs are used. English has three moods: imperative, indicative, and subjunctive. Also see *imperative mood, indicative mood, subjunctive mood.* (42f)

narrative writing Writing that tells a story. (11f)

Netiquette Coined from the word *etiquette,* Netiquette is good manners when using e-mail, the Internet, and online sites such as bulletin boards, chat rooms, and the like. (22d)

noncount noun A noun that names "uncountable" things: *water, time.* (69a)

nonessential element See *nonrestrictive element.*

nonrestrictive clause A clause that is not essential to the sentence's meaning. (Quick Reference 44.2, 57f)

nonrestrictive element A descriptive word, phrase, or dependent clause that provides information not essential to understanding the basic message of the element it modifies; it is therefore set off by commas. Also see *restrictive element.* (57f)

nonsexist language See *sexist language.*

notes (content notes) Notes people take to record the ideas or information contained in a source. The notes are usually in the form of a quotation, summary, or paraphrase. (28g)

noun A word that names a person, place, thing, or idea. Nouns function as subjects, objects, or complements. (41a)

noun clause A dependent clause that functions as a subject, object, or complement. (41n)

noun complement See *complement.*

noun determiner See *determiner.*

noun phrase A noun along with its modifiers functioning as a subject, object, or complement. (41m)

number The attribute of some words indicating whether they refer to one (singular) or more than one (plural). (43a, 44a, 48a)

object A noun, pronoun, or group of words that receives the action of the verb (*direct object;* 41k); tells to whom or for whom something is done (*indirect object;* 41k); or completes the meaning of a preposition (*object of a preposition;* 41g).

object complement A noun or adjective renaming or describing a direct object after certain verbs, including *call, consider, name, elect,* and *think: I call* daily **joggers** [object] **fanatics** [object complement]. (41l)

objective case The case of a noun or pronoun functioning as a direct object, an indirect object, an object of a preposition, or a verbal. A few pronouns change form to show the objective case (for example, *him, her, whom*). Also see *case.* (44j)

outline A technique for laying out ideas for writing in an orderly fashion that shows levels of generality. An outline can be formal or informal. (8h)

overstatement Deliberate exaggeration for emphasis; also called *hyperbole.* (54e)

paragraph development Rhetorical strategies for arranging and organizing paragraphs using specific, concrete details (RENNS) to support a generalization in the paragraph. (11a, 11d)

parallelism The use of equivalent grammatical forms or matching sentence structures to express equivalent ideas. (11e, 52a)

paraphrase A restatement of someone else's ideas in language and sentence structure different from that of the original. (31g)

parenthetical documentation Citation of source information enclosed in parentheses that follows quoted, paraphrased, or summarized material from another source. Such citations alert readers that the material comes from a source other than the writer. Parenthetical documentation and a list of bibliographic information at the end of a source-based paper together document the writer's use of sources. (Chs. 33 and 36)

participial phrase A phrase that contains a present participle or a past participle and any modifiers and that functions as an adjective. Also see *verbal*. (41m, 52g)

participle A verb form that indicates the present tense (*-ing* ending) or the past tense (*-ed, -d, -n,* or *-t* ending). A participle can also function as an adjective or an adverb. Also see *present participle, past participle*. (Chs. 41–42)

passive voice The form of the verb in which the subject is acted on; if the subject is mentioned in the sentence, it usually appears as the object of the preposition *by:* for example, *I was frightened by the thunder* (the active voice form is *The thunder frightened me*). The *passive voice* emphasizes the action, in contrast to the *active voice,* which emphasizes the doer of the action. (42g)

past participle The third principal part of a verb, the past participle is formed in regular verbs by adding *-d* or *-ed* to the simple form to create the past tense. In irregular verbs, the formation of the past tense varies from merely adding a letter or two to the simple form: *break, broke, broken.* The past participle functions as a verb only with an auxiliary verb as its partner. (42b)

past perfect progressive tense The past-perfect-tense form that describes an ongoing condition in the past that has been ended by something stated in the sentence: *Before the curtains caught fire, I had been talking.* (42e)

past perfect tense The tense that describes a condition or action that started in the past, continued for a while, and then ended in the past: *I had talked.* (42e)

past progressive tense The past-tense form that shows the continuing nature of a past action: *I was talking.* (42e)

past-tense verb The second principal part of a verb. In regular verbs, the past tense is formed by adding *-d* or *-ed* to the simple form. In irregular verbs, the formation of the past tense varies from merely adding a letter or two to the simple form: *break, broke; see, saw.* (42b)

perfect tenses The three tenses—the present perfect (*I have talked*), the past perfect (*I had talked*), and the future perfect (*I will have talked*)—that help to show complex time relationships between two clauses. (42e)

periodicals Magazines, newspapers, and journals published on a regular basis. (29d)

person The attribute of nouns and pronouns showing who or what acts or experiences an action. *First person* is the one speaking (*I, we*); *second person* is the one being spoken to (*you*); and *third person* is the person or thing spoken about (*he, she, it, they*). All nouns are third person. (43a, 48a)

personal pronoun A pronoun that refers to people or things: *I, you, them, it.* (44k)

persuasive writing Also called *argumentative writing,* persuasive writing seeks to persuade the reader about a matter of opinion. (8b, Ch. 13)

phrasal verb A verb that combines with one or more prepositions to deliver its meaning: *ask **out,** look **into.*** (72b)

phrase A group of related words that does not contain a subject and predicate and thus cannot stand alone as an independent grammatical unit. A phrase can function as a noun, a verb, or a modifier. (41m)

plagiarism A writer's presenting another person's words or ideas without giving credit to that person. Documentation systems allow writers to give proper credit to sources in standardized ways recognized by scholarly communities. Plagiarism is a serious offense, a form of intellectual dishonesty that can lead to course failure or expulsion. (Ch. 31)

plural See *number.*

positive The form of an adjective or adverb when no comparison is being expressed: *blue, easily.* Also see *comparative, superlative.* (45d)

possessive case The case of a noun or pronoun that shows ownership or possession. Also see *case*. (44j, 60a)

possessive pronoun A pronoun that shows ownership: *his, hers*, and so on. (60c)

predicate The part of a sentence that contains the verb and tells what the subject is doing or experiencing or what is being done to the subject. A *simple predicate* contains only the main verb and any auxiliary verb(s). A *complete predicate* contains the verb, its modifiers, objects, and other related words. A *compound predicate* contains two or more verbs, modifiers, objects, and other related words. (41j)

prefix Letters added at the beginning of a root word to create a new word. (54c, 64b)

preposition A word that conveys a relationship, often of space or time, between the noun or pronoun following it and other words in the sentence: *under, over, in, out.* The noun or pronoun following a preposition is called the *object of the preposition.* (41g, Ch. 72)

prepositional phrase A group of words beginning with a preposition and including a noun or pronoun, which is called the *object of the preposition.* (41m)

present participle A verb's *-ing* form: *talking, singing.* Used with auxiliary verbs, present participles function as main verbs. Used without auxiliary verbs, present participles function as nouns or adjectives. (42b)

present perfect progressive tense The present-perfect-tense form that describes something ongoing in the past that is likely to continue into the future: *I have been talking.* (42e)

present perfect tense The tense indicating that an action or its effects, begun or perhaps completed in the past, continue into the present: *I had talked.* (42e)

present progressive tense The present-tense form of the verb that indicates something taking place at the time it is written or spoken about: *I am talking.* (42e)

present tense The tense that describes what is happening, what is true at the moment, and/or what is consistently true. It uses the simple form (*I talk*) and the *-s* form in the third-person singular (*he talks, she talks, it talks*). (42e)

present-tense participial phrase A verbal phrase that uses the *-ing* form of a verb and functions only as a modifier (whereas a gerund phrase functions only as a noun). (41m)

prewriting A term for all activities in the writing process before drafting. (Ch. 8)

primary sources Also called *primary evidence,* these sources are "firsthand" work such as written accounts of experiments and observations by the researchers who conducted them; taped accounts, interviews, and newspaper accounts by direct observers; autobiographies, diaries, and journals; and expressive works such as poems, plays, fiction, and essays. They stand in contrast to *secondary sources.* (28b)

progressive forms Verb forms made, in all tenses, with the present participle and forms of the verb *be* as an auxiliary. Progressive forms show that an action, occurrence, or state of being is ongoing. (42e)

pronoun A word that takes the place of a noun and functions in the same ways that nouns do. Types of pronouns are demonstrative, indefinite, intensive, interrogative, personal, reciprocal, reflexive, and relative. (Ch. 44)

pronoun-antecedent agreement The match required between a pronoun and its antecedent in number and person, as pertains to personal pronouns and to gender. (44a)

pronoun case The way a pronoun changes form to reflect its use as the agent of action (*subjective case*), the thing being acted upon (*objective case*), or the thing showing ownership (*possessive case*). (44j–44s)

pronoun reference The relationship between a pronoun and its antecedent. (44f–44i)

proper adjective An adjective formed from a proper noun: *Victorian, American.* (65c)

proper noun A noun that names specific people, places, or things; it is always capitalized: *Tom Thumb, Buick.* (65c)

public writing Writing intended for readers outside of academic and work settings. (8b, Ch. 23)

purpose The goal or aim of a piece of writing: to express oneself, to provide information, to persuade, or to create a literary work. (1c, 8b)

quotation Repeating or reporting another person's words. *Direct quotation* repeats another's words exactly and encloses them in quotation marks. *Indirect quotation* reports another's words without quotation marks except around any words repeated exactly from the source. Both direct and indirect quotation require documentation of the source to avoid plagiarism. (31f)

References The title of a list of sources at the end of a research paper or scholarly article or other written work used in many documentation styles, especially that of APA. (Chs. 36–38)

reflexive pronoun A pronoun that ends in *-self* and that reflects back to its antecedent: *They claim to support **themselves**.* (44s)

regular verb A verb that forms its past tense and past participle by adding *-ed* or *-d* to the simple form. Most English verbs are regular. (42b)

relative adverb An adverb that introduces an adjective clause: *The garage **where** I usually park my car was full.* (41f)

relative clause See *adjective clause.*

relative pronoun A pronoun—such as *who, which, that, whom, whoever,* and a few others—that introduces an adjective clause or sometimes a noun clause. (41n)

RENNS test A memory aid for the specific, concrete details used to support a topic sentence in a paragraph: reasons, examples, names, and numbers. (11d)

restrictive clause A dependent clause that gives information necessary to distinguish whatever it modifies from others in the same category. In contrast to a nonrestrictive clause, a restrictive clause is not set off with commas. (Quick Reference 44.2, 57f)

restrictive element A word, phrase, or dependent clause that provides information essential to the understanding of the element it modifies. In contrast to a nonrestrictive element, a restrictive element is not set off with commas. Also see *nonrestrictive element.* (57f)

revising A part of the writing process in which writers evaluate their rough drafts and, on the basis of their assessments, rewrite by adding, cutting, replacing, moving, and often totally recasting material. (10a)

rhetorical strategies Various techniques for presenting ideas to deliver a writer's intended message with clarity and impact, including logical, ethical, and emotional appeals. Reflecting typical patterns of human thought, rhetorical strategies also include arrangements such as chronological, spatial, and climactic order; stylistic techniques such as parallelism and planned repetition; and patterns for organizing and developing writing such as illustration, description, and definition. (11f)

Rogerian argument An argument technique using principles developed by Carl Rogers in which writers strive to find common ground and thus reassure readers who disagree with them that they understand others' perspectives. (13f)

run-on sentence A sentence in which independent clauses run together without the required punctuation that marks them as complete units. Also known as a *fused sentence.* (Ch. 47)

search strategy A systematic way of finding information on a certain topic. (28a)

secondary source A source that reports, analyzes, discusses, reviews, or otherwise deals with the work of someone else. It stands in contrast to a primary source, which is someone's original work or firsthand report. A reliable secondary source must be the work of a person with appropriate credentials, must appear in a respected publication or other medium, must be current or historically authentic, and must be logically reasoned. (28b)

sentence A group of words, beginning with a capitalized first word and ending with a final punctuation mark, that states, asks, commands, or exclaims something. The vast majority of sentences have at least one *independent clause. A simple sentence* consists of one independent clause. A *complex sentence* contains one independent clause and one or more dependent clauses. A *compound sentence* contains two or more independent clauses joined by a coordinating conjunction. A *compound-complex sentence* contains at least two independent clauses and one or more dependent clauses. Sentences are also classified by their grammatical function; see *declarative sentence, exclamatory sentence, imperative sentence,* and *interrogative sentence.* (41o)

second person See *person.*

sentence fragment A portion of a sentence that is punctuated as though it were a complete sentence. (Ch. 46)

sentence outline A type of outline in which each element is a sentence. (8h)

sexist language Language that unfairly or unnecessarily assigns roles or characteristics to people on the basis of gender. Language that avoids gender stereotyping is called *gender-neutral* or *nonsexist language.* (55b)

shift An unnecessary change within a sentence in person, number, voice, tense, or other grammatical framework that makes a sentence unclear. (Ch. 48)

short quotation A direct quotation that occupies no more than four lines of type in an MLA-style source-based paper (for prose) or no more than three lines of poetry. In an APA-style source-based paper, a short quotation has no more than forty words of prose. Short quotations are enclosed in quotation marks. (61a)

simile A comparison, using *like* or *as,* of otherwise dissimilar things. (54e)

simple form The first principal part of a verb, the simple form shows action, occurrence, or state of being taking place in the present. It is used in the singular for first and second person and in the plural for first, second, and third person. The simple form is also known as the *dictionary form* or *base form.* (42b)

simple predicate See *predicate.*

simple sentence See *sentence types.*

simple subject See *subject.*

simple tenses The present, past, and future tenses, which divide time into present, past, and future. (42e)

singular See *number.*

slang Coined words and new meanings for existing words, which quickly pass in and out of use. Slang is inappropriate for most academic writing except when used intentionally as such. (54d)

slanted language Language that tries to manipulate the reader with distorted facts. (13h)

source A print or online book, article, document, CD, other work, or person providing information in words, music, pictures, or other media. (28b)

specialized database A database of sources covering a specific discipline or topic. (29d)

specialized reference work A reference work (such as a dictionary, encyclopedia, biographical compendium) covering a specific discipline or topic. (29e)

split infinitive One or more words coming between the two words of an infinitive. (49c)

squinting modifier A modifier that is considered misplaced because it isn't clear whether it describes the word that comes before it or the word that follows it. (49b)

standard English See *edited American English.*

subject The word or group of words in a sentence that acts, is acted upon, or is described by the verb. A *simple subject* includes only the noun or pronoun. A *complete subject* includes the noun or pronoun and all its modifiers. A *compound subject* includes two or more nouns or pronouns and their modifiers. (41j)

subject complement A noun or adjective that follows a linking verb, renaming or describing the subject of the sentence. (41l)

subjective case The case of the noun or pronoun functioning as a subject. Also see *case.* (44j)

subject-verb agreement The required match in number and person between a subject and a verb. (Ch. 43)

subjunctive mood The verb mood that expresses wishes, recommendations, indirect requests, speculations, and conditional statements: *I wish you were here.* (42f)

subordinate clause See *dependent clause.*

subordinating conjunction A conjunction that introduces a dependent clause and expresses a relationship between the idea in it and the idea in the independent clause. (41h)

subordination The use of grammatical structures to reflect the relative importance of ideas in a sentence. The most important information falls in the independent clause, and less important information falls in the dependent clause or phrases. (51c)

suffix Letters added at the end of a root word to change function or meaning. (54c, 64b)

summary A critical thinking activity preceding synthesis. It extracts the main message or central point of a passage or other discourse. (7b, 31h)

superlative The form of an adjective or adverb that expresses the greatest degree of quality among three or more things: *bluest, least blue; most easily, least easily.* (45d)

synonym A word that is close in meaning to another word. (9a)

synthesis A component of critical thinking in which material that has been summarized, analyzed, and interpreted is connected to what one already knows (one's prior knowledge) from reading or experiences. (1d)

tag question An inverted verb-pronoun combination added to the end of a sentence and creating a question that "asks" the audience to agree with the assertion in the first part of the sentence: *You know what a tag question is, don't you?* A tag question is set off from the rest of the sentence with a comma. (57h)

tense The time at which the action of the verb occurs: in the present, the past, or the future. (42e)

tense sequence In sentences that have more than one clause, the accurate sequencing of verb forms to reflect logical time relationships. (42e)

thesis statement A statement of an essay's central theme that makes clear the main idea, the writer's purpose, the focus of the topic, and perhaps the organizational pattern. (8g)

third person See *person.*

tone The writer's attitude toward his or her material and sometimes to the reader, especially as reflected by word choice. (2b, 10c)

topic outline An outline in which items are listed as words or phrases, not full sentences. (8h)

topic sentence The sentence that expresses the main idea of a paragraph. (11c)

transition The word or group of words that connects one idea to another in discourse. Useful strategies for creating transitions include transitional expressions, conjunctive adverbs, parallelism, and planned repetition of key words and phrases. (11e)

transitional expressions Words and phrases that signal connections among ideas and create coherence. (11e, Quick Reference 11.3)

transitive verb A verb that must be followed by a direct object. (Ch. 42)

understatement Figurative language in which the writer uses deliberate restraint for emphasis. (54e)

unity The clear and logical relationship between the main idea of a paragraph and the evidence supporting the main idea. (11c) As a design principle, the term refers to whether the elements (color, text, images) work together visually. (24b)

URL *URL* is the abbreviation for *Universal* (or *Uniform*) *Resource Locator.* It is the address of a site or page on the Web. (30b)

verb A word that shows action or occurrence, or that describes a state of being. Verbs change form to show time (tense), attitude (mood), and role of the subject (voice). Verbs occur in the predicate of a clause. Verbs can be parts of verb phrases, which consist of a main verb, any auxiliary verbs, and any modifiers. Verbs can be described as transitive or intransitive, depending on whether they take a direct object. (41c, Ch. 42)

verb phrase A main verb, along with any auxiliary verb(s) and any modifiers. (41m)

verbal A verb part functioning as a noun, adjective, or adverb. Verbals include infinitives, present participles (functioning as adjectives), gerunds (present participles functioning as nouns), and past participles. (41d)

verbal phrase A group of words that contains a verbal (an infinitive, participle, or gerund) and its modifiers. (41m)

voice An attribute of verbs showing whether the subject acts (active voice) or is acted upon (passive voice). (42g)

warrants The writer's underlying assumptions, which are often implied rather than stated. Warrants may also need support, also called *backing.* (13e)

Web site A collection of related files online that may include documents, images, audio, and video. Web sites typically have a *home page* that provides links to this content. (25a)

wordiness Writing that is full of words and phrases that don't contribute to meaning. The opposite of *conciseness.* (Ch. 50)

word order The order in which words fall in most English sentences. Usually, the subject comes before the predicate. Inverted word order can bring emphasis to an idea. Multilingual writers are often accustomed to word orders in sentences other than those used in English. (Ch. 71, 52h)

working bibliography A preliminary annotated list of useful sources in research writing. (28e)

Works Cited In MLA documentation style, the title of a list of standardized information about all sources cited in a research paper or other scholarly written work. (Ch. 34)

writing process Stages of writing in which a writer gathers and shapes ideas, organizes material, expresses those ideas in a rough draft, evaluates the draft and revises it, edits the writing for technical errors, and proofreads it for typographical accuracy and legibility. The stages often overlap. (4a, Ch. 8)

writing situation Elements for writers to consider at the beginning of the writing process: their writing topic, purpose, audience, context, role, and special requirements. (1c)

CREDITS

TEXT:

Figure 1.1: Courtesy of Myspace.com; Courtesy of Facebook; Courtesy of Google; Reprinted with permission of the Doctors Without Borders; **Figure 2.1:** Reprinted with permission of The Ad Council; **Figure 2.2:** Copyright © 2005 EBSCO Publishing. All rights reserved; **p. 17:** From *Angela the Upside-Down Girl* by Emily Hiestand. Reprinted by permission of Beacon Press, Boston; **p. 33:** From "Beyond Kyoto," *Foreign Affairs,* July/August 2004; **p. 37:** Cathy Newman/National Geographic Image Collection. Used with permission; **p. 60:** Reprinted with permission of Steven Johnson. Originally published in *Wired Magazine,* May 2005; **p. 61:** Excerpt from *Fast Food Nation* by Eric Schlosser. Reprinted by permission of Houghton Mifflin Harcourt Publishing Company. All rights reserved; **p. 62:** Reprinted with permission of Cassandra Tate; **p. 65, top:** Excerpt from *Barrio Boy,* Ernesto Galarza, University of Notre Dame Press, 1971. Reprinted with permission of the University of Notre Dame Press; **p. 65, bottom:** *The Story of My Life,* Helen Keller. Reprinted with permission of the American Federation for the Blind; **p. 69, top:** Reprinted with permission of Rockwell Stensrud; **p. 69, middle:** Excerpt from *The Language of Clothes* by Alison Lurie. Copyright © 1981 by Alison Lurie. Reprinted by permission of Henry Holt & Company LLC; **p. 102:** Yusef Komunyakaa, "Blackberries," from *Please Dome* © 2001 and reprinted with permission of Wesleyan University Press; **Figure 24.1:** Courtesy of the Ad Council; **Figure 25.2:** Courtesy of the National Museum of the American Indian, Washington DC; **Figure 26.1:** Reprinted with permission of David Krewinghaus; **Figure 29.1:** Reprinted with permission of the Illinois Central College; **Figure 29.2:** Courtesy of Milner Library, Illinois State University and Endeavor Information Systems, Inc.; **Figure 29.6:** The PsycINFO screen shots are reproduced with permission of the American Psychological Association, publisher of PsycINFO databases, all rights reserved; **Figures 30.1 and 30.2:** Courtesy of Google; **Figure 34.2:** From *The Creation of the Media,* by Paul Starr. Copyright © 2004 by Paul Starr. Reprinted by permission of Basic Books, a member of Perseus Book Group; **Figure 34.3:** Copyright © 2003 by the National Council of Teachers of English. Reprinted and used with permission; **Figures 34.4 and 34.5:** Copyright © 2005 by EBSCO Publishing, Inc. All rights reserved; **Figure 34.6:** Reprinted by permission of The Scientist.

PHOTOS:

Page 14: Peter Vadnai; **p. 87:** Douglas Hesse; **p. 89:** Douglas Hesse; **p. 96:** AP Wide World Photos; **p. 104:** © Patrick Johns/CORBIS. All Rights Reserved; **p. 147:** AP Wide World Photos.

INDEX

Where can I find what I need to know about . . . ?

Quick Reference Card for Research & Documentation

Materials you might need for research

1. A copy of your assignment.
2. This handbook, especially Part 5, or access to the Internet so that you can read the book online and use its guidelines.
3. Your research log.
4. Index cards for taking notes (unless you use a laptop). If you use different colors of index cards, you might color-code the different categories of information you find. Also, you might use one size for bibliography cards and the other for content note cards. Another coding strategy is to use pens of different ink colors or self-sticking dots of various colors.
5. Money or a debit card for copy machines or printers.
6. A flash drive or other means for storing downloaded source materials, if you're not exclusively using your own computer.
7. If you use index cards and other paper, a small stapler, paper clips, and rubber bands.
8. A separate bag or backpack with wheels to carry research-project materials and books you check out from the library.

Learning your library's resources

- How do you get access to the library's catalog and databases, both from inside the library and through the Internet? What are the log-in procedures?

- How does the library's catalog work?

- What periodical indexes or databases does your library have, online or in print? (*Indexes* and *databases* are lists of articles in journals and magazines, grouped by subject areas.)

- Where is the general reference collection? (You can't check out reference books, so when you need to use them, build extra time into your schedule to spend at the library.)

- Where is the special reference collection? (Same rules apply as for general reference books.)

- Are the book and journal stacks open (fully accessible shelves) or closed (request each item by filling out a form to hand to library personnel)? If the latter, become familiar with the required procedures not only for asking for a book or journal but also for picking it up when it's ready.

- Where are the library's physical collections of periodicals (journals, magazines, and newspapers) stored? Libraries are increasingly moving from paper to digital storage, but some publications might still exist only in print. Most libraries place periodicals published recently in open areas, and they place older ones in bound volumes, on microfilm or microfiche, or online. Learn to use whatever system is in place at your library.

- How do you identify when periodical articles exist digitally, in versions that you can read completely online rather than from a paper copy? When you find that an article has a digital version, how do you access it?

- What, if anything, is stored on microfilm or microfiche? If you think you'll use that material, take the time to learn how to use the machines.

- Does the library have special collections, such as local historical works or the writings of persons worthy of such an exclusive honor?

Tips on using search engines and directories

- Use keyword combinations or BOOLEAN EXPRESSIONS unless you have a very specific, narrow topic with unique keywords. A search for even a moderately common topic may produce thousands of hits, many of which won't be relevant to your topic. You might also switch to a subject directory.

- Most search engines attempt to search as much of the World Wide Web as possible. But because the Web is vast and unorganized, different search engines will give different results for the same search. Try using more than one search engine, or use a **metasearch engine** that searches several search engines at once, such as Dogpile (http://dogpile.com).

ARRANGEMENT OF ENTRIES

Alphabetize by author's last name. If no author is named, alphabetize by the title's first significant word (ignore *A, An,* or *The*).

AUTHORS' NAMES

Use first names and middle names or middle initials, if any, as given in the source. Don't reduce to initials any name that is given in full. For one author or the first-named author in multiauthor works, give the last name first. Use the word *and* with two or more authors. List multiple authors in the order given in the source. Use a comma between the first author's last and first names and after each complete author name except the last. After the last author's name, use a period: Fein, **Ethel Andrea, Bert Griggs, and Delaware Rogash.**

Include *Jr., Sr., II,* or *III* but no other titles and degrees before or after a name.

CAPITALIZATION OF TITLES

Capitalize all major words and the first and last words of all titles and subtitles. Don't capitalize ARTICLES (*a, an, the*), PREPOSITIONS, COORDINATING CONJUNCTIONS (*and, but, for, nor, or, so, yet*), or *to* in INFINITIVES in the middle of a title.

SPECIAL TREATMENT OF TITLES

Use quotation marks around titles of shorter works (poems, short stories, essays, articles). Italicize titles of longer works (books, periodicals, plays).

When a book title includes the title of another work that is usually italicized (as with a novel, play, or long poem), the preferred MLA style is not to italicize the incorporated title: *Decoding* Jane Eyre. For an alternative that MLA accepts, see the MLA documentation chapter.

If the incorporated title is usually enclosed in quotation marks (such as a short story or short poem), keep the quotation marks and italicize the complete title of the book: *Theme and Form in "I Shall Laugh Purely": A Brief Study.*

Drop *A, An,* or *The* as the first word of a periodical title.

PLACE OF PUBLICATION

If several cities are listed for the place of publication, give only the first. MLA doesn't require US state names no matter how obscure or confusing the city names might be. For an unfamiliar city outside the United States, include an abbreviated name of the country or Canadian province.

PUBLISHER

Use shortened names as long as they are clear: *Random* for *Random House.* For companies named for more than one person, name only the first: *Prentice* for *Prentice Hall.* For university presses, use the capital letters *U* and *P* (without periods): Oxford UP; U of Chicago P

PUBLICATION MONTH ABBREVIATIONS

Abbreviate all publication months except *May, June,* and *July.* Use the first three letters followed by a period (*Dec., Feb.*) except for September (*Sept.*).

PAGE RANGES

Give the page range—the starting page number and the ending page number, connected by a hyphen—of any paginated electronic source and any paginated print source that is part of a longer work (for example, a chapter in a book, an article in a journal). A range indicates that the cited work is on those pages and all pages in between. If that isn't the case, use the style shown next for discontinuous pages. In either case, use numerals only, without the word *page* or *pages* or the abbreviation *p.* or *pp.*

Use the full second number through *99.* Above that, use only the last two digits for the second number unless to do so would be unclear: 113-14 is clear, but 567-602 requires full numbers.

DISCONTINUOUS PAGES

A source has discontinuous pages when the source is interrupted by material that's not part of the source (for example, an article beginning on page 32 but continued on page 54). Use the starting page number followed by a plus sign (+): 32+.

MEDIUM OF PUBLICATION

Include the MEDIUM OF PUBLICATION for each Works Cited entry. For example, every entry for a print source must include "Print" at the end, followed by a period (if required, certain supplementary bibliographic information like translation information, name of a book series, or the total number of volumes in a set should follow the medium of publication). Every source from the World Wide Web must include "Web" at the end, followed by a period and the date of access. The medium of publication also needs to be included for broadcast sources ("Television", "Radio"), sound recordings ("CD", "LP", "Audiocassette"), as well as films, DVDs, videocassettes, live performances, musical scores and works of visual arts, and so on.

ISSUE AND VOLUME NUMBERS FOR SCHOLARLY JOURNALS

Include both an issue and volume number for each Works Cited entry for scholarly journals.